Men as Managers,
Managers as Men

Men as Managers, Managers as Men

*Critical Perspectives on Men,
Masculinities and Managements*

Edited by

David L. Collinson

and

Jeff Hearn

SAGE Publications
London • Thousand Oaks • New Delhi

HD 38.2

·M462

1996

First published 1996

SAGE Publications Ltd
6 Bonhill Street
London EC2A 4PU

SAGE Publications Inc
2455 Teller Road
Thousand Oaks, California 91320

SAGE Publications India Pvt Ltd
32, M-Block Market
Greater Kailash – I
New Delhi 110 048

British Library Cataloguing in Publication data

A catalogue record for this book is
available from the British Library

ISBN 0 8039 8928 8
ISBN 0 8039 8929 6 (pbk)

Library of Congress catalog record available

Typeset by Mayhew Typesetting, Rhayader, Powys
Printed in Great Britain by The Cromwell Press Ltd,
Broughton Gifford, Melksham, Wiltshire

Contents

Preface

It is both rather strange and quite predictable that such an obvious matter as the relationship between men, masculinities and managements should be a subject for silence. This cannot be explained by either carelessness or conspiracy: the silence around these issues is built into the very process of their reproduction. The pervasiveness and taken-for-grantedness of this silence reinforce one another. It is another problem that has no name (cf. Friedan, 1963). Having worked separately for many years on questions of gender relations, men, sexuality, organizations and management, we realized in 1989 that we were thinking on very similar lines around the need to focus on the massive links between men, masculinities and managements. This led to the decision to work on these latter questions both in our own joint and separate research and writing and in co-editing this book.

The process of producing this book has run from 1992 to the end of 1995. It has involved contributors drawing upon a diversity of perspectives – from social psychology, sociology, history, accounting, organization analysis and management theory, to women's studies, studies on gender and critical studies on men. All the contributors have been committed to rethinking their work in ways that can analyse both men *and* managements without re-excluding women. This has often been a demanding intellectual, political, practical and personal project. Accordingly, we would like to thank all the contributors for their willingness to engage in this process over the past few years. Addressing men, masculinities and managements *simultaneously* does seem to produce the effect of questioning concepts, assumptions and disciplinary boundaries.

Finally, we would like to thank Sue Jones for her encouragement and support of the initial idea, and Margaret Collinson for her constructive criticism throughout.

Leamington Spa
December, 1995

The Contributors

Beverly H. Burris is Professor of Sociology at the University of New Mexico, where she teaches courses in sociological theory and the sociology of work. She has published two books: *No Room at the Top: Underemployment and Alienation in the Corporation* (Praeger, 1983) and *Technocracy at Work* (SUNY Press, 1993). In addition, she has published articles on contemporary theory, women and work, and computerization of the workplace. Her current research is focused on the Internet and electronic communication.

David L. Collinson is Senior Lecturer in Organizational Behaviour at the University of Warwick. Author of *Managing the Shopfloor* (de Gruyter, 1992), co-author of *Managing to Discriminate* (Routledge, 1990) and co-editor of *Job Redesign* (Gower, 1985), he has conducted research and published papers on various aspects of shopfloor culture and resistance, gender, selection, management control, humour, and safety practices on North Sea oil installations. His theoretical interests concentrate on the examination of power, culture and subjectivity in the workplace.

Jeff Hearn is Professorial Research Fellow in the Faculty of Economic and Social Studies, based in the School of Social Policy, University of Manchester. His publications include *'Sex' at 'Work'* (Prentice-Hall/Harvester Wheatsheaf, St Martin's, 1995) with Wendy Parkin, *The Sexuality of Organization* (co-editor: Sage, 1991), *Men in the Public Eye* (Routledge, 1992), and *Men, Masculinities and Social Theory* (co-editor: Unwin Hyman, 1990). He is currently researching organizations and violence.

Wendy Hollway is a Reader in Gender Relations in the Department of Psychology, University of Leeds. She has researched and published on questions to do with subjectivity, gender, sexuality, the history of work psychology, and gender relations in organizations. In addition to co-authoring *Changing the Subject* (Methuen, 1984), her published books are *Work Psychology and Organizational Behaviour* (Sage, 1991) and *Subjectivity and Method in Psychology* (Sage, 1989). She is currently working on an ESRC-funded project on 'Gender Difference, Anxiety and the Fear of Crime' with Tony Jefferson and a book entitled *Mothering and Ambivalence*, with Brid Featherstone (Routledge, 1997).

Deborah Kerfoot is Lecturer in Organizational Behaviour at the School of Business and Economic Studies at the University of Leeds. Her research interests and publications are in the fields of the sociology and critical study of management, work and organization; empirical research on employment and management practices; post-structuralism; and gender and sexuality in organizations. She is currently working on an ESRC-funded project on the management of change, with a critical focus on Total Quality Management and HRM, in addition to a co-authored book *Management, Masculinity and Organization* under contract with Sage. She is book review editor for *Journal of Management Studies* and an associate editor of *Gender, Work and Organization*.

David Knights is Professor of Organizational Analysis and Director of the Financial Services Research Centre at UMIST, Manchester. His research has included projects on management strategy and control, the management of information technology, equal opportunity, and theoretical contributions to debates on power, managerialism and subjectivity. He is the co-editor with Jill Rubery of *Gender, Work and Organization*. His most recent books are *Managers Divided: Organizational Politics and IT Management* with Fergus Murray (Wiley, 1994), and *Resistance and Power in Organizations* co-editor with John Jermier and Walter Nord (Routledge, 1994).

Cheryl R. Lehman, Professor of Accounting and Business Law at the Frank G. Zarb School of Business, Hofstra University, is general editor of *Advances in Public Interest Accounting* and associate editor of *Critical Perspectives on Accounting*. She has published *Accounting's Role in Social Conflict* (Marcus Wiener/Paul Chapman, 1992), has co-edited *Multinational Culture: Social Impacts of a Global Economy* (Greenwood, 1992) with Rusty Moore, and is on the editorial board of *Accounting, Auditing and Account-ability*, and *Gender, Work and Organization*. Her research and professional work include accounting's role in a global economy, public policy and regulation, ethics and gender issues.

Patricia Yancey Martin is Professor of Sociology at Florida State University and does research on gender and organizations. In 1995 she co-edited with Myra Marx Feree *Feminist Organizations – Harvest of the New Women's Movement* (Temple University Press), and published a paper with Marlene Powell on the social construction of rape victims by legal organizations in *Law and Social Inquiry*. She has recently completed interviews and observations of gender relations and dynamics in large, for-profit corporations, for a project on the changing demographics of organizations. She is currently writing a monograph on the local politics of rape processing.

David Morgan has lectured in sociology at the University of Manchester for over thirty years. His main interests are in the sociology of gender, with particular reference to studies of men and masculinities and the sociology of marriage and the family. He is the author of *Discovering Men* (Routledge, 1992) and is the joint editor of a series, *Gender, Change and Society*, for Taylor and Francis.

Kate Mulholland is a Research Fellow at the School of Industrial and Business Studies, University of Warwick. She previously worked at Leicester University on ESRC research project on Gender Power and Wealth Creation from which her chapter is drawn. Her research interests are in gender and work.

Craig Prichard is currently a PhD student and Graduate Teaching Assistant in the Department of Continuing Education at the University of Nottingham. His research addresses the construction of 'the manager' in further and higher education in the UK and particularly this development's gendered inflections. In previous 'lives', Craig has been a journalist and musician. Most recently he was Research Officer with the Department of Management Development at the University of Central Lancashire at Preston.

Rosslyn Reed is a Senior Lecturer in the Faculty of Humanities and Social Sciences at the University of Technology, Sydney. Her teaching and research interests are in the sociology of labour, industry and organizations, with particular emphasis on equal employment opportunities for women. She has carried out research on technological and occupational change in the newspaper and general printing industries. Her current research interests are in the employment experiences of older women working in the retail industry. She is the author of *Strategies of Regulation: Labour Market Segmentation in the Melbourne Newspaper Industry* (University of New South Wales, IRRC, 1990) and *Women in Printing: Employers' Attitudes to Women in Trades* (The Women's Bureau, AGPS, 1993).

Michael Roper teaches social and cultural history in the Department of Sociology at the University of Essex. His book, *Masculinity and the British Organization Man since 1945* (Oxford University Press), was published in 1994. He is currently researching the post-war rise of management education in the UK, focusing on the articulation of masculine discourses in new forms of management thought.

Alison E. Woodward is Professor in Social Sciences at Vesalius College of the Free University of Brussels and teaches in Flemish interuniversity graduate programmes in Women's Studies and European Studies. Her research and articles focus on public policy, organizational culture and gender, especially in relation to elite formation and the European Union. Her most recent books are *Municipal Entrepreneurship: A Five Nation Study* with Tom Burns and J. Ellig (Gordon and Breach, 1994) and *Women and Management* (editor: Vrouwenstudies, University of Antwerp, 1995). She directs the Belgian unit of the Comparative Leadership Study on women and men in politics and business.

1

Breaking the Silence: On Men, Masculinities and Managements

David L. Collinson and Jeff Hearn

Most managers in most organizations in most countries are men. Yet the conditions, processes and consequences of men's historical and contemporary domination of management have received little scrutiny. There has been a strange silence, which we believe reflects an embedded and taken-for-granted association, even conflation, of men with organizational power, authority and prestige. This book examines why and how the association of men and managements persists both in 'theory' and 'practice' and explores the consequences of these interrelationships for organizations, employees and managers themselves. Acknowledging the multiple and diverse meanings of management, the volume brings together a wide variety of contributions from three continents to examine management theories, the institution and occupation of management itself, and the power, functions and practices of men as managers and managers as men. By highlighting the interrelations of men, masculinities and managements, this book seeks to break the silence and to develop new perspectives, understandings and approaches that can more adequately analyse the conditions, processes and consequences of 'man'-agerial work.

It is important to begin by examining the scale of men's 'occupation' of management from the boardroom to junior levels. Women comprise less than 5 per cent of senior management in the UK and US while in Australia and many other countries, it is closer to 2 per cent (Sinclair, 1995). A Hansard Society Commission survey (Hansard Society, 1990) found that only 5 per cent of the UK Institute of Directors and less than 1 per cent of chief executives were women.[1] Despite slow but steady progress by women into more junior managerial hierarchies within UK corporations in the 1980s, recent research suggests a reversal in these trends. The 1994 National Management Survey (Institute of Management, 1995), for example, found a fall in the number of women managers from 10.2 per cent in 1993 to 9.8 per cent in 1994. While women constituted only 2.8 per cent of directors, they were: concentrated in junior managerial grades, twice as likely as their male counterparts to have resigned in the previous twelve months and paid less than their male counterparts by an average of 15.2 per cent. A 1992 survey of forty-three broadcasting organizations across the twelve member states of the European Community found that women comprised under 11 per cent of management at the top three levels (Equal Opportunities Commission, 1992).

Research in the United States suggests that those few women who reach senior managerial positions are much more likely than their male counterparts to report feeling stressed and burned out, as a result of juggling work and a disproportionate load of family obligations (*New York Times*, 1993). They are also less likely than their male counterparts either to receive training (Tharenou et al., 1994) or to be assigned tasks with high responsibility, visibility and the opportunity to demonstrate the levels of competence needed for future advancement (Ohlott et al., 1994). Moreover the few women in US corporations who become company directors are often channelled into 'peripheral' committees like public affairs while their male counterparts sit on committees deemed central to corporate governance such as executive and finance committees (Bilimoria and Piderit, 1994). Hence, although not all managers are men, the male domination of most hierarchical levels within management tends to persist not only historically, but also across different societies. The development of transnational organizations, international trade, communication and world financial systems is likely to reinforce the globalized nature of these male-dominated networks and processes.

Reflecting and reinforcing this numerical dominance is a masculine or masculinist imagery that frequently pervades the managerial function and perceptions of it. This gendered imagery is reflected in the etymology of the verb to 'manage' derived from the sixteenth-century Italian word *menagerie*, which meant handling things and especially horses (Williams, 1976). As Mant (1977: 20) argues, 'In this derivation it was ultimately a masculine concept, to do with taking charge, directing, especially in the context of war.' Indeed throughout the history of management thought and practice there has been a recurrent association between gender, hierarchy and organization on the one hand and militarism and warfare on the other. Early management writers tended to draw on military experience and language when making sense of organizational problems (Morgan, 1986; Shaw, 1990). Central to such thinking was the prioritization of the leader and manager as heroic warrior (Grint, 1995). The masculinity of this imagery is illustrated more recently by a 'Heathrow management text' (Burrell, 1992b) that applies to contemporary business the 2,500-year-old teaching of Sun Tzu on military strategy and the management of warfare (Krause, 1995). Its prescriptions on the 'Art of War for Executives' and the ruthless 'Principles of Success' regarding competitive strategy and 'defeating the enemy' are deeply imbued with masculine images and assumptions.

Biographies and autobiographies of famous twentieth-century entrepreneurial male managers/owners such as Ford (Ford, 1923; Sward, 1948; Beynon, 1980), Iacocca (Iacocca, 1984), Geneen (Geneen, 1985) and Maxwell (Davies, 1992) often reveal an evangelical, personal and lifelong preoccupation with military-like efficiency, ruthless practices and autocratic control. Many of these accounts of dictatorial business leaders also demonstrate how the managerial search for efficiency can become an all-engulfing obsession. Equally, they implicitly disclose the masculine assumptions and practices that frequently predominate in management. Morgan argues that from an early age Frederick Taylor (1947) was an obsessive anal-compulsive character 'driven by a relentless need to tie down and master almost every aspect of his life' (1986: 204). Scientific management, one of the most influential managerial theories of the twentieth century, is found to be the product of 'a disturbed and neurotic personality' (ibid.: 205). The life history of Howard Hughes, the American innovator, entrepreneur and tycoon, is an extraordinary example of these obsessive tendencies towards control and mastery (Drosnin, 1987). Driven by a fear that his father did not respect his achievements, Hughes created a massive business empire that increasingly reflected and reinforced his concern with personal control and efficiency. He prescribed in minute detail the rules of behaviour to which his employees should adhere. Hating emotion of any kind, Hughes sought to control not only the women in his personal life, but also those who starred in his films, closely defining and monitoring their daily routines. His detachment, isolation and obsession with control grew to the point where he could no longer bear to breathe the air of other human beings because they might be germ carriers. Consequently, Hughes had his headquarters hermetically sealed and in his later years he lived totally alone in a room that was neither cleaned nor ever saw the light of day. His life history illustrates the self-defeating consequences that can ensue from an obsession with personal control through autocratic management. We would argue that the preoccupations of all these famous male entrepreneurs with work, discipline and emotional control are also indicative of highly masculine modes of thought and behaviour that prioritize 'mastery' over self and other.

In the 1980s especially, journalistic profiles of male executives or 'captains of industry' consistently presented 'heroic', 'macho'[2] images emphasizing qualities of struggle and battle, a willingness to be ruthless and brutal, a rebellious nature and an aggressive, rugged individualism (Neale, 1995).[3] Managers and senior executives were frequently depicted and portrayed themselves as 'hard men', virile swashbuckling and flamboyant entrepreneurs who were reasserting a 'macho' management style that insisted on the 'divine right of managers to manage' (Purcell, 1982; see also Mackay, 1986; Edwards, 1987; Denham, 1991). Masculine, abrasive and highly autocratic managerial styles were widely valued and celebrated as the primary means of generating corporate success. 'Man'-agement came to be defined in terms of the ability to *control* people, events, companies, environments, trade unions and new technology. In the 1990s, managers and their performance are increasingly being evaluated. One central criterion of these evaluation practices is the masculinist concern with personal power and the ability to control others and self.[4] Such masculine discourses are also embedded in conventional managerial language which is frequently gendered, for example both in terms of highly (hetero)sexualized talk about 'penetrating markets' and 'getting into bed with suppliers/ customers/competitors', and in the extensive use of sporting metaphors and sexual joking in making sense of and rationalizing managerial decisions and practices (Scase and Goffee, 1989; Collinson et al., 1990). Designed to measure performance, annual revenue, sales and productivity figures are often treated as symbols of corporate and managerial virility (Gherardi, 1995). Equally, managerial presentational styles (especially those of management consultants) which emphasize 'professional', 'competent' and 'rational' self-images infused with an air of total confidence, detachment and control frequently reveal masculine assumptions, particularly when presenters use sexist and racist jokes as 'icebreakers' (Cockburn, 1991). Participation in male-dominated sports can significantly shape managerial interactions and indeed career progress within and between organizations, networks, labour markets and professional alliances where men seek to relate to one another as colleagues, employees, clients and customers, as well as competitors and team-mates (Jackall, 1988). A considerable amount of business is also conducted through the 'entertainment' of client 'guests' in male-dominated sporting spheres such as tennis and golf clubs, in 'executive boxes' at football grounds and in the men-only business clubs of which many managers and executives are members (Elliott, 1959; Rogers, 1988; Allison, 1994).

Despite – possibly even because of – this frequently pervasive association between men, power and authority in organizations, the literature on management (and indeed organization theory) has consistently failed to question its gendered nature. Here again images of middle and senior management seem to be imbued with particular notions of masculinity. Whether we refer to the 'ideal'[5] *prescriptive* models of management of early academic writers (for example Barnard, 1938; Fayol, 1949; Simon, 1945), *descriptive* accounts of managerial work (for example Mintzberg, 1973; Stewart, 1976a; Drucker, 1979) or even more *critical* contemporary analyses (for example Willmott, 1987; Reed, 1989; Mangham and critics, 1995), the masculine imagery of management and managers seems to be taken for granted, neglected, and thereby reproduced and reinforced.[6] This neglect is illustrated by the unreflexive use of book and chapter titles such as: 'The organization man' (Whyte, 1956); 'Men who manage' (Dalton, 1959); 'A thinking man's management', 'Manager for himself'' (Sampson, 1965); 'The men at the top' (Elliott, 1959; Burns and Stalker, 1961); 'The man and the corporation' (Guzzardi, 1966); and 'The manager and his work' (Drucker, 1979). Failing to consider the gendered questions to which their titles seem to allude, all of these studies tend to say a great deal more about management than they do about men.

Yet, there is another derivation of the verb to manage, drawn from the French *ménager*, an eighteenth-century meaning which Mant (1977: 21) sees as 'a more gentle, perhaps feminine usage' emphasizing careful house-keeping and domestic organization.[7] Developing this theme, Wensley (1996) has recently identified several important implications of Mrs. Beeton's (1861) *Book of Household Management* for the analysis and practice of corporate management in the 1990s. This alternative meaning makes a point which is central to this volume, namely that management, as a function, profession and practice, need not *inevitably* be dominated by masculine styles, discourses or processes generally, or by men in particular. Feminist writers have questioned the inevitability of this association between men, management and power by demonstrating how management often excludes women, especially those who are black and/or from ethnic minorities (DiTomaso, 1988; Bell and Nkomo, 1992). This book attends to the Other side, that is taken for granted in malestream discourses, and is theorized implicitly and sometimes explicitly in feminist discourses; the problem of men, masculinities and managements, of men's continued domination of management.[8] Its purpose is to examine critically the conditions, processes and consequences of men's persistent dominance of management. Why, when we 'think manager' do we still tend to 'think male' (Schein, 1976)? In order to highlight how such questions are neglected in the literature, this first chapter reviews some of the studies that conceptualize management, gender, men and/or masculinities in the workplace from prescriptive, descriptive and particularly from critical perspectives. Seeking to demonstrate the importance of breaking the silence, we begin by briefly considering the ever-proliferating dominant discourses on management.

Dominant discourses

Facilitated by the separation of ownership and control (Berle and Means, 1932), the growth of management and large-scale organizations has been one of the most significant features of modern society (Burnham, 1945; Chandler, 1977; Pollard, 1965). Indeed Mintzberg (1989) has characterized the twentieth century as the 'age of management'. The emergence of management as the central organizational activity of modern corporations is reflected in the burgeoning literature, especially from the United States, that explores the assumptions, responsibilities and practices of contemporary managements (for example Likert, 1961; Sayles, 1964; Lawrence and Lorsch, 1967; Child, 1969; Mintzberg, 1973, 1989; Drucker, 1979; Kotter, 1982; Cole, 1982; Deal and Kennedy, 1982; Stewart, 1986; Kreitner, 1989; Bennis, 1989; Hannaway, 1989). Adopting a prescriptive and/or descriptive perspective, conventional discourses rarely question managerial power, the elitist nature of most decision making in organizations or the terms and conditions of employment that are associated with the function. While these dominant modes of analysis are immensely varied, most share a reluctance to explore questions of gender that would otherwise tend to disrupt taken-for-granted ways of thinking about management.

This neglect can be seen in the development of management theory, from scientific management to human relations, systems and contingency theories, and more recently population ecology and institutional perspectives. It is also evident in recent broad-ranging reviews of the management literature (Hales, 1993; Thomas, 1993). In conventional organizational psychology, where the major contribution to the prescriptive study of leadership has emerged (for example Fiedler, 1967; Vroom and Yetton, 1973), a pervasive domain assumption has been that leadership is synonymous with men and that gender is not an issue worthy of exploration (Hearn and Parkin, 1988). A recent review of the leadership literature in organizational psychology (Hollander and Offerman, 1990) devotes only two sentences to women in organizations and totally neglects issues of men and masculinity in relation to power and leadership. Within the foregoing dominant discourses, management is usually presented as if it is a gender-neutral activity, whereas in reality it is clear that managerial hierarchies remain largely dominated by men in most organizations and sectors.

The empirically based descriptive work of Mintzberg (1973, 1975, 1983, 1989) has been particularly influential in the dominant discourses on management. Challenging the prevailing highly rational, objective and 'scientific' view of management, Mintzberg reveals a less ordered, inherently subjective reality characterized by political alliances and strategies played out by managers in their search for power, influence and organizational security. In many ways, such descriptions of managerial work are similar to those of Dalton's (1959) classic study which graphically examines the hidden agendas of intra-managerial collusion and conflict. While both authors may be writing primarily (or even exclusively) about men, they fail to analyse men and masculinities as socially produced, reproduced and indeed changeable. We are given no indication of how men managers are socially constructed *as men* through either the practice of managing or the impact of other social forces such as the processes of boys becoming adult men, the organization of domestic life or broader cultural and religious practices. Mintzberg uses 'manager' and 'he' interchangeably throughout his influential text, and even when he critiques the 'Great Man' theory for revealing 'almost nothing about managerial work' (1973: 12) he remains silent about its inherently gendered imagery and assumptions. Hence while both writers explore the alliances, interrelations and conflicts within management, neither questions the gender of those about whom they write or the hierarchical power of management, nor do they locate the function in its structural position within the organization. Yet relations between men in senior organizational positions, whether conflictual, co-operative or both, are frequently highly gendered. As this text seeks to illustrate, within, between and across managerial and organizational hierarchies, masculine discourses and practices are often a crucial basis for alliances, divisions and conflicts between men in senior positions.

Having highlighted this tendency to ignore gender completely in the dominant discourses on management, we also emphasize that this book is not intended to be an extension of the 'women in management' literature that characterizes much of the debate on gender and organizations (for example Loden, 1985; Jelinek and Adler, 1988; Helgesen, 1990; Rosener, 1990; Sekaran and Leong, 1992; Fagenson, 1993). Such analyses have also tended to neglect a critical examination of the hierarchical and/or gendered power and practices of either men as managers or managers as men. Their recurrent emphasis upon women's different ways of organizing, managing and leading and the need to develop women's skills to fit into contemporary managerial hierarchies reflects a focus primarily upon women that is always in danger of blaming the victim and/or essentialism. Recent research has found few consistent differences between female and male managers in terms of managerial behaviours, commitment, decision style, stress or subordinates' responses (Powell, 1988; Donnell and Hall, 1980; Boulgarides, 1984).

Primarily concerned to prescribe more effective techniques of managerial control, dominant discourses on management fail to address two interwoven forms of organizational power: the first related to hierarchy and management and the second related to gender and men. By contrast, more critical studies have questioned the conditions, processes and consequences of various aspects of control within the workplace. In particular, they have generally examined and problematized either *managerial* power, control and ideology or *men's* power, control and ideology. Possibly reflecting the difficulties of integrating their respective insights, these two critiques have tended to develop quite separately, their interrelations and overlaps remaining relatively underexplored. The next two sections of this chapter will briefly review the respective insights of critical studies: of management and of gender. Each of these overall perspectives provides a partial critical analysis of the interrelations between hierarchical and gendered forms of power and control in organizational practices. The third section considers the relatively few critical studies that have sought to develop a more integrated analysis of gender, men and managements.

Management without gender

Critical analyses of management emerge from critiques of dominant discourses. They seek to make explicit and then to question management's extensive power and control. Inspired by Braverman's (1974) analysis of the labour process, writers such as Friedman (1977), Edwards (1979) and Burawoy (1979, 1985) highlighted the structural economic imperatives of capitalist production and emphasized how managerial practices are shaped by a primary concern to control the labour process based on the separation of conception and execution. This perspective regards managers as the bearers of an economic logic in which labour is controlled and directed for the benefit of profit and sectional interests (Nichols, 1970; Marglin, 1974).

Increasingly, critical writers have also recognized that an exclusive focus on the structural basis of managerial power tends to attribute a unity, homogeneity and omniscience to management that fails to address the complex realities of the function. Accordingly, recent contributions have contextualized managerial power and discretion within broader social, economic and political conditions (Willmott, 1984, 1987; Hales, 1986; Linstead et al., 1996). Through an additional focus on subjectivity and agency, they have also examined the diversity, differences and contradictions that can characterize managerial hierarchies (Knights and Willmott, 1986). For example, dependence on the agency and consent of labour limits managerial control (Hyman, 1987) and sustains the possibility of employee resistance (Jermier et al., 1994). Control strategies can therefore produce contradictory effects, generating employee opposition rather than compliance. Equally, it has been recognized that managers are concerned with sales and marketing, financial controls, the supply of components and product quality, as well as the control of labour (Kelly, 1985).

Research has also highlighted the way in which management can be fragmented between and within functions. For example, Armstrong (1984, 1986, 1989) explores the battle between the managerial professions of accountancy, engineering and personnel to secure ascendancy for their own approach to the control of the labour process. Strategic solutions to management's 'control problem' could therefore be competing and internally fragmented. Managers may also be highly sensitized to career advancement (Clements, 1958; Sofer, 1970). While this might generate motivation and co-operation, it can produce tension and conflict, power struggles and communication breakdowns as managers seek to differentiate and elevate themselves and their departments (Collinson and Hearn, 1994). Various studies demonstrate how the following vertical and/or horizontal differences are routine characteristics of management: functional discipline and organizational specialism (Reed, 1989); hierarchical position and status (Collinson, 1987; Hyman, 1987); careerism and ambition (Offe, 1976); age (Collinson et al., 1990); cultures, countries and religions (Clegg, 1990; Hofstede 1993; Hickson and Pugh 1995); identity interests and orientations (Nord and Jermier, 1992; LaNuez and Jermier, 1994). Jackall (1988) reveals how such differences between corporate managers are often the medium and outcome of intense rivalry, anxiety and competitive strategies to secure power and status. Outlining the patronage, intrigues, conspiracies and impression management characterizing relations within management, he describes how managers seek to survive by 'currying favour' with senior managers and 'managing reputation' (e.g. 'team player', 'promotable', 'buoyant optimist') with colleagues. Despite highlighting important contradictions within managerial hierarchies, Jackall's study, like many of those discussed in this section, would be greatly enhanced by a gender analysis of these processes (see also Martin, Chapter 10, note 8, in this volume, pp. 208–9). For, as Legge (1987) demonstrates in examining the historical development of personnel management as 'women's work', these intra-managerial struggles can also reflect and reinforce specific competitive masculinities that subordinate women.

Critical analyses of management examine the function's overriding concern with the control of labour and the extraction of production and profit. Recent contributions also consider the differences, fragmentations and contradictory organizational and subjective effects of managerial control. Yet this literature has not given sufficient attention to the continued predominance of men in managerial positions at various hierarchical levels, the relatively limited presence of women and the processes, networks and assumptions through which the latter are intentionally and unintentionally excluded and/or subordinated. Indeed in many cases these gendered processes are totally neglected.[9] The challenge to managerial power and control posed by critical analyses requires further consideration of gender, men and masculinities in organizations. It is to the literature which more explicitly considers gender that we now turn.

Gender without management

Adopting a wide range of theoretical and methodological perspectives, including Marxist feminism and dual systems approaches, feminist studies constitute *the* major influence in developing the explicit analysis of gender in organizations. Feminist writers focusing on patriarchy as a separate system of men's control over women (Hartmann, 1979b; Cockburn, 1983; Walby, 1986b, 1990) reveal how organized groups of male workers (in the United States and the UK in particular) have historically opposed the entry of cheap female labour by demanding the 'breadwinner wage' and by controlling both the provision of training and gendered definitions of skill. They disclose how male workers contribute to the segmentation of labour markets and to the way in which 'skill has become saturated with sex' (Phillips and Taylor, 1980: 85), wherein men are associated with skilled work and women are automatically regarded as unskilled labour. Middle- and working-class men have exaggerated and mystified their own skills so as to secure job demarcation and labour market closure (Witz, 1986).[10]

In a similar way to the post-structuralist developments in critical management studies, recent feminist analyses develop more sophisticated accounts of gendered power relations that combine a focus on structure with that of agency, contradiction and difference (for example Hollway, 1984a; Ferguson, 1984; Pringle, 1988; Martin, 1990; Kondo, 1990). Examining the contradictions of male power and control as well as highlighting female agency and resistance, such studies criticize theories of patriarchy for treating 'men' and 'women' as unified groups and undifferentiated categories. For Connell (1985, 1987), such 'categorical' (1987: 54) theories about patriarchy neglect differences and relations that can shift over time and place. Exclusively structural analyses of gender relations caricature men's power and women's subordination and ignore the analytical significance of the organizational practices through which these categories are constituted. Post-structuralist feminism has increasingly recognized men's and women's diverse, fragmented and contradictory lives in and around organizations. Attention has focused on gendered subjectivities and their ambiguous, fragmented, discontinuous and multiple character within asymmetrical relations. In deconstructing or decentring 'the subject', some writers argue that all subjectivities are fundamentally non-rational and frequently contradictory (Henriques et al., 1984).

Informed by this growing interest in gendered power, subjectivity and agency, critical studies on men highlight not only male power, but also the material and symbolic differences through which that power is reproduced. They argue that both men and masculinities (or femininities) are by no mean homogeneous, unified or fixed categories but diverse, differentiated and shifting (Connell, 1987, 1995; Hearn, 1987, 1992b; Hearn and Morgan, 1990; Morgan, 1992). Hence the preference for the term *masculinities*, rather than just masculinity (Carrigan et al., 1985). These studies examine relations between men themselves as well as between women and men (Brod, 1987; Chapman and Rutherford, 1988; Kimmel and Messner, 1989; Segal, 1990). Likely to vary in specific situations, in different historical times, in various cultural milieux, particular masculinities may also be internally contradictory and in tension (Brittan, 1989). Paralleling developments in the critical analysis of management, this diversity and heterogeneity of men has been shown to include differences and competing divisions according to age; class; ethnicity; religion; bodily facility; sexuality; world view; region; nationality; appearance; paternal/marital kinship status; leisure; occupation and career; size; and propensity for violence (Hearn and Collinson, 1994). These debates have in turn led to critiques concerning the increasing diversity of what is meant by 'masculinity', the imprecise nature of some usages, and the need to focus on 'men's practices', material and discursive (see McMahon, 1993; Hearn, 1996).

Yet most of the foregoing gender analyses have not applied these insights to men in positions of formal organizational power, such as management. This is particularly surprising in the case of critical studies on men, given their recurrent focus on the way that 'hegemonic masculinities' (for example white, heterosexual, middle class) may dominate other masculinities (for example black, gay, working class). When we try to apply the notion of 'hegemonic masculinities' specifically to *organizational* analysis, its meaning is not always obvious. For example, white, male-dominated shopfloor masculinities may be simultaneously hegemonic in terms of gender or ethnicity but subordinated with regard to class and hierarchy (Collinson, 1992). Masculinities (for example white, gay masculinities or black, middle-class masculinities) can carry internal contradictions between elements confirming or undermining power and identity. In a gender, hierarchical and class sense, however, it is men in management, especially those in accounting, engineering and strategic functions, who often most closely represent 'hegemonic masculinity/ies' in the workplace. While their attempts to control employees, colleagues and self may produce contra-dictory effects, men's organizational dominance both as managers and as men needs further detailed analysis.[11]

Typically, it is with the managerial function that organizational power formally (and often informally) resides. In most contemporary organiz-ations, managerial prerogative in key decisions remains the taken-for-granted norm. Whether decisions concern strategic issues of capital investment, product development, pricing, market position and so on, or human resource matters such as recruitment, supervision, promotion, appraisal and training, managements' influence over these practices remains unquestioned and unchallenged even by trade unions. This assertion of managerial prerogative itself can be seen as part of a highly masculine discourse. Managerial masculinities are also hegemonic within organiz-ations in the sense that these senior positions enjoy comparatively high salaries and ancillary remuneration packages through secretarial support, share options, company cars, pensions, extensive holiday entitlements and other material and symbolic benefits. Even when they are dismissed, managers frequently receive substantial 'golden handshakes', and poor performance does not seem to prevent re-employment in other lucrative, high-status managerial positions (Pahl, 1995).

There are also innumerable ways in which the authority and status of manager can signify 'men' and indeed vice versa, just as there are many signs that can simultaneously signify the power of both 'manager' and 'men'. These cultural processes of signification include the size and position of personal offices; the office furniture and the display of pictures, paintings and plants; the use or control of computers and other technological equip-ment; and of course the choice of clothing. While business suits appear to have a transnational significance, their style, cut and cost are also import-ant, not least as a means of managing impressions through 'power dressing' (Feldman and Klich, 1991). The colour and style of shirts, braces, shoes and socks as well as the size and pattern of ties (see Gibbings, 1990) can all carry totally embodied and context-specific meanings for both managers and men that may reflect and reinforce their organizational hegemony. In the 1980s, for example, male managers in the UK often 'dressed for success' with very bright yellow and pink ties and deep red trouser braces.

Men's continued domination of senior positions results in many interconnections between particular masculinities and managerial practices, for example paternalism, entrepreneurialism, careerism and personalism (Collinson and Hearn, 1994). Specific managerial masculinities, such as paternalism, may not only reinforce the power of those men concerned but also confirm the 'rights' of management and men to manage. In practice, both managers and men frequently seem to take for granted these asymmetrical power relations, often disregarding the hierarchical nature of organizational life and/or neglecting its gendered character. It is with these frequently taken-for-granted 'hegemonic masculinities' of management, as they are reproduced through formal and informal power dynamics, their interrelations, networks and practices, that this book is primarily concerned.

Our brief review of the critical literatures on management and gender suggests that both perspectives have become increasingly sophisticated in their analyses of power and control. Acknowledging the asymmetry of managerial and male power, they recognize the multiple, ambiguous and differentiated nature of organizational and gendered relations as well as the contradictory consequences of managerial and men's control. Although men's power as managers should not be underestimated, it is more contradictory, precarious and heterogeneous than often it at first appears. Power relations are fragmented, shifting, partial, incomplete and characterized by disjunctures and multiple subjectivities (Kondo, 1990). Despite such insights, most of these critical studies have not explicitly considered the interrelations of men, masculinities and managements. Critical management studies explore managerial power without considering gender, while many feminist and related studies problematize men and masculinity but do not examine the power and practices of managers. We continue to be confronted by a dualism between critical studies of *either* management *or* men. Highlighting how labour resistance itself can simultaneously constitute a form of control over women, feminist analyses of male-dominated trade unions have made some links between these two separate forms of critical analysis. However, these studies have given little, if any, regard to the possible exclusionary practices of managers and their justifications and rationalizations. They seem to overestimate the labour market power of organized labour and underestimate that of management, especially in the United States where the influence of trade unions has declined dramatically in recent years (see also Brenner and Ramas, 1984). Equally, as Acker (1989) argues, they tend to subscribe to a 'dual systems' perspective that artificially separates the analysis of 'patriarchy' from 'capitalism'. The next section considers a few exceptional studies that *have* attempted to overcome this dualism by examining either gender *and* management generally or in a very few cases the persistent dominance of management by men and masculinities more specifically.

Gender, men and management

A path-breaking study, which pre-dates many of those discussed in the previous section, is Rosabeth Moss Kanter's *Men and Women of the Corporation* (1977; republished in 1993). Its explicit focus on the interconnections between men as managers and managers as men probably makes it still *the* most relevant text for our concerns. Kanter argues that scientific management, with its emphasis on rationality and efficiency, is infused with an irreducible 'masculine ethic' which assumes that only men have the requisite qualities of the 'new rational manager': a tough-minded approach to problems, analytical abilities to abstract and plan, a capacity to subordinate personal concerns in order to accomplish the task and a cognitive superiority in problem solving. Despite its emphasis on the social group rather than economic remuneration, human relations theory also rests on the image of the rational manager who remains, 'the man who could control his emotions whereas workers could not' (Kanter, 1977: 24).[12] Stereotyped as 'too emotional', women are consequently excluded from managerial positions with the exception of the few who display an ability to 'think like a man'. Meanwhile, men's managerial careers are often constructed with the help of the invisible support of women as secretaries and wives (see also Finch, 1983; Grey, 1994).

Revealing some of the organizational processes through which the power of men and managers can be reproduced, Kanter refers to 'homosexual reproduction' (1977: 48) to describe the practices that exclude women from managerial posts and 'homosocial reproduction' (ibid.) to characterize the processes by which certain managers and men are selected and differentiated according to their ability to display appropriate social credentials. In the former case, Kanter suggests that senior managers frequently appoint in their own image. Men are selected for managerial positions because they are perceived, especially by male selectors, to be more reliable, committed and predictable, free from conflicting loyalties between home and work. In the latter case, Kanter argues that the extensive pressures on managers to conform to corporate expectations and demands can exclude not only women, but also many men. Emphasizing the difficulty of formally identifying the necessary criteria for effective managerial performance, she contends that social credentials can become substitutes for ability measures. Suggesting that the typical profile of managers is 'invariably white and male, with a certain shiny, clean-cut look' (1977: 42), Kanter draws upon Dalton's (1959) classic study to argue that US managers are usually Protestant, from an elite school, often members of the Masonic order and of prestigious sports and country clubs, Anglo-Saxon or Germanic in origin, and Republican. Only certain types of men, it seems, display the necessary commitment, trustworthiness and potential to be a manager.

Kanter's notions of homosexual and homosocial reproduction usefully *describe* how the power of men as managers and managers as men may persist in organizations. Raising important questions regarding the ways that managerial nepotism and favouritism can be mediated through gendered informal criteria, channels and procedures, she shows how elitist practices in management (for example, related to school, family, university, religion and class connections) may exclude women and other minority groups (see also Ibarra, 1995). Yet her study is less valuable in helping to *analyse* these persistent interrelations and networks (see also Pringle, 1989; Acker, 1991; Witz and Savage, 1992). Kanter explains homosexual and homosocial reproduction with reference to what she believes is the nature of management itself, namely its inherent and pervasive uncertainty. She argues that conditions of market uncertainty reinforce the corporate requirement for trustworthy employees, particularly those in high discretion positions. It is the 'uncertainty quotient in managerial work' that leads managers 'to develop tight inner circles excluding social strangers; to keep control in the hands of socially homogeneous peers; to stress conformity and insist upon a diffuse, unbounded loyalty' (1977: 49).

Subscribing to a Weberian conception of power that eschews notions of domination in organizations, Kanter does not consider that the senior managerial concern with predictability and control of (managerial) subordinates may *also* be related to the highly competitive and contradictory nature of capitalist organizations, the preoccupation with appropriating private profits through socialized production and/or the concern to sustain a middle-class career, masculine identity and sense of personal power.[13] Equally, it is not merely management but all organizational members who are likely to be exposed to unpredictability and uncertainty. Men, especially, may try to manage this uncertainty by seeking, through 'identity work' (Thompson and McHugh, 1995), to *control* social relations and particular notions of self (Collinson, 1992). Their attempts to establish a stable and well-defined sense of masculine identity frequently involve defining oneself and one's masculine/hierarchical difference, status and power through the subjective processes of *identifying* with some men (for example with a specified group or with individuals), while simultaneously *differentiating* themselves from others (other men and from women). Such attempts to control identity can often characterize men's routine relations, discourses and practices as they are embedded in the reproduction of inter- and intra-organizational networks and asymmetrical power relations. Between men managers, for example, these formal and informal relations, networks and alliances may involve mutual identification through old school, university or professional association connections, kinship or religious ties, shared sporting interests or even heterosexist joking relations (Jackall, 1988).[14] Yet this search for predictability can entrap individuals in a self-defeating and unachievable preoccupation with trying to maintain control and stable hierarchical and masculine identities in a changing, highly complex world. Entrapment is likely to be intensified by the difficulty that men (managers) often face in conceding that they may not be in full control of others, of events or even of themselves. The combined assumptions that managers are employed to control organizations and their environments and that being in control is a central characteristic of men and dominant masculine identities, often precludes the possibility of reflecting upon the contradictory nature of the processes in which managers and men are embedded. The consequence can be intensified levels of stress and anxiety.

In explaining the managerial preoccupation with control, predictability and order, the (middle-class) *masculine* discursive practices of senior managers could be as important as unpredictable organizational and market forces. Within patriarchal organizations, men may seek to differentiate self and exercise power and control over other men as much as they try to control women. Why this might be so is not addressed by Kanter.

She does not *explicitly* analyse men and/or masculinity(ies). Artificially separating 'power' from 'sex' (1977: 202), Kanter contends that what appear to be differences between men and women in organizations are related not to gender, but to work position and the structure of opportunity. In seeking to deny difference, she fails to recognize how power in organizations is frequently heavily gendered. Her concern to separate 'sex' from 'power' reflects and reinforces a neglect of the way that particular masculinities may be embedded in and might help to reproduce and legitimize managerial power and authority.

While few writers have sought to develop Kanter's ideas on 'homosexual' and homosocial' reproduction within management, others, often informed by more critical theoretical perspectives, have begun to examine the gendered nature of the function. In the main they have tended to emphasize the oppressive nature of masculine managerial cultures from the perspective and experience of women managers. Martin (1990) shows how women managers can be forced to organize Caesarean operations to fit in with both the launch of new products and the masculine expectations of senior management. Calás and Smircich (1993) predict that more junior managerial positions, confined to national-level concerns, will continue to be feminized, downgraded and deskilled, while men move into and colonize the more powerful, prestigious and strategic globalized functions of transnational corporations. Exploring women managers' strategies for acceptance within male-dominated managerial hierarchies, Sheppard (1989) concludes that neither resisting nor trying to blend into the dominant male culture was effective (see also Scase and Goffee, 1989; Davidson and Cooper, 1992). Frequently experiencing a 'no-win' situation (Cockburn, 1991), women managers may decide to resign, possibly to become self-employed (Goffee and Scase, 1985; Kanter, 1993). Marshall (1995) found that the dominant reasons why some women managers decided to 'move on' were: male-dominated organizational cultures (characterized by hostile, tense relationships, isolation and stress), seeking more balanced lifestyles and avoiding roles that had become impossible or demotivating. Often surprised at the highly aggressive, sometimes vindictive territorial and status-conscious processes within the male-dominated ranks of senior management, women managers felt isolated, excluded, placed under attack and/or continuously being tested on masculine criteria of success such as toughness, political skill and total commitment (see also Davidson and Cooper, 1983). Disillusionment with senior male managers was a primary influence on their decision to leave.

Another response might be to strive for professional credentials, for example through obtaining MBA degrees. Yet Sinclair has argued that the current culture of the MBA 'is a powerful agent for the perpetuation of the masculinity of management' (Sinclair, 1995: 310). Women students often experience MBA programmes as exclusionary and disempowering. Sinclair argues that in terms of curriculum and course content, pedagogical methods, learning styles, valued careers and the understanding of private lives, dominant MBA cultures are often deeply imbued with masculine values and practices. Reflecting and reinforcing the masculinity of management in theory and practice, large MBA classes can be conducted in a gladiatorial atmosphere with teachers who intimidate and cajole students, often receiving highly positive feedback (Burrell, 1992: 70). Similarly, T. Watson's (1994) ethnographic study of managerial practices reveals how expectations of working long hours, especially in the evening, can marginalize women managers. Men managers deliberately stayed at work late into the evening, artificially extended meetings during the day and criticized those managers, especially women, who left, for example at 7.15 p.m. (even though women managers might begin work much earlier in the morning). Watson does not, however, examine these processes as part of an explicitly critical examination of men, masculinity and management. Indeed, notwithstanding the foregoing accounts that examine women's experiences in male-dominated managerial cultures, there are still very few studies that focus primarily on the interrelations of men, masculinities and management in contemporary organizations.

This neglect is all the more important in the light of changing forms and practices of management worldwide. These include the introduction of more tightly controlled performance targets and work schedules for managers themselves, their increasing employment on fixed term, insecure contracts and the possible proletarianization of some, perhaps many, managers (Smith, 1990; LaNuez and Jermier, 1994). While this applies most obviously in the private sector, with the intensification of the world competitive system, it is equally relevant to state organizations, with their own economic imperatives, internal markets and transformation through the application of private sector methods. This increasing tendency across private and public sectors for managerial work to be intensified, measured, evaluated and even delayered problematizes the view discussed earlier that management constitutes the most clear-cut form of hegemonic masculinity (Collinson and Collinson, 1995). In the changing organizations of the 1990s, managers are self-evidently objects as well as subjects of the organizations which they constitute. These empirical patterns require more sophisticated analyses that incorporate the contradictory and ambiguous practices through which are reproduced the authority and status of men as managers and managers as men.

Among the few studies that have tried to 'break the silence'[15] on men and management are several written by contributors to this volume. Roper (1991, 1994a) considers how men managers in the post-war era frequently identified strongly with machinery and products. Undervaluing the role of labour in the manufacture of products, male managers engaged in a kind of fetishizing of the masculine self through the idolization of products. These managers were persistently concerned to display confidence and control and to conceal anxiety and self-doubt. Similar themes are developed by Kerfoot and Knights (1993) who contend that paternalism and strategic management are concrete manifestations of historically shifting forms of masculinity in operation. Arguing that these managerial approaches both reflect and reinforce 'discourses of masculinism', they suggest that 'paternalistic masculinity' and 'competitive masculinity' have the effect of privileging men *vis-à-vis* women, ranking some men above others, and maintaining as dominant certain forms and practices of masculinity. Highlighting the self-defeating nature of the search for masculine and managerial identity in these discourses of control, they show how the desire for a secure and stable sense of self tends to reproduce rather than eliminate anxiety and insecurity.

Our own work has included studies of the historical establishment of management in the late nineteenth and early twentieth centuries (Hearn, 1992b); the relationship of multiple masculinities, the variety of discourses of masculinity/management (Collinson and Hearn, 1994, 1995, 1996); the ways in which (men) managers can routinely discriminate against women in contemporary recruitment and promotion practices while also privileging male candidates (Collinson et al., 1990); how men managers can mismanage cases of sexuality and sexual harassment as well as engage in sexual harassment of women colleagues (Collinson and Collinson, 1989, 1992, 1996; Hearn and Parkin, 1995); how the working of long hours can become a test of manhood, with some men managers enjoying 'the buzz' of staying late at the office such that management is re-colonized as an inherently masculine function (Collinson and Collinson, 1995) and the possibilities of simultaneously changing men and management (Hearn, 1989, 1992a, 1994a).[16] It is against the background of these wide-ranging debates on gender, men and management that the present volume was conceived and developed.

Men as managers, managers as men

The following chapters present new theoretical, historical and empirical analyses of men, masculinities and managements which propose a radical reformulation of the way that management is analysed. Together, they argue that theorists of management should explicitly turn their attention to the genderedness of those in positions of hierarchical power within organizations. This applies both to the *content* of managements (for example how many men are present, with what power and authority, on what conditions) and to their *form* (for example how these distributions relate to the style, organizational process, hierarchy, culture, traditions, strategies and practices of managements). In pursuing this new intellectual current in the analysis of management, these chapters examine two interrelated sources of men's power: first as managers and second as men. Demonstrating that the hierarchical and gendered power of men managers is not homogeneous, monolithic or inevitable, they also recognize that gender issues are characterized by asymmetrical power relations which are both material and discursive.[17]

While the contributors take different theoretical perspectives, they all share the view that gender relations are socially constructed and therefore historically and culturally variable. Equally, they seek to problematize the conditions, processes and consequences of workplace control strategies by managers and men (over, for example, labour, other men, women, technology and self). Although concerned to highlight the neglect of gender, men and masculinities in much of the relevant literature, the following chapters do not suggest that management or indeed organizations are the product simply of gender relations – hence the interrelated focus on other questions such as class, culture, hierarchy and sexuality. While management and managerial functions are usually highly gendered, they are not exclusively so. Conversely, all the contributors insist that in the analysis of management the complete neglect of gender, men and masculinity can no longer be justified or sustained.

The initial four chapters examine men, masculinities and managements through historical and theoretical work.[18] Chapters 2 and 3 reread from the perspective of gender and men the classical theories of twentieth-century management. In Chapter 2 Wendy Hollway focuses on the specific historical transition from scientific management (and the management of 'factory hands') to human relations (and the management of 'sentimental workers'), through the lens of the effects of competing masculinities. Rereading previous work (Hollway, 1991), she develops an analysis of the transition from the disciplining of bodies (scientific management) to self-regulation (human relations) in terms of diverse masculinities. This is pursued through the application of psychoanalytic theory located within a social analysis of gender, and in particular asymmetrical power relations, both between women and men, and between men. Highlighting the reproduction of 'defensive masculinities' (p. 40), Hollway outlines a variety of forms of splitting, desire for control and mastery over the other. Attending to the implications of her analysis for women in management, Hollway concludes that forms of masculine psyche are not to be subsumed within a structural gendered division of labour; they themselves are partly determinant of gender and gender relations in organizations and managements.

In the next chapter, David Morgan builds on his own earlier work (Morgan, 1992) and that of others (for example Sydie, 1987; Bologh, 1990), to present an extended critical reflection on the modern history of bureaucracy, and in particular its sociological study. His main purpose is to reread and re-engage with classic contributions in order to show some of the concealed themes around gender that lie within these apparently genderless texts that subsequently influenced the theory and practice of management. Additionally, men were and are more likely to carry out managerial functions within bureaucracies, while bureaucracies were, and are, major sites for the development and elaboration of modern masculinities. Morgan engages with these issues through a number of interrelated themes: ideal types, the dynamics of bureaucracy, dysfunctions of bureaucracy, rules and negotiations and metaphysical pathos and impersonality. In each case, he makes explicit the gendered nature of these themes with particular reference to the articulation of men, masculinities and managements.

Several of the issues raised in Chapters 2 and 3, around control and scientific management, and rationality and bureaucracy, are developed further in Chapter 4 by Beverly Burris. She concentrates on the inter-relation of technocracy, patriarchy and management and the specific implications of this triad for men and masculinities. Burris discusses both the general usefulness of the concept of patriarchy, and the specific types of and shifts in patriarchy and their association with different forms of organizational control. This sets the scene for the main analysis of the chapter on *technocratic patriarchy* – a new type of patriarchal practice which is gendered and managerial. The key features of technocratic patriarchy include polarization of both occupational status and gender segregation; the valuing of expertise as authority; 'adhocracy', informality and, indeed, sexuality, among the expert sector; and technocratic patriarchal ideology. These developments significantly shape the gender identity of managers and the gendering of others.

In Chapter 5, Deborah Kerfoot and David Knights develop this concern with issues of masculine identity in management. Beginning with the broad sweep of the history of management, their analysis examines the contem-porary and *privileged* form of masculinity that has become associated with dominant (in both senses) management practice. This is abstract, rational, highly instrumental, controlling of its object, future-orientated, strategic, above all, masculine and wholly *disembodied*. More precisely, the link between managements and men is understood through the search, rarely if ever successful, for a secure and stable masculine identity. The arguments of this chapter make certain connections with the theoretical approach to 'defensive masculinities' developed by Hollway, the substantive problem of rationality discussed by Morgan, and the interplay of control and identity suggested by Burris.

Whilst these initial chapters interrogate histories and theories of organiz-ations and managements from diverse critical perspectives on men and masculinities, the remaining seven chapters are more concerned with detailed organizational and managerial dynamics, processes and practices within specific empirical settings. Accordingly, they lay the basis for a more comparative analysis across and within sectors, and more specific and differentiated examinations of men, masculinities and management. Chapters 6 and 7 both address a particular form of management and of manager-entrepreneurialism, and the so-called 'self-made' man. Highlight-ing the gendered nature of entrepreneurialism, Rosslyn Reed uses bio-graphical case material to examine changes in Australian management over the last century. Two lives of individual male entrepreneurs are discussed in some detail: David Syme (1827–1908), the nineteenth-century, Scottish-born Australian publisher of *The Age* newspaper, and Rupert Murdoch, the contemporary Australian-born international media entrepreneur. While

Syme conformed to the Weberian image of the sober, self-made modern capitalist who adopted a paternalistic and dutiful approach to management, Murdoch's style is adventurist, in keeping with the spirit of the 1980s, and more akin to pre-modern forms of capitalism and management. Reed's contribution connects with the historical surveys of the first four chapters, as well as with previous debates on paternalism and management (Kerfoot and Knights, 1993; Collinson and Hearn, 1994).

Chapter 7 by Kate Mulholland draws on research findings from an ethnographic study of seventy of the richest entrepreneurial families in a Midlands county of England which illustrates the continuing significance of family capitalism. A key dimension is the consistency with which men claim all of the credit for their success. The interviews with men, and in many cases wives, provided detailed information of the interconnections of entrepreneurialism and domestic life. In particular, Mulholland's research reveals the links between the hidden services provided by women in the household and the construction of particular masculinities and capital accumulation. Two individual men are examined in depth. In the first case, of 'the company man', technical expertise, product and company took priority over profits. In the second, of 'the takeover man', quick profits through financial manipulation overrode loyalty, or indeed rationality or paternalism. Clear comparisons can be made with Syme and Murdoch.

The remaining chapters are more concerned with corporate management forms rather than entrepreneurialism *per se*, although it is important to note that the latter may emerge in corporate contexts as well as in the development of small businesses. Chapters 8 and 9 highlight important questions regarding cross-national practices. Cheryl Lehman argues that dominant accounting and accountancy practices both reflect and reinforce specific masculinities, which in turn construct the 'accounting person'. Her chapter compares accounting practices in the West with those in the rapidly changing political economies of Eastern Europe, especially Russia. Lehman also outlines a more general critique of the male-dominated assumptions and practices that persist in the discipline of economics which, in particular, render women invisible. She elaborates on the more specific analysis of the hidden domestic services provided by women to male entrepreneurs presented by Mulholland in the previous chapter.

In the next chapter Alison Woodward examines a different kind of transcendent 'rationality', that of the European Union administration, designed on the 'rational' principles of bureaucratic practice in order to be above national and party loyalties. Using a framework which emphasizes the interconnections of gender, organization, systems, culture and power, Woodward examines international organizations as gendered bureaucracies in which the 'male' norm is dominant and masculine practices of resistance to female leadership persist. Her chapter provides a highly contemporary empirical example of the kinds of masculinity that can characterize bureaucratic forms of management examined earlier by Morgan. She pays special attention to the processes of recruitment and promotion of

Eurocrats within the European Commission, and how these structure masculinities and femininities. Her chapter is equally important in considering the interplay of nation, culture and gendered organizations and managements; questions which are likely to be increasingly significant with the growth of multinational and global organizations.

The final three chapters all report on *practices* of men in management. Focusing on the exercise of power through the appointment, promotion and evaluation of employees, they draw especially on material from the education sector, particularly universities. These chapters illustrate the ways in which management is not just a topic to be studied *from* academia but is also a topic for academia itself. In Chapter 10 Patricia Yancey Martin makes explicit her assumptions of the cultural and structural embeddedness of gender in organizations, the importance of power as a constitutive aspect of gender relations in organizations, and the proactive gendering of members of organizations through the discursive, relational and material dynamics and arrangements of organizations. Drawing on a range of research data from universities to research and development laboratories, she outlines three vignettes that explore the themes of 'promoting men', 'rejecting women' and 'blaming women'. Martin identifies three evaluational frames which link masculinism and patriarchal masculinities: 'differing potential' (of men and women); 'normative legitimacy' (in rights to hierarchical power); and 'performance' (valuing men's and women's contributions and failures). She also describes four major styles of gendered interactions: 'promotion of men', 'requests for paternalistic aid', 'open criticism of women, not men', and 'ganging up on a woman'. The focus of this chapter is on the active and interactional *doing* of gender and of masculinity in organizations and managements.

Chapter 11, by Michael Roper, explores relations between men, not simply in terms of power, authority or competition, but specifically in terms of homosocial desire. Examining management as a complex series of processes that involve and invoke seduction and succession between men, his analysis suggests that these seductive/successive power relations may entail flows of power from the less formally powerful to the more formal, as well as vice versa. Using detailed case study material from a management college, Roper argues that the relations between men in management can consist of circuits of desire. In marked contrast with the model of impersonal relations described by Weber and his successors, Roper's analysis suggests that organizations and managements are locales of emotion which are managed by men both within and between them. There are clear linkages here with themes examined earlier of defensive masculinities (Hollway), the gender of bureaucracy (Morgan), disembodied/embodied masculinities (Kerfoot and Knights), and the doing of emotion work (Mulholland) and of gender (Martin).

The final chapter by Craig Prichard reviews some of the changes that are currently under way in further and higher education in the UK and then, drawing on interviews with senior university staff, outlines how recent moves towards managerialism have had contradictory or potentially contradictory effects. On the one hand, such reorganizations may reaffirm or reinforce previously existing patriarchal relations in universities; on the other, change of this kind may open spaces for women managers to act in ways that were previously unthinkable. This short chapter brings together many of the earlier themes of styles of management, women and men in organizations, and promotion and succession, and raises the possibility of future organizational change.

This book was produced in order to *stimulate* debate, theorizing and empirical research. It does not claim to provide an exhaustive theoretical or empirical analysis of these highly complex features of hierarchy, gender and power and control in the workplace. Our intention is that this collection, drawn from a diversity of perspectives, should begin to develop analyses that simultaneously examine the persistent masculinity of management and the management of masculinity in contemporary organizations. In so doing, the volume seeks to challenge both conventional and more critical perspectives on management by revealing their neglect both of the dominant masculinities that are often embedded in managerial discourses and practices and of the organizational effects of this embeddedness. This challenge raises a whole series of further questions around the analysis of men and masculinities in management. For example, could the continued dominance of management by men and masculinities and the exclusion of alternative views actually constitute crucial barriers to 'effective', 'efficient' and 'rational' decision making and organizational practices? Will women managers challenge or reproduce the masculine hegemony of management? Conversely, how is men's power in management maintained by the gendered structuring of largely unpaid domestic work and child care? Less obviously, what are the implications for both women and men of the tendency for increasing organizational power in management to be associated with growing encroachments of business into personal and domestic time? Important issues also need to be addressed regarding the impact of gender on the historical emergence of particular managerial functions (marketing, production, sales, etc.) and in relation to the different (gendered) meanings and values associated with managements in various cultures and societies.

These issues suggest major changes in the business of education most broadly, and the theorizing of management more particularly. As the final three chapters illustrate, the management of higher and further education tends to remain largely male-dominated in ways that crucially shape the form and content of what counts as knowledge and education. As we discussed earlier, management theory itself until recently has remained very much a domain of men. These arguments raise important questions: What perceptions and priorities are emphasized and neglected by men management educators? Why do men as management and organization theorists find so many 'good reasons' for avoiding these issues? Self-reflexive questions such as these speak to the very heart of management theory and practice as it has been constructed historically. Not least, they critically examine what counts as 'theory', and how 'theory' is developed, defined, written, refereed, rejected or acclaimed, published and circulated. The practice of critical self-reflexivity, we argue, is an essential precondition for the development of management theorizing. For all these reasons, this volume seeks to highlight the pressing need for explicit, critical, feminist/ pro-feminist and self-reflexive studies on the enduring dominance and interrelations of men, masculinities and managements. How is it that the 'great' and 'classic' theories of management have consistently managed to avoid these obvious questions?

Notes

1. In 1976, women constituted 0.4 per cent of directors in the top 250 UK enterprises (Scott, 1989) and of these eleven women, none held more than one directorship. The 'inner circle' of directors with multiple, interlocking directorships was exclusively male.

2. The term 'macho', as in 'macho management', could be said to carry connotations of racism, in associating certain kinds of tough aggression with Hispanic men. This is a particularly important issue in different localities and regions where Hispanic people are an oppressed group.

3. The tendency to define managers, entrepreneurs and owners as mavericks, radicals and revolutionaries in the media and in biographies is somewhat paradoxical in that they are very much the agents of power and control within contemporary society. Comparatively, they benefit considerably from the status quo and will therefore tend to seek to conserve present arrangements. The changes they introduce are likely to be designed to reinforce rather than transform dominant power relations.

4. Even male shopfloor workers may use these masculine criteria when criticizing managers for being weak 'wimps' who are not strong, authoritative and assertive managers (Collinson, 1992). Indeed it might be argued that there are some close and interesting parallels between the 'tough' masculinities of both management and the shopfloor.

5. These 'ideal models' of management failed to recognize the socially constructed nature of management power and practices. A primary objective of this volume is to argue that gender and masculinity are central factors in these processes of social construction. Equally, their socially constructed nature means that they are always able to change and be transformed.

6. This raises the question of to what extent such apparently diverse masculinities are predicated on similar psychosocial structures. Common themes include the assertion of inde-pendence, the denial of dependency, egocentric views of the world and an absence of nurturing of others (see Jefferson, 1994). Further related questions could include the extent to which men as managers feel compelled to achieve and how far this desire for success is fuelled by particular relationships, for example with parents (Pahl, 1995).

7. Together these two meanings of management, one related to the 'public' and one to the 'private' sphere, also reflect the separation between 'home' and 'work' that occurred in the industrial revolution and that intensified the masculinization of the paid workplace.

8. This decentring of men is premised on the inversion of the dominant portrayal of women as Other (de Beauvoir, 1953). For discussion of the potentials and pitfalls of recasting the one, men, as the Other, see Middleton (1992), Silverman (1992), Hearn (1994b).

9. For example, although corporate culture initiatives have been critiqued in terms of their manipulative and totalitarian tendencies (e.g. Kunda, 1992; Willmott, 1993), the gendered imagery which informs managerial claims about teamworking and 'happy families' has largely escaped attention. Similarly, the way in which men's heterosexuality can be incorporated into managerial practices, for example in Japan where geishas routinely entertain men managers after work in the evening, requires further attention.

10. This focus on the gendered nature of skill needs to be extended to include managerial competencies. To what extent are conventional assumptions about managerial capabilities themselves gendered?

11. Adapting the ideas of C. Wright Mills (1956) on the power elite, one author has recently argued that the 'managerial revolution' of the twentieth century has resulted in the triumph of 'an overclass' or managing elite (Lind, 1995). This managerial elite, he argues, has almost completely replaced older aristocracies as the dominant social group in every industrial democracy.

12. The human relations emphasis on shared interests and mutual responsibility is often associated with the masculine managerial strategy of paternalism (for example Norris, 1978; Lawson, 1981; Pollert, 1981; Westwood, 1984; Reed, Chapter 6, this volume). Paternalism encourages personal loyalty and worker identification with the organization in order to ensure cohesion, stability, production and profit (Collinson et al., 1990). Managers insist on a reciprocal working relationship, the need for moral co-operation and the development of 'personal', trust relations, an approach which often emerges when management's economic power is weakened, for example in the context of labour shortages, high product demand or severe competition. Paternalism may reflect and reinforce the partriarchal imagery of the conventional ('happy') family, where employers' power is legitimized by their concern to 'protect' the workers' 'best interests' (Lown, 1983; Bradley, 1986).

13. In order to examine the managerial and masculine preoccupation with predictability and control it is necessary to refer to more critical studies both on management – sometimes refered to as labour process theory (a perspective that Kanter explicitly rejects because, she contends, its notion of power is 'too simple': (Kanter, 1977: 260) – and on gender. While we would concur that an *exclusive* focus on structural forms of asymmetrical power is insufficient, because this would ignore the complex processes and consequences of its reproduction, complete neglect is equally problematic. In Kanter's work it results in a very partial explanation of 'homosexual' and 'homosocial reproduction'. As already discussed, critical studies question management's and men's extensive power and control in organizations. Moreover, they demonstrate that the managerial concern with predictability is frequently unsuccessful (see also MacIntyre, 1981). The changing, complex and multiple nature of organizational realities renders the managerial search for order and control highly unlikely to be achieved. Elitist forms of management may well reinforce employee resistance and hence render the workforce even less predictable (Collinson, 1992, 1994). Moreover, the numerous scandals in the 1980s involving senior executives and finance capitalists suggest that the gendered selection processes described by Kanter are not necessarily effective on their own terms in securing stable and trustworthy employees.

14. Selecting new managers in one's own (gendered) image, as described by Kanter, constitutes an important way in which this 'identity work' may characterize organizational practices.

15. For a recent discussion of the general theoretical and practical implications of the concepts of 'silence' and 'din' in organizations see Harlow et al., (1995).

16. Tensions persist between the theoretical analysis of men/management and the transformation of men/management towards less oppressive practices.

17. The relationship of the material and the discursive is a question of major theoretical concern both in general gendered social analysis (Hennessey, 1993) and in focused studies of men, organization and management (Collinson, 1992; Hearn, 1992b, 1993).

18. It is important to remember that patriarchal relations dominated all areas of social life before the modern phenomena of organizations and management and their associated discursive practices of organizing and managing.

2

Masters and Men in the Transition from Factory Hands to Sentimental Workers

Wendy Hollway

The reduction of the workman to a living tool . . . must either demoralize [him] or . . . produce resentment and result in serious difficulties between *masters* and *men*. (Cadbury, 1914: 105, my emphasis)

In this chapter I look at a specific historical transition in the management of subordinates from scientific management to human relations principles, in order to consider the effects of competing masculinities within that transition. Managerial practice is a product of a history in which management has developed in tandem – as simultaneous cause and effect – with certain regularities in subjectivity characteristic of that subset of white men who have always been the managers. The production and reproduction of the discourse has been the historical vehicle for management to become what it is. The contradictions concerning workforce regulation were set in motion during the period in question – the first few decades of the twentieth century – and these still define Western approaches to the management of the workforce.

In previous work (Hollway, 1991), I have detailed the transition in management discourses from scientific management to human relations and their contested effects on management practices. By employing a Foucauldian analysis to describe a partial movement of management practices from the discipline of bodies to self-regulation, I raised the question of the production of subjectivities through the practices of workplace regulation. In that work I was not blind to the sex of employees, the gendered division of labour and the subordination of women at work. Yet the resulting analysis of workforce regulation was not informed by an understanding of the effects of gender conceptualized psychodynamically, which I now believe adds a crucial dimension. In keeping with the focus of this book therefore, I examine masculinities psychodynamically, not primarily in relations between women and men, but as they are expressed in relations between men and men at work.

In my earlier account (Hollway, 1991), I characterized the transition from the discipline of bodies to self-regulation as a shift in managements' construction of workers from 'factory hands' to 'sentimental workers'. In the language of the time, 'hands' referred to simple labour power, unproblematized except by the need to apply whatever sanctions are required to extract it. 'Sentiments' constructed a dimension of the worker as an individual with feelings or emotions which affected his or her relation to work. Sentiments were formalized in management discourse with the beginning of the human relations approach and materialized in the practices of employee counselling, interpersonal skills training, and later management training.

Mayo's characterization of the counsellor as 'someone intelligent, attentive and eager to listen without interruption' (1949: 65) developed to become the human relations paradigm for a new type of supervisor or manager who, by virtue of treating another person with respect, could establish co-operative relations at work: 'in matters pertaining to collaboration, the sentiments and their interactions are very important' (Roethlisberger, 1949: 39).

Human relations approaches involved a shift in the target of regulation to a deeper 'core' of the worker. It was an uncertain and partial transition, often resisted not only in practice by workers, supervisors and managers, but in management discourses (for example Lee, 1982, 1985). Nonetheless, it continues to survive, albeit in changed forms, because:

> there are many circumstances when the exercise of authority fails to achieve the desired results. Under such circumstances, the solution does not lie in exerting more authority or less authority: it lies in using other means of influence. (McGregor, 1960: 31)

Here I argue that 'the exercise of authority', and resistance to it, can be illuminated by exploring the various clashes of masculinities amongst and between three groups of men in work organizations: manual workers, supervisors and managers.[1]

I draw on my previous analysis of masculinities as insecurely established, resulting in unconscious dynamics which work through power relations dependent on gender difference to construct an inferiorized 'other' (Hollway, 1984a, 1984b, 1989). Anxieties, which by the time of a child's entry into language are firmly connected to gender difference, result in the continuous operation of defence mechanisms. The most important ones for the purposes of an analysis of gendered power relations are the defence mechanisms that operate between people to produce various kinds of splitting; for example that between rationality and emotionality (Hollway, 1984a, 1984b). By examining in detail the way that such splittings are articulated through gender-differentiated positions in discourse, and reproduce – or modify – gendered power relations, I have tried to locate psychodynamic theory within a social analysis of gender.[2] In previous work, both mine and that of others, analyses have concentrated on relations between the sexes.

In this chapter I want to apply some of the same theoretical principles to an analysis of relations among men in the world of work organizations. This results in two working hypotheses: that a psychodynamic analysis of the gendered character of relations among men in hierarchically ordered positions of authority and subordination is crucial for understanding management; and that relations among men in the hierarchy are not about power in itself, but about power through which defensive masculinities can be rehearsed and reproduced in relation to one another.

In the following section, I start with an outline of women's positions in relation to work. I develop a psychodynamic dimension to this history in which men's mastery at work, and the relations among men, are premised on woman as 'Other'. Then, in the next section, I explore the implications this has for relations among men as workers, supervisors and managers by rereading scientific management and human relations as gendered phenomena. In the final section I consider where these clashing masculinities leave women in organizations.

Mastery and the other

The term 'mastery', as well as being a self-evidently gendered term, connotes the infusion of actions and relations with the desire for control. Mastery takes two forms, according to the dictionary definitions; mastery over others and mastery over objects.[3] In the sense of being infused with competition, or the desire for victory or to subjugate, mastery appears to be about something which is above and beyond the evident requirements of the situation, whether that be production and transformation of objects or the organization of others' labour to that end.[4] A third meaning concerns mastery over self, typically expected of men in a form which involves rational control of weakness or impulse.

Work has always been done by women and men (and children) and the formal workforce has consisted of men, women and children (until legislation prevented employment of children and ousted women from some occupations such as mining). In early industrialization, the mode of regulation in factories, which were small, family-owned firms, was quite simply based on the pre-industrial patriarchal family out of which they had emerged – a family which included master–servant relations. By the late nineteenth century, these traditional relations of mastery were impossible to sustain in the face of 'the centralization and specialization of labor that marked the transition from market capitalism to corporate capitalism' (Ferguson, 1984: 4). These changes, precipitated by the shift of production from a domestic to a factory mode, involved a redefinition of the relation between public and private spheres, also redefining women's and men's relations to work and domestic life. Victorian femininity, initially in the middle class, was defined on the basis of the desirability of women having no part in productive work, helping to produce the construction of 'masculinity' and 'femininity' as categories of psychological difference between the sexes (Hall, 1992).

The worker came to signify as a man, and paid work as the legitimate sphere of men:

> The abstract worker transformed into a concrete worker turns out to be a man whose work is his life and whose wife takes care of everything else. Thus the concept of a job is gendered, in spite of its presentation as gender neutral, because only a male worker can meet its implicit demands. Hidden within the concept of a job are assumptions about separations between the public and private spheres and the gendered organization of reproduction and production. (Acker, 1992: 257)

At a psychological level, this enables work generally to be valued by being counterposed to an inferiorized woman's realm where domestic work is marginalized and rendered worth-less. The extension of this principle to gendered divisions of labour in formal employment has enabled 'men's work' to derive status from the inferiorized 'other' of women's work, which is usually linked to the domestic sphere.

The gendered separation into public and private spheres helps to produce, and is reproduced by, the production, through difference, of a feminized other. To understand the processes whereby this is achieved at the level of subjectivity, it is necessary to outline some psychodynamic principles as they can be applied to understanding relations among men in organizations.

Self-mastery and the other

The concept of the other has occupied an important place in critical and postmodern theory, largely because it serves to bridge psychological, philosophical and social analyses. Classically the other is approached as in opposition to self and is seen as playing a formative part in the development of self, for example in Habermas's understanding of intersubjective relations. In feminist theory, the other has an unchallenged place through De Beauvoir's *The Second Sex* (1953) in which she argued that, in relation to men, all women are the Other. She goes on to account for this through theories of biology, psychoanalysis and economics.

A reference to woman as Other therefore stresses the way that 'woman' has been produced as the negative of the masculine. I use the capital 'O' to indicate the way that the Other (unlike in the self/other usage) is a psychic production: that is, it is a product of collective masculine phantasies. By analytically separating the signifier 'woman' from actual women, it is possible to explore the workings of meaning and ideology in the construction of gendered subjectivity in a way which does not reduce to socialization theory.

In Lacanian psychoanalysis the concept of the 'Other' occupies a central place, understood – through the Oedipus complex – as a product of patriarchal dominance. In Lacanian psychoanalysis, the development of the self is premised on a lack:

> being the negative of the masculine, women come to represent to men the possible place of fulfilment of the absence which is encapsulated in their desire . . . it is not simply, as in object relations theory, that women are desired because they seem to promise a return to the mother–son bond of imagined childhood; it is also that

men fantasise women as the Other who can provide fulfilment in the place of the experience of lack which operates under the sign of patriarchal law. (Frosh, 1987: 200)

Lacan captures the difference between actual women and woman as the Other of masculine desire as follows: T̶h̶e̶ woman. Although (or because) fulfilment of desire for the Other (= mother = woman) is an impossible phantasy, its function 'is to provide men with an idea of the possibility of their own coherence and the attainability of their desire in the unreality of t̶h̶e̶ woman' (Frosh, 1987: 200).

Within psychoanalytic thinking, establishing boundaries between self and other is a continuing developmental struggle, the product of which is anxiety. The absence or vulnerability of the infant's boundaries, the dependence on the breast (the first object from which the infant must attempt to separate) and the imperative to reduce anxiety, lead to defences which operate across the boundaries of self and other, notably projection, introjection, projective identification and idealization. Broadly speaking, these defences all involve splitting, that is, the splitting up of parts of the self, based on primitive experiences of what is 'good' and 'bad', in order to separate them from each other and protect the 'good' on which the infant depends – or so it feels – for its survival. According to Melanie Klein, these defence mechanisms, called the 'paranoid-schizoid' defences, can be largely replaced by those characteristic of the maturing ego, which has more secure boundaries (the depressive position). However, evidence is overwhelming that high levels of anxiety and profound social divisions mean that splitting mechanisms operate consistently enough to create dominant splittings, for example between 'masculine' and 'feminine', or more specifically between 'rationality' and 'emotionality' (Hollway, 1984a, 1984b).[5]

In summary, such splitting is a defence against anxiety. The irrational need to control others, which I am associating with mastery, can be explained as an attempt to protect the vulnerability of one's (gendered) identity. The vulnerability is a product of the instability of defence mechanisms which operate in relations between people. Since splitting relies on the continuous production and reproduction of difference through discourse and practice to create an inferiorized 'other', men and members of other dominant groups are, paradoxically, most vulnerable, in this specific sense. My contention is that, to a greater or lesser extent, depending on their anxieties, defences and statuses, men project parts of themselves on to others of different categories, in order to experience themselves as living up to a masculine ideal. In this theoretical context, mastery over self can be understood as working, not just through rational processes, but through projecting unwelcome parts on to others. In this way men 'master themselves', bringing themselves into line with whatever they regard as acceptable ways of being men.

The main recipient of these projections is 'woman'. However, the picture is complicated because of different masculinities and the dominant power of white, middle-class men, particularly in work organizations. The typical manager may:

> project his 'inferior' parts onto the other categories: onto women the weakness of emotionality and lack of autonomy; onto working-class people the absence of self-control and perspicacity, the lack of ambition; onto black people 'animal nature' and lack of responsibility. All these characteristics involve a lack of rationality. He cannot accept these things in himself, so he cannot respect them in others. Because his ego depends on finding others to be inferior, he cannot relate to the parts in them that he must monopolize for himself. (Hollway, 1989: 125)

To some extent, all these splittings can lead to a 'feminization' of subordinated groups,[6] since woman is the overarching 'Other' for men's masculine defences. Either way, these dynamics do not just operate between men and women, since women function as the psychic 'Other' whether they are absent or present in the organization itself. The threat of being positioned as the inferiorized other – as less of a man – is a weapon in the competition among men to achieve mastery.

To come back to my starting point: where work is defined as 'men's work' in the gendered division of labour, we find that it relies on the other of women's work to invest it with masculine prowess or status, and thus on the exclusion or subordination of women.[7]

Mastery over objects

Throughout the history of industrialization, male workers have fought hard to exclude women from certain categories of work, usually on the grounds that the work required a man's physical strength (Walby, 1986b). The physical strength or skill supposedly involved in labour has been gendered as masculine, despite the fact that, with the deskilling of work, most labour has in practice been degraded, allowing of little skill, no autonomy or control, and often requiring little or no physical strength. However, for this very reason it needs to be invested with masculinity in order to shore up a threatened source of status (for example Cockburn, 1983, 1985). Cockburn sums this up as 'the cross-valorization of masculinity and manual labour' (Cockburn, 1983: 139). Willis (1979) concludes: 'we may say that when the principle of general, abstract labour has emptied work of significance from inside, a transformed patriarchy has filled it with significance from outside' (quoted in Cockburn, 1983: 136). As he notes, despite the rarity of really heavy jobs, 'the distinctive complex of chauvinism, toughness and machismo' characterizes the culture of the shopfloor (Willis, 1977: 53).

Mastery through technology and science

While labour transforms and controls nature, technologies extend this transformation and render it more powerful. Skilled craftsmen, who controlled their own technology prior to the appropriation of craft skill by management, were of higher status than unskilled labourers. Again women have been constructed as other, historically by being excluded from the craft guilds and trades (Hall, 1992; Walby, 1986b; Cockburn, 1983). Technologies developed as an extension of labour power, controlled by the one who laboured, and thus provided an extension of the masculinity invested in mastery over objects directly through the body.

Technology and masculinity derive their status from each other in a mutual process which depends on the feminine other, who stands as the antithesis of science and technology; she stands for nature. Francis Bacon, writing in the early seventeenth century, 'identified the aims of science as the control and domination of nature' (Keller, 1985: 33). Keller argues that the metaphors which couple science and nature have relied on the gendering of science as male and nature as female; metaphors which range from 'a chaste and lawful marriage between Mind and Nature' (1985: 36), to servitude ('I am come in very truth leading you to Nature with all her children to bind her to your service and make her your slave', ibid.: 39) to something akin to rape ('the power to conquer and subdue her, to shake her to her foundation', ibid.: 36). Keller argues that, by the process of gendering science and technology, 'nature is objectified', and the relation between science and nature 'consummated through reason rather than feeling. The modes of intercourse are defined so as to ensure emotional and physical inviolability for the subject' (ibid.: 79).[8] In summary, the argument is that science as we know it (like management) has been produced since the Enlightenment in a defensively gendered opposition based on the masculine need for mastery over nature, into which the feminized other has been unconsciously split.

The location of masculinity in science and technology has implications not only for the masculinity of labour, but also for management through science and the technologies of planning, organization and regulation. Science has signified as the epitome of an Enlightenment tradition (Easlea, 1981), based on the notion of a rational unitary subject who is male (Venn, 1984). Management is one of the extensions of this tradition. The unitary rational subject is the dominant subject of post-Enlightenment discourse, but this subject is produced in identities at a psychic cost, when parts which are undesirable in its terms are split off. The most obvious costs are a failure of empathy (because empathy relies on identification with the other through accepted similarities); defensiveness in relation to others leading to aggression and/or a rigid closedness to ideas which emanate from others, and the loss of the kind of understanding which is accessed through emotion rather than reasoning.[9]

Mastery over others' labour

Control over others' labour power is a defining feature of patriarchy (Walby, 1986b). According to Hearn, 'patriarchy is founded on men's appropriation of reproductive labour powers . . . of others, particularly women and children, but also other men' (1992b: 81). Early forms of work organization were an expression of this principle. A man's ideal was to be master in his own domain: master of his family and also over his own work. The father/owner controlled and the rest of the family provided labour in an informal hierarchy based on age, sex and class. As in the family, authority might be exercised in a benevolent or autocratic manner, but either way it was paternalistic. Sons, subject to patriarchal authority through the age hierarchy, could be used to disseminate the authority of the father to those who laboured, thus prefiguring the management tiers of an organizational hierarchy.

Changes to this simple model, where the patriarchal head of household controlled by 'natural right', were wrought by bureaucratization (Ferguson, 1984: Chapter 2), where relations of control and subordination were defined by a more complicated hierarchy, governed by rules. As in Foucault's description of Bentham's Panopticon, bureaucracy is 'a machine in which everyone is caught; those who exercise power, just as much as those over whom it is exercised. . . . There are certainly positions of supremacy and privilege, but they stand within a context of universal domination' (Ferguson, 1984: 93). The new class of managers, therefore, were in an ambiguous position for the exercise of mastery.

While the conflicting interests of capital and labour broadly defined the lines of control and resistance, an analysis of patriarchy operating in work relations among men requires attention to the age dimension. Younger men – the 'fratriarchy' (see Hearn, 1992b) – may resist the authority of their seniors, in the process investing masculinity in challenges to authority and control. Again it is useful to draw on a psychodynamic analysis. Younger men's challenge to older men's authority is a feature of human culture captured in Western civilization by the story of Oedipus, which represents the desire of the son to kill his father in order to have access to the mother. In Freud's reading of that myth, the desire for the mother and its traumatic passage through Oedipal conflict with the father produces the masculine psyche. According to this account, relations between younger and older males will be dominated by transferences from father–son relations basically driven by desire for the mother/Other, idealization, power inequality, anxiety and potential resistance. Patriarchal power is based on age as well as sex, and age, unlike sex, offers a passage of the subordinated into the position of authority – the passage from son to father. To this extent the authority of the patriarch is necessarily unstable over time. The idea of career progression through a male organizational hierarchy mimics this older principle. The patriarch is never secure in his mastery, at least at an unconscious level, and so power relations among men invariably undermine the rational principles of bureaucracy.

What part does 'woman' play in the articulation of these relations among men? How does the 'opposite sex' construct masculinity, in this case managerial masculinity? The Oedipal myth does not simply describe the struggle of son and father, but contains a third term: woman. The desire for the mother/Other as the symbol of successful masculinity is projected on to woman. Again we find that it is necessary to incorporate the Other as a third term in the analysis of relations among men. Whether or not women are actually there in the office, for example being subjected to sexual harassment as part of inter-male rivalry, 'woman' as Other is there as a projection of the masculine psyche, the premise for the acting out of competitive masculinities in relations among men in the organizational hierarchy.

To sum up, I have outlined two main principles through which masculinity at work is conventionally invested: control of others' labour power and control of nature through the transformative action of one's own labour power, directly or extended through technology. Control over others' labour power involves others of both sexes: women and other men. If this control is defensively invested, it takes one form of what I have called mastery – mastery over others. Mastery over nature spans forms of control from physical labour, through technology, to mental labour through planning and science. In all of these, the object to be mastered – nature – is gendered at an unconscious level, thus gendering the subject of work as masculine. Labour, skill, technology, science and planning all draw on the archaic gendered opposition of nature and culture (Ortner, 1974) to produce and reproduce a masculine superiority through an opposition with a feminized other. In the case of management, mastery is overdetermined through control over others' labour via the use of abstract and removed forms of control over production (mind commanding body) which characterize organizations: the 'rationality' of bureaucracy, the impersonality of technology, the 'objectivity' of science.

In the next section I apply these principles to the positions of three groups of men occupying different levels in the hierarchy of work organizations – manual workers, supervisors, managers – and their relations in the transition from scientific management to human relations.

The gendered contradictions of workplace regulation

Scientific management

Management emerged in a context in which conventional patriarchal forms of mastery were on the defensive, first with the breakdown of the patriarchal family as a form of work organization and then with an assault on the control male workers exercised over their own work. Managers were a class of men charged by the old masters (owners and rulers of the state) with the control of a male workforce whose mastery over their own work was to be systematically removed. The old traditions of authority, what Burris refers to as 'an easygoing collegiality' (see Chapter 4 of this volume) no longer worked. A traditional, if precarious, balance had been upset, a balance of masculinities between 'master' and 'man', where both retained a share of what defined them as the superior sex: the former, mastery over others' labour; the latter, mastery over their own labour in the transformation of objects in production.[10]

Within the dominant paradigm of workers as bodies, whose actions should parallel the efficiency of machines, scientific management aimed to systematize and rationalize workers' job performance, increasing productivity and eliminating waste through management control of the labour process. The task idea, 'the most prominent single element in modern scientific management' (Taylor, 1911: 64), meant that 'the task of every workman is fully planned out, and each man usually receives written instructions describing in the minutest detail the work which he is to accomplish, as well as the means to be used in doing it' (Cadbury, 1914: 101). The 'mind' of management appropriated knowledge from the 'body' of labour.

Scientific management claimed to offer the means to achieve 'the rule of law, procedure and science' rather than workplace discipline based on arbitrary personal authority (a derivative of traditional patriarchal authority), personified in the early twentieth-century factory by the foreman or supervisor. In this discourse, consistent with the rise of bureaucracy and the wider status of natural science at the time, science functions as the neutral arbiter, outside the interests of both management and labour. The appeal to science denies power relations, since it produces 'natural' laws which management too must observe: 'It substitutes joint obedience of employers and workers to fact and law for obedience to personal authority' (Taylor 1911, quoted in Hoxie, 1915: 9). In practice 'every protest of every workman must be handled by those on management side' (ibid.): this 'science' was produced on behalf of management. More broadly 'by claiming to be the nonideological instrument of technical progress, bureaucracy clothes itself in the guise of science and renders itself "ideologically invisible"' (Ferguson, 1984: 16).

Mental labour stepped in to fulfil a vision of work organization as 'a world which is thoroughly reduced to certainty' (Agger, 1975, quoted in Ferguson, 1984: 10). The defining principle of bureaucracy, whether in factory or office, is to create something that is 'capable of rational management' (ibid.). Just as science and technology can be defined as the prediction and control of nature, bureaucracy or the organization of work can be seen as the attempt to predict and control others' labour.

The application of scientific management is gendered in multiple ways. First, we have men stripped of an important support to their masculinity by the appropriation of their craft skill. Second, we have the struggle for control of the powerful technologies of the production line, with the masculine investments in that control, given that its object is (female) nature. Third, there is management's dependence, not on abstract labour, but on the bodies of male workers who struggle to retain their masculinity, mechanization notwithstanding.

On the management side, with a restructuring of traditional patriarchal authority into an organizational hierarchy, direct supervision is separated from the control exercised by 'mind' through bureaucratic means. Both management and supervision are separated from the body, which is claimed by manual labour, along with its masculinity. As Keller argued, the application of 'rational' science and rule served to establish 'a mode of intercourse' (with the workforce) which 'ensures emotional and physical inviolability' (Keller, 1985: 79).

The basic conflict set in motion by the establishment of management in hierarchical structures and expressed in the principles and practices of scientific management is still in evidence in contemporary workplaces. Willis's ethnographic account in *Learning to Labour* provides evidence of the way that relations between management and workers ('masters' and 'men') revolve around a contest of masculinity. He quotes a foundry worker who talks with pride about working in a noisy, hot shop, in charge of a six-ton hammer, where he enjoys being watched by the managing director and the progress manager: 'You have to keep going . . . and it's heavy work, the managers couldn't do it, there's not many strong enough to keep lifting the metal' (Willis, 1977: 53).

In Willis's study, it is evident that the lines are already drawn between manual and mental labour in schoolboy subcultures. The culture of the 'lads', like the culture of the shopfloor, is chauvinistic, tough and macho, in opposition to the 'ear'oles', whose connection to educational achievement renders them 'cissy'. Willis argues that part of the 'lads'' choice to shun educational achievement (with its promise of mental labour) is because they 'affirm themselves through manual labour' which signifies, not just through class, but through gender: 'manual labour is associated with the social superiority of masculinity and mental labour with the social inferiority of femininity' (1977: 148). Thus 'ear'oles' are derogated through feminization ('cissy') and through challenges to their masculine (hetero)sexuality ('wankers', 'poufters'). The attempt to establish a superior masculinity means that Joey, one of the 'lads', must render his own sexuality superior to that of the 'ear'oles': when told that one of them had a girlfriend, he comments 'I can't see him getting to grips with her, like we do' (1977: 15). Reference to girls is exclusively a way of parading masculine sexuality. For Joey, the foundry worker's son, sex beats education in the masculinity stakes: to the question 'Would you go back to college?', he replies 'I don't know, the only thing I'm interested in is fucking as many women as I can' (Willis, 1977: 199).

Willis describes what I regard as the fundamental and enduring clash of masculinities involved in the conflict of manual and mental labour, of body and mind. 'Rationality' and 'mind' at work were appropriated by management with the appropriation of skill; but in opposition to body, as in the mental/manual labour split. In human relations a new dualism was introduced, also gendered, in which sentiment as irrationality was juxtaposed to rationality.

Human relations

With the destruction of the craft tradition and the introduction of machine-paced jobs, the control of the workforce became an issue of the utmost importance to employers. Absenteeism, restriction of output and sabotage were rampant, even though supervision was intense in an attempt to impose discipline on the labour force (Goldman and van Houten, 1979). Scientific management did not achieve the desired social regulation but exacerbated worker resistance (Hoxie, 1915; see Hollway, 1991: 21–33).

In the course of the contradictory injunctions which followed regarding worker regulation, management's 'inviolability' was shored up at the expense of the 'front line' supervisor, who was left with the shreds of an authority characteristic of the traditional patriarch, flawed by his subordinate position in the managerial hierarchy (often exacerbated by the youth of his superior), further compromised by his separation from 'masculine' labour and finally complicated by Oedipal-style resistances as a result of the age dimension of patriarchal authority. Mayo worriedly described the problem of this type of supervisor:

> The fact that one man has been set in control of others has usually been taken to imply that he is expected to give orders and to have them obeyed. So supervision has frequently come to mean 'ordering people about'. There is only one objection to this, and the objection is not in any sense political, it is simply that the method is exceedingly stupid. If there is difficulty or delay in obedience, or eccentricity or 'slackness', the supervisor is expected to yell or bawl or swear, or what is worse, to indulge in lengthy admonition. So he 'talks' and does not 'listen'; and he never learns what is really wrong. The workers are often terrified, they harbour a grievance and at last, if they express it, they tend to overstate or distort. . . . At once the overstatement is seized for attack, and the possibility of understanding is lost. (Mayo, 1930: 331)

Despite the claims of scientific management to promote co-operation in management–worker relations (for example in Taylor's idea of the 'functional foreman'), it signally failed to curb the foreman's arbitrary personal authority and in this way ushered in human relations, which became influential on the basis of its claim to train supervisors (and later managers) in interpersonal skills in order to promote worker co-operation, which in turn would get workers to regulate themselves (Hollway, 1991: Chapter 5).

The Hawthorne counselling programme, and the later supervisory training, were attempts to alleviate grievances at a psychological level: for example, one ex-counsellor at Hawthorne said that they were instructed to deal 'with attitudes towards problems, not the problems themselves' (Baritz, 1965: 105). In a different discourse, feelings could have been taken as reliable indicators of grievances which needed redressing, but in practice 'Comments on supervision, more than those in any other area, could not be taken at face value' (Roethlisberger and Dickson, 1970: 292). Management, in charge of 'objective information', was involved in a psychological construction of the individual worker as beset by irrational emotions: the new 'sentimental worker' of human relations.

Consistent with this analysis, one could hypothesize that the gendering of irrationality/emotionality as feminine would result in resistance by (male) workers invested in their masculinity.[11] However, the picture is complicated by a movement in human relations towards the location of sentiments in managers. During a period of over two decades, the focus of human relations shifted from workers to supervisors to managers, and this shift corresponded to a change in the construction of employee subjectivity which refined the notion of the sentimental worker. The target of management training shifted deeper into the subject because (male?) workers were not fooled by the cheery 'how's your wife' from the supervisor trained in interpersonal skills when it was not followed up by fair treatment (Hollway, 1991: 93). Training was therefore to involve 'a modification or change in himself as well as a change in his relation to his environment' (Roethlisberger, 1954: 16). By the 1960s, in the continuing search for methods to produce self-regulating workers, the manager was required to be authentic and even the executive should have sentiments.

Human relations, though supposedly gender neutral, appears in the light of this analysis to be gendered as feminine.[12] How then did it get not only produced but extended to management by a class of male managers and professionals, who, I have argued, were defensively invested in rationality and traditional patriarchal forms of control?

I hope it is clear from the foregoing analysis that changes of some kind in forms of work regulation were urgently required, because the effects that Mayo described at the supervisory level were perceived not to rest there but threatened increasing trade union militancy, and the competitive failure of North American manufacturing industry (in this case), in terms of both price and quality, in an increasingly global market. Bearing in mind that there was precious little chance of transformations in the mode of production, the scope was narrowed to attempts to change the *relationship* of labour to the dominant modes of production through newly developing social-psychological paradigms.

The purpose of self-regulation, as defined by human relations, was precisely to reinvest workers with *some sense of mastery* over their work. At its most radical, this was approached by restructuring work, more cautiously through 'job enrichment' and most typically through the impression of autonomy fostered by the interpersonal relations typical of a 'democratic' leadership style (listening, empathy, consultation), while impersonal rules and technology governed the actual control one could exercise over the job. Discipline of the body has not ceased. Commentators as far apart politically as Braverman and Drucker are of the opinion that scientific management was not superseded but was built into the technology of the production line: 'Taylorism dominates the world of production; the practitioners of "human relations" and "industrial psychology" are the maintenance crew for the human machinery' (Braverman, 1974: 87).

So, to the extent that human relations practices did preserve the (masculine) dignity of workers in their relations with other men at work – even (more rarely) providing them with an experience of a little more autonomy in relation to the actual job – they would be successful in extracting some compliance where traditional authority had failed: 'the chief importance of human relations to management is that they are manageable' (Gellerman, 1966: 1).

Self-regulation as a strategy of worker regulation did not appear out of the blue: the ideal of work autonomy was not only deeply inscribed in patriarchal relations, but the practices continued to exist in pockets of craft, trade, skilled work, small enterprise, smallholding, art, the professions and so on. Moreover, there had always remained workplace practices which owed more to benevolent paternalism than to coercive personal authority (Hollway, 1993). Child (1969: 155) argues that some British employers were practising human relations before 'human relations' was formalized and legitimized through social science research.

A further analysis of the conditions of possibility for the emergence of human relations discourse, given that it was not gender neutral, depends on breaking down the broad categories of worker and management by specifying variations in the relation of different groups to mastery. First, women workers, on whom manufacturing industry has also depended, have to be brought back into the frame. Women workers too resisted the dehumanizing conditions of factory work, but it follows from my analysis that they would not resist the feminization potentially involved in being positioned as 'sentimental' in a human relations discourse. It was because it worked so well in the all-women Relay Assembly Test Room at the Hawthorne plant that 'the lure of the miraculous' took hold (Baritz, 1965: 49).[13]

The case of male supervisors' rejection of human relations is probably the most clear-cut if, as I have argued, they were closest to the traditional mode of patriarchal control over others' labour. Their traditional patriarchal mode of mastery proscribed empathy, which was the condition for the 'authentic' exercise of interpersonal skills with subordinates. Already deprived of a masculine investment in manual labour and technology, supervisors were likely to resist a discourse which feminized them by removing the outward forms of their traditional patriarchal authority. It is no wonder, in the light of my emphasis on the vulnerability of masculinity, that supervisors – indeed any managers who engaged directly in workplace regulation – were reluctant to change their behaviour. It may be 'exceedingly stupid' behaviour, as Mayo complained, but behaviour that is so heavily invested with the requirements of vulnerable self-identity is not easily changed by the demands of senior management, however 'rational'.

When human relations principles began to be applied to managers themselves, the expectation that they should know themselves as sentimental beings – indeed as anything other than rational (inviolable) – provided a direct challenge to the legitimacy of management. The picture in contemporary European and North American organizations is therefore one which is surprisingly close to the old 'theory x' models of managerial style or leadership,[14] despite over half a century when – especially in the US – human relations *discourse* has dominated the human resource management field and when billions of dollars have gone into promoting human relations style management through training, research and consultancy (see Hollway, 1991: Chapter 7 for two 1970s cases).

Managers are not an homogeneous group, as is amply testified by the evidence in organizational studies of failures of co-operation between departments and functions. For both managers and professionals, the masculinity of mind is bolstered by the formal hierarchy which underpins their patriarchal authority and also their technical expertise. While line managers' stance is similar to that of supervisors, at this level they are more invested in control through mind and less directly threatened by the challenge of the masculinity of the body on the shopfloor; nor can they use that discourse of masculinity to protect themselves against the threat to masculine rationality. Human resource managers (as they are now called) take their positions concerning work regulation from a different cultural and professional history, one whose origins (in Britain) are in women's welfare work (Hollway, 1991: 37ff.; Niven, 1967).

Those who are defined as professionals, whether personnel managers or academic researchers, rely for their mastery on different practices and different interpersonal encounters. For example, Mayo was able to formulate what was wrong with supervisors' behaviour, not necessarily because he was free of masculine defences, nor even because he had undergone personal psychoanalysis, but because, presumably, he was sufficiently secure of his (masculine) identity defined within different practices and discourses.

We thus have variabilities relating to gender not only between the sexes, but between and among groups of managers and professionals which depend on structural positions and levels and locations of defensiveness. The resulting picture is one of a complex of forces, acting in different directions, which attest to the multiple effects of masculinities producing, reproducing, contesting and changing the previous equilibrium between masters and men. In these divergent masculinities, I have traced a common theme, which also helps to identify differences among men.

Where does this leave women at work?

Although the structures of work organizations make it very difficult for most women to compete on equal terms with men, built as these structures have been on the premise of women's reproductive labour in the home, I do not believe that this wholly accounts for the scarcity of women in management and other senior positions in work organizations. The dominant form of the masculine psyche and its relation to the feminized other has its own set of effects which help to reproduce, but should not be subsumed under, a structural gendered division of labour. Many masculinities resist women in positions of power and authority, a resistance institutionalized in the patriarchal family. In the organization, this traditional masculinity is overlaid by the investment in (masculine) mind and rationality and, while the direct competition is between this masculinity and the masculinity of the body, the third term, as I have argued, is 'woman'. It is for this reason that when women are present in organizations there is usually an unrelenting attempt to sexualize them because, by positioning women through masculine discourses concerning sexuality, men are unconsciously working to unsettle women in positions of potential equality and to move them back to positions approximating the psychic 'Other'.

Throughout this chapter I have focused exclusively on masculinities, with femininity only figuring, by implication, as the 'other'. I believe this is theoretically justified for two reasons. First, I wanted to explore an analysis which looked at masculinity as a product of relations among men (although this required a third term; the recognition of 'woman' as Other). Second, although women have been present in most organizations, a remarkably watertight gendered division of labour, both horizontal and vertical, has ensured that, in general, they can be positioned as different. Into this difference, woman as the psychic Other has fitted neatly, reproducing and being reproduced by it.

However, it is important to theorize the difference between women doing actual jobs and 'woman' as Other; that is as a series of defensive projections of masculine psyches. Moreover, it is important to bring back actual women into the picture in order to bring back actual men: neither women nor men are entirely captured by gender differences, and by keeping in view the variability of women and men, it is possible to avoid the danger of a simplistic dualism which is characteristic of dominant thinking. Actual women, occupying specific jobs, often do not provide safe vehicles for men's projections of their unacceptable parts: a woman with skill at her job; an authoritative woman supervisor or manager; a woman who is a professional expert (particularly in a 'man's' domain); an unskilled woman doing the *same* boring, dirty, repetitive, demeaning job. The conditions under which women, as the main other, introject or remain independent of defensive masculine projections is an important area for further theoretical development, as is an understanding of the effects of women's projections on to men. If we fall into a discourse determinism, which assumes that women can be positioned as other because of the dominant positions of men in patriarchal discourses, we are no further forward than if we use a traditional socialization model. The political importance of psychodynamic approaches is that they explain the difficulty of achieving traditional masculinities and femininities, as well as their inducements (Rose, 1987: 184). The defensive masculinities I have described are not determined, either in childhood development or in organizational structure, although organizational structures have developed in tandem with the histories of masculinity. The investment of masculinities in human characteristics and practices is a continuous, dynamic achievement, requiring power and never securely established. Masculinity is insecure to the extent that it depends on the achievement of asymmetrical power in relations with the 'opposite sex' through the continuous ideological reproduction of difference. Variations among men in the extent to which they invest in this through their defensive masculine subjectivity can be explained in terms of unique emotional histories, which to a greater or lesser extent give rise to splittings based on gender difference as a defence against anxiety. The conditions for changing those defensive psychic structures – and the organizational and domestic conditions which allow them to be reproduced – are surely one of the key political issues in the theory of organizations.

Notes

1. Much of the available historical material refers to manufacturing industry and consequently this analysis does not incorporate clerical workers, who fit none of these categories.

2. There is a strong and theoretically sophisticated tradition of applications of psychodynamic theory to work organizations deriving from the Tavistock Institute of Human Relations in London and often represented in earlier volumes of the journal *Human Relations* (see Hollway, 1991: 114). In this tradition, Jaques's Kleinian notion of defences against anxiety (1947–8, 1955) was of central importance (see for example Menzies, 1960). Not surprisingly, none of the work in this tradition contained a gender analysis.

3. The *Shorter Oxford English Dictionary* gives the following definitions, among others: '1. Authority, sway, dominion; an instance of this. 2. 'Upper-hand'; victory. Now only victory resulting in the subjection of the vanquished. 3. Superior force or power. . . . 5. An exercise or work of skill or power. 6. A competitive feat of strength or skill.'

4. An example of the dominance of control over rationality is the case, cited by Ferguson (1984), of a foundry worker not allowed to repair his machine, though he knew how to do it, which the repair team did not, even when they eventually arrived after hours of waiting: 'he expressed the widespread resentment by factory workers against a work organization that prefers a loss of profit to a loss of control' (Ferguson, 1984: 114).

5. For evidence from organizational case studies see Menzies (1960), Miller and Gwynne (1972) and Jaques (1951). Also, Sherwood (1980), in a detailed field study based on in-depth interviewing, demonstrates these mechanisms operating in the racist constructions by white families of black families in their neighbourhood.

6. In *The Feminist Case against Bureaucracy*, Ferguson sees 'feminization as the structural complement of domination' (Ferguson, 1984: 121). She argues that the bureaucrat is feminized by being positioned in the relations of domination and subordination characteristic of modern bureaucracies; hence her notion of the bureaucrat as 'second sex'.

7. For example, work in British munitions factories was unproblematically seen as men's work (heavy physical work) by employers and workers alike until women were needed to replace them during the First World War, when it was found that they were not that different from men. After the war, the ideology of difference had to be reproduced (Walby, 1986b; Braybon and Summerfield, 1987).

8. I explore the implications of this in detail in Hollway 1989, Chapter 7.

9. Keller (1983, 1985) has developed these ideas in detail in relation to Barbara McClintock, a cytogeneticist whose genius seemed to depend on an identification with nature (the chromosomes she was studying) rather than a defensive differentiation.

10. Willis (1977: 53) points out that in his experience of shopfloor culture in the Midlands, the men (as opposed to managers) actually controlled crucial aspects of production like manning and speed. Willis cites the case of a foundry worker (Joey's father, quoted elsewhere), for whom the competitive edge in his relationship to management was balanced by respect: 'and the managing director, I'd say "hello" . . . they'll come around and I'll go "alright" (thumbs up) and they know you' (Willis, 1977: 53). He and the managing director laid claim to different masculinities, and a balance had been achieved that enabled co-operation rather than

resistance (albeit a co-operation dependent ultimately on the fact that they could feel superior to woman as the other of both their masculinities).

11. For theoretical purposes, this illustrates an interesting question about the relationship between discourse and subjectivity: what effect had management discourse, through its positioning of male workers, on the subjectivities of those male workers, despite its dominant position? At a psychodynamic level, one could frame the same question in terms of managers' projections of the rejected 'irrational/feminine', and the susceptibility of workers to introject these qualities.

12. During the 1970s, a new 'women in management' position, closely based on human relations premises, became apparent in the management literature. It was characterized by the claim that women would make better managers because of their superior interpersonal skills (see, for example, Gordon and Strober, 1975).

13. The failure of the Hawthorne researchers to analyse the sex of workers in their two major studies, the Relay Assembly Test Room (all women) and the Bank Wiring Room (all men) is relevant here. It was the 'miracle' of increased productivity in the former, as a result of researchers' attentions, which justified the strength of conviction that attitudes or sentiments were such an important mediating variable between the worker and 'his' (*sic*) job.

14. McGregor (1960) identified two contrasting sets of management assumptions which guided managers' behaviour: theory x reflecting scientific management beliefs and practices, and theory y incorporating human relations values. Generations of managers worldwide have been taught that theory y is more desirable than theory x as a set of principles on which to base management–subordinate relations. When it comes to practice, however, theory y principles, like 'democratic leadership style' and 'system 4' (Likert, 1961), suffer from the defences occasioned by the similarly vulnerable masculine identities of a majority of management trainees.

3

The Gender of Bureaucracy

David Morgan

I suppose that my sociological training was not unique in that it included an exploration of the theme of bureaucracy along paths that were, even in the 1960s, fairly well worn. Subsequently, of course, I took further generations of students along these paths, taking in some additional diversions along the way. Like some well marked out nature trail the path began with Weber and took the ramblers through Merton, past Gouldner and Blau, taking in Burns and Stalker, Crozier and Etzioni, and possibly leading the more adventurous explorers through Strauss and out into the wilderness of ethnomethodology. The fact that all these contributors to these debates were men was a fact that escaped my attention, as it escaped the attention of my students.

There seemed to be something peculiarly satisfying about such an expedition. It possessed a degree of intellectual coherence that was rare in academic, or at least sociological, discourse. There was a neat interplay between middle-range theorizing and empirical case studies and it was possible to believe in a genuinely cumulative social science that engaged with matters of real concern. Here were debates which seemed to provide links between scholarly enquiry on the one hand and the applied worlds of management and administration on the other. Finally, it seemed to highlight the contrast between lay common sense and social scientific analysis and hence seemed to legitimize not only this particular field of enquiry but the whole sociological enterprise.

The aim of this chapter is to return to some of these earlier, and doubtless still familiar, debates. The point does not need labouring that these accounts and debates were remarkably ungendered. Issues of gender did not appear at all and women, even where they appeared in the case studies, were ignored while questions of men and masculinity were so far removed from the discourses as to seem to belong to another discipline altogether. I am attempting here to recover some of the concealed gender themes within these apparently gender-less texts. In so doing, I am attempting to follow my own suggestions that one strategy that might be adopted in the study of men and masculinities is a critical re-engagement with some classic texts within the discipline (Morgan, 1992). It is easy enough to criticize such texts for their gender-absence; it is more complex, although possibly more rewarding, to interrogate such texts in order to en-gender them.

I do not need to stress that the point of departure for these debates was Weber's ideal type. The editors of one of the earliest (and several times revised) readers on sociological theory define this contribution in characteristically masculinist terms as 'seminal' and go on to argue that 'Weber's theory is now neither accepted nor rejected, but it is put to use' (Coser and Rosenberg, 1976: 353). Merton, editing a detailed collection of papers on bureaucracy, sees the ideal type as the 'fountainhead' and Weber as the 'founder of systematic study of bureaucracy' (Merton et al., 1952: 17). Much later, in an Open University collection on the sociology of organizations, Salaman and Thompson call for 'a return to the spirit of Weber's work on rationalities of organisation, as exemplified in his discussion of bureaucracy' (1973: 3).

I do not intend to provide a detailed and gendered re-analysis of Weber's original ideal type. The strengths and weaknesses of Weber's treatment of gender themes, in the study of bureaucracy and elsewhere, have already been the subject of some detailed analysis (Bologh, 1990; Sydie, 1987). Rather, the aim is to explore some of the subsequent developments and elaborations of Weber's ideal type through a re-examination of a set of themes emerging from a series of studies that retain something of the status of classics.

In so doing, I also hope to highlight the relevance of these past debates for more recent discussions of men and management. In the first place, these debates about bureaucracy constituted one important influence on the evolving theory and practice of management. Management has developed as a set of increasingly specialized statuses and practices within organizations and as a body of theory and research focusing on these practices. Second, the managerial functions associated with the development of bureaucratic organizations tend to be associated, in imagery and in practice, with men. As elsewhere, we are dealing with a two-way process: men are more likely to be found carrying out managerial functions within bureaucracies while bureaucratic offices constitute major sites for the development and elaboration of modern masculinities. Of possible relevance here is Collins's argument that those who are more likely to be found giving orders are also more likely to develop a degree of identification with the organization for which they work (Collins, 1991). Further, since an emphasis in the following discussion will be upon tensions, ambiguities and contradictions within bureaucracies these sources of variation will also have their impact upon the constructions of men and masculinities.

Some reference, however brief, to the point of departure is essential. Weber's discussion of bureaucracy was part of a wider analysis of the rational character of modern Western society and this, in its turn, was part of a wider exploration of the different bases of legitimate authority and the social systems upon which these were based. Bureaucracy is seen therefore as not simply a type of organization that is common, increasingly so, within Western society, but as a reflection of the very principles upon which a modern society is based. In order to explore the nature of bureaucracy and its wider significance, Weber draws up an ideal type, a heightened and exaggerated model of some of its key and interrelated features. Having established such a model, it becomes possible to explore actual organizations and the extent to which they might depart from this ideal typification. Key features of bureaucracy in this model include a clearly established division of labour, the setting up of 'offices' based upon established rules and codes of practice, clearly defined lines of authority and hierarchy, impersonality and the deployment of technical expertise. A common feature in subsequent discussions of bureaucracy was the contrast between this model and more commonsense, pejorative usages of the term 'bureaucracy'. Popular understandings of bureaucracy are almost entirely negative, focusing on red tape and inefficiency. Weber, while expressing considerable reservations about the rational drift of modern society, stressed the efficiency and technical superiority of bureaucratic systems of organization. The implied contrast was with the nepotism, graft and corruption associated with more traditional systems of authority and organization.

Feminist critiques and after

Feminist critiques of much of this enterprise are now well known in organizational analysis and are reflected in other chapters in this volume. Not only did such an enterprise ignore women, but the whole tone of the analysis, often at a relatively high level of abstraction, tended to exclude any consideration of such messy matters of gender. But even where, as was often the case, the original analysis was worked out through case studies and even where it was clear that at least some of the personnel in these case studies were women, the gender themes were not followed through. In these analyses black-coated and white-bloused workers (see Anderson, 1988) were interchangeable.

We have some account of the gender breakdown in Blau's two case studies (Blau, 1963) but the further possible significance of this fact is not followed through. There is more of an attempt at a gendered analysis in Crozier's study (Crozier, 1964) a point which is recognized by Acker and Van Houten (1992). Yet they go on to demonstrate that Crozier's analysis would have been greatly strengthened had he taken these gender themes further, linking issues of gender more systematically to questions of power and control. Elsewhere, in the studies by Selznick (1966) and Blau (1963) for example, questions of race are given greater prominence than those of gender.

If women were ignored in these analyses, the same may be said, perhaps even more strongly, of men. While most of the accounts deal with men, often in senior managerial positions, the influence of their gender is never a topic for investigation. The wider feminist critique of sociological analysis, however, had the inevitable consequence of problematizing men and masculinities as well as drawing attention to the failure to consider women. As Hearn writes: 'the connections between bureaucracies and masculinities are *socially and historically intense*' (Hearn 1992b: 160, emphasis in original).

Feminist critiques of organizational analysis, as with sociological analysis more generally, were not simply concerned with noting the absence of references to gender. It was also a question of criticizing, and reformulating, the actual practice of organizational analysis itself. A point of departure would inevitably be the distribution of women and men in different sections and different levels of the hierarchy. But the re-analysis did not end there. There was also a consideration of the gendered character or culture of organizations as a whole and the extent to which they were dominated by masculinist notions of rationality. This was not simply a question of the internal composition of particular organizations but also of their position in the wider society and the way in which they took on assumptions that prevailed in the wider culture. At the same time it was argued that not only were organizations themselves gendered, numerically and culturally, but similar considerations applied to the actual modes of analysing these structures and the assumptions guiding these analyses. This might apply especially to the use and elaboration of ideal types.

Ideal types

As has already been stressed, Weber's model stimulated an extraordinary succession of studies and further elaborations. While some voices were more sharply critical than others, there appeared to be a general willingness to use the ideal type at least as a launching pad, rather than to reject it altogether. There were some who were sceptical about the whole ideal-type methodology, at least in relation to the study of bureaucracy (for example, Friedrich, 1952) although a more common criticism was that Weber had generalized on the basis of a relatively narrow range of organizations. Thus Friedrich found in Weber a 'Prussian enthusiasm for the military type of organization' (1952: 31) and felt that the ideal type was best reflected in armies, businesses with no worker representation or totalitarian parties. Somewhat later, Etzioni was to make a similar point – that Weber's analysis seemed to work for some organizations and not for others (Etzioni, 1975: xii–xiii).

However, most critics used such departures and limitations not so much as causes for the wholesale dismissal of Weber's type and his method but as evidence of the fertility of such an approach. In real life we would expect to find departures from the model and a mixture of types. Thus, for example, Gerth explored the mixture of the charismatic and the bureaucratic within the Nazi party (Gerth, 1940). More systematically, Pugh, Hickson and others used Weber's model in a more formalized way in order to explore different degrees of bureaucratization within organizations and to explain these discovered variations (Pugh and Hickson, 1973).

Suppose we were to introduce the theme of gender into these critical approaches to Weber's use of the ideal type? One rather simple line of enquiry might be to suggest that the more an organization conforms to the key dimensions of Weber's ideal type, the more that organization will be masculinist in its composition and guiding assumptions. In using the term 'masculinist' here I am referring not simply to the numerical composition of the organization under consideration but also to its dominant ethos, one which conforms to and reproduces features of the hegemonic forms of masculinity present in the wider society (Connell, 1987). Many organizations might be described as 'masculine' but only some of these may be defined as 'masculinist' in this more overt or 'up-front' sense. This is implied in Friedrich's argument and, indeed, in the argument of all those who maintained that Weber was generalizing from Prussian experience. This might be a fruitful line of enquiry but possibly a limited one, if only because of the danger of drawing upon essentialist or stereotypical constructions of men and masculinity.

A more complex line of analysis would entail asking whether the ideal-type methodology, exemplified in almost casebook clarity here, was itself based upon masculinist assumptions. Thus rationality is not only the topic under investigation it is also the methodological resource which is called upon in the analysis of bureaucracy. Certainly, the links between the themes of rationality and masculinity have been explored in some detail in recent years (for example Seidler, 1994). There are also fruitful connections which can be made between Weber's mode of theorizing and his stress on rationality and features of his own life, including his relationships with his father and his extended nervous breakdown (Bologh, 1990; Gane, 1993).

But perhaps of particular relevance here is some implied hierarchy of levels of analysis in terms of degree of abstraction. The ideal type is clearly an abstraction, a 'utopia'. Questions of gender, implicitly, belong to a lower order of abstraction along with other considerations such as race, age or class. Indeed, the very notion of impersonality, at the heart of the ideal type, not only describes bureaucracies but also describes the mode of their analysis.

This does not, however, seem to provide a reason for the wholesale abandonment of the ideal-type methodology. For one thing, as many commentators subsequently pointed out, Weber was merely formalizing what social theorists and analysts do all the time. The difference is the degree to which this is done implicitly or explicitly. Key terms within feminist analysis, such as patriarchy, also have some of the characteristics of ideal types. Walby's systematic analysis of patriarchy, for example, might be viewed as a version of ideal typical analysis allowing for the exploration of historical and cultural variations (Walby, 1990). More important, perhaps, is the fact that while the ideal-type approach did draw, implicitly, upon some of the principles of rationality that were simultaneously under critical examination, rationality was a topic for critical enquiry as well as a resource to be deployed. Hence, Weber problematized rationality and its realization in bureaucratic structures, opening the way for further problematization in terms of gender.

Finally here, it may be noted that if subsequent critical examination of the original ideal type opened the way for a consideration of a wider range of types of bureaucracy and organization these developments could be combined with a more gender-aware analysis in order to explore a range of sites in which masculinities are deployed, shaped and modified. In short, the analysis may point not to 'the organization man' but to 'organization men', pluralizing men and masculinities as well as organizations. This would also be in keeping with Hearn's pluralizing of the term 'patriarchies' (Hearn, 1992b).

Somewhat speculatively, for example, we might deploy different mixes of Weber's types of authority in order to highlight different managerial practices. If we recognize that there are no purely rational structures, then we may begin to identify managerial styles which approach the charismatic (the manager as hero), the traditional (the paternalistic family firm) as well as the more or less straightforwardly rational. Even in the latter case, as my later discussion of Burns and Stalker illustrates, there may be a variety of managerial styles. The point to stress here is that these are not simply managerial styles, the subject of numerous scientific or popular texts, but also ways of 'doing masculinity'. When men manage, they not only manage other men (and women) but also manage masculinities (Collinson, 1992).

Dynamics of bureaucracy

One line of research was in the exploration of a range of bureaucracies and managerial practices, with different mixes of the various elements of the ideal type or incorporating other, non-bureaucratic, principles of organization. But one of the strongest and most enduring lines of enquiry was the exploration and elaboration of the movement that took place within bureaucratic structures. Here the argument stressed that bureaucratic structures were not things, despite the somewhat technological language that might be used to describe them, but dynamic processes. Bureaucracies were subject to process and change and the source of these dynamics often lay within the organizations themselves as much as in the pressures or processes in the outside world.

Organizations, it was argued, tended to develop lives of their own: 'Though formally subordinated to some outside authority, they usually resist complete control' (Selznick, 1966: 10). Total institutions (Goffman, 1961) might be seen as one particularly dramatic illustration of this general tendency. Organizations create within themselves informal structures which may ultimately modify the goals of that organization. The distinction between the formal and the informal within organizational structures became, indeed, a stable feature of organizational and industrial sociology, appearing and reappearing in various guises right up to the present day. A recent feminist historical analysis of the 'clerking sisterhood' in the American department store found informal practices and an occupational culture that were similar to those previously identified as occurring in male occupational groups. For example, 'grabbers' were subjected to informal sanction and ostracism (Benson, 1992).

Several sub-themes may be noted. There was the tendency for social actors to become identified with the means, that is to say with their own particular patch or location within the structure, rather than with the wider goals of the organization. There was the fact that organizations existed within a wider social order and that there were inevitably tensions arising out of the interplay of organization and environment. Selznick, in his analysis of the Tennessee Valley Authority, explored the patterns of formal and informal co-option whereby individuals or representatives of agencies outside the bureaucracy would be incorporated, reflecting 'a state of tension between formal authority and social power' (Selznick, 1966: 15).

A major theme in this analysis of the interplay of the formal and the informal was the division between those occupying administrative positions and those whose legitimacy was based upon professional competence: that is, between those who managed people and those who managed things or ideas. Parsons and Gouldner were two of the best-known critics to note that many organizations included both those whose authority rested upon the office that they occupied and those whose authority rested more upon their professional skills as accountants, engineers, research scientists or whatever (Parsons in Weber, 1947: 58–60; Gouldner, 1955a: 22–4). Many tensions and conflicts within organizations could be understood in terms of a clash between these two bases of authority, bases which Weber had tended to merge in his original model. This was less a manifestation of a clash between the formal and the informal and more of a contradiction between two bases of authority which claimed equal legitimacy.

Within the developing studies of masculinities there are echoes of these earlier debates around the dynamics of bureaucracy. There has always, it seems, been a tension between individualistic models of masculinity, striving, competitive and heroic, on the one hand and more collective models focusing on the elaboration of masculinities in group contexts. For example, the 'man of violence' may be an individual expressing his own aggression or frustrations in individual acts or he may be a member of a group organized around a commitment, partial or complete, to acts of violence.

Elaborating this further we may see a tension between the principle of hierarchy and solidarity in the generation and reproduction of masculinities. Another way of stressing this contrast is as a tension between patriarchy and fratriarchy (Remy, 1990). Men express their dominance in and through hierarchies, formal and informal. Strong and dominant images of masculinity draw on familiar hierarchical images of the captain of industry or the leader who does not suffer fools gladly. But there are also images of men focused on group solidarity, camaraderie or the equalities of men sharing a common fate. These modes of doing masculinity within organizations may at times reinforce each other (in the officers' mess, for example, or in conferences for senior managers) although they may also cut across or contradict each other.

Bureaucracies, within a modern society, become major sites for the elaboration of these competing models of masculinity. Hierarchy, one key dimension of bureaucracy, is to do with the exercise of legitimate power. Senior managerial offices are filled on the basis of competition, perhaps based upon examination or some other formally recognized procedures, which itself tends to reinforce values of individualism and competition. In this sense, hierarchy reinforces the dominant models of masculinity that are readily associated with men of power.

At the same time, as case studies of the dynamics of bureaucracy have pointed out, hierarchies also create solidarities at particular levels. These solidarities may be fragile, always prone to the eroding forces of competitive striving within the hierarchy, but they may also be enduring and act as a powerful counterbalance to the other hierarchical tendencies. This will be especially the case where, for reasons of class, education or ethnicity, opportunities for promotion may be severely limited. While such solidarities need not be exclusively male, there are clearly links between such solidarities and other masculine values such as those to do with 'mateship' or collegiality.

So the tension between hierarchy and group solidarity, a major element in the dynamics of bureaucracy, can also be seen as a tension between two modes of 'doing masculinity'. We may similarly locate organizationally situated masculinities in other tensions mentioned above: that between the administrators and the professionals or, in a slightly different guise, that between line and staff management. The analysis of these tensions is not new and is, indeed, a stable feature of organizational analysis. What may be novel is the possible gendering of these tensions. Some of the rhetoric involved in the construction of the culture and self-images of these different groups may involve the deployment of gendered imagery. Administrators or mere bureaucrats may be seen as being less than fully masculine, perhaps afraid to take risks or clinging to the security of their positions and the rule book. Scientists or sales personnel may, on the other hand, be seen as lacking insight into the realities of life, as lacking a firm grounding in corporate rationality, as less responsible. Again, this is not to say that women cannot and do not participate in such processes. However, given that organizations continue to be dominated at the higher levels by men, it is likely that many of the everyday and built-in bureaucratic tensions will be conducted in terms that deploy or reproduce the language of gender and aggressive sexuality. The use of the term 'wanker' as a popular term of organizational abuse is one such illustration, showing the fusion of organizational processes and the dynamics of gender and sexuality.

An illustration of the potential for rereading gender themes in relation to organizational process may be found in Burns and Stalker's *The*

Management of Innovation (1961). This has frequently been acknowledged as a classic study in the Weberian tradition (for example, Marshall, 1990) and is, at the time of writing, about to be reissued. Although based upon some detailed case material, focusing largely on electronic firms after the Second World War as they moved from production for the war and for the government to production for the market, this study barely mentions gender and certainly contains no gendered analysis. In a recent self re-assessment, Tom Burns notes several developments since the book was first published but does not include the rise of gender or feminist analysis among them (Burns, 1994). We are left to assume that most of the protagonists are men, although this is never spelt out.

With the benefit of hindsight it is possible to recover some gendered themes from this account. The study hinges on three main themes. In the first there is an important elaboration of Weber's original ideal type, focused on a distinction between Mechanistic and Organic systems of management (Burns and Stalker, 1961: 119–22). The former corresponds roughly to Weber's model and is, the authors argue, especially appropriate for firms or organizations operating under relatively stable conditions. The latter is more appropriate to dynamic, uncertain or changing conditions and involves a blurring of hierarchies and rules and an emphasis on teamwork. Modern debates about flexibility rework many of the arguments here. Mechanistic systems tend to be somewhat less demanding, at least on the individual personality. The bureaucrat can, as it were, leave his bureaucratic identity on his desk when he returns home. This is a traditional model of masculinity, focused on the male breadwinner and the man who, through the sexual division of labour, can readily compartmentalize his life.

In the Organic system, matters are not so simple. Increasing demands are made upon individual personalities: 'the centre of gravity shifts significantly away from family and the outside world and towards his working life' (ibid.: 234). More important than the unexplored gender assumptions here, perhaps, are the equally unexplored issues of models of masculinity. In the latter case, the work identity subsumes all other identities; in the Mechanistic system work and family identities are held in roughly equal, and separate, balance. A traditional model of masculinity is giving way to a more complex and less stable one.

The next theme which is explored in Burns and Stalker's study is an elaboration of the old formal/informal distinction. They write: 'In every organised working community, therefore . . . individuals seek to realise other purposes than those they recognise as the organisation's' (ibid.: 97). It is interesting that they use the phrase 'men and women' when elaborating this argument (for the first and probably the only time) although this is not developed. They refer to the informal system as 'latent social identities' and break it down into the political and the status system. The elaboration of this more complex model of the tensions between the formal and the informal sets the stage for a more multi-stranded deployment of masculinities. We may ask, for example, whether the pejorative use of the term 'long-haired types' to describe scientific experts (for example on p. 140) has gendered connotations.

The third area where Burns and Stalker make important elaborations of Weber's model is in the analysis of the 'man at the top'. Again, although the male term is used, there is no explicit discussion of masculinity. But in a sense this would be unnecessary since the analysis is redolent of masculinities. It shows how the man at the top often symbolizes or personifies the organization; hence the actual man becomes a symbolic man and the organization becomes explicitly masculinized. The socially isolated position at the top is certainly in keeping with many powerful images of masculinity and of the lone managerial hero. Yet these are not identikit men. They may exploit their position in a charismatic way, they may overplay or underplay their role, they may seek all kinds of ways to escape from the isolation at the top. The man at the top has a degree of leeway to deploy a range of possible masculinities and hence to masculinize the organization. Thus sexual or male family images may dominate interactions at the top (Roper, 1994a).

Dysfunctions of bureaucracy

The interplay of the formal and the informal was often combined with another distinction between the functions and the dysfunctions of bureaucracy, a distinction originating largely in the influential essay by Merton on bureaucratic structure and personality (Merton, 1957). Weber had claimed that bureaucratic rationality represented a maximization of efficiency in terms of the goals of the organization. Merton argued, in contrast, that bureaucracies also had dysfunctional elements, elements which were not simply abnormal or pathological but which were built into the very logic of this mode of social organization. Merton focused on themes of trained incapacity and the lack of flexibility often to be found among bureaucratic personalities. He noted that groups located at particular points on a hierarchy tended to develop group loyalties and a sense of *esprit de corps* that led to a displacement of goals. Preservation of the integrity of a particular office or a particular established way of doing things became more important than the overt goals of the organization. This was especially the case where the bureaucracy was formally supposed to serve the general public. Merton argued that the inflexibility and impersonality displayed by bureaucratic officials in their dealing with members of the public was not an individual aberration but was built into the very processes and principles of bureaucratic organization.

To members of the public, these insights were probably scarcely news since they conformed to popular perceptions of bureaucracies as unfeeling, soulless and dominated by red tape. 'They just didn't want to know' has always been a common complaint about bureaucracies. Gouldner, in a relatively little-known but important essay, submitted the very concept of red tape to sociological analysis trying to tease out, through qualitative analysis, the range of meanings and understandings associated with this term (Gouldner, 1952). He noted the way in which accusations of red tape were often associated with conservative rather than radical agendas and suggested that in many cases blanket accusations of bureaucracy missed the point. The problem was often a lack of bureaucracy, in the fullest sense, rather than its presence. In some ways more recent debates about feminism and bureaucracy rework these debates in a gendered context (for example Due Billing, 1994).

As with other themes, the discussion of the possible dysfunctions of bureaucracy edited out considerations of gender. Yet it is not difficult to engender such debates. In the first place, the themes of red tape, trained incapacity and bureaucratic inflexibility have some affinities with feminist constructions of masculine moralities and perceptions of the world. Men, it is argued, are more likely to seek to construct the world according to abstract rules rather than according to a more diffuse and particularistic ethic. Gilligan's distinctions between a morality of rights and an ethic of responsibility are not too far removed from these constructions (Gilligan, 1982). Although this distinction is not straightforwardly mapped on to men and women, masculinity and femininity, it can inform a gendered under-standing of routine organizational and managerial practices. The popular image of red tape is of the mechanical application of abstract rules to the varied complexities of individual human needs and experiences. At a simple level, it might be possible to see such inflexibility as reflecting the imposi-tion of a strong masculinist view of the world, one reflecting a conformity to rules and established procedures which may themselves be legitimized by reference to abstracted notions of rights.

However, the analysis cannot remain here. For one thing it runs the risk of accusations of essentialism. For another, it once again plays down the varieties of masculinities that may be deployed within a bureaucratic context. The 'bureaucratic personality' may be a dominant feature of many such organizations but it is not the only one. Indeed, one study of men in bureaucracies suggested that the respondents tended to be less inflexible and more imaginative than the stereotype would lead one to suppose. In part, it was argued, this was due to the greater job security and other benefits enjoyed by bureaucrats (Kohn, 1971). What is important, however, is the identification of bureaucratic organizations as an especially favourable site for the construction and deployment of masculinities. In such organizations, it might be argued, certain masculine identities gain prominence and are allowed to develop.

Perhaps the classic application of Merton's approach was Blau's *Dynamics of Bureaucracy* (1963). Blau deployed the notion of manifest and latent functions and dysfunctions to explore the processes whereby bureau-cratic rules were adjusted, modified and amplified on a day-to-day basis. Thus statistical records were not simply impersonal guides to office performance but were also used as mechanisms of managerial control. He describes how new performance records were introduced by a new, in this case female, head of department, and how this contributed to a kind of displacement of goals. In other words adherence to the need to conform to these indicators tended to subvert the original public aims of the organization. Elsewhere, he shows how rules were subverted in order to favour more individualistic needs. Thus, in the Federal agency, workers were supposed to consult only their supervisors if they had any need to seek advice. In practice, however, they often sought the advice of their peers since it was felt that an individual consulting upwards would run the risk of exposing himself or herself as being less than fully efficient at the job.

Blau skilfully demonstrates how bureaucratic organizations can be understood as dynamic structures, in constant processes of modification from within and below as well as from without or above. He therefore demonstrates that bureaucratic inflexibility is not an inevitable feature of such structures but one story amongst several and that it is open to challenge and modification. What is missing from this account is the gender dimension, especially important since Blau did recognize the mixed gender composition of the organizations concerned. It would undoubtedly be too crude to see the bureaucratic and less bureaucratic tendencies within a single organization as reflecting gender differences, and this does not appear to be wholly supported by Blau's study. Indeed, a historical study of the nineteenth-century American civil service indicates more complex relationships between the emerging bureaucratic structures, class and gender (Aron, 1987). However, one can argue that different gender mixes, at various levels of the organization, are almost certainly part of the story in the examination of bureaucracy as a dynamic process.

Rules and negotiation

Combining the analysis of the informal system with a discussion of the mixture of functions and dysfunctions contributed to the establishment of a more dynamic, processual model stressing the processes of adjustment, modification and amplification of rules (Blau, 1963). Matters did not rest there, however. Rules came to be seen not as fixed, given codifications from which departures and modifications could be measured but as processes which were the outcome of continual negotiations (Strauss, 1978). The order which emerged was not a stable and once and for all order based upon a conformity to rules but a negotiated order in which rules were the subject of continuing interpretation, reinterpretation and bargaining. More ethnomethodologically inclined accounts emphasized the processes by which rules were used, how actors used their understandings of rules to provide accounts of and for their actions (Bittner, 1973; Zimmerman, 1973). However, such accounts also provided a more radical critique of the whole tradition and mode of theorizing represented in the bureaucracy literature. The more wide-ranging critiques from the symbolic interactionist and ethnomethodological perspectives, while themselves being relatively silent on gender issues, did open up the possibilities for a more gendered approach to the study of organizations. If we are called upon to take the actor's point of view seriously, the further question has to be, 'Which actor?' The 'official' assumption that workers in bureaucratic organizations are straightforwardly defined by the goals and practices of those organizations gives way to allowing bureaucratic actors to define themselves in other terms including their gender, class, ethnic or age identities.

The approach to a study of the negotiated order of an organization also opens the way for a more fluid understanding in which, again, gender may play a part. In other words, gender is one of the counters which social actors might use in their day-to-day involvement in the processes of the organization. Nurses, for example, may reach an understanding which includes not only their identity as women, for the most part, but also the identities of (most of) their employers as men. This does not occur as a matter of course, arising out of the simple presence of women and men in different positions within the hierarchy, but may come to the fore in particular circumstances. Thus the reintroduction of male nurses might be the occasion for a development of a more gendered understanding of nursing practices.

There are, however, some possible limitations to an approach stressing negotiation. It needs to be remembered that the term is, itself, a metaphor implying the language of labour relations or international diplomacy and applied to the everyday conduct of life in a wide range of formal and informal institutions. It is a metaphor, in its origins at least, strongly associated with the affairs of men in the public sphere. It is, moreover, one which is based on certain rationalistic assumptions, assumptions which again have a complex but historically discernible relationship with the development of masculinities (Seidler, 1994). There is a danger that an approach couched in the form of a negotiation model may run counter to the understandings of at least some of the social actors in this context, especially women. While in theory the concept of negotiation can take on board issues to do with the unequal distribution of power within an organization, for some actors questions of power, especially gender power, may loom so large as to call into question the metaphor of negotiation.

Metaphysical pathos and impersonality

The ethnomethodological critique of bureaucracy theory may, in a sense, be seen as one terminus at which this particular line of investigation came to rest. But there were other tracks to follow. These were concerned with the wider framework within which bureaucracy, and theorizing about bureaucracy, might be placed. Weber's discussion included an account of the conditions that were favourable to the growth of bureaucracy although there was a tendency, overall, to see this process of growth as irreversible. Eisenstadt, however, argued that we could see bureaucracies existing in a kind of stable equilibrium in their environment, while in other contexts there might be an increase in bureaucratization. Furthermore, it was possible in other contexts to see processes of de-bureaucratization (Eisenstadt, 1959). Bureaucracy was not inevitable and some social circumstances might favour moves away from it.

This recognition that bureaucracy was not inevitable reflected a wider set of critical issues. These focused either on the adverse consequences of bureaucracy or on Weber's pessimistic approach to bureaucratic processes, or on both. Weber was, of course, well aware of the wider consequences of rationalization within society and the general sense of disenchantment that would follow from this. Merton focuses, among other things, on the theme of impersonality: 'The structure is one which approaches the complete elimination of personalized relationships and non-rational considerations' (1957: 196). He follows Weber in seeing this as an elaboration of the Marxist notion of alienation. Wider control, domination and surveillance result:

> The enemy is not an exploitative capitalist or an imperialist general or a narrow-minded bureaucrat. It is no man. It is the efficient structure of modern organisations which enable the giant ones and their combinations to dominate our lives, our fortunes, and our honour. (Blau and Schoenherr, 1973: 23)

Selznick provided a more muted, indeed morally ambiguous, account of the same process. He notes how social engineering almost inevitably creates divisions and power differences between officials and the general public. Within the bureaucratic machinery, officials have greater knowledge and hence greater access to power. His evaluation of this process is ambiguous, to say the least: 'The rise of the mass man, or at least the increasing need for government to take into account and attempt to manipulate the sentiments of the common man, has resulted in the development of new methods of control' (1996: 219). The slightly ambiguous note here gets close to the heart of the matter. Is the sociologist simply the messenger, who should not be blamed if the message is unwelcome? Or does the sociologist play a more active part in the creation of the bad news? Gouldner tended to argue for the latter, pointing to what he (citing A.O. Lovejoy) called 'metaphysical pathos' (Gouldner, 1955b). The theory of bureaucratization and rationalization (together with related theories such as Michel's 'iron law of oligarchy') appealed to deep-seated sentiments rather than, or as well as, to rational arguments. Thus they tended to have affinities with widespread and fashionable themes of fatalism and pessimism. In short, it was the messenger as much as the message that was to blame and sociologists did not do enough to counteract the tendency for their discipline to become the new dismal science. As Levinson notes: 'Human personality has been virtually excluded from traditional organization theory' (Levinson, 1973: 224). It is the theory that is held up to account, not the institution of bureaucracy itself:

> There is no place in Weber's ideal type for the ties of affection, the competitive strivings, the subtle forms of support or of intimidation, so commonly found in even the most 'rationalized' organisations. (ibid.: 225)

What is striking, with hindsight, is that none of these critiques raised issues of gender. However defined, it is difficult to develop an understanding of personality which excludes gender. A theory or a social arrangement such as bureaucracy which apparently regards men and women as interchangeable seems to reflect a very high degree of impersonality. Bureaucracy, it would seem, ungenders individuals. This appears to be the implied message of much of this debate, although it is never mentioned. Yet if bureaucratic power develops to the extent of rendering gender irrelevant, this has staggering implications that demand further elaboration. Alternatively, perhaps it was the theorists who ignored gender, and with further scrutiny their work will yield up tales of men and women – certainly of men.

For the present, two themes suggest themselves. In the first place, feminist theory (and any theory claiming some inspiration from feminist scholarship) appears to be firmly placed amongst those critical approaches which refuse to see human agents as simply the product of law-like forces outside their own volition. The iron law of oligarchy would be rejected along with any theory proclaiming the inevitability of patriarchy. Any research agenda in this area would contain investigations of countervailing forces, of patterns of resistance to bureaucracy and bureaucratization.

In the second place, as has already been suggested, the theme of impersonality would need to be gendered. The popular critique of 'man as a cog in a machine' is often literally about men. Men feature in the key images (Chaplin in *Modern Times*), and the humanity which is being denied by modern bureaucratic or working practices is, by implication, an individualized man, fulfilling his particular talents and aptitudes. Merton's 'bureaucratic personality' is, by implication at least, a man. Conversely, it is difficult not to see male figures in Marx's celebrated vision of the non-alienated worker. Women, although certainly involved in routines as repetitive and unfulfilling as those that characterize bureaucratic organizations, are not conventionally brought into the ambit of discussions of impersonality. The impersonality of modern rational society seems, implicitly, to belong to the public sphere, the sphere of men. In some popular understandings, the introduction of women into the workplace is said to 'humanize' the workplace and the male workers who are present there. In an untheorized way, and somewhat below the surface, women represent the personal and the human values that modern bureaucratic society seems bent on denying.

But again we cannot allow matters to rest there. To assume that the mere presence of women in bureaucratic structures necessarily changes the character of those organizations is to run the risk of treating gender as a fixed given in social life. Yet to assume that women will become more like the men who dominate, numerically and/or hierarchically, such structures is to allow too much to the bureaucratic imperative. To see bureaucratic structures as sites for the shaping of gender identities and relations is to allow for a fluidity in these gendered processes, a fluidity which is shared by the very settings themselves.

Conclusion

These debates about bureaucracy were never solely about particular, if increasingly dominant, organizational structures. The debates were also about the interplay of agency and structure, about organization and environment, about the methodology of the social sciences, the responsibilities of social scientists and the very character of modern societies. While consideration of some of these factors may help us understand how gender came to be ignored in the course of the debate they can also help us to understand how there can be fruitful interchanges between the continuing developments in the sociology of gender and the established and also developing study of organizations. Each can learn from the other.

While there has been a strong cumulative set of themes emerging in the study of bureaucracy there have also been some contradictions and paradoxes. Thus 'bureaucratic' has become a near-universal term of abuse, although one often associated with radical or left-wing critiques. Yet bureaucracy can often be contrasted with corruption or nepotism. Yet, again, bureaucratic rules can also be appealed to or used in defence of specific rights or minority claims and 'bureaucratic', as Gouldner reminded us, can also be an element in right-wing rhetoric. Much of the debate about the European Social Chapter reflects some of these paradoxical features.

A consideration of gender and an incorporation of gendered understandings into the analysis of bureaucracy may heighten some of these paradoxical or contradictory features. For example, feminist analysis and political practice put issues of sexual harassment on the agenda and opened up an examination of the interplay of organizations and sexualities (Hearn et al., 1989; Hearn and Parkin, 1987, 1995). 'Classic' analysis of bureaucracy, it needs hardly be said, had nothing to say on this topic. Had it been asked to comment on this issue, it might have viewed sexual harassment or even sexual relationships as non-rational carryovers from traditional patterns of master–servant relationships or as some other form of pathological departure from bureaucratic rationality. Only an understanding of gender which sees it as a fundamental, not an incidental, part of organizational analysis could begin to recognize the dimensions of sexuality, gender and power raised by a consideration of sexual harassment. This entailed going further than reformulating the formal/informal distinction in gender terms; it demanded a much more thoroughgoing critical examination of bureaucracy and organizational theory in general.

The paradoxical element comes in once sexual harassment has been recognized as a problem that demands a solution. One common response involves the definition of sexual harassment, the codification of definitions and the application of sanctions against those found guilty of this particular offence. Individual offices may be allocated special responsibilities for the investigation of sexual harassment and the receipt of complaints. Despite these attempts, power imbalances still make the use of formal procedures as a mechanism for gaining redress a hazardous and uncertain business. So bureaucratic solutions to issues of sexual harassment in organizations may not in themselves guarantee success. Similar observations may be made about equal opportunities policies. Moreover, there may be something paradoxical about the application of a form of control, derived initially from a masculinist rationality, to issues placed on the agenda by feminism. It is here that a return to some of the earlier, ungendered, debates might be of some help. It might be helpful to reconsider, in relation to gender, Gouldner's distinctions between mock, punishment-centred and representative bureaucracy (Gouldner, 1955a). Similarly, there may be something to be gained from thinking through the mechanistic–organic distinction or the interplay of the various systems of control that coexist within a bureaucratic organization (Burns and Stalker, 1961). Or again, we may need to return to gendered discussions of themes to do with negotiated order or a much more dynamic and fluid understanding of the concept of rules within the day-to-day life of organizations.

Recent debates about feminism and bureaucracy have put many of these themes on to the agenda (for example Due Billing, 1994; Ferguson, 1984; Savage and Witz, 1992). A feminist argument against bureaucracy would seem to follow inevitably from wider critiques of masculine rationalities and an increasingly gendered understanding of organizational and managerial practices. Yet such a critique also brings further problems and paradoxes to do with, for example, the dangers of essentialist and fixed understandings of gender, a recognition of the ways in which bureaucratic managerial procedures may be used to the benefit of women, and the complexities that emerge when increasing numbers of women are to be found at all levels of modern organizations, even where such bodies may still be effectively controlled by men. The working through of such complexities brings more fluid and dynamic understandings of gender as well as of the organizations themselves.

In relation to issues more specifically focused on men and management we can see the emergence of similar degrees of complexity. Models of bureaucracy often seem to *imply* a straightforward parallel with the organization of hegemonic masculinities. Men manage other men and/or women where these other men or women are either lower participants in an organization or clients, or both. Yet the recognition of men in different positions in relation to bureaucracies suggests a more varied range of masculinities, around themes of dominance and subordination. Closer examinations of 'managerial styles' or managerial careers may again point to different ways of doing masculinity within the context of such organizations. Men manage their gendered identities through managing others in the day-to-day work of bureaucracies. The increasing presence of women and the increasing recognition of the need for a more gendered under-standing of organizational processes produce further complexities in the management and deployment of gendered identities.

The debates around bureaucracy did not come to an end with Strauss and the ethnomethodological critique. A gendered and feminist analysis clearly identified problems with all the main lines of development in the debate but also allowed for further critiques and developments. Yet, even here, there may be a case for a critical rereading of the classics.

4

Technocracy, Patriarchy and Management

Beverly H. Burris

Men's and women's lives have changed dramatically during the past few decades, leading to a diverse array of masculinities and femininities. However, gender remains closely allied with male dominance, to the extent that some theorists see the two as identical (MacKinnon, 1987: 51 and *passim*). Our task is to make sense of a contemporary reality in which there are many more options for women and men, and yet most paths lead towards the familiar reality of male dominance and patriarchal control, a reality that restricts both women and men.

I believe that recent changes in gender relations cannot be understood except in the context of changing occupational structures. As several theorists have pointed out, a shift from *private patriarchy* to *public patriarchy* has occurred (see Walby, 1990; Hearn, 1992b; also p. 64ff. below), with the latter emphasizing female subordination in state and occupational sectors. In advanced industrialized societies, paid employment is now central to the lives of the majority of both women and men, and workplaces are some of the most important arenas in which the drama of gender is staged.

Given the salience of gender within work organizations, what is striking is the general inattention paid to gender in the literature on organizations and management; as Acker (1992: 255–6) points out:

> What is problematic is the discontinuity, even contradiction, between organizational realities obviously structured around gender and ways of thinking and talking about these same realities as though they were gender neutral. What activities or practices produce the face of gender neutrality and maintain this disjuncture between organizational life and theory?

In order to reach a fuller understanding of both contemporary gender relationships and contemporary work organizations, this ideology of the gender neutrality of work must be questioned, and the gendering of the workplace must be more fully explored.

One way in which organizational gender has been acknowledged and discussed is through the substantial literature on 'women and management'.[1] Although this work has made a contribution to our understanding of gender in organizations, it also has the potential to divert attention from other important foci. In particular, given the fact that the large majority of high-level managers are men, greater analysis of men, masculinity and management would seem pertinent. To focus on women in management runs the risk of exaggerating their numbers and importance, and of ignoring the important ways in which male dominance and patriarchal norms of conduct have influenced modern management practices and work organizations. Female and male managers alike often operate in a clearly patriarchal context.

Work organizations have changed dramatically since the Second World War, as what has been termed a 'second industrial revolution' has occurred (Piore and Sabel, 1984). The changes in work organizations are intertwined with changes in gender relations in complex ways: changes in gender relations have been both a contributing cause and an important effect of changes in the workplace. Neither the dynamism (for example new options, new definitions of masculinity and femininity) nor the static dimensions (for example male dominance, female subordination) of gender can be understood without exploring the linkages between gender and the new forms of organizational structure and control. New types of workplace organization require new forms of management, which create new patterns of gender construction.

Elsewhere I have theorized that a new type of organizational control structure, which I call *technocracy*, has become apparent in diverse work settings (see Burris, 1986, 1989a, 1989b, 1989c, 1993). Particularly in workplaces centred around advanced technology, such as high-tech research and development firms, highly automated production workplaces, and service corporations reliant on computerized systems (for example telecommunications, finance), technocratic organization and control have become apparent. Such interrelated factors as the internationalization of the division of labour, enhanced worldwide competition among core firms and a corresponding emphasis on innovation, implementation of computerized automation and advanced telecommunications technology, expanded need for the management and planning of complex economic systems, and rising educational levels and equal opportunity pressures have led to the emergence of technocratic control.

Organizational control structures include structural characteristics and corresponding ideologies which work together to ensure managerial control of the labour process, subordination of the workforce, and legitimation of this subordination (see Etzioni, 1965). Different forms of organizational control have evolved through an historical process of rationalization: pre-capitalist craft/guild control, simple control, technical control, bureaucratic control, professionalism, and finally technocratic control. Technocratic control has arisen as previous forms of control became inadequate to deal with social and technological changes. Like previous forms of organizational control, technocracy is gendered, and reflects a type of male dominance that I call *technocratic patriarchy*. Technocratic managers utilize different managerial strategies and skills, and these differences shape both their own gender identity and the gendering of others.

In this chapter, first I discuss the concept of patriarchy, how it has been defined, and how I believe it should be defined in order to be useful. I then explore the different types of patriarchy which have been associated with the different types of organizational and managerial control. I go on to discuss technocratic patriarchy: how gender and new types of organizational structure and managerial culture have shaped one another so as to create workplaces which are both innovative and yet still strongly gendered. I conclude with a discussion of the implications for the future of gender in organizations.

The concept of patriarchy

The concept of patriarchy has generated considerable controversy. It has been defined in rather different ways, and rejected completely by some feminist theorists (as well as by many non-feminists). Given the centrality of the concept of patriarchy, it is worth reviewing some of these debates so as to situate the present analysis within them.

The classic social scientific definition of patriarchy is a social system in which the fathers or heads of households rule over all women and younger men. This definition goes back to Weber (1978a) and has affinities with Freud's discussion of the primal horde (Freud, 1938, see also Hearn, 1987; Pateman, 1988; Walby, 1990). This usage of the term 'patriarchy' suggests a rule by older male patriarchs in societies where kinship structures are central to the sociopolitical system.

Feminist theorists have often adopted the term, but have typically altered the meaning. Many feminists use the term rather loosely, as a general term for male dominance. More precisely, Walby (1990: 20) defines it as 'a system of social structures and practices in which men dominate, oppress, and exploit women'. Some feminists, however, retain the emphasis on male dominance over men as well as women; Pleck (1989: 27), for instance, says 'Patriarchy is a dual system, a system in which men oppress women, and in which men oppress themselves and each other' (see also Hartmann, 1979a). Here the literal rule of the father becomes a more general distinction between powerful and less powerful men: more powerful men dominating less powerful men and women, while also limiting themselves in the process. As Cockburn (1991: 8) puts it: 'Patriarchy corrupts the man at the top and mutilates the one at the bottom.' This usage of the term raises further questions about power, and the interaction of gender inequality, class, race, and other types of inequality.

Some have rejected the concept of patriarchy altogether, contending that the term points towards ahistoricity and a false universalism (Barrett, 1980). As Cockburn (1991: 7) notes, however, this criticism is valid only in certain cases. Feminist theorists such as Cockburn (1985, 1991) and Walby (1986b, 1990) have devoted considerable time and energy to the question of how and why patriarchy has changed over time (see also Hearn, 1992b; and below). Moreover, Cockburn (1991: 7) clearly takes the position that 'patriarchy is only one of other possible sex/gender systems'.

The shift from *private patriarchy* to *public patriarchy* (Walby, 1986b; Hearn, 1992b) has received considerable attention. With capitalism and societal rationalization, male dominance has been institutionalized, and familial dominance by husbands and fathers is amply buttressed by state and occupational structures. These societal transformations imply fundamental changes in gender relations and patriarchy. As Hearn (1992b: 67) argues, public patriarchy might be understood as combining elements of both patriarchy and *fratriarchy*, more collegial, shared power among brothers of equal rank. Hierarchical work settings, for instance, are more patriarchal, and post-bureaucratic occupational settings are more fratriarchal.

I believe that the concept of patriarchy, defined as a system of male dominance in which some men (and women who adopt patriarchal values and practices) dominate other men and most women, has the potential to be useful. What we need are detailed historical and contemporary analyses of the micropolitics of patriarchal practice and the various patriarchal ideologies that support these practices: how they have changed and how they have remained constant, the continuities and discontinuities over time. In particular, this chapter explores the ways in which patriarchal values have been and continue to be embedded in organizational control structures so as to reflect and reinforce different configurations of masculinity and management.

The changing face of patriarchal organization

Pre-capitalist workplace control centred around family-based production and craft/guild control, both of which were buttressed by ideologies of traditionalism and religion. Theocratic ideology promoted the submission of women to men, and of everyone to the 'authorities, particularly the Highest authority' (Bendix, 1956: 205). Women were excluded from religious leadership positions, craft unions and property ownership. Paternalism and *noblesse oblige* were extolled as virtues: the rich were to be 'in loco parentis to the poor, guiding and restraining them like children' (Mill, 1848, in Bendix, 1956: 47), and men had similar responsibilities for their wives and children. Patriarchy, literally understood as rule by the familial and church fathers, was clearly a central organizational principle of pre-capitalist work organization.

However, the stringency of the theocratic patriarchal ideology made possible considerable flexibility within families and guilds. The hierarchical relationship among masters, journeymen and apprentices, like the division of labour within the family, was relatively collegial and fluid (Braverman, 1974; Reckman, 1979). Within the family, production was organized according to a clearly gendered division of labour, but gender roles were seen as practical rather than psychological in nature, and were routinely crossed when necessary. Women's work was socially respected and valued, and women had the additional responsibility of being 'deputy husbands', clearly subordinate to men, but also expected to take on male tasks and responsibilities in the event of their husband's absence or death (see Ulrich, 1982). Theocratic patriarchy combined a stringent ideology of male superiority, of men as closer to God and therefore with unique leadership abilities and responsibilities, with relatively relaxed and collegial forms of work organization. The theocratic masculine ideal was spiritual, charismatic, skilled and paternalistic: a strict but benevolent leader.

With the emergence of capitalism, these pre-capitalist forms of work organization became perceived as insufficiently stringent in terms of control of both the work process and the product (Clawson, 1980; Marglin, 1974). The emerging factory system relied on simple, direct control:

> The personal power and authority of the capitalist constituted the primary mechanism for control. . . . Alone or perhaps in concert with a few managers, he watched over the entire operations of the firm. He supervised the work activities directly; he maintained a close watch on his foremen, and he interceded immediately with full power to solve any problems, overriding established procedures, firing recalcitrant workers, recruiting new ones, rearranging work schedules, reducing pay, handing out bonuses, and so forth. (Edwards, 1979: 25)

Simple control would not have been possible without the corresponding legitimating ideology of entrepreneurial prerogative. Storey (1983) discusses how this entrepreneurial ideology may comprise several aspects. First, there were ownership rights and responsibilities. Second was the belief that 'there are persons naturally identifiable as "leaders," and others who perform best when led' (Storey, 1983: 104), an outgrowth of social Darwinist ideas of the survival of the fittest. Given the Darwinian struggle for capital, capitalists were seen as having proven their superiority by accumulating capital. Third was the idea that because of this natural superiority and ability to lead, capitalists can best serve the *general* interest by exercising workplace control and making their enterprises profitable.

This entrepreneurial ideology was clearly gendered, although typically discussed in gender-neutral terms. Social Darwinism exalted white males as the natural leaders (see Ehrenreich and English, 1979), and early capitalist societies rigged the competition for capital by restricting property ownership rights of women and non-whites. As Walby (1986b: 97ff.) points out, 'this effectively precluded the possibility of female capitalists'. Capitalism and patriarchy began their long relationship in a symbiotic manner, although the history of this relationship has also been marked by conflict and contradiction.

With the emergence of capitalism, simple control and entrepreneurial patriarchy, masculine management norms changed. The more relaxed and collegial types of work characteristic of the pre-capitalist period were replaced by a more ruthless, competitive and acquisitive spirit. Masculinity was something that had to be proven in the crucible of the capitalist marketplace, and success was increasingly seen in terms of affluence and capital accumulation. Women were viewed as constitutionally unfit for the ruthless world of capitalism; men were expected to be 'good providers' who could afford to cloister their wives in the home.

By the mid-nineteenth century, industrialization and the consolidation of capital led to larger enterprises and a crisis of control (see Edwards, 1979). Three separate types of control emerged as alternatives and adjuncts to simple control: technical control (in blue-collar production workplaces), bureaucratic control (in white-collar, corporate settings), and professional control (in non-routinized, skilled work settings). All three of these organizational innovations represent more structural types of control than the more personalized control characteristic of both pre-capitalist and simple control. 'Rather than being exercised openly by the foreman or supervisor, *power was made invisible in the structure of work*' (Edwards, 1979: 110). As we shall see, patriarchy also became more structural, with its dominant strategies increasingly less transparent and more cleverly legitimated by various corollary ideologies.

Technical control is embedded in the design of machines and mechanical systems, so that they set the pace and form of work (Edwards, 1979). Workers are constrained by the design of the machine technology to work at a certain pace and in specific ways. The clearest manifestation of technical control is continuous-flow production, as used by the early textile industry and (most famously) the automobile assembly line. Technical control depends upon three separate legitimating ideologies: technological autonomy/neutrality, technological determinism, and technological progress.[2]

Although workplace technology is presented as driven by its own progressive dynamic, rather than by particular interests, in actuality it has been shaped by patriarchy (as well as by capitalism). The form of masculinity exalted by technical control emphasized technical ability and physical strength. Work on the early assembly lines was dirty, noisy and tiring, and soon became defined as 'man's work'. As one worker nostalgically told Cockburn (1983: 52): 'I like to do a man's job. And this means physical labour and getting dirty.' The technology was designed to be used by working-class men, and generated a distinctive class/gender culture (see Cockburn, 1983 for a fuller discussion).

The work in this era was often dangerous as well, and protective labour legislation excluded women from work seen as unfit for them. Paternalism, a benevolent but condescending fatherliness analogous to *noblesse oblige*, was therefore endorsed as a central patriarchal strategy for managers in the early twentieth century. As Walby (1986b: 111) argues, in her discussion of the British Factory Acts, 'the factory legislation . . . represents a political response from patriarchal interests striving to re-establish patriarchal control which was threatened by the emerging capitalist reorganization of the sexual division of labor'.

In contrast with technical control, bureaucracy rests on an expansion of formal/legal rationality within work organizations: formal rules, task differentiation, hierarchy, and in general an organizational structure that emulated the machine (see Mintzberg, 1979). As Beninger (1986: 6) points out, bureaucracy emerges as a 'critical new machinery . . . for control of the societal forces unleashed by the Industrial Revolution'.

Unlike the personalized culture of both craft work and simple control, bureaucratic rules purport to constrain workers at all levels of the organization, even as they protect workers from arbitrary exercises of power. As with technical control, bureaucracy is legitimated on the grounds of impartiality and neutrality: clearly defined rules that ostensibly apply to everyone and allow all to compete fairly and equally. To discuss the gendering of bureaucracy is therefore to challenge directly its central legitimating ideology.

As Kanter (1977), Ferguson (1984) and others have revealed, bureaucracy is deeply gendered and male dominated (see also Morgan and Woodward, Chapters 3 and 9 in this volume). Women are marginalized by the male culture of inflexibility, efficiency, rationality and instrumentality. In the context of bureaucratic patriarchy, male managers (and a few female managers) are expected to be unemotional, objective, impartial, efficient and closely bound by the rules. Women are defined as antithetical to this culture: as emotional, irrational, particularistic, subjective, focused on family rather than work (see Kanter, 1977; Ferguson, 1984 for fuller discussions). Initially excluded from offices altogether (Davies, 1974), when women did enter bureaucratic organizations it was as a marginalized group, segregated into a clerical/secretarial ghetto where the conditions of powerlessness tended to create 'feminine' characteristics and a self-fulfilling prophecy of male superiority (see Walby, 1986b: 154ff.; Kanter, 1977).

Professionalism arose simultaneously with technical and bureaucratic control during the latter half of the nineteenth century. Professional control differs from technical and bureaucratic control in that it allows for more professional discretion in dealing with clients and more autonomous and collegial forms of work organization. Professionals are alleged to possess esoteric skill and knowledge which requires self-regulation and collegial control, in contrast to the external control of bureaucracy or technical control. Professionals are expected to deal with clients as unique individuals, and to utilize formalized knowledge and skill to deal with crisis situations (see Friedson, 1984; Wilensky, 1964; Larson, 1977; Burris, 1993).

The model of early professionalism was essentially male, and women were seen as antithetical to professional norms of conduct: as lacking in self-control, as unpredictable in a crisis. Women were excluded from early professional schools in order to ensure that the professions would be male (see Walby, 1986b). Professional patriarchy emphasized qualities such as rationality, tacit knowledge, and wisdom in the face of crisis, traits that became defined in clearly paternalistic terms: the professional as surrogate father.

In recent years, certain aspects of technical control, bureaucracy and professionalism have been integrated into a more complex and heavily legitimated type of technocratic control. As we shall see below, technocracy has fostered unique forms of patriarchal management. However, it would be a mistake to view the previous types of organizational control and patriarchy as superseded; on the contrary, they persist and flourish today in different contexts. A central reason for the contemporary complexity of gender relations is this overlapping pattern, this *pentimento*, of different types of organizational and managerial patriarchy: theocratic patriarchy, entrepreneurial patriarchy, technical patriarchy, bureaucratic patriarchy, professional patriarchy, and, finally, technocratic patriarchy.

Technocratic patriarchy

A new type of workplace organization and ideology, technocracy, is becoming apparent, particularly in workplaces centred around computerized technology. Although the reasons for the shift to technocratic organization are complex, one impetus appears to have been the equality movements of the 1960s, and their demands for equity and fairness. Technocracy purports to be a more objective, rational and just system, more of a meritocracy. The questions then become: with regard to gender relations, in particular, are technocratic organizations more equitable than previous types of organizational control structure? How has technocratic reorganization led to new types of managerial strategy, and how are these gendered?

As certain factories, bureaucracies and professional organizations are restructured around advanced technology and technical experts, similar changes in structure have become apparent. The basic characteristics of technocratic organizations include a polarization into 'expert' and 'non-expert' sectors, the de-emphasis on bureaucratic rules and reliance on informal, *ad hoc* organization within the expert sector, importance of technical expertise rather than rank position as the primary basis of workplace authority, and technocratic ideology of decision making derived from technical imperatives.[3] Each of these dimensions of technocracy is gendered, resulting in new types of patriarchal practice, what I call technocratic patriarchy.

Polarization

In technocratic organizations, polarization according to occupational status is paralleling and reinforcing gender segregation and circumscribing the mobility prospects of non-expert sector workers (Cornfield et al., 1987; Feldberg and Glenn, 1983, 1987; Gutek, 1983: 164; National Research Council, 1986; Noyelle, 1987; Zimmerman, 1983: 147). In the UK, recent studies reveal that in high-tech industries women are in the majority in non-expert production jobs such as 'stuffing boards', but that '94% of technicians, 99% of craft workers and 97% of managers were men' (Cockburn, 1985: 225). Similarly, Feldberg (1980) found that the computerization of the large US insurance company she studied led to a more bifurcated organizational structure, with men increasing their domination of upper levels due to their over-representation in high-level technical jobs, which Feldberg found to be 95 per cent male. Strober and Arnold (1987) in their study of computer-related occupations in the US, found that men represented 95 per cent of computer engineers.

This polarization and the concomitant demise of internal job ladders have implications for equal opportunity and affirmative action policy. As Noyelle (1987: 14–15) puts it:

> A central principle behind these [Equal Employment Opportunity] decrees was to eliminate discrimination by extending the benefits of internal labor markets to women and minority workers. Had everything else remained unchanged, the EEO challenge would probably have considerably weakened sex and race discrimination in the workplace . . . but at the same time that EEO policies were gaining speed, other forces came into play that began weakening the role of internal labor markets across a broad range of industries. Hence a basic dimension of EEO strategy – aggressive internal promotion of women and minority workers – was undermined. Some women and minority workers continued to advance to higher echelons, but their progress became increasingly dependent upon a different set of factors, involving educational credentials.

In the bifurcated technocratic organization, then, middle-level positions are dramatically reduced or eliminated, and internal job ladders are much less operative. One male manager described this structural transformation in heavily gender-laden and sexualized terms:

> 'We are moving from the pyramid shape to the Mae West. The employment chart of the future will show those swellings on the top and we'll never completely get rid of those big bulges of clerks on the bottom. What we're trying to do right now is to pull in that waistline [expensive middle management and skilled secretaries]' (Garson, 1981: 35).[4]

Indeed the elimination of middle management positions is a central feature of technocratic reorganization, and one which has increased the competition for upper-level managerial positions.

The fact that the polarized technocratic organization is also gendered implies imbalances of numbers and distinct gender cultures in expert and non-expert sectors. As early as Kanter (1977) we have had clear evidence that imbalances of numbers heighten gender relations in organizations. In technocratic organizations there is both continuity and change in gender cultures. Gender imbalance and segregation persist, while the culture and organization of the expert sector (in particular) is fundamentally changed (see Kanter, 1983).

Working conditions are dramatically different for expert and non-expert sectors. Expert sector workers enjoy considerable autonomy from supervision, collegial working relations with co-workers, and generous salaries and fringe benefits. Non-expert workers, on the other hand, are typically organized in a more traditional manner: isolated from co-workers and closely supervised, often through the computerized system, which can count errors and monitor productivity. Technocratic managers, then, are forced to adopt a bifurcated and gendered managerial strategy: a *laissez-faire* strategy for expert workers, who are disproportionately male, and a strategy of close supervision of the non-expert, largely female sector, often using the computerized system to augment and extend this control.

This technological and social restructuring necessitates fundamentally different managerial skills. Top managers interact less with middle-level managers, and more with technical experts and computers; new types of technical expertise are therefore required for managers (see p. 71 below). Technocratic organizations, often worldwide in scope, both generate and require large amounts of data, and upper-level managers may feel inundated by large amounts of information which make it difficult to understand the past, manage the present, and plan for the future (see Burris, 1993). Like other types of computerized work, management in the context of computerization implies a greater reliance on abstract, formalized knowledge rather than concrete experience (see Zuboff, 1982, 1988). One manager described the change in managerial orientation in the following manner:

> 'If I didn't have the Overview System, I would walk around and talk to people more. I would make more phone calls and digress, like asking someone about their family. I would be more interested in what people were thinking about and what stresses they were under. When I managed . . . without it, I had a better feeling of the human dynamics. Now we have all the data, but we don't know why. The system can't give you the heartbeat of the plant; it puts you out of touch'. (Zuboff, 1988: 326)

Expertise as authority

In expert and managerial sectors, with their majority of men and minority of women, one of the most salient aspects of the workplace culture is the emphasis on demonstrated expertise and the need to prove oneself and one's expertise. Traditional authority of position becomes less important than expertise, leading to new types of 'conspicuous expertise' and the constant need to appear knowledgeable (see Burris, 1983, 1993).

In her analysis of various types of computerized workplace, Zuboff (1988) writes of the pronounced insecurity within the expert sector, the constant fear of 'not being the expert' (p. 252) and the conscious effort on the part of managers to monopolize information and use it to impress others and consolidate their power. She argues that the ability to speak knowledgeably is emphasized, and quotes one worker as saying '"The people who get the highest rankings do the most talking, but it can be a real snow job. The managers can't see the work, but they can hear you talk, so that is what they pay attention to"' (1988: 295). One manager agreed: '"Since it's hard to see what people do, you tend to get rewarded if . . . you make it sound like you did great"' (ibid.). Kanter (1983) also discusses the increased need for managers to persuade and convince, rather than being able to rely on rank authority.

In technocratic organizations where managers have attempted to rely on rank authority, and where they may have less technical knowledge than their subordinates, conflict has been a frequent occurrence (see Kraft, 1977; Hodson, 1988). Such managers have found that their rank authority provides insufficient legitimacy, leading to worker perceptions of managerial incompetence and ensuing problems of authority. Increasingly, managers need technical expertise, external credentials and managerial expertise in order to maintain legitimacy within technocratic organizations. Technical expertise is becoming an important precondition for traditional managerial functions: supervision, planning, marketing, etc.

Gender is intertwined with expertise in several ways. First, conspicuous expertise is more consistent with traditional male gender, giving men some advantages in the new types of micropoliticking. Masculinity has traditionally been associated with proving one's expertise, particularly in technical matters; as Wajcman (1991: 38) puts it: 'Men's affinity with technology is . . . integral to the constitution of male gender identity.' If technical expertise is more consistent with masculine self-identity, there is also the greater likelihood of *insecurity* among men in the expert sector: fear of being unmasculine if one's expertise is questioned. As Cockburn (1985: 178) points out, the competition among men to demonstrate technical competence is pronounced:

> Male self-identity is won in a costly tussle with other men for status and prestige, and this applies in technological work no less than in other situations. Those men who seek their masculine identity in technological competence find themselves obliged to manoeuvre for position and negotiate their rank relative to other men. There are comparisons of competence: the cognoscenti versus the rest.

Moreover, the threat from women in the expert sector is another source of insecurity; to be perceived as less competent than a woman would constitute a double threat to one's masculinity.

'Adhocracy' and informality among the expert sector

Another feature of technocratic organizations with clear gender implications is the emphasis on more flexible and collegial types of work organization within the expert sector. Task forces, horizontal communication and 'adhocracy' (Mintzberg, 1979) prevail in this sector. Given this informality, the micropolitics of small group interaction, heightened by gender insecurity, becomes increasingly salient. The de-emphasis on bureaucratic rules and norms can serve to heighten subjectivity and permit discrimination.

Josefowitz (1983), for instance, found that in small group discussions, men often failed to hear women's comments, or attributed them to a male participant. Similarly, Murphree (1984) observed that gender discrimination was apparent in task force interaction, and Gallese (1985) found that high-level male corporate managers did not fully accept women, even those with elite credentials, into the upper echelons of corporate life. It appears that one tactic used by expert-sector men to protect themselves from female competition and perceived threats to their expertise and masculinity is to deny expert-sector women recognition and visibility. As Wajcman (1991) notes, one consequence of the traditional association of skill with masculinity is that skilled women are often not perceived as such.

If expert-sector women are often invisible, non-expert-sector women (and a few men) are, conversely, constantly visible and often subject to computerized surveillance, a modern Panopticon: 'information systems that translate, record, and display human behavior can provide the computer age version of universal transparency with a degree of illumination that would have exceeded even Bentham's most outlandish fantasies' (Zuboff, 1988: 322). In technocratic organizations, then, we have a disproportionately male expert sector subjecting the disproportionately female non-expert sector to a supervisory gaze that is legitimated on the grounds of expertise but that also has clear gender, and even sexual, overtones. The imbalance of power and privilege between expert and non-expert sectors corresponds to traditional gender relations of domination and subordination.

With technocratic restructuring, the workplace is sexualized in ways which involve both continuity and discontinuity with earlier patterns. Within the expert sector, the de-emphasis on bureaucratic rules and norms, and the more relaxed and informal atmosphere of small group interaction, encourages sexualization of the workplace. Cockburn (1991: 156ff.), for instance, has documented how such informality, combined with the waning of traditional gender assumptions, has promoted a new type of masculinity:

> Women had identified this new type of male. . . . What distinguished him was an overt and confident machismo. Women everywhere made reference to the 'codpiece wearing jocks' of the policy unit, the 'new men' of the advertising department. This masculinity does not share the woman's-place-is-in-the-home mentality of the old guard. These men expect to find women in the public sphere. Nominally at least they welcome women into this exciting new world because their presence adds sexual spice to the working day. (1991: 157)

In the context of competition and insecurity, as well as the general culture of what Hearn (1987) calls 'hierarchic heterosexuality', this sexualization is laden with politics. The workplace culture is sexualized in such a way as to promote male solidarity, compensating for the competition over technical expertise (even though a good-humoured male competitiveness over sexual expertise is also common). As Cockburn (1991: 158) puts it: 'Such sexualized discourse is a necessary part of the cementing activities with which senior men seek to bond men beneath them firmly into the fraternity, healing the contradictions of patriarchal and class structures that threaten to divide them.' Women are disadvantaged by workplace sexuality, even consensual sexual relations, because of cultural and organizational stereotypes and double standards. They are in a no-win situation: if they attempt to participate as equals in sexual discourse and practice, they are perceived as dangerous *femmes fatales*; if they resist or question sexualization they are labelled 'iron maidens' (Kanter, 1977; see also Cockburn, 1991; Hearn et al., 1989).

Given the politicized context, sexuality always has the potential to become sexual harassment. Within the expert sector, where masculine insecurity over technical expertise and perceived threats from competent women are common, sexual harassment becomes one way in which 'emergent and potentially powerful women . . . [can be] cut down to size' (Cockburn, 1991: 141). Sexuality becomes a trump card of masculine privilege, a way of asserting power when other avenues fail. Given the imbalances of numbers and the isolation of women within the expert sector, resistance by expert-sector women to such harassment can be difficult.

The dynamics of sexual harassment within the non-expert sector are typically somewhat different. In blue-collar settings where a traditional male culture has been feminized, the heightening of male sexuality and overt harassment of women to emphasize their intrusion upon men's domain is common (Cockburn, 1983). However, in white-collar, clerical sectors, where women comprise the vast majority of the workforce, sexual harassment is likely to come from male superiors. In such cases, the subordinate organizational position of women, corresponding to the general subordination of women in the culture, serves to make non-expert-sector women vulnerable to sexual harassment. Indeed, the polarized and sex-segregated technocratic organization can be perceived as a fraternal group of expert-sector men with a virtual 'harem' of non-expert-sector women providing various types of support for male activities. Some men undoubtedly see sexual services as part of the fringe benefits of occupying privileged positions within the organization.

Sexual harassment, then, has become an influential and controversial new discourse about workplace sexuality, and one which contradicts the organizational tendencies towards informalization and sexualization. By calling attention to entrenched norms of patriarchal sexual conduct, sexual harassment discourse has directly challenged patriarchal control, and hence has provoked considerable resistance from many men (and some women). Collinson and Collinson (1992, 1996), for instance, have found that male managers often mishandle sexual harassment complaints because they identify with the perpetrator and blame the victim, even when the evidence of sexual harassment is unequivocal.

However, sexual harassment discourse also raises further questions which merit attention. The rather narrow focus on coercive sexuality, and the frequent assumption that most, if not all workplace sexuality has coercive overtones (see Fitzgerald, 1992: 31ff. for a good review), may be overly restrictive. Can workplace sexuality ever be consensual and liberating? Is a desexualized workplace a desirable (or realistic) goal? Can sexuality be disentangled from power, or are the two inextricably linked? (see Burrell, 1984). A fuller examination of workplace sexuality needs to incorporate sexual harassment discourse, but also go beyond it (see Pringle, 1989; Burris, 1992).

Technocratic patriarchal ideology

Technocratic ideology is gendered in that technical expertise and abstract conceptual knowledge are socially defined as more 'masculine' traits. Technocracy exalts a type of objective, abstract, scientific rationality which allegedly eradicates politics from decision making altogether, as decisions are seen as purely technical and apolitical in nature: finding the 'one best way' to do things. This technocratic rationality rests on technical expertise, and is identified with contemporary forms of masculinity. Femininity, on the other hand, is seen as antithetical to technocratic norms: as subjective, emotional, irrational, unscientific, and technically incompetent (Bourdieu, 1984; Glennon, 1979; Hacker, 1989, 1990; Keller, 1985; Lowe and Hubbard, 1983). From her study of the impact of computerization in eleven different workplaces, Cynthia Cockburn concludes:

> How has hegemonic masculine ideology dealt with the shift of technology from heavy, dirty and dangerous (electromechanical) technology, to light, clean and safe (electronic) technology, given that masculinity was so clearly associated with the former qualities and femininity with the latter? The ideology has done a neat 'about turn.' The new technology is associated with logic and intellect and these in turn with men and masculinity. The complementarity is preserved by associating women and femininity with irrationality and physicality. (Cockburn, 1987: 5, 8)

These ideological assumptions are particularly salient in fields such as engineering and computer science. Hacker (1989, 1990), for instance, has documented the way in which engineering as a profession is gendered. She argues that 'engineering contains the smallest proportion of females of all major professions and projects a heavily masculine image that is hostile to women' (Hacker, 1990: 113). The engineers she studied said that engineering was a 'male' activity: hard, clean, predictable, abstract, technical, mathematical, controlling. Disciplines such as the humanities and social sciences, on the other hand, were seen as 'womanly': 'soft, inaccurate, lacking in rigor, unpredictable, amorphous' (Hacker, 1990: 116).

Hacker found that in engineering classes, the male professors often used jokes to put down women, bodily functions, racial minorities and the technically incompetent. Engineering magazines often included pictures of nude or partially nude women, and one included both a centrefold ('E-girl of the month') and a dirty joke page (Hacker, 1990: 113). Engineering was perceived as a male fraternity, with mathematics courses (in particular) serving a gatekeeping function. One statistics professor, for instance, when asked why students could not have more time for an exam, said, '"If we gave people more time, anyone could do it. The secretaries could even pass it"' (Hacker, 1983: 47).

The male engineers she interviewed reported limited experience with intimate, close personal relationships, difficulties in expressing emotion, and a sense that sensual pleasures were 'unmanly'. The men also reported a history of estrangement from girls and women: feeling shy, insecure, frightened and mystified by the female sex (Hacker, 1990: 115). Largely because of the childbearing ability of women, these male engineers associated women with nature. The men also reported painful childhood experiences of insecurity over lack of athletic ability, self-perceptions as 'sissies', as sickly and lacking in courage. What emerges is a pattern of compensation through academic prowess, compensation for lack of other masculine traits; as one man put it, he tried to compensate by being 'head of the class' (Hacker, 1990: 115).

Engineers were considered to be the most appropriate men for managerial positions 'because they can treat people like elements in a system' (Hacker, 1989: 36). Engineering was seen as closely allied with ideologies of control and dominance: control of non-expert workers, women, racial minorities, the body, and nature in general (Hacker, 1989: 35). The abstract rationality of engineering rests on a mind/body dualism and a strong sense of hierarchy: the reward for denying the body, emotionality and intimate relations is social privilege. It becomes apparent, however, that the male engineers themselves are also stringently controlled and limited by this discourse.

Conclusion

Managerial practices have evolved over time, as organizational patriarchy has been transformed along with organizational control more generally. Theocratic patriarchy gave way to entrepreneurial control which then was made more structural in various ways: technical control, bureaucracy, professionalism. Socially desirable traits have historically been defined as masculine: pre-capitalist theocracy declared men to be closer to God, industrialization exalted male physical strength, bureaucracy rests on a masculine ethos of predictable, rational behaviour (Kanter, 1977; Ferguson, 1984). Alongside these earlier types of patriarchal control, we now have technocratic patriarchy: a new and more sophisticated control structure that relies on computerized technology and emphasizes new types of expertise and workplace organization.

Technocratic restructuring of workplaces is associated with new forms of patriarchal managerial practice. Polarization and sex segregation promote distinct gender cultures and a new micropolitics of expertise within work organizations. In the context of an expanded emphasis on skill and expertise, male managers and experts experience intensified insecurity over their abilities, an insecurity which is exacerbated by the entrance of women into traditionally male jobs. Men respond by such strategies as conspicuous expertise, overlooking the competence and skill of women, and sexual politics. These male practices are buttressed by a gendered technocratic ideology which portrays women as antithetical to technocratic norms of scientific objectivity: as emotional, subjective and technically incompetent.

However, technocratic reorganization may also undermine gender discrimination in certain ways. In her analysis of computer conferencing, for instance, Zuboff (1988) found that computer-mediated communication had the potential to reduce the salience of gender, race and rank authority, bringing people together who might otherwise be separated by discriminatory barriers. She quotes one engineer who extolled the virtues of computer conferencing:

> 'DIALOG lets me talk to other people as peers. . . . All messages have an equal chance because they all look alike. The only thing that sets them apart is their content. If you are a hunchback, a paraplegic, a woman, a black, fat, old, have two hundred warts on your face, or never take a bath, you still have the same chance. It strips away the halo effects from age, sex, or appearance'. (1988: 371)

What is most noteworthy about this statement, however, is the fact that this man clearly associates women (and racial minorities) with physical and social handicaps, even while ostensibly espousing gender neutrality. Whether computer-mediated communication will become sufficiently prevalent substantially to undermine face-to-face discrimination is unclear, but in some workplaces the increased emphasis on knowledge and expertise may serve to de-emphasize types of discrimination based on ascriptive characteristics.

Turkle (1984), in her study of computer-mediated interaction among different age groups of children, also concludes that computer technology may have the capacity to undermine gender discrimination. She found that children approach the computer in two divergent ways: the 'hard mastery' of one's 'imposition of will over the machine through the implementation of control' (1984: 104), and 'soft mastery' which focuses on interaction, aesthetic considerations, and occasional anthropomorphizing of the computer. She found that these styles of interaction were correlated with gender, with the 'hard masters' being 'overwhelmingly male' (ibid.: 108). Turkle concludes that working with computers from an early age may provide 'an entry to formal systems that is more accessible to women' (ibid.: 118), opening up new opportunities to excel in mathematics, science and engineering. What is not clear, however, is whether 'soft mastery', intuition and creativity continue to be valued at more advanced levels of science and maths training, or whether they are primarily salient in early socialization experiences. Evidence indicates that the masculine 'hard master' approach continues to predominate in more advanced levels of science and engineering, as well as within managerial and expert sectors of technocratic organizations.

Technocratic patriarchy is a heavily rationalized type of gender domination, strongly legitimated by science, and yet also with deep roots in the past. Male (and some female) managers and experts now have a sophisticated technological apparatus with which to perpetuate their privilege, one which is viewed as gender neutral and grounded in impartial expertise. In actuality, work organizations remain heavily gendered, and the forms of patriarchy are more varied and more insidious than ever before.

Notes

The author thanks the editors for helpful comments on earlier drafts.

1. See, for instance, Adler and Izraeli (1988b), Bell and Nkomo (1992), Stead (1985).

2. Workplace technology, like technology in general, is presented as autonomous, as driven by its own dynamic rather than by particular interests. Technological design also tends to be viewed deterministically, as predetermined by technical considerations, and technological choices are typically not seen as such, but rather as inevitable manifestations of science and engineering. Finally, technological innovation is viewed as progressive, as inherently humane and liberating. Typically, technological innovation *does* involve some improvements in efficiency, a fact that contributes to the obscuring of technical control and decreases the likelihood that alternative forms of technological design and implementation will be considered. See Burris (1993) for a fuller discussion.

3. For a fuller discussion of technocratic organization, see Burris (1993).

4. This quotation amply illustrates the organizational trend towards informality and sexualization, particularly among experts and managers.

5

'The Best is Yet to Come?': The Quest for Embodiment in Managerial Work

Deborah Kerfoot and David Knights

Management, it may be argued, is a comparatively modern phenomenon, the seeds of its genesis being sown with the transition from domestic to factory production during the industrial revolution in the eighteenth century. While large agricultural estates had existed as far back as Elizabethan days, their administration as sources of revenue to the landed gentry was generally feudal and, thereby, legal-compulsory rather than economic (Pollard, 1965). The emergence of economic organizations designed to co-ordinate large-scale production for purposes of instrumental gain (i.e. profit) was a necessary though not sufficient, condition for the growth of modern management.

Largely concerned with the co-ordination and control of a diverse range of collectively organized work tasks, modern management becomes necessary once labour is transformed into a formally 'free' agent of production under economically organized systems of corporate capitalism. Prior to this state of affairs, subordinates were under legal or paternal obligation to fulfil the productive expectations of their masters or owner-managers. Where obedience is no longer built into the relationship, however, supply and demand mechanisms may be expected, at least partially, to fill the gap. The growth of modern conceptions of management has been largely a response to the problem of supplementing this economic relation between capital and labour in conditions where it is seen to exhibit weaknesses or measurable limits. Although such limits are inherent within capitalist production, it may be suggested that they have increased in severity as economies and industries have become more globally competitive and populations, driven by interest groups and the media, more demanding in what they expect, as consumers, from productive organizations.

The recent decline of manufacturing and expansion of services in Western economies places even more demands upon management at one and the same time as making those demands more difficult to deliver. The demands are greater because the service sector is far more labour intensive than manufacturing, thus increasing the responsibilities of management to provide the requisite levels of co-ordination and control. They are more difficult because service outputs are comparatively less visible and meas-urable than material goods since they reside substantially in the amorphous and uncontrollable set of social relations through which they are delivered. This is the background against which, in this chapter, we wish to discuss management as a site for the reproduction of what we refer to as 'mascu-linity' in contemporary organizations. Our concern is to identify and analyse one set of masculine discourses and subjectivities that is privileged within modern management but may be threatened as organizations seek to become more flexible, responsive and socially skilled in meeting the demands of diverse and fast-changing markets and consumers.

The chapter is arranged as follows. In the first section we attempt a brief outline of the development of modern management and how it relates to the discussion of masculinity that follows. This provides an historical context in which to develop an argument about the links between mascu-linity, management and work organization. The next section puts some flesh on these ideas to show how managerial work is not only a site for, but also a consequence of, the reproduction of masculinity. Masculinity, no less than femininity, is seen as manifest in a multiplicity of forms and not as a 'fixed' entity. Nonetheless, the argument of this section is that whatever their diversity, a common characteristic of those masculine discourses and subjectivities that are privileged in contemporary managerial and organiz-ational work is a preoccupation with a particular instrumental form of 'rational control'.[1] In the third section, we draw upon our understanding of managerial and masculine practices in organizations, suggesting that they are supportive not only of one another but also of a sense of self-estrangement and disembodiment. This section is informed by epistemo-logical critiques of Enlightenment liberalism and a concern to dissolve a conventional dualism between masculinity and femininity that, at first sight, it may appear we are reproducing. It then examines some contemporary changes in the management of organizations where hierarchical control is giving way to programmes of self-managed social relationships, ostensibly organized around a more autonomous office or shopfloor. Here we question the compatibility of such change with the instrumental rationality prevalent in existing masculine-dominated, managerial and organizational practices. In the conclusion we reflect upon the implications of our analysis of masculinity for management practice in organizations.

An incitement to control: the modern corporation as a site of masculinity

Before turning to a contemporary analysis of these issues, it is appropriate to sketch not so much the genesis of management *per se* as the way it has evolved, and continues to be sustained, predominantly as a masculine enterprise. This is the case, we would argue, even when partly due to equal opportunity policies but increasingly because of the feminization of many large corporations: more women are becoming managers.[2] Most accounts of the history of modern management indicate that, although women were very often to be found in factory employment or the mines, virtually no women occupied managerial positions during the industrial revolution (Pollard, 1965; Child, 1969; Anthony, 1986). In the early development of managerial work, then, men and masculinity were a dominant feature. Even today there are few promotions of women into senior managerial positions above what has euphemistically been described as the 'glass ceiling' (Cooper and Davidson, 1992). But even if women were able to secure managerial positions, this would not be sufficient to negate the description of management as a masculine enterprise. For, as we go on to argue, masculinity is neither exclusive to men nor exhaustive of their discursive being; nonetheless, contemporary organizations create, sustain and reproduce masculine modes of behaviour that privilege some men and generate difficulties for those women who are more conventionally feminine in their outlook. Initially, we need a definition of what we imply by a masculine discourse and then we can explore the earlier developments of management practice in its terms. But first, what do we mean by masculinity?

Accepting that there are multiple and diverse forms of masculinity, it is our view that contemporary masculine identities are discursively bound up with high levels of purposive-rational instrumentality characterized by an urge to be in control. The extent to which this is an extension, or the condition, of what Hollway (1984a: 231) describes as the 'male sexual drive discourse' is debatable but whether in sex, politics or business, the desire to be in control seems to be an end in itself. Only the never-ending supply of new conquests, challenges and uncertainties keeps those caught up in such masculine discourses forever trapped in a permanent striving to be in control. In these respects masculinity is compulsive. Given that one can readily define purposive behaviour as a distinguishing characteristic of what it is to be human, the mark of the individual as distinctly masculine in modern cultures could be seen as a compulsive desire to be in control and, thereby, to act instrumentally with respect to everything, including the self. The sacrifices that are made in transforming everything into an object of control are especially visible in the field of management where leisure, personal life, family, and even physical and mental health are subordinated to the greater goal of control or mastery. Of course this desire for control manifests itself in very many different and often contradictory ways, and sometimes might even be displayed as submission, for example when a man falls 'head over heels' in love with a heterosexual woman, or appears 'helpless' in dealing with matters for which he prefers others to take responsibility. But the submission, feigned helplessness or learned dependency, we would argue, might well conceal a displaced sense of remaining in control.

Whether or not it is possible to trace the genesis of this instrumentality to some psychoanalytic condition of anxiety wherein the male child separates from its mother in order to secure a masculine identity (Chodorow, 1978) is of less importance to us than understanding how it appears to be reinforced by management (and other) practices in organizations and workplaces. Equally, we are sceptical of this and other psychoanalytic literature that pathologizes or renders problematic those aspects of separation only in relation to the boy child. For, as we have intimated, instrumentality may likewise describe women and what may conventionally be referred to as features of 'feminine' behaviour. While recognizing that the search for identity may have numerous ontological, psychoanalytic and social sources, the focus of this chapter is merely to identify specific forms of its reproduction within managerial and organizational work. In developing an analysis of the relationship between masculinity and management, our concern is not to periodize precisely the genesis of a modern conception of management, largely because we wish to focus primarily on the way that masculinity is sustained through current practices. But this historical task has been attempted by others (for example, Pollard, 1965; Hoskin and Macve, 1988, 1991; Knights and Morgan, 1990, 1991) and we therefore draw upon these literatures to identify 'the point of discontinuity between the pre-managerial and the managerial world: to define and ascertain the difference that made the difference' (Ezzamel et al., 1990) in unravelling its complex relationship to masculinity.

MacIntyre (1981) sees the manager as the embodiment of a modern bureaucratic form of organization that arose out of the decline of traditional institutions such as the Catholic Church and the monarchy. Its appeal is to efficiency and effectiveness in the achievement of instrumental goals through the manipulation of others (McMylor, 1994: 130). One aspect of this early development of modern management that could be seen to relate more directly to masculinity was its association, as a discrete function, with engineering and other technological skills. There are few activities that are as technical (or non-social) and instrumental as engineering. Moreover, there is little doubt that the first managers were recruited from those with engineering skills and expertise or at least their children, since it was in mining, metallurgy, shipbuilding, civil engineering and textiles that the transformation to corporate production first took place (Pollard, 1965: 61–103). Perceiving engineering as a significant element in the development of that form of instrumentalism which reflects and reinforces masculine modes of being does not preclude us giving attention to other important conditions that have made modern conceptions of management possible. Although engineering dominated the early phase of capitalist development, social class was extremely important in the context of recruitment into, and the pay differentials of, the new managerial positions (Pollard, 1965: 139). This declined, however, 'after the 1790s in favour of payment for the job, not the man [*sic*]' (ibid.) and seemed to coincide with an erosion of the differential between proprietors and salaried managers, though the latter were usually the relatives of the former (ibid.: 145). In so far as managers were clearly beginning to be recognized as of equal importance to the absentee owners, this could be seen as a point of discontinuity between the pre-managerial and the managerial world (Ezzamel et al., 1990).

Hoskin (1990) seeks to pursue this theme with more precision, suggesting that modern management has its genesis in mid-nineteenth-century America with the development of the Pennsylvania railroad. By 'importing the practices of writing, examination, and grading', Hoskin (1990: 23) argues, it was Herman Haupt of the Pennsylvania railroad who changed the 'rules of business discourse' in the direction of being 'proactive and future oriented' or what we would now define as strategic. It is this orientation to strategic corporate decision making that Hoskin identifies as synonymous with the concept of modern management. This is seen as conterminous with the development and transformation of the internal discourses and practices of organizations into a written recorded and calculable form (Hoskin and Macve, 1986, 1988, 1991; Hoskin, 1990). Modern management, from this point of view, is grounded in the knowledge and power that makes it possible to control labour and the organization of production in pursuit of a set of strategic ends such as profit or corporate expansion (Braverman, 1974; Edwards, 1979; Wood, 1982; Knights and Willmott, 1990). It is accomplished through practices that turn everything and everyone into an object of management. Files on employees are written, recorded and stored, and the activities and competence of labour are continuously examined so that its behaviour is rendered calculable in terms of both present and future prospects for the corporation. In this account of modern management, there are close similarities with what would now be seen as management and accounting control. It involves quantifying, examining and grading both people and events to bring them readily within the disciplinary gaze and the techniques of surveillance of those exercising power and constituting knowledge in organizations.

But this concept of management also reflects and reproduces modes of discourse and behaviour that we identify as masculine.[3] They are abstract and highly instrumental with respect to controlling their objects, thus sustaining a mode of relating to externalities that is self-estranged and wholly disembodied. Rarely does masculinity embrace the world or even itself with a sense of wonderment, pleasure or engagement, for it labours ceaselessly in the struggle to control and possess the objects of its desire, while at the same time self-deceptively presuming itself to be free of desire. That is to say, the desire is so buried beneath a series of rationalities and rationalizations as to be virtually invisible to its agent. Yet it may be suggested that the hidden agenda behind masculine struggles for control is a desire to produce a stable world in which identity can feel safe and secure (Game, 1991; Clough, 1992).

Where this masculine preoccupation with ordering the world reaches its culmination in modern management is in its attraction to strategic discourse. As Big Boy Caprice in the film *Dick Tracy* puts it very neatly: 'A man is not a man without a plan.' Of all the managerialist concepts peddled by consultants and gurus, strategy has probably had a more universal impact than any other on modern management. In fact Hoskin (1990) treats strategy as synonymous with the genesis of modern management in the sense that it was the point when exact records and calculable decisions rendered the future amenable to the precise and predictable controls of a strategic plan. Whilst Hoskin does not focus on the gendered nature of these technologies of control, it is clear that strategic management coincides closely with those contemporary forms of masculinity that turn everything into an object of conquest (Seidler, 1989). It involves a disembodied and emotionally estranged conception of reason (Kerfoot and Knights, 1993) that attaches itself to a ceaseless pursuit of strategic goals, the attainment of which confirms the promise, though rarely the reality, of a secure masculine identity. In this sense 'the best is yet to come' is the illusion of perfect security, contentment and control that pushes masculinity towards ever more heroic and self-sacrificing struggles.

Corporate capitalism is both the vehicle for the expression of this masculinity and a major driving force. For in elevating competitive success and the ethic of accumulation or 'possessive individualism' (MacPherson, 1962) as *the* reason for existence, the capitalist corporation provides a legitimate outlet for masculine preoccupations with conquest and control. But as we have already indicated, it also reproduces the conditions that sustain masculinity. First, the corporation stimulates the pursuit of abstract, instrumental objectives, such as output, profit and growth, above all else, and this process both reflects and reinforces a disembodied and estranged relationship to the world. Yet simultaneously it generates the conditions of competitive uncertainty in which such pursuits constantly create individual insecurities. Since masculine projects are often a disguised or disavowed desire to order the world for purposes of establishing a secure identity, these insecurities only serve to reinforce the masculine drive for success. In short, the very pursuit of security through achievement, conquest, success and wealth generates precisely those self-same conditions of insecurity that make the pursuit compulsive and unending, thus closing the 'vicious circle' and denying masculinity the possibility of escaping from itself. Of course, in the sense that masculinity knows no other mode of being and denigrates discourses (for example, of femininity) that fail to sustain this way of relating to the world, it cannot even contemplate the necessity for such an escape. We now seek to locate and develop our analysis of masculinity and managerial work broadly within what may be described as a 'postmodern' framework.

Masculinity and managerial work

Adopting a framework of analysis influenced by postmodernist feminism (Butler, 1990; Hekman, 1990) and the theoretical insights on power and subjectivity provided by Foucault (1980b), our purpose is to address the relationship between masculinity and managerial work. Here subjectivities are to be understood as 'symbolic categories' (Saco, 1992) emanating from particular discourses. For example, masculinity offers a range of subject positions born of a discourse of gender – about what it means to be a 'real' man at any point in history. Since postmodernist feminism is not a wide-spread philosophical position, it is appropriate to provide a brief summary of its central features. Broadly, the concern of the position is to reject the Enlightenment epistemology of representation with its concern for pro-gressive and emancipatory knowledge (Benhabib, 1992), and its political counterpart in liberalism without abandoning a feminist philosophy and political theory. This is difficult, not least because feminism grew out of the liberal Enlightenment. Moreover, many feminists of both a liberal and a radical persuasion have sought to rebel rather than revolt against this epistemology[4] and, in particular, its privileging of male rationality. They have been concerned to reverse the dualism either by suggesting that female rationality is superior or that emotional being should be privileged (Hekman, 1990: 5). Both these strategies perpetuate the dualistic thinking (for example, rationality–irrationality, masculine–feminine, subject–object) of the Enlightenment that a postmodern epistemological critique seeks to discard. In so far as our own focus is predominantly on masculinity, it may appear that we are equally guilty of perpetuating the dualism between masculinity and femininity. However, in support of a postmodern feminism, our critical reflections on masculinity do not imply a privileging of femininity so much as an attempt to dissolve these dualisms through deconstructing or problematizing the conditions that make them possible. Our attention is drawn to a critical analysis of masculinity not because the discourse of femininity is beyond critique or to be idealized (see Kerfoot and Knights, 1995). Masculinity is our focus because it is the dominant discourse and subjectivity within contemporary Western power-knowledge regimes of management.

However, this is not to privilege the activities of managerial work in organizations as *the only* site for the production and reproduction of masculinity. Management and work organizations are but one such site for the construction and reconstruction of masculinities. Although generally we are concerned to understand how masculinity is produced and reproduced in a diversity of sites – in the home, the pub, the club or on the playing field – here our focus is primarily on the specific practices that constitute the realm of managerial work. In particular, we seek to show how these practices help to make 'real' or sustain the ascription of masculinity to men. In speaking of masculinity, we are using a shorthand form of expression for what we regard as a multiplicity of behaviours and actions, within and beyond organizational locations. Like all identities, masculinity is to be conceived of as multi-layered, fluid, and always in process (Butler, 1990; Kerfoot and Knights, 1994). It is contingent and shifting not least in the lifetime of individuals. While it is possible to document a range of expressions of masculinity or permutations thereof (see, for example,

Hearn, 1994a; Collinson and Hearn, 1994), we have chosen to emphasize a dominant form of contemporary masculinity that is privileged in modern management discourses and practices.

Where masculinity is not fixed but constituted in and through practice, the ongoing processes of inscription (how identities are written on to living bodies through textual devices much like commemorations on the gravestones of the dead) and reinscription are prevalent in a multiplicity of sites, not merely managerial work and the workplace. In this sense, masculinity is always 'becoming'. To talk of becoming in this way is to embrace a perspective that refuses inevitability, universality or constancy in 'what it means to be a man'. Yet the mere association of masculinity with men does not make it exclusive to them nor exhaustive of their being. Women can and do constitute themselves at least partially through masculine discourses and modes of behaviour, while many men may also display feminine characteristics. However, the materialism of modern existence and the social practices that flow from it reflect and reinforce masculinity, elevated and socially privileged as a way of being for men as well as some women. Evidence from case studies or ethnographies (for example, Watson, T. 1994, esp. Chapter 8) and autobiographical accounts (for example, Lewis, 1991; Seidler, 1989) suggest that some men feel uncomfortable with this mode of being, perceiving their lives as a struggle to become a 'real man'. Likewise, as Craig (1992: 3) expresses it: 'men who find it difficult or objectionable to fit into the patterns of traditional masculinity often find themselves castigated and alienated'. Flowing from this, we recognize even the terminology of 'traditional masculinity' to be problematic in that it gives the impression of a singular, unitary and all-pervasive masculinity that we have already questioned. Nevertheless, this questioning does not preclude our point that masculinity involves a compulsive desire to be in control; it merely suggests that this desire may take a multiplicity of forms. While sometimes it is explicit and overt when physical strength or intellectual prowess is pitted against an opponent; other times it is implicit or covert where masculinity is concealed behind some institutional programme or organizational strategy. At times masculine behaviour may indeed appear to display quite the opposite of a preoccupation with control but learned dependence can be a subtle form of control. It also has to be admitted that the striving for a secure masculine identity may subside with age, either through the realization that it is a self-defeating goal or as a result of becoming 'worn out' in the struggle. However, a more mature and apparently laid-back style of behaviour can readily conceal a desire that burns deeply beneath the calming embers of an individual's twilight years. We concur with Seidler (1989: 8): 'the point, in other words is that what is significant is not the category of "masculinity" per se, but rather the way the category normalises a distorted life experience'.

By referring to 'masculinity' rather than men, we are making a distinction between the biological category of sexed bodies (men) and the social constitution of gender difference that is colloquially or commonsensically designated as masculine. Our concern, in line with many academic and other commentators, is to render masculinity problematic. In using the term 'masculinity' we are invoking a definition that pertains to the socially generated consensus of what it means to be a man, to be 'manly' or to display such behaviour at any one time. Following from this, it is axiomatic that what 'counts' as masculine may shift over historical periods, over the lifetime of individuals and in differing spatial, social and cultural contexts. Moreover, since the designation is used equally, although no less unproblematically, with regard to women, we must extend the definition of masculinity to encompass those behaviours and expressions regarded as 'masculine' in females or when applied (often stereotypically and pejoratively) to their behaviours. For many women the experience, not least of organizational life, is one wherein they too are said, to varying degrees, to display traits associated with the common yardstick of masculinity. This is particularly the case where women seek to compete with men for managerial positions, because the gendered nature of management discourse and practice means that everyone is judged against a single masculine measure of competence.

In making masculinity problematic and exploring masculinity as a social rather than biological concept, we are concerned to explore how and in what manner masculinity is constituted at given 'moments' and in certain settings. Part of our concern is to interrogate contemporary designations of masculinity in contrast with those writers and commentators who accept them as given. This is to see gender and gender differences as in dynamic process where masculinity is an *outcome* or product of social processes as opposed to an *amount* that any one person may possess and as part of a wider discussion of gender relations. In speaking of masculinity as an outcome we refer to the dynamic constitution of gender identity wherein identity and subjectivity are conceived of as always in process – always 'becoming'.

In turn, to speak of becoming in this way is to align with a theoretical position informed primarily by the work of Foucault, where social subjects are understood to be discursively 'produced' by relations of power (Foucault, 1988). Broadly, such analysis is concerned to theorize subjectivity and identity as the product of a variety of different and often competing discourses; the individual is seen as produced amid a multiplicity of discourses. From this perspective, subjectivity is at once both contingent and precarious. Identity acquires the status of a 'project' to be constantly worked at, to be accomplished or achieved. This takes us to our next point. The lack of fixity and stability of subject positions forces us to consider the possibility of masculinity as a fluid concept. Masculinity is not fixed in time or place, nor does it exist as some transhistorical 'essence'. The definition of masculinity, of what counts as masculine or 'manly' (see Roper and Tosh, 1991) at any given moment, is itself diverse and in flux.

In a discussion of masculinity and managerial work elsewhere (Kerfoot and Knights, 1993) we have been concerned to isolate and analyse forms of masculinity contingent upon managerial and other practices in modern financial services organizations in the UK, although our elaboration of these 'styles' of management is perhaps readily applicable in diverse industrial and other sectors. Here we developed the concept of a 'paternalistic masculinity' in the financial services industry and argued that it was coming to be displaced by or superimposed upon a form of adversarial and aggressive 'competitive masculinity' in ascendancy in many organizations. Coterminous with the language and practices of strategic management, competitive masculinity sustains and reproduces a variety of behavioural displays consonant with entrepreneurialism, risk taking and an instrumental orientation toward others, wherein the 'other' becomes a site for and object of conquest. This is an instrumentality that discounts or precludes any other mode of being. It has the power to asphyxiate everything other than itself.

In charting the rise of masculinity and the British organization man in the post-Second World War period, Roper (1994a) has detected some resistances. Noting the decline of the family firm and the demise of the 'gentlemanly' culture of many such institutions, his study of managerial activities in what were often large bureaucratic structures reveals not only a form of masculinity geared towards the trained management 'expert' and the rational organization manager that was thought to be his personification, but also the quiet subversion of this masculinity by many managers themselves. In so doing and in their emotional connections with one another, managers sustained a counter-dialogue that both undermined, and yet paradoxically reinforced, a variety of masculinity geared towards managing commercial companies in an era of post-family capitalism (ibid.).

Femininities, like masculinities, cannot be understood as 'fixed features' (Hollway, 1984a: 228) identified exclusively with women. Whatever its manifestation, however, femininity represents ideal-typically a less disembodied mode of being. Femininity is not instrumentally attached to securing itself through projects and goals, and it can be more engaged with, rather than detached from, the world. This engagement is at once immediate, sensual and embodied, not driven by cognitive and goal-centred designs and preoccupations. While femininity may not engender a disembodied mode of being as does the cognitively goal-directed compulsiveness of masculinity, it is frequently associated with a passivity that lacks purpose and direction, other than that given to it by others. Consequently those whose identities are discursively constituted as feminine are invariably vulnerable to the demands of 'others', especially masculine subjects according to whose expectations feminine women often live their lives. Within the family, this subjection to the expectations and demands of others is indeed institutionalized such that the very conception of feminine time is perceived not as a linear process but as an embeddedness in embodied social relations (Davies, 1990; Knights and Odih, 1995). Clearly, we are not seeking to elevate femininity over masculinity; our concern is merely to contrast the gendered differential modes of engagement and their implications for changes in management practices and organizational life.

Furthermore, since 'arguments about gender are plagued by an assumption that what is natural is more "real" than what is social' (Connell, 1987: x), our aim is to provide a discussion of management as within the realms of the 'real' as produced in the day-to-day lives of people in organizations.

A certain privileged and pervasive form of masculinity is characterized by the modern manager whose *raison d'être* is to co-ordinate and control others in pursuit of the instrumental goals of production, productivity and profit. Defining them as managerialism, Ezzamel et al. (1990: 159) speak of these processes as a way of constructing time in a linear fashion and controlling the 'furthest reaches and the inner corridors of organisational space'. On this time/space dimension, managerialism involves forms of 'action at a distance'. This managing 'at a distance' is necessary because in large enterprises where absentee ownership is the norm, employee conformity and control become problematic. Employees no longer have personal obligation to the owner, and close supervision is not only costly but can be counterproductive (Gouldner, 1955a). Consequently, control by numbers and records rather than by interpersonal relations has become an established, if not unproblematic, norm of modern management. This distancing reflects and reinforces masculine modes of being, despite the rhetorical counter-claims of the 'excellence' and other literatures on the added value to be gained by harnessing the creative potential offered by labour.

It has been argued with some philosophical force that management is precarious and insecure because it lacks the knowledge which could ensure that its decisions and actions had precise and predictable outcomes (MacIntyre, 1981). This uncertainty surrounding its practice also raises questions of managerial legitimacy with those who are delegated to execute the decisions of management. Such philosophical examinations are supported by considerable empirical research (Mintzberg, 1973; Stewart, 1976b; Burns and Stalker, 1961) which also shows that management, in practice, is not the systematic, unambiguous and rational process of planning and control it is often assumed to be by outsiders. These critiques of management practice clearly demystify the claims of classical management theory (for example Fayol, 1949; Taylor, 1911) and much of what is taught, in the name of management, in many contemporary business schools (Sinclair, 1995). These prescriptive approaches make the assumption that management consists in 'a specialised body of knowledge (more than just informal know-how) . . . and a set of practices and processes of control' (Ezzamel et al., 1990) that not only can, but must, be taught both to existing and to potential managers.

It could be, however, that there is some validity on both sides of this argument. From the analytical science perspective of MacIntyre (1981; see also Mangham, 1995 and critics), managers clearly do not have the kind of knowledge that equates with the natural science capability to predict events by the application of abstract and generalized laws. But what this view fails to acknowledge fully is how knowledge is drawn upon in the exercise of power and how power stimulates the production of knowledge (Foucault, 1980b). So while management may not possess knowledge that can guarantee predictable outcomes, its deployment in exercises of power often produces self-fulfilling effects that give it the appearance of predictability. This is because management exercises hierarchical power over subordinates which, in turn, often secures employee compliance, given the unequal control of resources in conventional organizations. Not that resistance is precluded by managerial power and, indeed, compliance when combined with indifference and distancing behaviour may be seen as a form of resistance (see Jermier et al., 1994).

Of course, practising managers are rarely naive enough to believe that their knowledge has the status that is claimed for it in the pursuit of managerial legitimacy. They are also aware that what works at one point may not at another, and in order to legitimize their privileges they must forever be seeking new and exclusive knowledges. But the continuous necessity to search for, and apply, new knowledge is in itself anxiety-provoking and generative of insecurity (see Anthony, 1994, *passim*; Watson, T., 1994). There is, then, a double sense in which managers are insecure: first, they are aware that management knowledge does not have the certainty and stability of scientific knowledge even though managerial legitimacy is based upon a specialist 'expertise' that is dependent precisely on such uncertain knowledge. Second, these conditions make it necessary for managers continually to seek new knowledge. This, it may be argued, is one of the main reasons why those offering plausible prescriptions can very soon 'grow' into gurus. From scientific management to business process re-engineering, the history of management is littered with prescriptive knowledges that provide the most convincing response to the demand for solutions to uncertainty. But these solutions themselves promote continuous change that threatens routinized securities, especially given that the solutions often take the form of a fashion to be abandoned almost as speedily as adopted, once a new solution emerges. In combination, these insecurities exacerbate the anxieties that we have already identified as a feature of masculinity.

The dynamics of masculinity, management and organization

These larger managerial problems are embedded in dominant discourses in the everyday world that elevate control as a central and defining feature of what it is to be human. Seidler (1989: 20) expresses the problem of masculinity and men as follows:

> It is as if we only exist in our decisions, constantly judging and validating ourselves according to the correctness of the decisions we have made. Our life becomes a series of discrete decisions and plans. This is the way we feel good about ourselves, unable to give significance and importance to our relationships,

emotions and desires. We become so used to discounting our feelings and desires in order to do the 'right' thing, that we are barely aware of how this estranges us from ourselves.

Those individuals who invest themselves predominantly in these masculine discourses, it may be argued, experience this self-estrangement or dis-embodiment as a result of preoccupation with their own externally assessed competence and associated success and status. It is, however, an un-reflective estrangement since the rational pursuit of instrumental objectives and doing 'the right thing' leaves them bereft of emotional energy to question whether what they are doing is right, either for themselves or for their more intimate relations. It is our contention that there is an intensification of this sense of self-estrangement in contemporary manage-rial work. This is because of the highly instrumental nature of economic production and the self-interested careerism that accompanies its hierarchical forms. Whether through self-selection or acculturation, managerial work is predominantly populated by self-estranged masculine subjects. Arguably a defining feature of such subjects is the form that this self-estrangement takes: self-estrangement sustains a way of relating to themselves, others and the world around them in terms of control. That is to say, both masculinity and management practice sustain a transformation of *all* relations into forms of instrumental control. On the one hand, organizations reflect and reinforce this instrumental control by virtue of the pressures to produce, distribute and compete in the marketplace. In everyday organizational life, hierarchical structures leave management distant both physically and mentally from employees, and in order to sustain productive output, abstract quantifiable targets and other often coercive controls are imposed upon workforces. This accentuates the already existing instrumentality of employees (Goldthorpe et al., 1969; Palm, 1977; Collinson, 1992), reproducing self-estranged and disembodied labour forces where for many men the sense of individual significance is sought through exaggerated macho masculine sexual prowess which, often through humour, stigmatizes or denies the value of all that is associated with the 'feminine' (Collinson, 1992). We recognize and go on to discuss later the way in which conventional bureaucratic hierarchical forms of organization are under threat as a function of the demand for flexibility in turbulent markets. But it is debatable whether the substance, in contrast merely to the form, of bureaucratic structures is in transition. In our view this transition to new organizational forms does not negate the argument surrounding instrumentality, since the legacy of bureaucratic hierarchy remains, despite the formal commitment to alternatives (Kerfoot and Knights, 1995).

While for both managers and employees the workplace reproduces the instrumental behaviour that is both a condition and a consequence of self-estrangement, masculine discourses reinforce this instrumentality as subjects seek to control social relations as a way of managing the experience of disembodiment and self-estrangement itself. For although self-estrangement is partly an outcome of instrumental control, the isolation of the individual generates increased anxiety about the uncertainty and unpredictability of social relations. As a consequence, it stimulates even further the desire to control social relations that is ultimately self-defeating since, by definition, human behaviour is beyond absolute control. This desire takes the form of an unceasing preoccupation with purposive action in the drive to be 'in control'. But more than this, the desire becomes compulsive. By displacing non-instrumental modes of being, masculinity denies or discounts the possibility of alternatives that are *not* preoccupied with control: control becomes *the* way of relating to others. When unable to control the other, indifference or a mental distancing from the circumstances which are, so to speak, 'out of control' frequently occurs. This is because the only way a masculinity 'out of control' can retain some dignity is by feigning uninterest in the conditions that lead to such a situation.

The instrumental preoccupations of masculinity are directed towards the achievement of goals or projects and the excitement associated with their attainment. But the thrill that such success provides is always fleeting, compelling its self-induced victims continuously to repeat the experience. Moreover, however momentary, the corporeal 'feel' of success that this provides must always be bitter-sweet given that it depends crucially on the approbation of others. Since it is neither self-contained nor self-assured, masculine subjects require the metaphorical 'pat on the back' not only from workplace peers, subordinates or superiors but also from partners, spouses, family and friends. Where masculinity requires constant confirmation from others, its short-lived thrill can only be resuscitated if it is embellished and elaborated in countless freeze-framed dinner table, bar room or clubhouse tellings amongst the middle class or in more direct macho behaviour at football matches, on the street, in pubs, or on the shopfloor within working-class communities. In both sets of situations the sexist elevation of men and masculinity over women and femininity predominates even though its expression varies. As everyday conversation so clearly reveals, spouses are frequently enrolled as reluctant witnesses to unseen instances of their partners' heroic success. Accounts of organizational encounters become tales of organizational heroism, or targets met, meetings conquered and moments of weakness, failure or despair retold and reconstructed as personal triumphs over adversity, hopelessness or social impotence. Masculine subjects thus constitute the organizational and managerial world as a series of discrete challenges, in order to rise above them. The act of conquest, however fleeting, becomes its own validation. Yet it remains transient, caught up in the necessity to be reflected back by the 'approving other' and made potent in the telling. Masculine subjects are dependent not only on the thrill of conquest but on the need for constant confirmation from onlookers, real or otherwise. But the confirmation can only be maintained if the recipients continue to take on new conquests and struggles.

From this discussion, masculine subjects can be characterized as carving up the social and organizational world into a series of projects designed to manage the insecurity of their separation from themselves and others. Management is a site for the production and reproduction of this form of masculinity and for the continued insecurity of managerial subjects. To say this does not imply that management is in some way superimposed upon masculinity, that masculinity is superimposed upon management, or that one is in any way prior to the other. Our conception of the dynamics of masculinity and management envisages an alternative theoretical and empirical scenario wherein masculinity and management are at once mutually embedded and reproductive of one another. Self-estrangement and emotional distance from others occurs not in some form of psychological vacuum: it is created, sustained and reproduced in social or managerial practices.

In sum, this form of masculinity is a disembodied, self-estranged and socially disengaged mode of being wherein alternative relationships with self and others are displaced by the desire to control and to use others instrumentally in its service. Thus, masculine subjects 'know no other' than control and the instrumental use of others to secure that control, however momentary or precarious. In addition, masculine subjects control not least themselves. The self acquires the status of a project to be worked upon, policed for weaknesses, fought against, pushed and honed to meet the refinements of the ideal – this in spite of the often very real sensation of fear, weakness, or failure to live up to the image of the masculine ideal. This then is the dynamic process through which self-estrangement is sustained, and disembodiment produced and reproduced. The question is how compatible is this form of masculinity with the new forms of organization that are being cultivated by the change management gurus? – for much of this change is encouraging an emphasis on the productive value of *social* relationships.

Masculinity and 'new wave' management practices

Our interest here is to note a shift in the means of managing organizations and to document some of the practices (for example, service quality, teamworking, flattening hierarchies, the internal market) *vis-à-vis* workforces that are both their condition and consequence. We are less concerned with producing an exhaustive map of modern management practices than with sketching the conditions under which social relationships, or rather their productive value in organizations, have come to achieve a contemporary significance. Moreover, in delineating some key features of this shift, our objective is to suggest that the increased reliance on social relationships as a means of managing complex organizations and workforces renders masculinity doubly problematic.

It has been argued by numerous commentators that so-called modernist forms of bureaucratic control are, in large part, giving way to what might be argued to be more sophisticated ways of managing (for example, Child,

1984; Clegg, 1990). This trend, although contested in the scale and scope of its elements, draws together a number of key features suggested by many writers on the topic. First, there has been the transition to service industries and concomitant decline in manufacturing industries and employment. Not least in Britain, employment and other statistics indicate that this shift towards the service sector is strengthening. Second, accelerating competition within and between industrial sectors fuelled by economic deregulation has led to the demand for organizations to be more 'flexible'. Clearly this flexibility has several manifestations and, in its most developed form, involves what has been referred to by some commentators as 'flexible specialization', where companies can switch product lines at a moment's notice (Piore and Sabel, 1984). But in general terms, flexibility is required with respect to output of goods and services, in management processes and in the flexibility of employee behaviour. Nonetheless, for our purposes, an effect of the perceived drive for flexibility amongst the ranks of senior managerial hierarchies is the concern with the flexibility of workforces. In particular, in many service and retail sector industries, employees are expected to draw upon ordinary everyday social skills in the service of organizational goals and profit (see Fuller and Smith, 1991). But the provision of a service that is flexible with respect to a diverse and ever demanding consumer requires employees to use their social skills instrumentally.

A commonly held view is that, as a response to changes in the broader socioeconomic environment, the new 'flexible' organization is to be grounded in the collapse of large-scale bureaucratic hierarchies and the consequent restructuring, decentralization and delayering, the last not least in the arena of managerial jobs. Whether these changes are characterized as mere description or grotesque euphemism, they are nonetheless a managerial phenomenon that finds resonance in numerous sectors and industries, both public and private. Accompanied by a decline in the dominance of bureaucratic divisions of labour, newer 'leaner' structures, so the argument goes, necessitate the removal or weakening of vertical lines of control together with the break-up of the traditional functional groupings and specialisms of management.

In place of the 'old' order then, hierarchically flatter, horizontal structures are to be found which draw on peer networks cemented by greater autonomy and responsibility under the rubric of empowerment, participation and increased involvement (Kerfoot and Knights, 1995). Conventional forms of managerial control and supervision are thus rendered problematic amid the legions of project groups, multi-function work groups and forms of teamworking. But if the 'flexibility' offered by such working practices can render employees more productive in terms of output, a question arises as to the parallel 'success' of the abilities of their management.

More particularly, a new emphasis rests on the question of the means of managerial control in these newer, more commercially responsive organizational structures. For the new breed of manager can offer little by way of vertical promotion up through conventional hierarchies, whilst the exercise of authority in such structures on the basis of status is undermined within flat systems whose rhetoric, if not their immediate practice, is that of egalitarian partnership and equality. What remains then is the position whereby the success of the modern manager, to a degree at least, rests on the ability to manage and negotiate ever tighter groupings of employees by means of personal influence and interpersonal skill. 'Social skills' training packages for managers, for example, may be the flavour of the month, and dismissed as such, but their significance and frequency in companies is indicative of an accelerating trend in modern management towards the 'added value' that can be had from social relationships in organizations. If earlier regimes sought to strip employees of their discretion in tasks and render the social aspects of labour subordinate to the whims of an authoritarian management, then what of the new?

In aiming to align 'personal desires with the objectives of the firm' (Miller and Rose, 1990: 26), management increasingly has to rely upon transforming organizational cultures (Peters and Waterman, 1982; cf. Willmott, 1993) so that employees give consent and commitment to the ever-changing and flexible demands of the work. A further point concerns the exposure of workforces to the language of the market and an increased emphasis on staff as a productive and flexible resource. Through human resource management (HRM), service quality, corporate culture and total quality management (TQM), for example, this new entrepreneurialism has challenged the conventional bureaucratic wisdom of 'protecting' staff from the end customer.[5] In its place management are seeking to improve and maintain corporate profits, and render staff more creative with respect to their relationships with customers and with one another. This increased emphasis on the management of social relationships as a commercial resource involves some recognition on the part of senior management that conventional means of 'managing at a distance' (Cooper, R., 1992) are problematic. What seems to be demanded of new managers is that they have to reveal themselves as human beings with all the associated weaknesses and vulnerabilities – which under the conventional managerial practices of more bureaucratic regimes could be hidden.

So what are the implications of this discussion for masculinity as a hitherto predominant discourse in organizations? A number of questions need to be examined. If what we have termed 'management at a distance' is compatible with self-estranged and disembodied masculine modes of being, then these new practices of entrepreneurialism in management may be extremely threatening. This is because in contrast to numbers and files, 'real' human beings are unpredictable, uncertain and not easily controllable. But the threat is not only one of control; it is also a problem of relating to people rather than mere data. For those dominated by masculine discourses, this is not a straightforward task nor simply an act of individual or managerial will. For managers to engage more fully with those under their supervision, they first have to become more comfortable with themselves, no longer hiding from the scrutiny and judgement of others with respect to their social skills. Masculine preoccupations leave individuals ill-equipped to break from the grip of self-estrangement and disembodiment and thus generate a sense of subjective well-being appropriate to the new circumstances. 'Managing at a distance' has traditionally provided a smokescreen from the flaws or cracks in the social abilities of masculine subjects who are threatened by the calls for human engagement presented by new methods of managing wherein the role of social relationships is paramount. For there is not much doubt that masculine subjects preoccupied with instrumental control find difficult, and are often made tense by, ordinary everyday social interactions where there is an absence of such control. If one such smokescreen appears in the form of bureaucratic authority, another is the various claims to technical expertise on the part of managers. Paradoxically the methods of bringing about the new regimes where social relationships are paramount can be appropriated by some managers as expertise that, once again, can shield them from the intimacy that masculine subjects find problematic. Those managers unable to appropriate this expertise, in effect, become victims of what is euphemistically described as the 'delayering' process – where often extensive swathes of managerial hierarchies are considerably reduced or removed altogether – and managers either change their function or are forced to take redundancy.

Another implication concerns the future of masculine subjects in relation to management, work and organization. There is a commonsense association of femininity with the interpersonal skills necessary for the new entrepreneurial organization grounded in regimes of management through social relationships that is currently being cultivated by a number of managerial gurus (for example, Tom Peters). Consequently, in the minds of senior managers, women are assumed to be the more productive category of employee with respect to these social skills. Even before these new regimes emerged, of course, women had become dominant numerically in service and retail organizations, largely because of their presumed flexibility and more particularly their comparatively lower employment costs. The displacement of men within these industries was partly a function of low wages but also a result of the self-generating image of feminized work and men's consequent desire to distance themselves from it. Now, however, this trend toward the feminization of employment is given an additional boost such that traditional men are in danger of becoming redundant in ever-increasing numbers. In relation to management, this redundancy is not simply a literal one in terms of their future in employment; for those remaining in work it is also metaphorical, since it places a question mark over the productive value of distanced forms of instrumental management control. This is not to argue that at the very senior levels women will replace men but it is indicative perhaps of an even greater degree of insecurity and competitive ambition for masculine subjects whose opportunities may be diminishing as a result of the development of management practices that are not entirely compatible with instrumental and distanced forms of control.

A caveat needs to be added here in that while we are suggesting that meaningful social relationships require individuals first to be comfortable with themselves – a condition that we have argued is rare for masculine-dominated subjects – the amorphous and continually shifting character of social relations renders them capable of being manipulated instrumentally. Consequently, the attributes or the outward presentation of these social skills can be readily reproduced on demand (Goffman, 1959). But in the world of managerial work where interactions must be continually repeated, these social skills appear as a parody – a performance instantly recognized as superficial and synthetic. The attempt to render social relationships manageable as an instrumental goal or to give them instrumental purpose will probably fail or be self-defeating since instrumentality is often recognized as such. Nonetheless, however artificial or forced, the instrumental use of social skill can still be buttressed by hierarchical authority regardless of how it grates on employees. Despite the tensions that relating to other human beings encompasses for masculinity, social skill can still be instrumentally appropriated so as to shield individuals from the contradictions of their masculinity.

Summary and conclusion

This chapter has focused on the discursive constitution of a certain form of masculinity privileged in contemporary managerial and organizational work. It is a masculinity that is preoccupied with setting itself challenges, missions and targets and with controlling the social and technical means of achieving them. This masculinity brooks no opposition and continuously searches for new targets and challenges as the thrill of success from one mission or accomplishment subsides. Driven by a conviction that the 'best is yet to come', it strives ceaselessly and compulsively for the ultimate yet elusive achievement. It does this through seeking to control rather than relate meaningfully to others. By virtue of a preoccupation with instrumental control, the tendency for masculine subjects to be disembodied or separate from themselves as well as from others is sustained. A significant part of the drivenness of this masculinity paradoxically is to overcome this disembodiment so as to feel more at ease with itself and with others. However, the strategy of resolving this disembodiment is part of the problem not the solution. For in seeking to control others and the world outside themselves, masculine subjects become even more disembodied and further from a sense of contentment or being at one with the world. We have contrasted this compulsive masculinity with the discourse of femininity where identities are secured through subordinating the self to the demands or desires of others; feminine subjects passively fading into the background for fear of stealing the limelight from those masculine subjects whose fragile identities have to be massaged and supported. Whilst on the surface it may appear that femininity is more easily managed, it is equally difficult to sustain a feminine identity as a masculine one. But it is managed more passively, since to be assertive is a violation of what it means to be feminine, despite the very real feeling of frustration and tension that might result. Until the contemporary development of feminist movements, women had no legitimate means through which to express their dissatisfactions and little space within which to behave differently and create alternative subjectivities. Clearly these dissatisfactions were a major stimulant in the growth of feminism as a political and social movement but they are also intensified by it and provide the conditions for social change in organizations and elsewhere.

Because of their overly rational, disembodied and instrumental pursuits, modern management and work organization are particularly important sites for the reproduction of masculine discourses and practices. In one sense management might be seen to legitimize this disembodied instrumentality, making it appear wholly self-evident and unproblematic, such that there is no space for alternatives. However, the extent to which this gender myopia can continue is questionable when, on the one hand, feminist discourses – in the media, leisure, politics – are challenging masculine domination and, on the other, organizations are seduced by management gurus who are peddling 'soft', human-oriented managerial philosophies which are in tension with traditional 'hard' systems of management control.

In the final section we speculated on this changing nature of organizations where for reasons of employment adaptability, flexibility and cost, not only are women beginning to outnumber men in non-managerial work but also the demands of diverse and fast-changing markets and consumers are rendering traditional masculine control mechanisms in management increasingly vulnerable. Culture change, quality management and customer service, especially in service industries, are all demanding a less abstract, distanced and disembodied approach to managerial and other organizational work. Even business process re-engineering (BPR), which may be seen as something of a masculinist technical backlash, is attractive for reasons that go beyond its power to reintegrate increasingly fragmented functions; it also takes labour away from time-consuming routine procedures. It is often adopted so as to 'free up' staff to engage in the more social and relational, 'value-added' activities that are seen as essential to maintain or promote corporate competitive advantage through improved service quality and a distinctive customer image.[6] However, many of these new organizational philosophies and procedures hit the barriers of deeply embedded masculine and hierarchical means of control, where relations are purely instrumental and social encounters *pre-scripted*. Given that new managerial innovations (e.g. quality management, culture change) are usually implemented, if not designed, through such masculine imbued understandings, it is not surprising that they often fail or gain only limited success. We are not suggesting that management and organizations are becoming less masculine as a result of the new philosophies. On the contrary, masculine managers appropriate any new vocabularies and behaviours as an instrumental technique. In the case of these more social and human-oriented management philosophies, this is wholly contradictory to their espoused ethos since it undermines the very basis of social co-operation and collaboration.

Notes

1. A similar concern has been expressed by Collinson and Hearn (1994), who seek to analyse the unities and differences between men and masculinities and the ways in which they overlap within specific organizational discourses and practices.

2. As David Collinson pointed out to us, while more women are entering management as a whole, the actual numbers at senior levels are declining. Calás and Smircich (1993), on the other hand, suggest that feminization is creating a situation where jobs, regardless of the sex of the job holder, become 'women's work' with associated low salaries or wages (see also Ferguson, 1984).

3. While throughout this chapter we emphasize the multiplicity and diversity of masculine identities or masculinities, the singular term masculinity or masculine identity is also used to convey certain ideal typical features such as disembodiment, instrumental rationality, and a preoccupation with control that are commonly though variably produced and reproduced in all masculine discourses.

4. In case this phrase is a little obscure, it simply refers to the tendency for feminists to replace masculine representations with feminine ones rather than eradicate the epistemology of representation altogether.

5. The qualifier 'end' has to be included here to distinguish between customers internal to the value chain and those who actually consume the product or service eventually. This is because, since the development of the internal market as a major managerial practice to improve service quality, everyone is a customer of someone else.

6. This observation comes from our research on quality issues and innovations in financial services.

6

Entrepreneurialism and Paternalism in Australian Management: A Gender Critique of the 'Self-Made' Man

Rosslyn Reed

Two developments in the last twenty years which have contributed to research interest in the relationship between masculinity and management have shaped this study. The first is the debate on Harry Braverman's (1974) reformulation of Marxian labour process theory and the second is a growing body of feminist theory and research on women and work. Although Braverman's rigid adherence to the original Marxian theory of the labour process resulted in a flawed analysis, the debates on the nature of managerial control and the different functions and interests within management as an occupational group have opened the way for a critical evaluation also of the gendered nature of management practice(s). Similarly, the critique of Braverman's craft notion of skill generated the debate on the politics of skill and especially its uses in the social construction of male dominance and female subordination on the shopfloor as well as working-class masculinity. More recently, these now related debates have been integrated and have generated a revitalized sociology of organizations with a focus on the linkages between various managerial discourses, strategies, styles and practices and different forms of masculinity, particularly in the United Kingdom (Collinson and Hearn, 1994; Hearn, 1992b; Kerfoot and Knights, 1993).

In this chapter I will address two pervasive forms of management which have been discussed in management and organization literature: paternalism and entrepreneurialism. This discussion will attempt to link them to forms of masculinity rather than assuming them as gender-neutral forms or styles. These two approaches to management are often seen as separate and distinct but this analysis will show they can be, or rather have been, mutually overlapping forms of management in particular economic and cultural contexts. It will also be shown that there is no necessary link between them, as one can occur without the other in a different temporal context.[1] In particular, I will highlight the importance of exploring these masculinities and overlapping strategies of entrepreneurialism and paternalism through a case study of the life and management style of David Syme (1827–1908), the nineteenth-century Scottish-born Australian publisher of

The Age newspaper and a leader of liberal political thought in the colony of Victoria. In his public activity, he was almost 'ideal typically' Weber's (1930) sober, self-made modern capitalist entrepreneur. Syme's entrepreneurialism is linked to his paternalism through his commitment to the pursuit of 'duty' in a 'worldly' calling. In the context of newspaper publishing, Syme's paternalism also coexisted with and was developed alongside craft and growing trade unionism, especially by printers. The management practices established under his influence continued in attenuated form within a context of compulsory industrial arbitration in the twentieth century and changed organizational ownership relations until the 1980s. This and other evidence is suggestive of one approach to management in Australian firms in the second half of the nineteenth century which is not unlike that in some British family-managed firms of early capitalism.

Against this historical background of paternalistic entrepreneurial masculinity, the chapter then presents a provisional analysis of 1980s entrepreneurship. The example here is the Australian-born international media entrepreneur, Rupert Murdoch. The paternalism illustrated in the Syme case is absent from Murdoch's entrepreneurialism. While Murdoch benefits from the paternalism of older men, his entrepreneurialism is less driven by 'duty' in a 'worldly' calling than by adventurism – a pre-modern form of capitalist activity, according to Weberian analysis. Murdoch appears as an independent individualist, the apotheosis of Maccoby's (1977) 'gamesman'. This chapter therefore addresses specific and limited examples of entrepreneurialism and paternalism and their links to particular masculinities. It is recognized that other types both can and do exist, including types of entrepreneurship associated with women and including feminist approaches (see Goffee and Scase, 1985; Still, 1990).

My interest in Syme derives from doctoral research that I carried out at *The Age* in the mid-1980s. I examined the consequences of the introduction of automated typesetting equipment for three occupational groups. The study adopted a labour process framework taking account of the feminist critiques of the politics of skill within labour process debates, included attention to organizational aspects, and adopted an interpretative methodology. In addition to access to archival company records and union (chapel) minutes, formal and informal interviews with management, union officers and workers, I was able to observe the labour process of the three work groups studied over a two-year period. In addition, labour histories (Fitzgerald, 1967; Hagan, 1966) and two biographies of David Syme (Pratt, 1908; Sayers, 1965) provided historical background.

My theoretical interests lay in the construction of one type of working-class masculinity through craft skill on the one hand (Reed, 1988, 1990) and devaluing of women telephonist clerks' skills (Reed, 1987) on the other. While I noted the career path to management via journalism in the twentieth century (Reed, 1991a), I was more aware of the enduring influence of Calvinism on Syme's entrepreneurship in the nineteenth century

(Reed, 1991b) and its consequences for organizational culture (Reed, 1993). Only much later did the possible links between his entrepreneurial motivations, paternalistic management practices and type of masculinity become apparent.

If I have had multiple sources of data in relation to the Syme case study, the opposite is true for Rupert Murdoch. Much, of course, has been written about Murdoch in the media but these are generally unreliable sources for this type of analysis. In addition, a number of biographies have been written during his entrepreneurial career. They are often limited to specific sets of events (for example Leapman, 1983) or his early career (for example Regan, 1976). While Regan's emphasis on Murdoch's business approach is useful and Munster's knowledge of his Australian context a counterpoise to the assumptions and anti-Australian biases of overseas journalists, there is a sense that the later biographies 'feed off' the earlier ones. Part of the reliability problem lies in the refusal of sources within the publishing industry to be acknowledged and Rupert Murdoch's limited public writing and action/statements (Regan, 1976: 98) apart from his reputed intervention in his paper's editorial and other content. Hence, my analysis of Murdoch is programmatic rather than definitive.

The next sections of this chapter will address theoretical developments in the study of nineteenth-century entrepreneurialism and paternalism and their relationship to men and middle-class masculinity. The case studies of David Syme and Rupert Murdoch will follow. A comparison of these contrasting types of masculinity will reveal not only the differences in action and outcomes across time and in different contexts, but also the similarities in terms of producing repressed and repressive forms of humanity (Bologh, 1990: 11).

Entrepreneurialism and masculinity

Entrepreneurship has been examined within a number of academic disciplines. Both economics and psychology have produced taxonomies of requirements and character traits for continued entrepreneurial activity. While they tend to emphasize a range of actions and behaviours normally associated with men such as *total* commitment (my emphasis), drive to achieve and 'hero making' (Chell et al., 1991: 47–8), they do so in individualistic, voluntaristic, abstracted and agendered terms, even when using non-sexist and inclusive language (see also Mulholland, Chapter 7 in this volume).

Sociological analysis of entrepreneurial activity which takes account of specific economic, political and cultural factors begins with Weber's analysis of those who established industrial capitalism. Weber argued that a set of complex material factors gave rise to capitalism. This was accompanied by a specific 'ethos' which legitimized a break with traditional approaches to life, work and business activity on the part of a section of the middle class. This ethic of 'duty' in a 'worldly' calling derived from Calvinist theology, not in any direct sense, but through the development of a particular approach to the use of one's life, time and capital in order to obtain some evidence of 'election' or eternal salvation.

Through compulsion to extract calculable returns on investment, the process of capitalist accumulation was set in motion. Having created a process with its own dynamism, the relevance of the ethos itself is negated. In other words, it is not necessary for ascetic Protestantism to be sustained for either entrepreneurial or capitalist activity to continue. Weber does allow that a 'disillusioned and pessimistically inclined individualism' persisted in people with a Puritan past, and it could be found among the 'rising strata of the lower industrial middle classes' of industrailized countries in the nineteenth century (Weber, 1930: 52–177).

This is not an all-encompassing definition of entrepreneurship within industrial capitalism. Other types are possible, including the more openly aggressive exploitation of the economically weak and powerless found in other historical accounts of the industrial revolution. Whilst written in gender-neutral terms, the emphasis is masculine. Weber neglected gender in his writings as a result of his national identification (Bologh, 1990), which may partly explain his neglect of masculinity (also see Morgan, Chapter 3 in this volume). In different ways and with different conclusions, Ferguson (1984) and Due Billing (1994) have addressed the untheorized masculinity of bureaucracy in Weber's work. The broad sweep of his work on religion, economic history and organization on the one hand and methodological preoccupation with abstracted ideal types on the other ignores the relational as well as bodily features of bureaucracy and entrepreneurship.

Poggi argues that Weber refers only to the emerging 'burgher' or middle class (1983: 93–5). This type of nineteenth-century entrepreneurialism can be further defined in terms of Davidoff and Hall's (1987: 24) gender-sensitive categorization of internal distinctions within the English middle class. The lower ranks were more likely to be in single person enterprises, using mainly family labour with limited credit and mainly Methodist, Baptist or independent Anglican backgrounds. The higher ranks were in partnership or trust, employers of a workforce with wives full-time at home. Credit was obtained from banks and property was left in trust for dependants at death. Religious backgrounds were Quaker, Unitarian, Congregational or Anglican. It is the latter stratum or group rather than the former with which I am concerned here. In the case of Syme to be discussed below, religion remains a latent influence, his early Calvinist childhood having given way to a commitment to a secular liberal ideology which influenced his life and work. Nevertheless, an analysis of the biographies of Syme (Pratt, 1908; Sayers, 1965) and other histories drawing on the documentary sources of the time (Fitzgerald, 1967; Macintyre, 1991), indicates the influence of Calvinism on Syme's personality, particular liberal philosophy, approach to business investment and his management of the employees in his newspaper publishing organization (see Reed, 1991b).

As a former Calvinist, Syme epitomized the masculine 'elect' influenced by the Protestant Ethic as theorized by Weber and elaborated by Poggi (1983: 69), albeit without recognition of the gendered assumptions of the type of action described:

> The elect is active . . . his activity is directed by his intellect . . . the timespan of his effort is lengthy . . . his activity is continuous . . . he takes charge of his life . . . nor does he trust events to go his way; he plans his existence and takes responsibility for its temporal outcome, does not bless or curse fate: he struggles to impose order and control over the things and people surrounding him, does not allow or expect them to determine him.

Poggi's limitation of the Weber thesis in time and space and his specific elaboration of the traits of those (men) influenced by Calvinism is important because it answers many of the conventional academic criticisms levelled at Weber by economic historians (Tawney, 1938), theologians (Fischoff, 1959), sociologists (Parkin, 1982; Marshall, 1982; Dickson and McLachlan, 1989) and feminists (Bologh, 1990). While most of these are indeed justified, some may well have emphasized the 'letter' and missed the 'spirit' of his analysis. For example, Dickson and McLachlan (1989) draw attention to the inconsistencies in Weber's selective evidence from Franklin's (limited) writings. An alternative reading of the sections they criticize is also possible. Franklin himself seems to regard the first unascetic phase of Weber's life with some sort of sense of 'shame' in the reference to this as 'errata' (Dickson and McLachlan, 1989: 85). Furthermore, is it necessary to insist on a rigid and lifelong asceticism in the Calvinist to provide evidence of a contrasting approach to capital and wealth to the ethos of lavish consumption and/or the dissipated lifestyles of the aristocracy? Comfort and ability to buy quality goods and pursue other interests like writing in later years can hardly be seen as inconsistent with frugality and industry (Dickson and McLachlan, 1989: 86–7), but as alternative applications or a broadening of the notion of calling (cf. Campbell and Bouma, 1978).

More telling in its conclusions is Bologh's (1990) critical evaluation of Weber's (1978) overall approach to writing and research, which identified his interests with national political aspirations and masculinity. The world constructed through emphasis on the separation of public and private, of rationality and irrationality or emotion, of work, production and men from family, reproduction and women produces repressed and repressive forms of life (Bologh, 1990: 11): 'Within this patriarchal political economy, the private world of personal life and love is dependent upon, shaped by and subordinate to the public world of power and politics premised on a repressive rationality.'

Entrepreneurship in a capitalist sociopolitical context, then, marks the emergence of public patriarchy as distinct from traditional patriarchal and patrimonial relationships. The ascendancy and dominance of the public sphere is premised on its separation from, and the subordination of, the private sphere. Public patriarchy, even as differentiated patriarchies (Hearn,

1992b: 68), is a form of social organization produced through the separation of men from women. The public sphere to which men are linked is dominant over the subordinate private sphere to which women are linked. These relationships of masculinity and femininity are reproduced through these structural separations, transcending the aspirations and actions of individual men and women. While some women may engage in entrepreneurial activity in late capitalism (Goffee and Scase, 1985; Still, 1990), entrepreneurship continues as a 'normal' masculine domain.

Davidoff and Hall's (1987) historical analysis of the English middle class concurs and lends support to the notion of such a specific middle-class masculinity emerging in the late eighteenth and early nineteenth centuries. The middle class (and middle-class men specifically) were not just focused on the pursuit of profit, but also sought to carve out a public role for their class. Middle-class men also wanted to provide for their families in simple but comfortable ways. As they say, it was for the affections of wife and family that they were prepared to 'hunt the world for business' (Davidoff and Hall, 1987: 17). While the men concentrated their efforts to develop their 'pride in business prowess' (ibid.: 20), their wives were expected, consistent with Protestant values for women (Potter, 1986; Marshall, 1989; Pedersen, 1992), to economize in the home in support (Davidoff and Hall, 1987: 18). A revival of Puritan values occurred in England at this time in 'serious' evangelical Christianity – especially among the middle class – within the religious denominations identified above. Activity in the market was a *means* (my emphasis) to a proper family, moral and religious life in which the home represented a haven from the market, comfort, stability and morality for the protection and control of women (Davidoff and Hall, 1987: 21–2).

There is an emphasis here on the instrumental rather than the substantive rationality of entrepreneurial action but this does not altogether undermine Weber's argument, due in part to the passage of time. Furthermore, instrumental and substantive rationalities are only analytically separate. Motivations are seldom uncontaminated. They are not 'ideal types' which can be pure because they are only heuristic devices. This religious revival revolved around individualism and action in the world, that is, the public sphere of business and politics, but also included humanist compassion tempered with the desire for order and control (Davidoff and Hall, 1987: 25), a softening of the harshness of the earlier Calvinist world view. Those subscribing to this ethos, however, were also those most attracted to a rational and scientific world view (ibid.: 26).

Davidoff and Hall, therefore, present a broader picture of the middle class of early and nineteenth-century capitalism and entrepreneurialism in England, one which shows the relations within the family and especially those of the higher strata, but one which is consistent with both Poggi's elaboration and Bologh's critique of Weber. These developments in England are significant in locating Syme's type of entrepreneurialism and masculinity in its Australian context. Davidoff and Hall also identify links between entrepreneurship and paternalism to be discussed in the next section and which are crucially related both to the separation of public and private spheres and to men's and women's activity and the attribution of matters of 'head' or rationality to the former and the relegation of the non-rational or affective to the latter.

Current sociological and organizational literature on management, entrepreneurship and masculinity also notes the drive to order and control through notions of 'breadwinning' and the activity of 'providing' for the organization. These practices have their origins in the historical developments referred to above and have been reproduced through the separation of the public and private sphere so that they appear as unquestionable and natural. The contemporary discourse of entrepreneurialism in critical management literature emphasizes production for profit, risk, aggression and even ruthlessness. In organizational terms, those who participate in this discourse see themselves as 'breadwinners' for the organization (Collinson and Knights, 1986). Historically, as seen from the feminist labour process critiques of skill and the struggle for equal pay, breadwinning became a policy of the labour movement in nineteenth-century struggles between capital and labour (Seccombe, 1986). The breadwinner's wage is 'won' by a (male) husband/father on behalf of a (female) wife/family. The size of the wage was used by printing tradesmen, for example, to indicate their manliness (Baron, 1992: 72).There are links here to paternalism, but breadwinning in the modern discourse of entrepreneurship is also located in the notion of both aggression in 'winning' and the pursuit of further rational goals. In the newspaper publishing industry, for example, these meanings of masculinity can forge the bonds of a fratriarchal (Hearn, 1992b: 67) gender class which remains in tension with economic class interest cleavages.

The 'hard-nosed' competitive aspects of entrepreneurialism are also associated with recent management styles which emphasize economic efficiency and management control to the exclusion of all else (Collinson and Hearn, 1994: 14). Infused with the masculinist language of 'penetrating markets', imbued with a camaraderie of those who share the competitive ethos and are prepared (and able) to work long hours and be geographically mobile, these discursive practices marginalize those who do not share such values, including some men and those who are unable to participate in these practices because of family and domestic commitments, usually women (Collinson and Hearn, 1994: 14). This latter form of entrepreneurialism is masculine in that it marginalizes and excludes women both culturally and as organizational members according to their ability to separate 'work' and 'home' and maintain distance from the domestic sphere rather than their ability to 'juggle time' (Bittman, 1991) for work and family responsibilities. Entrepreneurialism, now as in earlier periods, relies on the separation of the public and private spheres and freedom from the obligations and responsibilities located in the private sphere. It is associated with male norms of paid employment processes and practices, such as the length of the working day/week/year which rest on a domestic support structure maintained by women.

Paternalism and masculinity

Paternalism is also linked to patriarchy through images of the 'provider' and 'father' figure who takes action and makes decisions on behalf of 'lesser' individuals or groups in his 'care' or protection. It has links to patriarchy in its most literal and traditional sense of the father exercising control over a family/household. Paternalism can be something of an attenuated form of patrimonialism – a system of patronage relations based on duty and obligation – but this is not the only form. Paternalism in organizations, then, and especially in relation to those managers who practise it, is a reflection of the separation of the public and private spheres and a shift from private to public patriarchy (Collinson and Hearn, 1994) and hence is related to the masculinity of management. Paternalism is also linked to other 'fratriarchal' (Hearn, 1992b: 153) relations. Printing trades have a long history of masculinity, and printing and newspaper offices have a history of paternalistic employment practices and controls. These have links to both craft and later trade union practices and the ownership histories of these sorts of firm but need also to be seen as negotiated – emerging as the result of the strength of organized labour and conflictual relations at the workplace where different discourses of masculinity clash and are reconstituted.

Different types of paternalism pertain in other political and national contexts such as in relatively isolated regional locations in the United Kingdom (Martin and Fryer, 1973) with a largely 'captive' and rural female workforce (Lawson, 1981: 47–66) as well as being embedded in practices as divergent as Fordism in the United States and elsewhere (Littler and Salaman, 1984: 75–6) and the management practices of large Japanese corporations (Littler, 1982: 151–6). Each of these different forms of paternalism has emerged in specific economic and cultural contexts and they have different consequences for employees, as well as different management styles.

While entrepreneurship appears more profit oriented in emphasis, paternalism suggests, in some circumstances, a preparedness to depart from profit maximization in the interests of enhanced employee welfare. It is likely, however, that the welfare measures are limited and/or sporadic, or perhaps as some compensation for low wages. The employee loyalty, commitment and motivation which are developed provide returns to employers that could not be obtained otherwise. Paternalism as a form of management control is dependent on sets of contextual factors outside the scope of this chapter but appears to be linked to a form of masculinity that values or accepts a relationship in which others are dependent on the administration of resources and/or largesse.

Paternalism suggests an alternative form of masculinity to that of entre-preneurialism: more benevolent, less aggressive, achieving its legitimacy and authority from 'protection' of the 'weak' and 'vulnerable' (i.e. 'lesser men' and women) from the harsh realities of decision making (Kerfoot and Knights, 1993: 665–7). Paternalism emphasizes the moral basis of co-operation and interdependence and mutual trust relations to secure com-pliance and motivation (Collinson and Hearn, 1994: 13). As Maddock and Parkin point out, there are overtones here of 'gentlemanly' (*sic*) behaviour which both appeal to older men and resonate with middle-class subcultures and have their origins in nineteenth-century, middle-class masculinity (cited in Collinson and Hearn, 1994: 13–14) and family ideology. Nevertheless, as discussed later in this chapter, paternalism can be quite consistent with the bureaucratization of organizations. (Bureaucratization, in turn, can be consistent with other more aggressive forms such as strategic management: Kerfoot and Knights, 1993: 668.) It was certainly consistent with the nineteenth-century entrepreneurialism outlined above.

Despite middle-class men's 'pride in business prowess' (Davidoff and Hall, 1987: 20) defining middle-class masculinity in nineteenth-century England, higher status and religiously influenced entrepreneurs, and employers more generally, experienced some degree of discomfort with the capitalist ethos and conflictual employment relations. They displayed some attachment to aspects of traditional and paternalist thinking, seeing themselves as providers and protectors of both family and employees (Davidoff and Hall, 1987: 20–1). Family were to be separated from the workplace, the market and the rigours of business decision making and this aspiration lent legitimacy to otherwise distasteful activity. The influence of the eighteenth-century religious revival meant, for these entrepreneurs, not only an emphasis on individualism, action and struggle, but also a humanist compassion for the 'weak' which tempered the drive for control and mastery in the public sphere associated with Calvinism and the Protestant ethic. Women, in this discourse, embodied the negative of the non-rational (i.e. weakness) but also the positive: innocence, nature and heart (Davidoff and Hall, 1987: 25–7) which had to be denied in the interests of the development of the rational active 'strong man' (Bologh, 1990: 36).

In relation to the principles of 'duty' and 'honour' which characterized the nineteenth-century phase of much personal entrepreneurial action, Hearn suggests a retitling of Weber's essay as *The Masculine Ethic* or *Protestant Masculinity and the Spirit of Capitalism*. As the earlier discussion of the 'elect' and the elaboration of paternalism indicates, '[m]asculinity was affirmed in management through a mixture of denial, earthly works, achievement and salvation. External works complemented internal denial: masculinity was a combination of doing and not doing' (Hearn, 1992b: 16). With the considerable weakening of religious motivations in the twentieth century and its direct links to a discourse of management and capitalist production for profit, shorn of any humanism or liberal values except the most utilitarian economic rationalism, contemporary entrepreneurialism has become severed from the discourse and practice of paternalism. Not that paternalism is itself negated as a form of management and masculinity, but it is more completely separated from other forms such as authoritarianism, entrepreneurialism and careerism (Collinson and Hearn, 1994).

David Syme: paternalistic entrepreneur

Turning to the case of David Syme, it is necessary here to outline only those aspects of his entrepreneurialism which are related to management and masculinity. David Syme was born in North Berwick, Scotland in 1827, the youngest son of a Calvinist schoolmaster and parish clerk whose actions generated considerable conflict but never, it seems, compromise with his principles. Syme was educated by his father in strict Calvinist fashion for 'duty' in a worldly calling but when his father died, he found himself untrained for any occupation or profession. Later, while at Bathgate with his brother George who had been educated for medicine, he tasted a variety of revivalist Christianity which appealed to him more than his father's Calvinism. He says:

> I came to know of a more rational plan of salvation for which the supernatural element was altogether eliminated. This was the plan formulated by the Rev. James Morrison . . . I confess this process of conversion appeared to me to be both scientific and scriptural . . . [which] came to me as a relief and a revelation. (Syme, in Pratt, 1908: 15)

Although he studied theology for two years, following a breakdown he travelled and studied philosophy in Germany for a year, eventually rejecting religion. After a brief period as a proofreader on a Glasgow newspaper, he migrated to California and Australia in the mid-nineteenth century in search of gold and his fortune and eventually achieved some success as a road-building contractor in colonial Victoria (Australia). Another brother, Ebenezer, who had been educated for the Church and was an itinerant Unitarian preacher in England, also came to Australia where he became a leader-writer for *The Age* newspaper which, at the time, was published by a workers' co-operative. Ebenezer Syme had connections with Radical thought in England,[2] and adopted an iconoclastic editorial style and practice. Within a short period the co-operative failed, but with the financial backing of liberal businessmen in the colony, Ebenezer Syme purchased *The Age*. David Syme joined his brother as a partner but when the paper could not support both families he returned to road-contracting, in which he appears to have been reasonably successful.

It was 'duty' to family and kin which shaped Syme's commitment to the 'worldly calling' of newspaper entrepreneur and resulted in *The Age* becoming and remaining one of Australia's and the world's 'influential' newspapers (Walker, 1982: 293–312). David Syme rejoined the paper in

1859 because his brother was dying of tuberculosis, and he remained after 1860 to support his brother's widow and her family. The biographies suggest that this partnership was characterized by conflicts and disagreements about the management of the paper rather than mutuality and familial affection. From the 1860s Syme was in virtual control of the organization and subsequently established sole proprietorship. On his death he left the business and considerable property acquired with its profits in a trust for his descendants.

Syme's sense of 'duty in a calling' extended to his management and control, which led to the pursuit of specific editorial policies that both built the paper's circulation (from lower middle-class and some 'respectable' working-class readers), such as campaigns against privileged access to land, corruption in colonial bureaucracies and 'sweated labour', and regularly jeopardized profitability through advertising boycotts and lawsuits for defamation. The paper's motto was 'Measures not men', which rested on the 'right of a newspaper to criticize the public actions of a public man' (Sayers, 1965: 172–4). By using his paper as a voice of 'advanced' (Macdonald, 1982: 23) or 'ameliorist' (Sawer, 1990: 217) liberalism, Syme could be seen as a paternalist in the wider societal context which facilitated his entrepreneurship. His politics, entrepreneurship and paternalism are thus all intertwined and appear to have constituted his personal identity and honour as a 'man'. His actions, although thoroughly secular, were infused with the sense of 'duty' and 'calling' to such an extent that religious metaphors abound when talking and writing about him and *The Age*. For example, *The Age* was a 'political pulpit' (Blainey, 1979: ix) and David Syme the 'apostle of restriction' (Sayers, 1965: 73).

The last reference is to his most noted campaign for tariff protection for local manufacturing against free traders, usually representing British merchant interests. It was this historically notable political action for which Syme earned the title 'the father of protection' – the subtitle of his first biography (Pratt, 1908) and the subject of subsequent academic debate. His biographers and others (Macintyre, 1991: 66–9) note his ability, via *Age* editorial policies, to 'make' and destroy colonial governments, although this view is challenged by others. Syme could, however, be seen as something of a public colonial patriarch. Space does not permit a full elaboration of Syme's risk-taking action. His was a largely rational approach to business, but not purely 'commercial' (instrumental) (Sayers, 1965: 35) because of his political commitments and sense of 'duty'. While the latter may be dismissed as a legitimizing rationalization for possibly otherwise untenable action, it surfaces often enough in his writing and rare public speeches in relation to 'honour' to have been more than superficial window-dressing.

As a highly profitable venture, *The Age*, along with other publishing ventures, allowed Syme to amass further carefully chosen property interests on good advice and to practise public philanthropy, sponsoring agricultural and scientific developments, expeditions for exploration and the like –

consistent with his rational and scientific world view. As a 'breadwinner' and 'provider' for his family and beyond, Syme developed impeccable credentials. His wife and only daughter certainly were shielded from the public world of commerce and paid work. Surviving photographs are of private domestic and family life.

In relations with his employees, Syme was known as a hard taskmaster although he opposed sweated labour. As the employer of a highly unionized masculine workforce and one which believed him to be a printer 'made good', such opposition was clearly in his material interests. His business was of a type and size that he was obliged to pay relatively high wages. He worked long hours himself from 10 a.m. to 2 a.m. in the early days, only going home at 5 p.m. towards the end of his life. Long hours of work were characteristic of labour-intensive newspaper publishing at the time. There is clear evidence that he paid all his debts – both financial and moral – including to those who had supported him financially when the business was threatened by advertising boycotts. He was known to be tolerant of 'peccadilloes' in those (men) who worked hard, and generous to employees, strangers in need and enemies in defeat. In other words, fratriarchal relations (Hearn, 1992b: 67) coexisted with those of paternalism.

Syme did not have the consistent welfare policies sometimes equated with paternalistic employment practices. These were inconsistent with and could have been opposed by a masculine, craft union organized workforce, even if he could have 'afforded' them, which is doubtful in the early years of his proprietorship. Like his philanthropy and generosity to strangers and enemies, his paternalism was sporadic (if sometimes substantial) and not entirely associated with relieving others (men) of responsibility for decision making, as is consistent with a commitment to duty and an independent masculinity or manliness.

By the late nineteenth century Syme's authority at *The Age* was secure because it was premised not only on his role as owner-manager, but also on the reputation of the paper and his public status. It was reinforced by the inaccurate image of him as a former printing tradesman (Fitzgerald, 1967: 39), and his fratriarchal support for the 'respectable' working-class aspirations of craft unionism based on securing the high 'breadwinner's' wage which underpinned shopfloor masculinity. Therefore, when Syme introduced Linotype machines in the 1890s, he provided pensions for older redundant compositors and settled others on farms or in small business. As Pratt (1908: 265) laments, in interesting language for my purposes: 'There are unhappily but few industrial employers with the patriarchal instincts of the founder of *The Age*.' This action is at once an action of paternalistic duty, public patriarchy and fratriarchal relationships. It is also economically self-interested, as the control of the printing craft union over the printing presses as well as non-mechanized typesetting processes had the potential to damage Syme in the market.

In another fratriarchal act of, in this case private, philanthropy, Syme is reputed to have given one of his most noted 'enemies', the railway commissioner Speight, £100 when he heard he had been ruined by Syme's victory in a defamation case which could alternatively have ruined Syme (Pratt, 1908: 255–6; Sayers, 1965: 278–9). He is also reported to have bestowed largesse on a young journalist employee who requested a loan against his wage to finance his marriage. This story which, like the other may be apocryphal, illustrates the nature of Syme's paternalism. It also illustrates his view of masculinity. As Davidoff and Hall (1987) point out, these acts of paternalism by nineteenth-century middle-class men were aimed at having other men act like them. While this sort of homosocial reproduction (Kanter, 1977: 48, 63, 68) is usually understood in terms of the control over uncertainty within organizational contexts which can never be totally 'rational', it is also a means of reproducing particular types of masculinity with particular sets of values.

Syme protects the young man's masculine status as a 'breadwinner' within the family by reinterpreting his request for a loan as a gift to the bride, avoiding a fall in family wages. These acts in the organizational and social context sustained traditional and rational legal authority relations and Syme's power as an owner-manager and a patriarch because of the loyalty and commitment they generated. In effect the patriarchal status of Syme, his paternalistic and philanthropic acts and the masculine identity they conferred meshed with and mutually reinforced the patriarchy, paternalism and 'respectable' working-class masculinity of the printers on the shopfloor as well as that of the journalists who lived in genteel poverty at this time in much the same way as clerks. How much each conditioned and shaped the other is difficult to gauge now but the strength of printing craft unionism in the 1870s and especially the 1880s in Australia would have been significant.

The best example of Syme's attempts to reproduce himself in other men is his relationship with Alfred Deakin who was a young lawyer encouraged by Syme to write for *The Age*. Syme sponsored Deakin's move into politics. Deakin also spent some periods with Syme at one of his rural properties, where the two discussed ideas and theories of liberalism. Deakin is regarded as one of the most successful of Australia's early prime ministers, and 'advanced liberalism' and 'protectionist' policies in the federal arena are referred to as 'Deakinite liberalism'. He wrote the 'Introduction' to Syme's first biography after his death, paying tribute to his mentor.

Pure ideal types are rare empirically by definition and Syme is not completely the Weberian 'sober self-made' capitalist. In some ways his location historically and structurally allowed him to develop a strange type of charismatic authority, paradoxically premised largely on his invisibility. For such a public persona, he made few public appearances. Consequently, his 'legendary' persona endured beyond his physical presence in the organization and his life-span. At the time of my research, employees at all levels from management to 'tea ladies' identified with *The Age* of David Syme. Some of these, but especially those with generational family links to the organization, had Syme family stories to tell – and in uncontrived ways, unlike the artificiality of the 'stories' which feature in much organizational culture theory.

The *Age* office was very much a 'household' culture but not a family business in the sense of all members of the family working in it. David Syme took his sons into the business, and as late as the 1960s the youngest and only surviving son, who was a director of the company at this time, was referred to as 'mister Oswald' (Souter, 1981: 415), carrying connotations also of traditional, even patrimonial authority. Some of his descendants acquired their own legends: Hugh Syme for his Second World War exploits rendering mines safe in Britain (Southall, 1967) and Kathleen as law graduate, board member, women's editor and charity organizer. Syme's sons, however, were neither charismatic nor entrepreneurial and appear as organizationally dependent 'company men' leading the organization conservatively from the early 1900s to the 1960s.

The links between kin and generational association with *The Age* extended to employment practices. Print union exclusionary practices of labour market regulation via apprenticeship by the Melbourne Typographical Society (MTS) (Fitzgerald, 1967; Hagan, 1966) made this and other associated trade areas highly masculine domains. This was reinforced by the maintenance of traditional controls over the labour process and a strategic location in the production process maintaining high wages and 'breadwinner' status. Fathers passed on both jobs and work values to sons and nephews (and other young men of their acquaintance). As much as Syme had an interest in encouraging middle-class men to emulate him, so these working-class men had an interest in reproducing their own masculinity. As they dominated the organization numerically as well as industrially, these values overshadowed other working-class values potentially held by unskilled ancillary workers. These are simply not on the record. In the working-class family, the union (especially the chapel or shopfloor level) and in the organization, masculine values were reproduced in myriad ways. While this can also be seen as facilitating some degree of control over the labour process for both union and management, it is the masculinities which are of interest here.

It would be inaccurate to represent this highly masculinized workplace as entirely hostile to women. Few, if any, women were employed in the nineteenth century. Consistent with his 'advanced' liberalism, Syme was supportive of 'women's movements' (Pratt, 1908: 268) for citizenship rights. Despite Kathleen Syme's employment as women's editor (a reflection of the separation of public [masculine] and private [feminine]), she and other female descendants have been board members in the twentieth century. Only after the routinization of second-wave feminism did some women, usually former journalists, come to occupy positions in middle management. Following Commonwealth legislation for affirmative action and equal employment opportunity (EEO) in 1986, however, the Syme organization employed two new female printing apprentices along with two males in typesetting and two female security officers, among other initiatives. For the telephonist clerks in classified advertising, the largest area of female employment which emerged after the Second World War, paternalism meant a benign employing organization which accommodated family and domestic responsibilities, provided 'permanent casual' employment and extended paid leave after fifteen years' service, benefits which many were able to claim. Reflecting the paternalistic, protective culture, these benefits were also the result of a post-entry closed shop and membership of a male-dominated operatives' union which achieved higher than usual wage rates for this type of work but which nevertheless carried its own patriarchal values and protection of the 'breadwinner' status of its male members (Reed, 1987).

As a higher-status middle-class man and entrepreneur, Syme was able to rely on bank finance and support from other businessmen in difficult times. He also appears to have had excellent (male) editors who carried out his policies exactingly. In terms of the public sphere, he was an independent entrepreneur. In terms of the private sphere, he remained dependent on his wife and family for support (cf. Hall, 1992: 262). The separation of the public world of business and the private world of family was complete until he took his sons into the business. That he frequently spent weekends at one of his rural properties suggests also an emotional distance from family. Records of letters confirm this and some degree of unease with it. In a letter to his wife following a missed wedding anniversary he wrote 'We two do not much indulge in sentiment when speaking to or of one another but we understand all the same. I am conscious of my shortcomings in my conduct towards you and am ever blaming myself' (quoted in Sayers, 1965: 214). One of his obituaries (*The Bulletin*, 27 February 1908) testifies to the nature of Syme's invisibility, charisma and public persona, including his appearance:

> Although one of the best known men in Victoria, he was one of the least seen. He could pass down Collins Street, and not one in a hundred know the tall, brown, all-bone pioneer. I sat facing him one afternoon on a tram, while the two men on his right abused Protection, *The Age* and David Syme – especially David Syme. The flinty Syme eye never faltered, the rusted cast-iron face never lost its metallic calm. It is simply not possible to write of Syme and keep iron out of it. His frame suggested to me the long iron cages we rode in at the mines; his face propounded a mask of boiler metal. If I were writing his epitaph it would be 'Rust to Rust'.

In photographs Syme appears like this – lean and unsmiling – or sitting before a large roll-top desk, symbolic of his work and public life. Like the dark-suited English middle-class men described by Davidoff and Hall (1987), his appearance was always restrained and plain. Nevertheless, as in the case of Franklin, wealth brought middle-class comfort to him and his family, but not luxury (Sayers, 1965: 219).

In the mid-1960s, Ranald Macdonald, Syme's great-grandson, became managing director of the Syme organization until he sold his shares and left the organization in 1983. The Fairfax organization, which was in partnership with the Syme organization during much of this time, shared a paternalistic ethos but not the liberalism of the (earlier) *Age*. Macdonald subscribed to the family values but was part of a generation of better educated Australians moving away from conservatism and the older liberalism. He was less of the 'company man' than Syme's sons and other descendants. Together with an editor frequently described as 'charismatic' by his peers, others in the organization and beyond, Macdonald revitalized the paper as a campaigning liberal voice taking on a strong investigative journalistic ethos, events and topics outside the scope of this chapter. Macdonald, however, was not located in a similar socioeconomic context to his great-grandfather and reflects a rather privileged upper middle-class, even ruling-class, background. After severing his ties with *The Age*, he invested most of the proceeds from his Syme shares in a health and fitness centre – an entrepreneurial venture of a more competitive type. He also engaged in much other public activity in sporting, cultural and government bodies. On the failure of his personal entrepreneurial activity Macdonald was quoted as saying:

> 'I think I was fairly slapdash about life . . . I worked damned hard and I didn't care much about the financial side. I've always done a lot and been pretty active, but never cared a lot, nor paid attention to my own affairs. . . . The negative side is that you obviously feel a failure.' (*Sydney Morning Herald*, 1987: 7)

Clearly the Syme family history is not unique. There are many tales of 'clogs to clogs in three generations', but this is not really one of those. Ranald Macdonald continues the professional practice of radio journalism and exhibits the middle-class 'gentlemanly' masculinity of his privileged, well-educated background. He is an idealist in an arena where there are relatively few (Souter, 1981: 414).

Neither is the Syme organization completely unique although it does have unique historically shaped aspects. David Syme fits the nineteenth-century sober self-made capitalist of Weber's thesis. Furthermore, his entrepreneurialism and paternalism, shaped as they were by a Calvinist childhood, a flirtation with revivalist Christianity, Enlightenment attachment to a rational and scientific world view but with some discomfort at the separation from traditional and private concerns in public life, are consistent with the masculinity of English middle-class entrepreneurial men of a similar period (in spite of his Scottish origins).

Syme's masculinity shares something with that of English middle-class intellectuals like John Stuart Mill and Thomas Carlyle, for whom writing was a highly masculine occupation (Hall, 1992: 264–8). The similarities in the descriptions of the appearance of Syme and Carlyle are especially striking in the portrayal of a 'particular form of male strength and seriousness' (ibid.: 266).[3] This style of entrepreneurialism, paternalism and masculinity would not have characterized many Australian organizations or managers at the time or since. Much entrepreneurship of the time was small scale and even more precarious than Syme's, closer to Davidoff and Hall's (1987) typification of the lower middle class in England. Moreover, in the colonial context there were few kin-based resources to soften the harshness of dependence on the wage. Face-to-face relations between workers and owner-managers in small business tend to be both coercive and exploitative in the pejorative sense and/or paternalistic in the sense of mutual accommodations. In spite of the persistence of some family-owned and managed organizations, corporate capitalism in Australia has developed towards impersonal ownership and control, and professional (that is non-owner rather than highly educated) management (Tsokhas, 1984: xiii).

These developments complicate the nature of entrepreneurialism and undermine the basis of the type of paternalism practised by Syme in the nineteenth century. By family background and education, David Syme belonged to one of the rising middle strata of the nineteenth century. As a middle-class man committed to duty in a worldly calling, he adopted the practices of entrepreneurship to meet his (and his family's) economic needs. At the same time, he adopted paternalistic management and other practices (for example, writing) in the public sphere which sustained his class and gender position and attempted to develop similar practices by other men. While he appears to have been successful in the public sphere, this success was built on a distance and separation from the private sphere of emotion and affection (Bologh, 1990: 11). For all Syme's identification with a humanistic ethos (Davidoff and Hall, 1987: 25), his resulting persona was of a repressed and repressive human being (Bologh, 1990: 11). While the entrepreneurial failure of his great-grandson attracts public attention, it may also demonstrate a weakening of the constraining power of Weber's 'iron cage' of the spirit of capitalism or, in Hearn's terms, an entrepreneurial masculine ethic (1992b: 163) and a less repressed and repressive humanity. Others, however, have pursued entrepreneurial action within late capitalism in a more instrumental form.

Entrepreneurship in the late twentieth century

In the economically stagnant 1980s the Australian government, like others, tried to promote a culture of entrepreneurial activity. In Australia, where small business constitutes about half of all economic activity, a few large-scale entrepreneurial ventures attracted attention as potential role models. Entrepreneurial actions were sometimes linked to the theories of Peters and Waterman (1982) and Kanter (1983) among others. Some larger-scale and publicly visible entrepreneurs became media personalities and even 'household names' in Australia. One Australian entrepreneur had entered the international arena earlier, and his activities spanned three continents in the 1980s. It is to an examination of the masculinity embedded in the entrepreneurialism of Rupert Murdoch that we now turn.

Rupert Murdoch: entrepreneur

Rupert Murdoch has similarities in family background to David Syme and links to the Syme family. He is a second cousin of Ranald Macdonald although not through the Syme lineage. The Scottish Presbyterian clergyman who read the funeral service for David Syme was Rupert Murdoch's grandfather. His father, (Sir) Keith Murdoch, obtained his first reporter's position at *The Age* through this connection. Contrary to some popular opinion which casts him as a 'colonial' outsider (Regan, 1976: 12, 202) his maternal grandfather was a successful entrepreneur and (Dame) Elisabeth and her family were part of the Victorian 'establishment'. Keith Murdoch died fairly early and although he had been a powerful media manager as well as politically influential, his only material capital legacy was the *Adelaide News*. The editor of the *Adelaide News*, when Murdoch inherited it, was the son of a family friend, Rohan Rivett, a grandson of Alfred Deakin. At Keith Murdoch's direction, Rivett had exercised a mentoring role over Rupert Murdoch during the latter's period at Oxford, visiting him when in the United Kingdom. It is from this base that Rupert Murdoch has built a media empire, as well as gathering other assets along the way (Munster, 1985: 257) across three continents. This is not the place to discuss the publishing strategies of Murdoch or debate the quality of the products. His managerial strategies and their entrepreneurial and paternalistic aspects and their implications for his masculinity will be our focus here.

Not unlike Syme and compared with other men of his social status and rank, Murdoch lives in relatively simple comfort (Leapman, 1985: 82; Regan, 1976: 206–10). Although a published writer in her own right, his wife Anna both maintains the domestic sphere (as did his first wife) (Regan, 1976: 60; Leapman, 1985: 42) and is a suitable adornment for a successful man. Although Murdoch goes to great lengths to provide for his family, he has a shorter time-frame for his activity and seeks primarily to leave a media empire for his son, which could be seen as a somewhat Freudian response to his own father's inability to do this for him (Regan, 1976: 209ff.; Munster, 1985: 258). Murdoch has received considerable support in both the public and private spheres. His mother and sisters provided their capital initially and their support is crucial to the maintenance of his control of News International (Munster, 1985: 258). (See Leapman's account of his mother's monitoring of Murdoch's achievements (1985: 21–2).)

The masculinity of Murdoch's persona includes elements of 'boyishness' (Regan, 1976: 15; Leapman, 1985: 17) although his toughness ('iron'), ruthlessness (Regan, 1976: 138, 175; Leapman, 1985: 17, 168) and instrumentality (Munster, 1985: 260) are noted. The latter is most apparent in his treatment, that is frequent sackings, of editors, managers and other staff. Murdoch's rationality is far more instrumental than that of the earlier type of 'self-made' man like Syme. His business philosophy is more utilitarian and social Darwinist (Leapman, 1985: 37). According to Regan (1976: 130), Murdoch offers his editors and managers a dream with purpose, challenge and idealism. Many accept the promise but after a short period they are 'burnt out' and exhausted. While their energies are depleted, they are the means (alongside respite within the family and domestic sphere) by which Murdoch recharges his own energy reserves. There are 'enormous rewards' in material terms for those who survive. This is the only means by which Murdoch creates other men in his own image (cf. Kanter, 1977: 48). Murdoch's paternalism is of the limited 'employer knows best' kind and his dealings with trade unions (and other employers in the industry bargaining context) are ruthless and aggressive, with little concern here as elsewhere for the dignity of other 'lesser' men as 'breadwinners'. Yet the 'boy publisher', with what Souter (1981: 345) calls 'the same winning charm' of his father, has been on the receiving end of the paternalistic actions of other older men (Regan, 1976: 207). Rupert Henderson of the Fairfax organization, for example, assisted his move into the Sydney newspaper market, which was reciprocated with strong competition in both tabloid and quality newspaper markets.

Murdoch's paternalism in relation to other men in the public sphere, then, remains limited and underdeveloped. It is likely that his entrepreneurialism would continue without it. If his paternalism is limited and instrumental, his entrepreneurialism is both instrumental and extremely risky. In Murdoch's hands, entrepreneurialism is gambling – for the fun of it as much as the profits, which are nevertheless considerable (Regan, 1976: 16, 56; Munster, 1985: 42; Leapman, 1985: 39, 80, 170, 277). Similarly, Murdoch's interest in horse-racing and playing poker machines in (private) leisure (Regan, 1976: 8, 12, 87; Munster, 1985: 42) is linked to his public action. Unlike the 'sober' entrepreneur of an earlier era, he is a 'gamesman' (Regan, 1976: 102).

Maccoby (1977) identified 'the gamesman' as a particular type of manager in high technology organizations. Although more of the 'intra-preneur' or internal organizational entrepreneur (Fulop, 1991: 26) than the independent entrepreneur, he has characteristics which match the accounts of Rupert Murdoch's entrepreneurialism: a fast-paced, semi-fantasy life, detached playfulness, compulsion to work and succeed, manipulativeness, toughness and domination (Maccoby, 1977: 107). While Maccoby does not acknowledge the masculinity of the traits he catalogues, the strength and continuing usefulness of his analysis lies in its attempt to locate types of management/leadership styles and entrepreneurialism in their social, political and cultural contexts. The types he identifies are related to specific periods of United States economic and cultural experience. But as genuine 'ideal types' they are not limited in their application, as the links to 1980s discourse show. Furthermore, it is clear that whilst the behaviours and characteristics Maccoby identifies can be adopted and emulated by women, they are most closely identified with men and masculinity. Fewer women managers, especially top women managers, tend to be married and more tend to be childless than men managers. Dominance and toughness, or at least contempt for weakness, are socially identified with masculinity although as Maccoby shows not always equally valued by all men or even all managers. There is, however, no suggestion here of space for leadership styles which focus on consultation and the nurturing or development of capacities among subordinates or of the longer-standing paternalistic approach to management which can be linked to entrepreneurialism in its earlier manifestations.

The intrapreneurial/entrepreneurial[4] discourse of the 1980s emphasized 'corner-cutting', 'skunk work, bootlegging . . . piracy' and 'horsetrading' (Fulop, 1991: 30–7). These are also aspects of action associated with men and masculinities. Alongside the traits listed above, these sorts of action are also associated with the entrepreneurialism of Murdoch (Regan, 1976: 121, 130; Munster, 1985: 42, 260; Leapman, 1985: 80, 85, 168). Included in the latter are references to an instrumentality in which all values, from employee loyalty to his nationalism and citizenship, are potential bargaining chips.

In his study of 1970s managers, Maccoby (1977: 75) found that advanced technology corporations encouraged 'qualities of the head'. He notes: 'In contrast, compassion, generosity and idealism, qualities of the heart, remain unheeded and underdeveloped.' 'Gamesmen' were not particularly happy; they lacked passion and compassion and were emotionally cautious, protected against intense experience. The cost of detaching the head from the heart to avoid painful experiences was to be 'only half aware' (Maccoby, 1977: 176–80). While Murdoch appears happier than this, his biographers note a certain one-dimensionality in his persona (Regan, 1976: 41; Munster, 1985: 5; Leapman, 1985: 272).

The media and other images of the 1980s entrepreneur (including Murdoch) invite epithets of 'cowboy' and 'buccaneer'. I find the latter attractive in theoretical terms, because it connects with an earlier form of capitalist activity discussed by Weber. According to Gerth and Mills, Weber distinguished the 'workaday enterpriser' of early capitalism from charismatic capitalists or 'economic super*men*' (masculine in original, emphasis added) (1948: 67). The latter were characteristic of 'adventure' or 'booty' capitalism, which refers to raids by groups of men on foreign countries to extract treasure, and which was associated with Spaniards in the Americas, English merchant adventurers and the Italian city-states (ibid.: 66–7). This suggests that the entrepreneurial activity of the 1980s (such as that of Murdoch) with its innumerable takeover bids, reflects, at least in part, a pre-modern rather than postmodern type and could be seen as an aberration in the ongoing development of modern capitalism. Clearly, Murdoch's entrepreneurialism is partly 'adventure'. But it also takes place in a constrained context. In order to maintain the family control necessary to deliver a media empire to his son – an act of patrimony of a traditional type – he is reliant on (initially) retained earnings and borrowed finance rather than the sale of equity. This appears to lead him into highly risky ventures which from time to time threaten the viability of his investments (Regan, 1976: 205; Munster, 1985: 258–60). Although, consistent with his 'gambling' instincts, he often makes huge profits from failed takeover bids (Leapman, 1985: 15, 152, 269–70).

There are continuities as well as discontinuities with the past. In his public appearances, for example, Rupert Murdoch dresses plainly in dark suits, white shirts and ties. The influence of a nineteenth-century, middle-class business presentation of self continues and is accentuated. It has become refined into a uniform which signals power and authority and also serves to marginalize matters of affect and humanity within the public sphere. It could also be that it serves to insulate those who adopt it from concerns which are not readily translated into market terms. While much has been said and written, mostly on a popular level, about the advantages and disadvantages of power dressing for women, men's clothing and appearance which constitutes the basis of power dressing remains unproblematic. This uniform has now been adopted widely within fratriarchal circles in Australia: businessmen, politicians, bureaucrats and some trade union leaders. Janine Haines, Australia's first woman leader of a Federal but minor political party, the Australian Democrats, has asked why it is that political 'minders' (advisers) 'make over' politicians to look like 'gangsters' (ABC-TV *Lateline* programme 15 February 1993). These fratriarchal images of a sort of 'Mafia' or 'brotherhood' are clearly masculine and exclusionary of women, gay men, people with disabilities and some ethnic minority groups whose own culturally based forms of dress and presentation of self can be sources of discrimination in organizational processes like promotion (see also Martin, Chapter 10 in this volume).

Independent entrepreneurship and i/entrepreneurialism of the 1980s was not only masculine because it was associated with men, individual men's actions and masculine images and representations. It was not only highly risky in the business and ethical senses, but it was also exceptionally instrumental, aggressive and ruthless, separating it from the sphere of 'heart', home and family much more than was the case in nineteenth-century upper middle-class entrepreneurialism. While families are increasingly acknowledged, they also play an ancillary public role as well as providing support in the private sphere. Rather than 'hunting the world of business' for the care and affection of family, the latter are harnessed to the search for profit. This could only occur in a context of male dominance, the precedence of the public over the private sphere and the tendency to commodify family relationships.

In Rupert Murdoch we can therefore see a mutually reinforcing entrepreneurialism and masculinity with elements of pre-modern adventure capitalist action. This kind of entrepreneurialism is no longer driven, consciously or unconsciously, by a set of moral imperatives. It is all but bereft of any humanistic discomfort with the harshness of market-driven action. After a century or more of separation of the public from the private sphere with men engaged in the former and women in the latter, contemporary entrepreneurialism as gamesmanship is a celebration of a type of life and work which has excluded women. Consequently many women and some men find it alienating. In the 1980s, entrepreneurialism was reduced to the basic 'spirit of capitalism' or an instrumental rationality.[5] Women entrepreneurs currently experimenting with traditional and other forms of entrepreneurship, including feminist ones, may yet develop alternatives which are less repressive. These could be adopted and emulated by some men as well as other excluded groups and may provide an opportunity for organizational and social change, while producing a less 'repressive rationality' (Bologh, 1990: 11) within entrepreneurs and other organization members. If the phenomenon of 1980s entrepreneurship has fallen into such a state of disrepute that it is all but dead, then few will mourn its passing.

Conclusion

This chapter has not dealt with the full range of possible types of entrepreneurialism. I have attempted only to draw on limited European, especially English middle-class history and culture to show how one type, a paternalistic entrepreneurialism, emerged and developed in the nineteenth century. Local economic and political factors in the colony of Victoria, including prevailing industrial relations regimes in newspaper publishing, were shown to condition that development and to shape the more routinized 'company' managerialism and masculinity which followed and was subsequently modified through a return to a more modern liberalism rather than via a renewed entrepreneurialism or even intrapreneurialism.

Twentieth-century entrepreneurialism, as identified here, is shorn of the humanistic discomfort which accompanied the nineteenth-century type. While it displays attributes of an irrational pre-modern 'adventure' type, in its emergence from the structures and constraints of earlier stages of modernity and industrial capitalism, it reflects the essence of (late) capitalism. Although there is increasing discomfort with so aggressive and ruthless a phenomenon, the search for new approaches to entrepreneurialism if not paternalism is unlikely to be over. There is space here for forms which are inclusive rather than exclusionary and which do not produce or reproduce repressed humanities. However, managers and entrepreneurs whose masculinity and identity are embedded in these practices and whose interests and careers are promoted and advanced through these and other forms of masculine managerialism are likely to resist change towards more rational (in the sense of reason), as well as less rational (in the sense of accommodation to the demands of the private sphere), open and accountable (for humanistic and equity objectives) management practices. For this reason, and despite the feminist critique of EEO as limited in its potential for organizational change, thoroughgoing promotion of EEO for women is a necessary if not sufficient condition for the de-masculinization of management.

Paternalism can limit women's advancement and influence within organizations through 'protective' policies and the covert allocation of privilege to 'deserving' young men (perceived as 'breadwinners') and others perceived to be cast in their mentor's image. There is, however, no indication that the absence of such a 'benign' environment and its replacement with one that is characterized by the attributes of the current 1980s discourse of entrepreneurialism (or any similar discourse grounded in masculine values and practices) is likely to generate cultures conducive to women's career progression, because their socialization and experiences may make such activities less consistent with socially constructed feminine identities. Alternatively, women who find themselves required to participate in these discourses may well choose, or be constrained to emulate, these practices successfully. The cost to them and to organizations and society may well be the reproduction of a limited and repressed humanity identified with men in increasing numbers of women also. More disastrously for them personally, such aggressive and ruthless behaviour as is incorporated into the i/entrepreneurial discourse outlined above may be deemed to be inappropriate for women by their superiors and limit rather than enhance their career prospects. Research shows that behaviours identified strongly with men can be interpreted negatively when displayed by women (Burton, 1991).

There is a growing body of research on men, management and different types of masculinity, of which this study is one small part. More work is needed to clarify the extent of similarities and differences in a range of national and historical contexts and their implications, especially for marginalized groups like women, gay men, people with disabilities and people from racial and ethnic minorities. The notion of 'intact' masculinity and 'intact' (heterosexual) male bodies, for example, requires some attention here. The extent to which the past is encapsulated or transcended in present processes and practices requires attention as a basis for dialectical transformation (see Hearn, 1990). Much more work is also required on the context and outcomes of 1980s entrepreneurialism in all its manifestations. This would need to pay greater attention to the sense of economic crisis in which the form of entrepreneurship and masculine alliance developed (Kelly, 1992: 14). It would require more than an analysis of biographies of some high-profile individuals such as Rupert Murdoch, authorized and unauthorized, which have been published to date. Eventually, other documentary evidence will be available to assist in this task. It is possible that the records and documents of failed organizations, or those where takeover bids were unsuccessful, may be more readily available than those of ongoing organizations which rarely grant the sort of access I had to the Syme organization. Interviews with employees and managers in relevant organizations, especially those which became targets for takeover activity, would allow for comparison between prior and later entrepreneurial forms of management. How these practices relate to men and masculinities remains an important analytical task and one which is particularly elusive under the pressures of the overarching 'naturalizing' effects of masculine domination in organizations and society.

Notes

This chapter has been developed through discussion and critical reflection. I wish to thank David Collinson and Jeff Hearn for their comments on earlier drafts and referral to a number of helpful sources. Kate Mulholland and Mike Roper also shared insights from their contributions. Any remaining limitations are the responsibility of the writer.

1. Broadly speaking, the nineteenth century in Australia was a time for establishing enterprises and institutions. In the late twentieth century processes of internationalization and globalization are unfreezing and rupturing established patterns. As in most historical developments, there are elements of continuity and change; of renewal of established practices and relationships and of dialectical transcendence. These disjunctions are not readily discernible, partly because of access to evidence and partly because it is difficult to ascertain whether the comparison is of the same or similar situations or actions in different contexts or emergent or new practices and patterns.

2. He worked on the *Westminster Review* and was associated with Chartists, Charles Dickens, Marian Evans and Herbert Spencer (see Elder, 1967; cf. Hall, 1992: 267).

3. This appraisal is supported by Macintyre who notes also the striking resemblance in terms of early Calvinist family influences in Scotland (Macintyre, 1991: 71).

4. Intrapreneurialism refers to enterprise for profit through internal corporate reorganization rather than external corporate development and expansion.

5. I am indebted to David Collinson for this insight.

7

Entrepreneurialism, Masculinities and the Self-Made Man

Kate Mulholland

This chapter uses case study data to explore the making of entrepreneurial masculinities. In particular it concentrates on two life histories depicting two rather different models of entrepreneurial masculinity but representative of first-generation wealth holders. It also examines the ways in which the processes of masculine entrepreneurialism impinge upon men's domestic role. Overall I highlight the links between the hidden services provided by women in the household and the construction of particular masculinities and capital accumulation through entrepreneurial activity. The following analysis suggests that women's domestic labour and the ideology surrounding femininity constitute invisible resources which play a fundamental part in building up the male entrepreneur and particular masculinities; these are sets of relationships which are themselves mutually reproducing. I show that men are able to construct masculinities around and from the activities in which they engage – these include public sphere activity, away from the non-engagement in private sphere activity and from the labour of wives.

Data for this chapter are drawn from an ethnographic study of seventy of the richest entrepreneurial families located in a Midlands county of England. Such wealthy families were involved in a range of very different entrepreneurial activities and were drawn from different sectors of the economy, but their principal concerns were in land, industry and commerce. Many of those interviewed were first-generation wealth holders and had gone into business for the first time in this country, whilst others had inherited the core of their family wealth. Forty-four families were first generation, and twenty-six had ownership and family origins dating back hundreds of years (see Mulholland, 1996). The masculine character of wealth ownership was encountered during the search for the sample families. The documentary sources, such as Burke's *Peerage*, local histories, business directories and press reports, all register the ownership of business to the male head, and these sources identified about half of the sample. The same gendered tendencies were also evident in consultations with community leaders as well as personal recommendation which helped identify the remaining sample. Despite the variety of sources most lead to a male head, with the exception of a few women who were wealth holders independent of men. The male head acted both as family 'voice' and 'gatekeeper' and controlled access to female kin. Sixty-five of the wealth-holding families were headed by men, and five by women. Over a hundred informants were interviewed and approximately one-third were women. Using the life history approach, for the most part men and women were interviewed separately using a semi-structured format. This approach had a number of advantages for it allowed the respondent to signal key life events, and in this instance it encouraged men to signal when they married. Although marriage was often significant to the development of the business, it was seldom given the recognition it warranted.

I was amazed by the consistency with which men took all the credit for their success (see also Roper, 1994a). Invariably the men told their stories as if they were the centre of the universe. In as many cases as possible wives were later interviewed, enabling the husbands' accounts to be checked. Since in some business sectors many of the respondents knew each other, and although the interviewees were guaranteed confidentiality, a few respondents acted as key informants, which further facilitated the checking of aspects of an interview. About half the interviewing was undertaken at the business headquarters, and the remainder in the homes of the respondents. The location of the interview was very significant. In many cases it measured the extent of access. Holding the interview in the business headquarters gave the respondent more scope to control the process, and in a number of cases it was simply regarded as another business appointment, and was constrained by time and the presence of support personnel. Accordingly, this was yet another dimension of male paternalism, preventing any outside gaze into the private sphere, the home. However, in the cases discussed below the different choice of location was intended to embody the sense of respondents' images and notions of success.

The naturalization of male entrepreneurialism

The literature addressing entrepreneurialism parodies the notion of neutrality in its presentation in routinely addressing a male audience and in assuming that the process is solely a male endeavour. This is reflected in the notion of entrepreneurialism based on human capital theory (Hebert and Link, 1989; Drucker, 1985) Its central focus is on the identification of very specific assumed qualities in human labour which are then portrayed as the cornerstone, or the format to successful wealth creation and regeneration. It then assumes that only men possess such human qualities upholding the further assumption that only men can be entrepreneurs (see also Chell et al., 1991). This literature is consistent with what Collinson and Hearn (1994) call 'malestream' organizational theory (see O'Brien, 1981). It places a premium on assumed entrepreneurial qualities, such as leadership, management potential, long-term strategic orientations, implying ruthless, financially astute, risk taking, rational and unemotional individuals. In many ways this literature leads to the 'charismatization' of individual entrepreneurs. It also tends to assume that successful wealth creation is an essentially masculine activity, dominated by men and excluding women (Kennedy, 1980).

The same emphasis and absences are apparent in a recent ethnographic study (Ram, 1994) which examines the survival strategies of Asian entrepreneurs in the clothing business. Whilst fully acknowledging direct female kin participation, it fails to question the class and patriarchal character of power relations within the business, or to problematize the gendered images of entrepreneurialism. Such gender inequality is explained as the policies and practices of a racist state and the experiences of living in a racist society, whilst class and patriarchal strategies remain unchallenged, protected by the sanctity of ethnicity and culture. Studies analysed in this vein simply add another layer to the processes that render gender and women in particular invisible, thus colluding in the naturalization of entrepreneurialism as male. However, the biggest flaw in this analysis is the denial that the material context in which such men operate and run their business and the kinds of resources available to them are often the key to their success. The euphemism 'family labour' conceals the identity of female kin, and vastly undervalues the extent and variety of their direct participation (Mulholland, 1993, 1996). Other literature does include women, but portrays them largely as *beneficiaries* and *consumers* of male wealth through marriage or inheritance(*Business Week*, 1992).

A further aspect of the male gendering of entrepreneurialism is the manner in which this process can also be observed in products (Roper, 1994a), while Allen and Truman's (1993) study indicates that female entrepreneurialism is service-oriented. But women's absence cannot be correlated with lack of participation.[1] The problem characterizing much of this literature can be gleaned from Collinson and Hearn's (1994) discussion – that although men have been the central focus, they have rarely been the object of scrutiny. Exceptionally, Goffee and Scase (1985) address the issue of female entrepreneurialism. In contrast with the mainstream literature, this study makes explicit that women are under scrutiny and the underlying assumption appears to be that women in business will operate somewhat differently to their male counterparts.

Summing up, much of this literature is problematic in a number of important ways. It ignores power relations embedded in material structures such as class and gender, whilst it reconstitutes the universalization and naturalization of entrepreneurialism as male. Ignoring the gendered character of labour power it promotes the link between masculinity and rationality. This denies that men do emotional labouring in the process of their economic activities, whilst it exonerates them from emotional labour within the family. Finally, it suggests that masculinity is monolithic and as such conceals the competitive character of entrepreneurialism which

reinforces fundamental divisions between men. The naturalization of entre-
preneurialism as exclusively male is a continuation of the kinds of discourse
which have helped to make women invisible, and as such is a manifestation
of patriarchal power. Whilst the feminist literature has said very little about
entrepreneurial activity directly, it has questioned these kinds of gendered
assumptions in a wide variety of workplace analyses, as the following
section shows.

Entrepreneurs and patriarchy

The notion of public patriarchy (Hearn, 1992b) can be historically under-
stood as the extension of male power from the private sphere into all
activities in the public sphere. Conceptualizing patriarchy in this manner
demonstrates how patriarchy can adapt to the changing material conditions
under capitalist relations of production characterized by the commodifica-
tion of goods and services. As capitalist relations have expanded, the
configuration of male power has gained territorially from the narrow
confines of the private sphere and the power of the father to the more
diffuse yet pervasive power of men in the control of public sphere activity.
In developing 'dual systems' theory, Hartmann (1979b) highlights the class
and material conditions that are the loci of male power. The alliance
between capital and men is mutually self-serving because of a shared
interest in the control over women's labour and sexuality, and over some
men. While men may be divided in many ways, they are united around the
shared interest in retaining control over women. This theorization has made
an important contribution in pointing to the significance of the control of
women in the systems of capital and patriarchy. It is inadequate however,
in that it makes no attempt to elucidate women's material or class position
and how this might regulate or modify the experience of male control.
Walby (1986a) does address this question in the notion of the cross-class
family. She makes a distinction between single and married women, arguing
that their class position differs. The class position of single women is based
on their direct labour market position, but I would argue that they are
subject to the impact of patriarchal practices and discourses in the public
sphere. By contrast, married women who are also housewives occupy a dual
class position: their direct job market position, and a second position
mediated by the circumstances of being wives married to husbands. Just as
single women (and arguably all women) are exploited by capitalist relations
of production, housewives are exploited by their husbands.

This argument is further elaborated by Delphy and Leonard (1992), who
suggest that the processes constituting housework can be understood as
production underpinned by the exploitation of women by men as social
categories. Women's labour including their sexuality is the site for
exploitation systematized through the institution of marriage. Pateman
(1988) elaborates on the links between marriage and female exploitation.

The male sex right cloaked in the duplicity of the marriage contract provides the mechanisms and is a prime site for male control of female sexuality and indeed labour (see also Erickson, 1993). The foregoing arguments, which highlight men's common interest in the control of women's sexuality and labour provide useful theoretical insights into the dynamics of the relationships between the male entrepreneurs and their wives. Of particular concern here are the ways in which the women's emotional labour has been consumed.

I will now turn briefly to the issue of how theories of patriarchy address the question of difference between men. There is a growing critical literature generated mainly by men identifying the problematic character of patriarchy. Whilst it hardly represents a conceptual shift, the notion of masculinities (Brod and Kaufman, 1994; Collinson and Hearn, 1994) denotes a subtle move away from the repercussions of male power on women, to a more central focus on men and power, and men and masculinity, while *still* retaining a concern with men's asymmetrical relationship to women. Critical of a static and monolithic view of male power as implied in ahistorical accounts of patriarchy (Millett, 1977), this approach suggests that masculinities are a shifting constellation of diversity, difference and unity anchored historically, culturally and materially (Brod and Kaufman, 1994). Men are divided by class (Collinson, 1992), ethnicity (Mac an Ghaill, 1994), sexuality (Mac an Ghaill, 1993), ableness and age. Accordingly, relations between men are then rooted between sets of oppositions – capitalist versus worker, nationality versus nationality, gay versus straight, able versus differently abled and old versus young, depicting differential positionings in power structures. Thus different masculinities are constituted and reconstituted in and through these sets of oppositions and in the subordination of women. By deconstructing masculinity this literature demonstrates the potential fragility of male power. It shows male power to be fragmented, in that men are divided by age, sexual identity, ableness, nationality, race and class. In terms of the capitalist class, while men are united around a class interest, that same class and their other interests divide them, and push them into rivalries and competition with each other. In the following study, I want to explore whether and how different types of entrepreneurial men who share the same class background and class aspirations, but who are differentiated by age, ethnicity, education and moment of business entry, differ in the manner in which they express or withhold their emotional labour in the household, and whether this makes any difference to the women who are economically dependent housewives.

In this section I discuss two life histories of first-generation entrepreneurs and their families. These cases are typical of particular types of entrepreneurial masculinity, although the men in question began their businesses in very different economic conditions. I want to explore what kind of entrepreneurial men they are becoming, and whether and in what ways they differ in their approach to wealth creation. The first model comprises a belief in internal growth and a low interest in financial management, while technical expertise and pride in the product and company take priority over profits. The second model is very different because it is moulded by an ethos of quick profits achieved through financial manipulation, where growth is facilitated by takeover. The men in the following study came from working-class backgrounds and had made good. In this sense I want to highlight their similarities and differences and how these embody a strategy, or strategies, for success in business. Are their shared poor backgrounds important in the construction of their masculinities? Do their different nationalities, education and age impinge upon the kind of men they become, and does this influence their approach to business? In what ways do men's relationships with their wives influence the construction of entrepreneurial masculinities? Seeking to tease out the dialectical relationship between different work-based identities and the creation of masculine entrepreneurialism, the following analysis now outlines the two life histories in turn. These accounts explore the contradictory character of particular masculinities and the ways they are bound up in specific material conditions such as migration, work activities, male working-class discourses and crucially in domesticity.

The company man

Aged seventy-six, Mr M. was still active as chairperson of the multimillion-pound, privately owned and run, civil engineering business he founded in 1952. His vision of successful entrepreneurialism is in building up a business identified by the product and service it provides, something substantial which can be transferred to his children. His eldest son is managing director, his daughter is a director, and a younger son is training for a senior position. His manhood and patriarchal identity are all bound up in the original business and its ethos, for its activities are still in the characteristically Irish sector of heavy plant machinery, lately diversifying into construction, open-cast mining and the speculation of industrial land. Such diversification is not mere opportunistic speculation, but a rather gradual development of the founding venture. In some ways Mr M. conforms to the model of the 'self-made', self-educated, 'hands on' practical man of the post-war industrial sector, whose prior commitment is to product development as opposed to quick profits (see also Roper, 1994a).

There is a sense in which he couches his achievement in a language which conspires to the ideology of the self-made man. One of the most striking features about interviewing rich and successful men and women is the sense of power and confidence they convey. This of course is stage-managed in the ambience of plush offices, or grand domestic settings. By contrast the office suites of Mr M. and members of his family are fairly modest. (Mr M. is coy about his private wealth; details were revealed by his children.) This setting is very much tied to the sort of image of himself he wishes to convey. Although he is chair, he wants to be recognized as a 'working man', someone who earns a living through hard work. Work and 'his' business remain the centre of his life, and he exudes an unrelenting energy and enthusiasm in telling the story of the company success – his success, based exclusively on his efforts. He relives the key moments of the business formation, filling out the contours of each stage with impressive detail, only remembering others' help when prompted. With regard to his wife's participation, there is an emphasis on a rigid division of labour, and a denial of any contribution from her to the business.

Toughness and a belief in the power of the body remain the touchstone of Mr M.'s vision of masculinity, an image which may be at odds with this small, slim man conventionally but immaculately dressed in a blue pin-striped suit. But the stress on physical toughness is partly linked to his earlier occupation and lifestyle. Beginning his career at the age of seventeen, when his father died in 1932 he migrated from Southern Ireland to Britain. As the eldest of eleven children he saw few prospects on the family's small farm. Assuming the role of breadwinner for his mother and ten dependent siblings, he worked initially in Britain as a farm labourer. Constrained by his lack of formal education and Irish migrant background, he, like many other Irishmen over the next twenty years, worked in the construction industry in a variety of manual jobs, moving to a different location with each new job. This job market has long been the ghetto for rural male Irish labour. Hearn (1985) makes a connection with forms of alienation and particular masculine behaviour. The characteristics of this kind of occupation foster rootlessness, alienation, isolation and an especially 'macho' culture. Although the image of the Irish construction worker as the drunken, brawling and tough 'navvy' conforms to a racialized stereotype, like some other stereotypes, it has some validity. It fosters a notion of toughness that is a mere cloak for the very exploitative work experience, which in reality requires physical stamina and emotional strength. Such men, finding themselves in these circumstances, are forced to act out 'macho' behaviour, and do internalize some of these values. But this can be explained by the alienation associated with migration and the conditions in which such men were forced to labour, and very often the poor domestic conditions they endured. This arduous work experience calls for physical strength and is a necessary socializing ritual in the construction of the particular masculinity. It is the rite of passage to this particular male club. Social rootlessness fosters a camaraderie between such men in which displays of muscle power, personal spending and drinking are seen as virtues – which suggest a lack of control, but may be a compensation for the absence of family and wives. The whole emphasis on the power of the body and the experience of social rootlessness generates the need for self reliance and independence from these constraining and destructive circumstances.

Notions of independence and breadwinning form dynamic themes in this version of manhood, for the boy acquired a man's responsibilities, a factor not unconnected with the theme of thrift. With his starting pay of £1 17s - 6d. in 1932, and after a stretch of twenty years' work, he explains: 'I had fourteen hundred pounds in the bank. I'd saved that. I'd earned good money during the war.' This challenges the racial stereotyping of Irish Catholicism, and rather conforms to Weber's model of the Protestant ethic of hard work and thrift. During this time, Mr M. gained an insight into business, also acquiring some technical and managerial skills. He learned to drive and maintain plant and machinery, and had worked as foreman for a number of years in his friend's contracting company. This was a key moment in his life, for he got married and simultaneously resigned from his job and became self-employed. Spending £200 of his savings, he invested in his first piece of machinery – a second-hand tractor. This event then is clearly linked to financial independence and is an acknowledgement of the dependence of others on him. Increasingly he became a workaholic, and made £8,000 profit in the first year.

> 'I went out on my own driving the machine, getting the jobs and doing them. I "broke" that machine. I worked seven days a week, sometimes fourteen hours a day. I was always going down the garden path by 6.30 a.m. That's how I did it.'

The premium is on individual effort – this time measured in a physical power which not only controls but also defeats the durability of inanimate objects – which conveys the superiority of human mastery over machinery, for, he explains, he 'broke the machine'. In other words, he worked the machine to its destruction, and beating it, he relishes its demise. The central issue here is the power of the body over the machine, another manifestation of the theme of physical toughness. Willis (1977) observes a similar vision of toughness among working-class men. The ideology of masculinity masks both the limits of this particular masculinity and its class basis, and also underplays his other possible skills. It is partly an accommodation to the racial stereotype of Irish male labour, where 'unskilled' labour alternatively relied on the power of the body, yet it is also a way of living with the indignity of a poor education, although clearly he had by this time acquired sophisticated managerial and business skills. During the interview the sense of indignity fostered by poor education was continually replayed in self-mockery.

Like the men in Sennett and Cobb's (1977) study, Mr M.'s apparent ambivalence about the merits of formal education may be a cloak for the pain he endures. Paradoxically, during his earlier career he learned several skills essential to becoming self-employed. He learned how to cost jobs and rudimentary accounting. Describing these coping strategies also allows him to demonstrate his intelligence:

> 'And I used to have my balance sheet in my pocket. When I looked at a job in those days I'd have to estimate how much I'd get for doing it. Against that I'd have to calculate my wages and the fuel, whether I'd be able to do the job, and how long it would take. I had no degree or anything, but I rarely made a mistake. Nowadays they have degrees and they'd be there measuring up and so. They still don't get it right. And me, I could tell by looking.'

His denigration of formally skilled engineers has parallels with the workers in Collinson's (1992) study who knew that formal education was one possible route out of one's class, but to admit to this is to devalue one's version of manhood. At the same time, formal education acts in opposition to working-class masculinities, for in one sense it feminizes 'real men' (Collinson, 1992; Roper, 1994a; Sennett and Cobb, 1977). These contradictions are again reflected in Mr M.'s approach to his children's education:

> 'Well they all went to University and got their degrees. Michael got his in Civil Engineering, but all of them including Pauline had to go on site and work. And I insisted, much to his mother's disgust that he did the hardest jobs, for my most cantankerous foremen. Michael had to prove himself learning to drive every machine and by being willing to do any job. And I mean Pauline did jobs in the yard. Their mother thought that they shouldn't get their hands dirty. But you see they did that and got their degrees.'

The rites of passage to supposedly authentic masculinity is the test to survive the demands of manual labour. His children, ironically, including his daughter, proved they were 'real' men. The logic of this is that it is a preparation for possible future 'hard times'. At the same time, by insisting on manual labour and formal education for his children, Mr M. has upheld the value of his version of masculinity whilst also transferring and fulfilling his hidden wish that his children be better educated. To admit or to dwell upon the limitation of his poor education would be to highlight the limits of his power and masculinity. This went against the grain of 'getting ahead' and setting himself apart from his equals and rivals:

> 'There was a big job out at Company X. There were many problems with it. The experts saw it and wouldn't touch it. And I suppose if I had seen the dangers I wouldn't, but I hadn't. But as I went along doing the job, I got better and better. They [colleagues and friends] all said, "It will be the last of him, it'll kill P." But that is where I made the money – on the jobs that other contractors wouldn't want.'

This sense of independence and the need to distinguish oneself from other men underlines his comments, and is consistent with some aspects of the rugged individualism espoused in conventional entrepreneurial theories discussed earlier such as risk taking. Whilst physical endurance and technical superiority are some of the hallmarks in his version of successful entrepreneurial masculinity, they are also part of working-class ideologies and discourses.

This brand of individualism stands juxtaposed to the family, class and ethnic solidarities which had been so central to Mr M.'s survival. Sustaining these loyalties is also limiting, and attempts to transcend such limits invite some risks:

> 'I had been with the G . . . [a very large private company] since 1948, and they were my friends. But I had done a lot for them, worked hard all hours of the day and night. In 1952 we had a big difference and I "jacked" the job in [resigned]. And my four years of high class college [ironically] with the G . . .s. I had done everything with them, I knew all my plant, machinery, the maintenance, and

above all, I could do evaluations. Anyway, what I really wanted was to do something on my own.'

This comment reveals several tensions. On the one hand, it resonates with the strong emphasis on independence, as an integral part of certain forms of working-class masculinity. On the other hand, the conditions of becoming an entrepreneur involve the interplay of class, ethnicity and a working-class masculinity. At one level, moving into self employment entails disloyalty to one's group, when identities and loyalties are subordinated to the needs of capital. In this case the respondent set up in competition with his former employer, gaining direct access to markets. At a second level this reveals the contradictory character of masculine solidarity, when friendships between men are challenged by the capitalist impulse. At a third level, unravelling the racialized stereotype of the irrational and untamed 'Irish navvy' revealed a regular saver, a cautious investor, a disciplined worker with an astute business sense.

Setting oneself apart through transforming one's class position creates another set of tensions between class and ethnic solidarity. A discrete notion of ethnicity may gloss over class contradictions (See Ram, 1994, who is reluctant to notice this) and partly conceals the tensions and conflicts, the capitalist essence of the wage labour relationship. Instead of being a worker employed under the conditions of 'lump labour'[2] drawing on his own ethnic group, he became an employer of such labour. This together with a climate of economic growth characteristic of the 1950s and 1960s and astute financial management were the essential elements in his model of entrepreneurial achievement. In this sense aspiring working-class ethnic masculinity reflects and reinforces middle-class entrepreneurial competitive values. The same lack of sentiment and rationalizing is adopted in relation to the employment of his brothers in the business:

'When it came to the business, there was no favouritism, and even now this applies to my children. They have earned their places. Now I had several brothers, two were great men and became directors, but some of the others, well – some swept the yard. What divides us is "keeping your head". I mean one went on the bottle and killed himself. And I can tell you so many hard men end in the sewer down and out. Then there are others – and they become gangsters – look at some of the Irish in America. Others never pay their taxes. I have always operated by the book, clean. That's why I have a good solid business. We are known for our reliability and service – that's better than dirty money.'

The process of setting oneself apart can be physical/geographical or social/psychological, which means rejecting some of the destructive values associated with masculinity and community. It entails personal self-denial and refusing the camaraderie of hard drinking and the seduction of making easy money. Mr M.'s honesty and hard work separate him from fellow countrymen and some male kin and justify his business achievements. At the same time, this shows how the suppression of sentiment and emotion is consistent with 'rational' decision making and control: the prerequisites of managerial professionalism (Hearn, 1987).

Financial acumen ran parallel with profitable capitalist activity and continued to be the hallmarks of Mr M.'s business progress, themes which strongly feature in images of middle-class entrepreneurial success. For instance, selling and re-buying his company is the nadir of his career. He sold 65 per cent of his company in 1965. Having negotiated a very good price he used the money to buy a 500-acre estate in Ireland with the intention of farming. However, during the following seven years he became unhappy with the manner in which the company was managed and organized a meeting with his partner, intending to sell his remaining 25 per cent of the company, which was underperforming. The meeting resulted in him buying back his company. Mr M. recalls the high points of his financial wizardry:

'They offered us a poor price, so we decided we'd try and buy back our 65 per cent of the company at the price offered to us for the 25 per cent. They finally agreed. Of course I had to sell my estate, but within six months I'd paid for my company, and then started it as a family company.'

Once the initial wealth is established, the emphasis shifts from muscle power to the financial wit of the entrepreneur in the art of boardroom negotiation. The process of creating a business and accumulating visible structures of wealth is also a sign of intragenerational class mobility, and to admit ignorance of such significant matters as finance at this stage would be to point to a dent in the armour of the invincible self-made entrepreneur. In the case of Mr M., aside from recruiting professionally trained financial advisers in the administration of his business, he learned accounting and acquainted himself with the broader issues relating to business. Attempting to emulate his perception of middle-class behaviour, he regularly reads *The Financial Times* and economic periodicals. For him a sound business is independent of the shackles of borrowing, and Mr M. gave a detailed account of how his bigger ventures were financed.[3]

The masculine discourse surrounding the triumphalism of financial wheeling and dealing often belies caution, but it engenders the feel for power. It makes men feel powerful, and it is the guile of power which they find so seductive; indeed this is not unconnected to workaholism:

'I don't take holidays, or days off, my leisure is the occasional meal in a hotel, and a rest on Sunday afternoon. Mind you, later I go out to survey some sites, my work is my pleasure. My wife of course would prefer if I was a dustman, I'd be home at five o'clock like her father was.'

In this case the proprietor of a multimillion-pound business in speculative house-building, motorcycle manufacturing and estate farming typifies the cult of workaholism. Workaholics pursue their work with such tenacity that it desensitizes them, so that other aspects of their lives are taken for granted. Wifely complaints are explained as the result of inappropriate socialization and the 'soft' masculinities of fathers. At the same time workaholism is a refutation of his wife's demand that he fulfil her expectations of him as a husband. Claims to workaholism, which is essentially activity outside the home, have long been associated with the notion of authentic masculinity. These spurious claims allow such men to evade domestic responsibilities, placing the burden of domesticity entirely on their wives. But the underlying issue is about the dynamics of the power relationship between the spouses and the ownership and control of wives' labour. By refusing to meet the five o'clock deadline men create space and time for themselves. The claims that 'real' men do not come home at five o'clock are ideologies masking the exploitation of wifely labour and the construction of masculinity. I found this a recurring theme during the interviews among first-generation wealth holders.

The emphasis such men as Mr M. place on workaholism has an additional explanation anchored in both the public and private spheres, and is contingent upon the question of emotional labour. The discourses of self-denial, sacrifice and punishing work schedule may well be market rooted. In other words the competitiveness in such markets calls for extraordinary effort endorsed by the ideologies of the breadwinning role. But work for such men is the site for emotional expression and rejuvenation. Work is without a doubt their first love. The experience of building a business – the 'lows' and 'highs' – are seductive and part of the creative process, which is felt intensely and personally. The wife and ex-working director of a very successful hygiene firm explained why she opted out of active management: 'Well, I'd done all these things, but the business was his idea, his baby, he lives for it.' Roper (1994a) captures this sense and meaning when he draws analogies between entrepreneurial success and giving birth. Workaholism also endorses masculine independence and strongly upholds the male breadwinner's role – thus sustaining the very mechanisms which reconstitute male dominance.

Mr M.'s success, power and wealth are reflected in a lifestyle of tasteful affluence. He lives with his wife in a period manor house, complete with swimming pool, fitness and games rooms. Adjoining cottages provide separate accommodation for one of his six children. He has an interest in art and has bought some minor paintings, has owned a yacht in the Mediterranean, a 500-acre estate, likes horses and regularly attends Ascot; interests and consumption patterns consistent with the upper middle classes.

I have attempted to map out the ways in which this particular vision of entrepreneurial masculinity has been founded upon changing class identities, ideologies and discourses. I have tried to show the contradictory character of a masculine identity founded upon the notion of manual labour. It both elevates and denigrates working-class masculinity. However, this cloak for class and self-exploitation, spurred on by gain through favourable economic conditions and a belief in competitive values, driven by the seduction of power, has the capacity to transform and to reconstitute working-class manhood in the realm of middle-class entrepreneurialism. These combinations of entrepreneurial masculine identity are embodied by the manly act of creating a business, something durable, solid, useful and productive. Equally, this masculinity has another hidden dimension – absence from family duties and the expression of emotional labour. Male emotion has been consumed in the construction of the business and in the making of money – powerful embellishments to masculinity. Yet, for all of this, while Mr M. can in material terms be objectively categorized as belonging to the property-owning class at heart, subjectively he is a man among men only in relation to his own earlier ethnic identity and class.

The takeover man

The resurrection of neoclassical economics promoting the virtues of the free market underlines the discourses and ideologies of recent popular managerial literature. When translated into notions of entrepreneurialism these advocate rugged individualism and the power of human capital and are presented as a panacea for the negative effects of the economic restructuring characteristic of the 1980s. New breeds of entrepreneurs have emerged espousing these principles. Aged thirty-eight, Mr A. belongs to this new generation of opportunistic, profit-oriented free-marketeers. Paradoxically his business ethos is founded in the aftermath of dramatic structural change, the shift from public to private ownership, the shedding and the casualization of labour and the legacy of boom and bust fostered by credit. Unlike Mr M., he is a beneficiary of economic restructuring, the hallmark of the 1980s economy. His prime business interests stem from company failure and the casualization of labour markets. He is chairperson with a 10 per cent share in a public company of which he is the founder, with a £40 million yearly turnover, specializing in contract labour, employment services and in the 'rescue' of small and medium-sized private businesses threatened with liquidation. Additionally he runs three private companies in London, one in advertising, one in the media, and one in laundry services.

Conducted in his home, this interview was intended to explore his lifestyle, patterns of consumption, class aspirations and sense of achievement – all of which embody a very different entrepreneurial masculinity in the making. This is indeed class bound, for his most cherished personal possession is the recently acquired manor house in a Midlands county, for which he paid £1 million. Since he purchased the house he has spent £200,000 in restoring it to its original style. This is not the tasteless grandeur of the *nouveau riche* – for that would betray his class background. A life-size portrait of his wife hangs above the huge mantelpiece, and the image conveyed is one of a country squire with an upper-class background. This sense of class and social status is very much endorsed by the fact that he lives in the 'big house' overlooking a small village of approximately ten cottages wherein the previous patrician owners and their tenants now live. Highly critical of privilege, he described the patrician family as 'wastrels', who had allowed the house to deteriorate and a 13,000-acre estate to be frittered away in financial profligacy. He clearly felt that despite his underprivileged background his talents and hard work had triumphed over the privileges associated with breeding and class. The former lady of the manor held him in equal contempt. In an earlier interview she suggested that the sources of his wealth and nature of his business remained an unfathomable mystery. But all of these threads are constituting embellishments to an image of traditional upper-class masculinity to which he aspired.

Beautifully dressed in expensive and perfectly matched tweeds, he displays impeccable manners which seem to be intended to complement the image of the country gentleman, a standard of dress that most such men did not match. The location of this interview also confirmed the idea of a leisured lifestyle associated with the moneyed classes, while also portraying him as a family man. This is both in the traditional sense as a family patriarch and head of the family, and in the sense of the 'new man' participating in child care and family life. As Davidoff and Hall (1987) and Veblen (1949) have argued, the family is part of the build-up of the successful capitalist, which also endorses paternalism, part of the construction of a specific and aspiring middle-class masculinity. In contrast to Mr M., who although he had established a large business still portrays himself as a workaholic, Mr A. draws on 'soft' masculine images, expressing a combination of the 'new man' taking an interest in domesticity and the seeming effortless grace of the traditional patriarch. At the same time, this seems to be intended to convey a sense of relaxed elegance which in turn gives the sense of man in control. Being married and having a family forms the crucial rite of passage to this particular masculinity. Family and leisure are used to convey a sense of wealth and status. In fact, Mr A. has three children, one of whom lives with his first wife, while Mr M. had six children and is surrounded by his children.

However, Mr A.'s class background belies this image. He was born in south London to working-class parents who were

'very, very working class, and very left-wing. My father worked for a London Council on the manual side. My mother was a Geordie, and there was five kids. She was brought up washing floors, and she was still cleaning when I was fifteen, or sixteen.'

Whilst for Mr M. association with one's class of birth and ethnicity proved a springboard to entrepreneurialism, Mr A.'s strategy is to distance himself from his roots, his class and his family. This sense of distance is strongly conveyed in the significance he gives to the house, which he explained was 'the roots and heart' of his family. Psychologically and geographically he left his natal family when a new identity was being formed assisted by education. This enabled him to acquire the social skills, grace, sense of relaxed superiority, of self-confidence and being in control – attributes long associated with the upper class. As he explained:

'I got an exceptionally good education because I was fairly musical, so I got several musical scholarships and various bits and pieces. I did a season on tour with the orchestra. I had various other opportunities in that line. So that got me a better education than I would have had otherwise. And it got me away from home, which was a good thing.'

By leaving home, socialization within the mix of working-class culture was avoided, and a middle-class value system and speech codes were acquired, skills essential to upward mobility. Yet having acquired this demeanour, Mr A. still endures the pain of his poor background. It is not that men like Mr A. are ashamed of their backgrounds; it is rather that they fear the repercussions and degradation of the harshness of working-class life. This theme forms a continuous strand in Mr A.'s career and personal development.

In the early 1970s he read politics and economics in London's most prestigious university, a route to upward mobility. Untypically perhaps, he did not enjoy student life, nor the political atmosphere there, preferring to abandon his degree to embark on a career in catering. Starting and soon tiring of work as a 'redcoat' at Butlin's, he went to work in a Paris hotel. In many ways this move can be accounted for by his class background and working-class values: some working people see little benefit in attending university and reading something as esoteric as economics and politics. Of course, very often there is a real need to earn money. However, Mr A. had a specific goal, which was to save money to buy a hotel. Using his savings of £5,000, he entered the property market, buying two houses in need of refurbishment. He then got a job as an interviewer with Brook Street Bureau, while his leisure time was spent repairing his property. Later these houses were sold at a substantial profit.

The cultivated image of leisurely affluence betrays the strategies involving thrift, and the celebration of the work ethic. Most young people would at least relish the experience of three years of student life. But Mr A. left and this reveals a working-class masculine ambivalence to studying, partly conforming to another version of the cult of toughness so strongly exhibited in the previous account. There is a sense in which this is not the real work of a man. This thrusting young man preferred the sense of purpose manifested in the frantic activity, risk and insecurity of moving between low-paid jobs, and the early penny-pinching. Unable to fully cast aside his working-class upbringing he had by this stage married and had a child. These critical points in his early life acted as part of the rite of passage to manhood and a very contradictory masculinity. Driven by an acquisitive, highly individual ethos, Mr A. explains that in the early 1980s he

'Canvassed a job with a London company. I went in there as a site negotiator, finding new sites for them. And they were turning over £200,000, and I found that I was fairly good at negotiating. After three years of doing that I was made managing director of the company. I took the turnover up to £2 million, of which £1 million was just profit. They wouldn't give me any equity, I was a paid managing director, I was paid very well.'

The need for independence is a feature of male working-class values, but the means of achieving this through managerial entrepreneurialism is more consistent with middle-class values and perceptions of money. Accumulating wealth is one aspect of a parallel process: while men gain control over money, they also enhance their masculinity. The power over money is what distinguishes them from men in other classes and lesser men in their own class. However, such drive and competitiveness is only achieved even by their standards at a price:

'If someone were to ask me "What is it that makes anyone successful?" I'd say three words: fear, greed and creativity, and I don't think there's anything wrong in that . . . well with fear I'd put insecurity until you reach a level of wealth where you decide "well hang on a minute, what is it all for?" People are afraid of failure, the insecurity breeds a fear, a fear that you are not quite as good, or you should be better. With that fear you have got loneliness. . . . It's a sense of urgency.'

Unlike the 'macho' invincible mask presented by Mr M., this respondent admits to self-doubt and human frailty, which is consistent with the ideologies of the 'new man'. He talks about his vulnerabilities, motivations and fears. This comment exemplifies some of the contradictions associated with masculinity and entrepreneurial activity. Pursuing the capitalist impulse creates feelings of loneliness, alienation, and a lack of solidarity and intimacy (see Sennett and Cobb, 1977; Fromm, 1978). Unlike Mr M. who appears to have found the process of building a business and creating wealth emotionally satisfying and fulfilling, Mr A. continues to feel insecure despite his wealth. This difference may be partly explained by the kind of difference in goals between the two men: Mr M. wants to embody his self in a tangible business, while Mr A.'s energy evaporates in the manipulation of financial deals. Sherrod (1987) suggests that friendships between men, and the relationships between men and women are transformed by the nature of work, noting that capitalism fosters competitiveness between men, which compromises their friendships with other men. Consequently, men transfer their emotional needs to women, whilst refusing to reciprocate affection. This has some resonance in the manner in which Mr A. evaluates his personal life against his entrepreneurial achievements:

'Well you see within two years I'd made £12,500, and became MD in that company, but I'd ruined a marriage. You get inside and you feel – I was married at nineteen. You grow together, or you grow apart. It is a question of whether your personality and interests take a parallel course. If you go through a few outside wars together, you grow together. It was not the pressure of work, because I didn't feel that I was working very hard. Well, you see it didn't seem at all like work. You see it was the fact that I came home on quite a lot of occasions and I realized that we couldn't actually talk to each other. Yep, it was a very hard decision, because there was a child involved. That dragged on, but it was an uncomfortable period, and you have to make decisions, and do things that are correct. As I say you grow together, or you grow apart'.
    KM: 'Did all that affect your business?
    'Not at all, not in the slightest, there was an enormous amount of luck involved at that stage. It was the height of the eighties boom . . .'

On the one hand, individualism, single-mindedness, instrumentalism – the basic tenets of the acquisitive enterprise culture – rationalized the tensions between the obsessive pursuit of material gain and personal loss. On the other hand, this comment again emphasizes the inseparability of home and work, and the manner in which men are able to channel the direction and consumption of their emotional energy. While this comment stands in stark contrast to his attitude and practice to his current family, it also demonstrates the way in which market-based activities mediate and shape the construction of a certain kind of entrepreneurial masculinity. A wife and family were not so essential to an aspiring businessman, but are considered very necessary to a rich and leisured aspiring 'gentleman'. Talking about his marriage failure, Mr A. appears more open about the repercussions of workaholism than the earlier respondent, but in a way it is retold in the same tone one might use when recalling a moment of business failure. Ochberg (1987) embraces the essence of such rationalizing when he argues that men have internalized a personal demeanour rooted in their external and public role. In this sense, one suspects that Mr A. does not address the real reasons for his marriage breakdown. He suggests that it resulted from a difference in personalities and an inability to grow together. But growing together would have been difficult in view of his absence from home and obsession with work. Yet responsibility for the breakdown of the relationship is transferred to the partner, who apparently was unable to adapt to the changing situation. Instead of dealing with this loss, his emotions and energies have been harnessed to the momentum of the casino economy which leaves little time for life review or self-reflection. Emotions are consumed in the 'buzz' of profit pursuit. There is no recognition that work has become an obsession. The separation of home and work masks the repercussions on men's personal lives but it is upon this façade that masculinities rest and thrive. Personal loss did not stand in the way of the pursuit of money, for he soon set up an advertising business.

On the one hand, themes of instrumentality and quick return inform his approach to business. Opportunism remains the underlying ethos, for by 1987 he had merged the company with another business, floating it to a £7 million capitation on the stock market before selling it. Unlike Mr M., whose personal constructions of masculinity were gradually built over time around a particular unit of capital, rooted in a specific activity, this respondent's activities are transient, ephemeral and difficult to quantify. On the other hand, it is an activity which he distrusts, for it is tinged with anxiety and uncertainty. There is almost a sense of disrespect for the process and this is manifested in low commitment to sustaining capital in any particular activity. As he explained: 'My motto is: to buy, float and sell.' Mr A. has now started another business in asset-stripping. The rapid expansion of his business empire began in 1989 with the accelerated collapse of small businesses. Since then he has bought ten companies, which had been firmly established but were undergoing some difficulty. Benefiting from the failure of others, he draws on bodily metaphors to describe the strategies in rationalizing such businesses: for instance 'picking off the heart of a business' means retaining its profitable elements.

The theme of financial machismo characteristic of a harder masculinity intertwines with a 'softer' masculinity more associated with the 'new man'. These contradictions are played out in individualism and self-interest in the pursuit of a quick return, which are the hallmarks of his business style. Yet the emphasis on his immediate family and the manner in which he exudes a sense of loss suggests a sensitivity which he continually strives to control. Driven by the fear of poverty he seeks to transcend his natal working-class background and adopts a highly detached relationship to business activities. He is unlike Mr M., since he does not identify with a specific product or indeed with any capitalist competitor. He does not conform to Penrose's (1980) model of the business manager for he is not interested in the notion of company expansion. His capital is kept liquid, accommodating and celebrating opportunism, which perhaps typifies the unregulated marketeer. He is more interested in accumulation. This model ties in very well with the point made earlier: his identity, unlike that of Mr M., is less embodied in the business and more in the idea of the family, which is symbolized by the grand house. Arguably, since identities are socially constructed in the public and private spheres and therefore transient, building an identity around the family and conveying a sense of lifestyle seems all the more important.

Most entrepreneurial men see virtue in sustaining arduous working schedules, suggesting that their established businesses embody their earlier struggles. What Mr A. wants to convey is something quite different – not the solid unit of productive capital sustained over time, but a lifestyle stemming from the private sphere which resonates with consumerism, the grand house and latest cars, and where the source of wealth is remote, apparently unconnected, and appears very detached from his working-class roots. Even Mr A.'s second wife complemented his brand of success. As he explained:

'No, my wife does not have a career now. I can afford her not to have one. Except of course, she has a very important career as my wife, and mother of my children. She is a wonderful, talented, intellectual woman. She is a graduate with a degree in Slavonic Studies and speaks several European languages including Russian. She, of course, has interests, she is secretary of the local English Speaking Society, is chair of the local branch of the Conservation Society in the village.'

Appropriate concerns for the helpmeet of a gentleman in the making. Part of her duty is to foster an image of the dependent and indulged wife, the essential accessory for an aspiring gentleman. At the same time, her involvement with worthy causes and her interests in a cultural high ground transmit an upper middle-class image essential to the construction of his particular masculinity.

Like those on the New Right, while Mr A. claims to despise and oppose the traditional upper classes, and the landowning classes in particular, he actually desires the status associated with their breeding and the superiority it exudes, and aspires to their image of power and lifestyle. The contradiction is that their political and financial power is now largely illusory. However, drawing upon a range of masculine working-class and middle-class entrepreneurial discourses and values, most of which hinge upon the role of breadwinner, he thereby reproduces a contradiction with not only the image he wants to foster, but the kind of lifestyle he wants to lead. The men and the class to which he grudgingly aspires reveal a much 'softer' and more feminine masculinity that he admires. The contradiction is that they fail to display the rugged individualism so central to his financial strategies, yet which he appears to despise.

I have argued that the mainstream literature on entrepreneurialism assumes a natural interchangeability of men and business. This is also mirrored in the foregoing case studies where entrepreneurial men tell their stories in ways which conceal several important features about the separation of home and work and the kinds of repercussion this has for both spheres. These respondents denied male emotion – and yet their energies and passions were channelled into the creative process of accumulating capital, rationalized in building a business and reconstituting their masculine identities. These men, who are also husbands, regard their unlimited claim to the space and time away from home as their undisputed right. Workaholism is simply the means to pursue the breadwinning role, the accumulation of capital and the construction of identities. But the impact of this is to free such men from all but the most perfunctory domestic duties, leaving them free to build their empires and to embellish their masculinities. Paradoxically, entrepreneurial masculinity hinges upon paternalism symbolized in the patriarchal image of the 'family man'. It is merely symbolic, for the whole panoply of domestic duties, especially the very demanding business of childrearing, is left to the wife. The men's patronizing (for example, Harvey Jones, 1991) accolades to their wives giving 'emotional support' merely conceals the value and scope of wifely labour but importantly fails to scrutinize the male claim to be 'family men'. It is this issue that I now wish to explore.

The entrepreneur's wife and family life: 'It's like being a one-parent family'

This section explores the dynamics of the sexual division of labour and the relationship between home and work. In particular I draw attention to a neglected dimension, the issue of male emotional investment in the domestic sphere. A dominant theme of this research is that the impact of male entrepreneurs' work activity is so pervasive that it invades and colonizes domestic life. This can also mean that the energies of the wives of such men are also indirectly consumed by the same activity. Kanter's (1977) study of women married to corporate managers shows the different ways in which the wives fulfilled the role of 'helpmeet' (Davidoff and Hall, 1987). As homemakers and emotional nurturers to their husbands, they helped to mould and hone the latters' careers and generally supported them as organizational men (see also Finch, 1983; Roper, 1994a).

The logic of this disconnected but necessary contribution is unproblematically explained in Veblen's (1925) work on entrepreneurs when he suggests that the notion of an 'idle' wife is fostered as part of the construction of the successful entrepreneurial patriarch. This is problematic in two ways: it suggests that women are economically inactive and are mere consumers and, secondly and more seriously, it denies the extent of the services wives provide in the home. The range and importance of these services are naturalized and taken for granted because they are regarded as women's tasks, associated with caring; it is wives generally who carry them out; and economically they are regarded as use values undertaken in a sphere of consumption the (family/domestic/private) distinct from the system of production. I take on board Delphy and Leonard's (1992) argument that the family is a unit of production organized on patriarchal, hierarchical lines. There are different permutations of this organizational hierarchy, but the husband and wife constitute one. My research findings suggest that men as husbands are able to appropriate wives' labour because of the rules of patriarchal marriage which place husbands as the virtual owners and controllers of their wives, enabling them directly to appropriate wives' labour as their own in what is conventionally regarded as productive work, for example working as a director in the family business.

There is another dimension to this which relates to the emotional labouring done by wives in the private sphere. This includes shielding spouses from domestic problems, acting as counsellors in nurturing spouses' confidence and relieving them of conventional responsibilities. (The recent proliferation of professional counselling amongst the middle classes is an indication of the economic significance of this work.) The case studies demonstrate that wives' emotional labour is consumed by their husbands/ entrepreneurs in the pursuit of business. I argue that such men's conventional paternal duties as husbands and fathers are largely reduced to that of breadwinner, apparently exonerating them from expending emotional labour within the family. Of course, the breadwinning role is primarily seen as an economic task characteristically associated with rationality, dissociating and denying that men utilize emotional labour, or indeed that they are emotional. The control of emotions is part of the construction of masculinity, and middle-class men are often involved in the control of the emotions of others such as their employees. This denial reinforces notions of personal strength, integrity, dependence and personal independence characteristic of masculinity generally.

Contrary to conventional accounts of entrepreneurialism, there is a growing literature which removes any doubt that emotional labour is part of modern organizations (Fineman, 1993). I think the important question here is who is expressing this emotion, and where is it channelled? Does it involve the creative energies of the particular individual, or is it merely the mediation of frustration associated with alienated labour? For example, what is interesting about Hochschild's (1983) study of flight attendants is not so much that the flight attendants' feelings were suppressed, but the manner in which the company harnessed and honed female sexuality and indeed emotional labour, with an ideology of female emotional labouring in the construction of the company's image and definition of competence of the flight attendants. As Hochschild demonstrates, the effects of this form of alienation were diffused through the individual anger of powerless workers. The entrepreneurial men portrayed in this chapter engage and express their emotions in the dialectical process of wealth creation and in the construction of particular masculinities. While such men gleefully extolled the virtues of being engrossed in the world of work, the dramas associated with workaholism and boardroom coups, they were reluctant to talk at any length about how much they were involved in the range of activities in the home, other than in the role of provider, and responded defensively to any further probing. Earlier sections reveal how the entrepreneurial process both necessitates and generates the expression of emotion from such men. Building a business as a creative process, mediated in male workaholism, also provides an invigorating outlet for men's intuition, energies and passions. Is this due to the ambiguity associated with men and emotion – entrepreneurial men whose image is rooted in assumed rationality and market-based activities?

But I want to make a rather different point: that these entrepreneurial men's relationship to emotional labouring in the private sphere is one of consumption – they are in effect the recipients of nurturing. Ochberg (1987) argues that even when men engage in the domestic sphere, they make little emotional investment, for they are merely 'acting' out of their conventional economic role: 'We have left unexplored the possibility suggested here; that men attempt to escape their private troubles by migrating – like souls fleeing diseased bodies – from their private lives into public ones' (1987: 190). This suggests that men are emotionally dissociated from domesticity. They refuse to confront and find solutions for familial problems. Their work provides the excuse to evade deeper involvement with problems associated with family life. While workaholism does emanate from the demands of entrepreneurialism, it is also endorsed by men's perceptions and the boundaries they draw around their domestic roles as family men.

There is indeed a link between this evasion of, and physical absence from the home and workaholism. That such men are able to do this is a result of the power and authority they enjoy as men, but particularly as husbands, in being able to direct and control their wives' labour. That this escapes question is related to the ways in which such men draw upon heroic themes such as self-sacrifice, and when hinged on to their conventional bread-winning role this acts as a powerful defence. The manner in which men come to terms with this is conveyed by Mr M.:

'Well I used to start work at six in the mornings, and I'd work till ten o'clock at night, weather permitting. At other times I'd be away from home for weeks on end. If I wanted to finish a job and couldn't afford to take time off at weekends, well I wouldn't be home. There were times when I didn't see my kids for weeks, they were not up before I left in the morning, and were in bed by the time I got home. But my colleagues used to say what a great woman P. was. You could never tell there was a child in the house. It was spick and span and she took . charge of everything.'

Self-denial, discipline and physical endurance are the hallmarks of his sacrifice. There is a sense in which being a good wife too becomes a sacrifice on behalf of her husband's goals, which means imposing a regulated and disciplined regime upon the family. The 'good' wife is the husband's faithful agent and unquestioningly accepts his plan, concealing her feelings and pursuing her duty in his absence. A good wife relieves her husband from the demands of fathering. Yet at the same time most men expect to be nurtured in their domestic lives:

'I have always been on the move and I used to do a lot of work in Europe . . . and since 1983 I have been involved with this [management buyout], and my preference is to commute with an emphasis on the quality of life. The best arrangement is for me to stay in . . . and be home at weekends. So I don't involve my wife in business matters. And I'm not chauvinistic at all. It is just that I can only work so long. I am usually in the office about 7.30 in the morning till seven at night. So that is an eleven-hour day and it's enough. I don't want to go back on a Saturday afternoon and feel that I have got to mow the lawn or I have to do this or that. My preference is that I don't like getting involved in domestic things, housework, gardening, repairs, you know, whatever. My wife looks after the domestic side, she will arrange everything for me. My free time is valuable to me and I want to play a round of golf, or have a game of tennis or go to my home in Portugal.

This respondent (an entrepreneur with a Master's in Business Administration and in the mould of the 1980s free-marketeer, with a share in a recent management buyout of a large retail jewellery business) expects his wife to provide a tranquil home environment – a cocoon wherein he refuses to discuss work, while he recovers from outside stresses. This mirrors the attitudes of male shopfloor workers (Collinson, 1992). By drawing distinctions between work and home both middle-class and working-class men preserve their right to leisure time. But this demand and claim to domestic tranquillity is also a way of not discussing domestic matters. To admit that the organization of domestic tasks such as gardening is a wifely duty masquerades as consideration, and compensates for the lack of a discussion of men's emotional work, and about what constitutes fathering in conventional terms, and the mundane difficulties associated with bringing up children. It is to trivialize and to overshadow the real domestic concerns. Insisting that they are the material providers, excludes men from emotional work, while also facilitating their access to emotional labour. It is important to question whether the ideology of role differentiation, characterized as it is by a rigid sexual division of labour, undervalues the significance of emotional labour in the processes of masculine entrepreneurialism and capital accumulation. Presenting effort as sacrifice is not only embedded in the breadwinning role, it is also the way for 'their' goals to be imposed upon their wives (see also Sennett and Cobb, 1977). One of the more interesting themes to emerge from my study is that first-generation entrepreneurial men see the receipt of nurturing as their right – claiming time for themselves as opposed to giving time to the family. Correspondingly, the most cherished wish of women in business partnerships was a little free time to devote entirely to themselves.

In exploring the question of whether time was allocated to his family, the respondent, a partner in the management buyout of a glass manufacturer, said: 'Not consciously. They ignore me when I walk in.' On the face of it, this comment suggests that the respondent is ignored and isolated by his family, and is in some ways a victim. But further probing reveals that this arrangement has advantages:

> 'I see my wife as a mother and housewife. That's probably not satisfactory to her. And she is trying to find things to do to occupy her, well no . . . she's busy with the children, I mean something to interest her.'

One of the central dynamics of such partnerships is the potential conflict and contestation about the allocation of emotional labour. It is a rather subtle demonstration of the way a husband's goals can be mediated to control a wife's labour within marriage. This respondent implies that he does not expect emotional labour to be expended on him personally, yet he is quite unprepared to engage in the emotional labour essential in the reproduction of domesticity. The following comment is quite insightful: 'No, no I don't work all the time, but I guess I'm thinking about work things all the time. I don't class it as work.'

This is the other side of workaholism.[4] In fact his comment neatly conveys the tenet of Ochberg's argument that some men sometimes intentionally disengage from the gendered politics of domesticity. It is only when we turn to the wives that these links can be revealed. Wives are aware that they are the 'sacrificial lamb', for as the wife, partner and founder in an expanding insurance and property business recognized:

> 'Well of course behind every great man there is even a greater woman . . . you know, the "little woman". You are the one to do all the backroom work. I mean here at home. I am behind him. Because even if they don't bring their work home they bring their worries home, and they don't even have to tell you. You know and of course then you have to make allowances for that. And if there is something you need to talk about – well you don't because – you think "I don't want to bother him".'

This comment demonstrates how the public sphere gradually invades the private sphere. This does not need to take the form of sweated manual labour. It is much more subtle. Acting on the capitalist impulse consumes the entrepreneur's own capacities, space and time. The wives of men in this situation consider it unreasonable to insist on reciprocating conjugal support. Seeing their spouses pressurized through what are their legitimate breadwinning activities, wives are forced to relieve their husbands of the burden of domestic matters. The wife and co-founder of a men's clothing and more recently property speculation business explains:

> 'I found it very, very difficult . . . and there are times when I have got very upset and resentful. I don't think you can avoid it. At one point the youngest boy became very difficult. He had tantrums each morning before school. It wasn't that he had problems at school. He was perfect there. I went out of my way to please him, and I used to take him fishing, even on the coldest days. But I think a lot of C.'s problem is his personality and the way I've handled him. . . . Anyway I got to such a low ebb I had to find someone to talk to, because when I tried to tell T. [spouse] he'd say, "Oh, do come on, you really must put your foot down, and make him do as he is told." And off he'd go to work. . . . In the end I had to tell C.'s form teacher, and it was agreed that T. would get involved and try and sort the problem out. When we left the school, T. said, "I'm sorry, I hadn't the slightest idea what you had been going through".'

This comment conveys some sense of the extent of the entrepreneur's investment in emotional work. Emotionally shut off in his world of work, and despite his wife's constant pleas for help, it was not until the problem was presented to him by an outside agency that it gained his attention. This example gives credence to the arguments debated earlier – the extent of power husbands still have over their wives' labour. The kinds of sanctions open to wives in such situations are fairly limited if they are to maintain the appearance of a cordial and happy marriage, set against the institutional powers and privileges granted by marriage to husbands and the conventional duties it imposes on wives. This is a most interesting example, because this spouse telephones his wife very frequently, and appears attuned to his family's needs, thus reconstituting the notion of the family man. However, much of the communication is business related. So not only does the wife take on what might reasonably be regarded as the husband's share in domestic matters, she is also involved with the business. Acting as his personal assistant she carries out a series of duties, some of which are secretarial and others can be categorized as public relations duties. In addition she does a lot of business-related entertaining at home, including having her spouse's business partners and clients to dinner. What is interesting is the manner in which she downplays the significance of this, passing it off as 'merely cooking a bite of supper', since such gatherings are informal. At the same time this creates the cosy image of the dedicated and involved family man. This example mirror's Ochberg's (1987) professional men 'acting' in their domestic role, who were not contributing as much as they might. But wives do not necessarily see it in this way:

> 'I think in a way . . . I mean part of it is not T.'s fault, because part of it is down to me wanting to protect him from it, not wanting to bother him with it, because he has got so many other things to worry about.'

Frequently such women feel guilt and a sense of failure – they are unable to meet the expectations of being a good wife and mother. Yet, interviews with wives also repeatedly demonstrate that discourses about 'protecting' men run alongside feelings of resentment. This discourse emanates from the conventional expectations and duties a marriage imposes upon a wife, and especially the tacit manner in which a husband can impose his vision of the 'good' wife.[5] But the other side of not complaining is sometimes interpreted as an act of wifely rebellion by some wives. This respondent, the partner and founder of the insurance and property business said: 'So I'm sort of rebelling with the two people, my daughter and my husband. But with him I don't tell him now, because unless he makes an effort, there is no point.' The rebellious wife refuses to inform her husband, thus depriving him of information essential to maintaining his role as patriarchal controller within the family. The wife takes on the responsibility of disciplining their daughter, therefore she undermines his authority. Despite the husband's ambivalence about sharing emotional work, this comment also expresses guilt, for the refusal to consult is seen as subversive – and inappropriate behaviour according to the ideal of the 'good wife'. Acting out the pre-scribed role of the 'good wife' is characterized by many contradictions. For instance, she feels guilty because she recognizes that this is a challenge to his authority. But the pressures to conform are strong, for during further rationalizing of the situation, she finally exonerates her husband: 'But you see I know he works hard and on top of that he's interested in various types of sport and other activities.'

In part this comment corresponds to Hochschild's (1983) study of flight attendants where it is suggested that women's greater tolerance of passenger abuse is explained as the result of their powerlessness due to inferior economic status relative to men. It is important to distinguish between women workers and wives, for the latter experience restrictions associated with status and duties unparalleled in the experience of women workers or indeed single women. Regardless of whether wives attain economic independence, wifely status assumes an unparalleled subordina-tion to a man in exchange for nurturing duties, which takes precedence over other considerations. The institution of marriage gives husbands enormous power over their wives should they wish to exercise it, a point compellingly made by Pateman (1988) and Erickson (1993) among others. But of course the means by which wives' labour is directed by husbands takes a more subtle form than mere coercion. Husbands' investment in workaholism can often be a disguise for their refusal to engage in emo-tional work and family responsibilities while they still manage to have leisure time. Exclusive male clubs and male-dominated sports activities constitute the playing ground for many entrepreneurial men. Yet the comment is manifestly resentful, because the husband's trustworthiness is seriously questioned. Such wives do not happily acquiesce in these explanations and no amount of male material success can make amends for the loss:

'That's what I fear most. My husband keeps telling me, "All right after I have done this, we'll settle down and do things together." But to be realistic I can't see that happening. He's a workaholic, he just can't keep away from work. It's ineffective. It gets in deeper and deeper. I don't want that in my life, because no matter how important the sacrifices I have made . . . but they are not living inside it.'

There is indeed a clear-eyed recognition that they have given up personal goals so that their spouses can pursue their life chances as capitalists. However, as the businesses grow so does the polarization of labour, with the women taking on more and more emotional labouring while male breadwinning is rationalized as obsessional and becomes acceptable, particularly when tied to the discourses and ideologies of sacrifice. Women then question the pursuit of material goals, when the quality of family life is undermined. This emerged as a dominant theme among the women interviewed. The price is often too great: 'Yes as the family grow up, and the children are very small and your husband is building up a business it is very hard on the wife, it is like being in a one-parent family.'

The result of this is to reinforce a rigid sexual division of labour, whereby men's increasing involvement with entrepreneurial activity greatly overshadows domestic involvement with their families, except in an extremely narrow sense as economic providers. Wives take on disproportionate responsibility for the emotional and reproductive work which is essential to the processes of wealth formation and to the construction of entrepreneurial masculinities.

But such entrepreneurs are not always prepared to admit the cost of their absences from home and the repercussions of their imposed expectations and goals on their wives. For instance, Mr M.'s lofty recommendations of his wife's virtues as his domestic ambassador conceal the hurt inflicted upon his wife. In a discussion about the problems of adapting to great wealth and success, Mr M. and indeed his children revealed that 'Mother couldn't take it'. As a result of this pressure she had become overweight and ill. It is not difficult to see that Mr M. correlated his version of successful masculine entrepreneurialism with personal fitness and good health, a precedent his wife failed to meet. In a paradoxical way it parallels the feelings of some of the wives who complained that they were expected to retain their sexual attractiveness while also being exhausted from work. The men interviewed here conformed to the very traditional pattern of seeing their wives in the conventional setting as their wives, and the mothers of their children engaged in caring and nurturing work. This raises many questions about femininity and the notion of the male as the family patriarch and the protector of women.

Conclusion

In this chapter I have drawn attention to the significance of emotional labour in the domestic setting and have argued that although it remains largely invisible it constitutes a major area of conflict and contestation in endorsing the supporting edifice of entrepreneurial masculinities and is indeed an essential input into capitalist accumulation. I have also argued in the context of this study that emotional labouring is in itself a gendered process whereby male entrepreneurs are able to exclude themselves even from conventional emotional tasks associated with fathering, thereby imposing a double burden of emotional work on their wives. The men studied are invariably psychologically separated from what happens in the household. This is an intentional strategy operated by such men, whilst they insist on 'wifely' support, which creates time to be spent in the public sphere. I consider this to be one of the most crucial inputs to their development, for it allows men to construct not only their businesses, but also their own masculine self-images.

In looking at two types of entrepreneurial masculinity I have attempted to show that despite the differences between such men, they had equally drawn upon and largely benefited from the domestic exclusionary practices they operated, while still benefiting from the processes of family production and reproduction. These included childrearing, continuous personal nurturing which in itself is a direct contribution to the enterprise, and appropriation of their wives' labour in tasks essential to the business but invisible. The discourses of workaholism, family man and so on both conceal and amplify the significance of the wives' emotional labour, enabling such men to prioritize business activity in the public sphere, endorsed by entrepreneurial ideologies and discourses. Although the two men differed, they shared a poor background and engaged in different kinds of enterprise. It mattered little whether they drew on working-class or middle-class ideologies of masculinity, for both types are compatible with middle-class male-gendered entrepreneurialism and capital accumulation. The central concern therefore remains the appropriation of wives' labour in the interests of men entrepreneurs.

Notes

I am particularly indebted to David Collinson and Jeff Hearn for their critical and continuing encouraging comments. I also thank ESRC who provided the grant R000 23 2711 for this research, and the Business School, University of Warwick for computing facilities.

1. Elsewhere I have argued that female kin made major contributions in the building up of business fortunes in a variety of ways during business start-up, but were later forced to withdraw from the active management of accumulated wealth through exclusionary patriarchal practices (Mulholland, 1993, 1996).

2. A system of casualized employment conditions and very poor safety regulations, long associated with the construction industry (Austrin, 1980).

3. Interviewing other entrepreneurs conveyed a strong sense that money could be accumulated providing the broader economy was favourable, and with a little luck and sense of financial intuitiveness, or maybe recognizing opportunities.

4. And indeed it is justified in the entrepreneurial literature discussed earlier.

5. 'A good wife' in the mould of Sennett and Cobb's (1977) Mrs O'Malley uncomplainingly takes on the burden of family stresses and pressures.

8

Quiet Whispers . . . Men Accounting for Women, West to East

Cheryl R. Lehman

I was weighted down with a power I did not want. I had knowledge before its time.

> (Zora Neale Hurston, *Dust Tracks on a Road*, 1942)

Democracy without women is no democracy at all.

> (Anastasia Posadskaya, Moscow Center for Gender Studies, 1993)

Money is for counting, women for beating.

> (Old Hungarian proverb)

Over the vast landscape of organizational practices that we have come to consider crucial for gender politics, accounting practice fails to raise many eyebrows. The green-eyeshaded-still-male accountant of Mr Cratchit-Charles Dickens imagery lingers, continuing to appear an innocent, if not innocuous and boring, actor within the firm. Yet for most participants in organizations – from the CEO reporting on quarterly earnings to Head Doctor reporting on patient–staff supply ratios, to miner on strike for back pay – there is a sense of subtle power held under the gaze of the bean counter-auditor.

Power held by an accountant, the likes of Mr Cratchit? An oxymoron?

Well aware that there are many meanings captured under the rubric of 'power', and that there are numerous forms of control and explanations of empowerment, this chapter is particularly concerned with the power of accounting, and the interrelationship of accounting and masculinity: the creation of an accounting practice that is masculine; the creation of an accountant that is masculine; and the importance of this imagery for a discipline sustaining a critical place in the hierarchy of business and its discourse. Why is there a continued association between accounting and men/masculinity? Does this resonate with the process of management and the evolution of managerial practices? How does accounting maintain its importance within managerial hierarchies? What would be the threat and challenges of a feminist accounting?

Utilizing contemporary gender research from diverse disciplines, I argue that an evolution has occurred, resulting in the reification and dominance of logocentric ways of knowing and organizing social existence. What have become privileged ways of conducting business, making organizational choices and managing business practices reside in the realm of logic and the rational, and this realm, crucial for what is considered 'good' accounting, manifests as well in the larger macro world of discourse and power: those in authority, politics, and in the dark-oak boardrooms of our major corporations 'should' be there: they possess those qualities of rational, objective, efficient, sharp, and hard decision making. They possess the characteristics identified with masculinity, an historically and socially defined category, with its shifting and renegotiated constructions. Management and accounting emerge, reinforce and co-create these privileges and social constructions (Cooper, C., 1992; Hines, 1992; Kirkham, 1992; Kirkham and Loft, 1993; Oakes and Hammond, 1993; Nelson, 1992; Roberts and Coutts, 1992; Reiter, 1995; Tinker and Neimark, 1987).

This chapter's focus is on the evolution of accounting's masculinity; it considers the variety of means by which the discipline practises its masculinity. The next section provides an overview of the strategies used in employment policies, including overt discriminatory, exclusionary and biased acts towards women, and the social construction of an accountant-person who reproduces what society deems masculine-sex-role identities. It elucidates the dilemma of dichotomizing masculinity and femininity, and the implications for social values, public policies and professional practices.

The third section examines the link between economics and accounting practices, and raises issues of valuation, which are fundamental to accounting. How do measurement issues and the proclivity for hard data, rationality and objectivity resonate with gendered ways of knowing? If women 'Counted' as queried by Marilyn Waring (1988) in her landmark book, how could the 'unpaid' work of women be unaccounted for in computations of gross national product? Given the pervasiveness and grand size of this exclusion, why this silence in the language of business? This section concludes that an accounting language emphasizing technique, as well as the discipline's obsession with rationality and the reasonable man *(sic)*, contributes to limiting the domain of the discipline.

This chapter reveals these methods and considers their consequences for the lives of women and men, East and West. Although 'the East' is narrowly confined to Russia, and 'the West' to the US (with some reference to the UK), I suggest there are many lessons to be learned for global gender politics. Without denying significantly different contexts and histories, we also find that even in these very different nation states there are similarities regarding the privileging of masculine ways of knowing and a silence on issues resonating with feminist concerns. The fourth section illustrates the discipline's efforts to reproduce the methods and strategies of exclusion and marginalization of women from the West to the East.

Two points are noted. The first is the significance of the historical locality of these imageries – they are part of the current imperatives in capitalist post-industrial societies. The rhetoric of accounting, business and management as rational, logical and masculine are outcomes of the maintenance of current hierarchies and structures. To recast financial statements according to non-logocentric criteria, to inculcate financial statements with qualitative factors of environmental degradation, and to include 'externalities'[1] would threaten the status quo and discredit the sacrosanct value of pursuing profit. As global competition and a variety of challenges threaten corporate profits, the containment of these threats is critical. Maintaining rationality in business practices does not fundamentally threaten the status quo; it does not question the importance of profit; it does not challenge the competitive and exploitative nature of capitalist economies. Embedded in social construction and control is an historical economic moment, and the contribution of a Marxist perspective of economic imperatives and class analysis is greatly acknowledged here. In this way, the present chapter seeks 'to see more clearly the part that gender takes in structuring relations between classes and promoting compelling systems of belief that justify and perpetuate domination' (Acker, 1988: 497).

Second, although this chapter reveals how women's position in accounting (and in other locations) is shaped by masculinity,[2] it is not a story of the *femme fatale*, nor a tragic history of woman as victim. Women – and men – have utilized and always will utilize a multiplicity of roles, positions and discourses to contest, challenge and reconstitute their world.

Men accounting for women in the West

Behind closed doors

The exclusion of women from the domain of accounting practice has a long history; from its early years as the discipline moved toward 'professionalization' (in the late nineteenth and early twentieth centuries) through the world wars, and into the years of the contemporary accounting 'industry', women accountants have been confronted with a variety of strategies that exclude and marginalize them. Kirkham observes that these mechanisms are an integrated part of the profession's knowledge and social practices – related to economic and social structures and ideologies, through gender as well as class relations (1992: 289). Assessing the gendered division of labour in Britain, Thane suggests it is a 'picture of powerful men acting in their interests against those of women' (1992: 311) where 'patriarchal instincts can collide with and override capitalist instincts' (ibid.). Similarly, the feminization and professionalization experience of accounting in the UK is seen by Roberts and Coutts (1992) as part of a wider discussion of the struggle of professions to maintain and extend their privileged position in society.

Documenting the resistance to women in accounting in the US for over eighty years, research reveals practices extending from total exclusion from the profession itself to resistance to high-level promotions (Lehman, 1992a). In the early 1900s men debated the entry of women to the profession, some stating 'That the admission of women into the profession is to be deplored' (*Accountant*, 1915: 127); and that 'by nature, women were impulsive, full of sentiment, and hasty in judgement – failings which condemned her against entry into the professions where justice, stern and unbending, but not sentiments, had a place' (ibid.: 129). Refuting the supposed equality of women and men, and fearful of corrupting women's virtues should they enter the professions, it was argued that the home was the proper sphere for 'the true virtuous Roman matron' (ibid.: 127).

At first denied access to accounting employment, and thus any chance of certification in the early years of this century, women were employed in the decades to follow, during the male-scarce period of the Second World War, only to be fired upon re-entry of the male population into the labour force after the war's end. In the subsequent decades of the 1950s, 1960s and 1970s the profession sustained a view of women as appropriately in the home, or in the profession within limited domains, and resisted the advance of women into top hierarchies. Gildea's 1952 summary of the four main arguments used in the profession for not encouraging women in accounting were: (1) it is a waste of time to train women, as they are likely to quit 'when [their] babies start to arrive'; (2) women are of limited value due to restrictions, such as their inability to perform inventory audits or work out of town; (3) clients do not believe women are capable of performing audits or tax work; and (4) women are unacceptable to male co-workers as seniors and supervisors. Tyra recounted that 'Women accountants are sometimes told at the time of their employment that they will never be promoted to supervisor or manager and that their sex makes them unsuitable for a partnership' (1969: 28). In different manifestations, these practices have been documented well into the 1980s and 1990s.

As reported in the Deloitte & Touche 1993 *Annual Report* (by Gabriel and Martin), a study of career progressions of male and female managers in twenty 'Fortune 500' companies revealed that although the two groups were alike in almost every way, 'women with equal or better education earn less on average than men, and there are proportionately fewer women in top positions' (1993: 18). This study, by Loyola and Northwestern Universities in Chicago, also showed that female managers and professionals with similar qualifications, education attainment, career orientation, jobs and ability to relocate had been transferred less frequently than their male colleagues, and that their salaries had increased far less rapidly over the preceding five years.

Are things likely to change? The president of the executive search firm Battalia Winston International wanted to know which of America's senior women executives were being groomed for the top rung of the corporate ladder, so she called a couple of hundred of them to find out. According to her phone survey, not one of these senior executives 'believed [she] would be able to overcome the barriers – both subtle and overt – to reach the top. . . . One third of the respondents thought that in five years the number of female senior executives at their companies would be the same or lower' (Gabriel and Martin, 1993: 18).

According to a 1992 Knight-Ridder article, accounting firms have been hiring men and women in equal numbers, but after six to eight years, only two women remain for every three men, and comparable findings have been reported in a recent University of South Florida survey. In 1989, only 4.1 per cent of the partners in the nation's largest accounting firms were women. 'Three years later, the needle had barely moved; figures for 1992 showed that just 4.9 per cent of the partners in those firms were women' (Gabriel and Martin, 1993: 18). In addition to the well-known 'glass ceiling' phenomenon (women can only look up and see the top offices, but are blocked from reaching them), the dilemma of reaching the top is now exacerbated by the 'glass wall' phenomenon – women are not given the breadth of horizontal training, but are placed in one division (frequently 'personnel' or human resource arenas), and thus never receive the diversity of experience that is required for moving vertically up the corporate ladder.

The above studies are useful documentations of accounting's marginalization of women, providing the seeds of my emphasis here: actions are taken within the profession to exercise control over women in the employment sphere. Yet beyond the acts of exclusion, I wish to examine the atmosphere of creating and shaping the accountant-person and its masculine identity.

Mirror mirror on the wall: the social construction of the accountant-person

Addressing images directly, Maupin and Lehman's research (1994) on sex-typed behaviour of male and female auditors sought to ascertain whether women (and men) could succeed in contemporary accounting organizations without conforming to a 'masculine model'. As stated by Kanter, 'Organizations clearly reproduce themselves. People in power (who are mostly masculine men) mentor, encourage, and advance people who are most like themselves' (1977: 72). Suggesting that women who achieve senior positions must resemble the men in power, Kanter states:

> a number of studies have shown that as women move up the organizational hierarchy, their identification with the masculine model of managerial success becomes so important that they end up rejecting even the few valued feminine managerial traits they may have earlier endorsed. (ibid.)

Maupin and Lehman's analysis of 461 auditors confirms this 'sex-switching' necessity for reaching the top. As revealed in their study, 'feminine-females'[3] comprise 46 per cent of audit juniors (the entry-level position for auditors), and 13 per cent of the entry-level females are sex-typed 'masculine'. However, in the partner category, there are *no* 'feminine' females, and the proportion of 'masculine' sex-role identities increases to 46 per cent (from the previous 13 per cent).

The message is that males and females alike are rewarded with promotions to the top hierarchy by conforming to a model of behaviour typically characterized by masculine traits. Yet the message for women is mixed, as revealed in the dramatic lawsuit pursued for almost ten years by a manager, Ann Hopkins, against the firm Price Waterhouse (a case that reached the US Supreme Court). As a manager in the 'Big 6' accounting firm, Ms Hopkins claimed her client base and performance for the firm would have secured her a promotion to partner, if she was a man, but she had been the victim of sex discrimination. Critics suggested she needed a course at charm school, and they considered her behaviour 'macho' as if she was 'overcompensat[ing] for being a woman' (Weisel, 1991: 46). Suggestions to improve her chances for promotion included: she should walk more femininely, talk more femininely, wear jewellery and make-up (ibid.). These standards are considered disparate treatment under the law, and Price Waterhouse was eventually required to promote Ms Hopkins to partner.[4]

Ironically, as Linstead (1995) points out, the adoption of certain perceived male virtues by women who seek to be taken seriously in the business world is not usually regarded as an extension of feminine repertoires, but a renunciation of the feminine. In contrast, when men adopt caring and sensitive behaviour towards their partners and children, it is considered an addition to male virtues; not an overturning of male domination but an elaboration and extension of it (Kerfoot and Knights, 1993, in Linstead, 1995). 'The image allows the colonization of certain attractive parts of femininity in order to re-centre rather than de-centre masculinity, and further marginalize the feminine by creating a more complete version of masculinity' (Linstead, 1995: 200).

Masculinity, like femininity, emerges as a historically socially defined category, within specific settings, and is socially constructed.[5] As it is constantly shifting, constantly emergent and negotiated, it reflects its intertextual nature. It is also defined in terms of the nexus of multiple femininities. Indeed it is within this social context that Naomi Wolf describes emergent femininity in her controversial book, *The Beauty Myth: How Images of Beauty are Used Against Women* (1991). Her account of the different costs for women to succeed professionally, the stereotypes and roles women must play, and the notions of sexuality, all add to the image of women as negativity and the other. Wolf points to the plight of urban professional women who are devoting up to a third of their income to 'beauty maintenance', and who consider it a necessary investment. *New York Women* describes a typical ambitious career woman who spends 'nearly a quarter of her $60,000 income . . . on self preservation' (Wolf, 1991: 52). Another 'willingly spends more than $20,000 a year' on workouts with a 'cult trainer'. Wolf concludes that the few women who are finally earning as much as men are forced to pay *themselves* significantly less than their male peers through the societally and self-imposed Professional Beauty Qualification (PBQ). It has engineered do-it-yourself income discrimination.

Wolf's message is not against 'beauty' *per se*, it is a concern with the disempowering, backlash propaganda which suggests that feminism forces women to choose between beauty and liberation. For Wolf the harm is not images of glamour and beauty or the harm that these images cause, but that they proliferate at the expense of most other images and stories of female heroines, role models, villains, eccentrics, buffoons, visionaries, sex goddesses and pranksters, in other words, the 'wide world of women' (1991: 3). Wolf's is not a conspiracy theory, it is a concern about the backlash against feminism that uses an ideology about beauty and images of women to keep women from reaching their potential.

Where are the men in all this? Documenting the tensions of sexuality in the airline industry, Linstead (1995) notes that advertisements for most Asian airlines feature beautiful, demure and sensual stewardesses, whose only apparent wish is to serve, typically smiling, but averting their gaze in respectful submission (Linstead, 1995: 197). Female flight attendants must manage the contradictory combination of femininities as 'proto-mother' and 'sex-queen' in the occupation, nurture and seduction being simultaneously demanded. Airlines themselves make no secret of their wish to entice a predominantly male clientele on board in the lucrative first and business sectors with gently erotic evocations (ibid.: 196), while male managers support these images (ibid.: 198).

For the professional – female – accountant, the dilemma requires two images to appear in the mirror. The demands in the accounting profession, from the Price Waterhouse testimony, suggest that a female accountant must 'look like a lady', be charming, and wear earrings. But in the evaluation of personality characteristics, a female must score 'masculine'.

Hines (1992) rejects the preoccupation with a male–female dichotomy, illuminating the more profound issue of the Universal Feminine and Universal Masculine, also called, in Chinese philosophy, the yin and yang, with the interplay, tension, complementarity and union of these opposites seen to pervade all existence. In Indian philosophy they are named Shakti and Shiva; in Western psychology anima and animus; and in science, negative and positive poles and charges. Both these polar 'opposites' exist within men and women, societies and the world of nature and environment. The two poles of yang and yin – associated with the firm and the yielding, the strong and the weak, the light and the dark, the rational and the intuitive – are mutually generative and supportive, not separable. The art of life is to keep the two in balance, because there cannot be one without the other (Watts, in Hines, 1992: 316).

Katha Pollitt (1995) laments the dichotomy and the ascription of particular virtues – compassion, patience, non-violence – to women, as having a long history, permeating just about every field, from management training to theology:

> Indeed, although the media like to caricature feminism as denying the existence of sexual differences, for the women's movement and its opponents alike, 'difference' is where the action is. . . . Rhyme is male. Plot is male . . . even logic and language are male. What is female? Nature. Blood. Milk. Communal gatherings. The moon. Quilts. (Pollitt, 1995: 44)

Haven't we been here before? Pollitt queries, and indeed we have. '[W]oman as guardian of all the small rituals that knit together family and a community, woman as beneath, above or beyond such manly concerns as law, reason, abstract ideas – these images are as old as time. Open defenders of male supremacy have always used them to declare women flatly inferior to men' (ibid.: 45).

> But the biggest problem with all these accounts of gender difference is that they credit the differences they find to universal features of male and female development rather than to the economic and social positions men and women hold . . . and questions of power, privilege and money. (ibid.: 48, 57)

Bacchi (1990) puts it this way: '[a]re women the same or different than men?' It is the wrong question: . . . an inappropriate way of thinking about important social issues, such as how society is to reproduce itself and the kind of society in which we wish to live. Asking questions about women's sameness to or difference from men only serves to mystify these issues, which in turn may help to explain the ubiquity of the question in popular discourse. If these larger questions about how we should organize our lives can be obscured, they can also be conveniently ignored. . . . if society catered appropriately for all human needs, men and women included, discussions about the sameness to or difference from men would be of little significance . . . the analysis stops short and fails to critique the *system* which encourages men to be a particular way – detached, competitive, individuated; . . . abstracted from, the personal needs and commitments involved in living arrangements (paraphrased from Bacchi, 1990: x, xi, xiv).

What becomes clear is that the dilemma of difference is inherently unstable and without solution. The reduction of complex issues of policy and theory to an equality/difference antithesis forecloses discussion of structural constraints, political context and alternative options (Vogel, 1993: 4). Declaring a dichotomous opposition to be an 'illusion' or 'intellectual trap' that must be transcended is one thing; actually doing so, another. As literary critic Ann Snitow shows, feminism moves in complex and unsystematic ways among commitments to equality and difference, sameness and specificity, essence and diversity. A position may be chosen, but the choice is never final. However frustrating the lesson, feminism must learn to 'embrace the paradox' for 'there is no third course' (Snitow, in Vogel, 1993: 5).

Thus what is at stake in these debates 'goes far beyond the suppression of women, to embrace the suppression of the values, perceptions, and ways of thinking, feeling, being and acting that are associated with the Universal Feminine or Yin' (Hines, 1992: 314). Policies, social practices, rights, values and future potentialities are at stake. Beyond the images of the feminine and masculine accountant-person are the basic and funda- mental practices of the accounting profession. These practices synchronize with and enhance what has been identified as the masculinity of the accountant-person. It is to these characteristics of the profession's practices that we now turn.

Does accounting matter?

Accounting's privileged access to specialized and 'inside' information regarding corporations, municipalities, federal bureaucracies, defence departments and schools places it in a unique position of power and knowledge. Accountants provide the 'facts': the hard data to assess buyouts and mergers, the costs of governmental weapons programmes, funding between local constituencies, and the benefits of pollution control devices.

Whether accounting is superfluous or critical in such managerial and social debates has generated a diversity of beliefs in the academy. In an efficient market, reason many, accounting is irrelevant, since accounting information is 'too late': the information is readily available from other sources, and thus already impacted in stock prices. For others, the irrelevance of accounting emerges from its inconsequential role in things that matter, i.e. if we were to change the world, we certainly would not start with accounting (Gray et al., 1987). Yet accounting is not related to nothingness, but to that which its presence promotes, enhances, denies or destroys. Accounting is used as 'the language of business', and the pro-liferation of accounting reports, budgets, forecasts, bankruptcy estimates, tax analysis and so on suggests that accounting collaborates as a social practice, beyond the trite and trivial, functioning as a ritualized method of resolving conflict and making choices. Should accounting disappear tomorrow it might not be 'missed', but other social practices would surely fill its void, providing the mechanisms for arbitration. The accounting we have today serves as this ritual practice and provides us with a means of making (a particular) semblance of the world.

Economic man and accounting

There is much emerging literature on masculinities (Bornstein, 1994; Brittan, 1989; Collinson and Hearn, 1994; Goodwin, 1995; Segal, 1990). In this section, we are guided by contemporary literature in *economics* with feminist perspectives. Intended here is to bring to light the emphasis on the 'economic man', and the implications for accounting and other business realms. Economic theories and the development of accounting research have long been intertwined, most notably in conventional accounting's usage of neoclassical economics, and more recently its reliance on agency theory, transaction costing, capital asset pricing models, efficient market hypothesis, etc. (Arrington and Francis, 1989; Neimark, 1994; Reiter, 1995; Whitley, 1986; Tinker, 1985; Williams, P.F., 1989). Even the models commonly used in behavioural accounting research are close cousins to economic theory models, and accounting's research methodology, such as mathematical modelling and analysis, are likewise borrowed heavily from economics research (Reiter, 1995). Given the interplay of economics and accounting – in the literature, in the classroom and in the academy – it is appropriate to observe what illuminations, benefits, restrictions or constraints this association has produced.

One perspective of feminist rewriting of economics elaborated by Nelson (1992) addresses how a certain way of thinking about gender and a certain way of thinking about economics have become intertwined through metaphor – with detrimental results – and how a richer conception of human understanding and human identity could broaden and improve the field of economics (substitute 'accounting') for both female and male practitioners. Dualistic, hierarchical metaphors for gender have permeated the way we think about what economics is, and how it should be done, and an alternative metaphor provides a more adequate base of understanding. Of course, there have been numerous challenges to the received methodologies and canons of economics; the challenge of interest here is the uprooting of masculine metaphors in economics, and seeing how organizational and accounting behaviour is imbedded in these metaphors as well (Nelson, 1992).

One of the major dialogues in feminist analysis has been the refutation that many of the traits assumed to be 'essential' male or female, in a biological sense, are not, and that they have very strong cultural components. Thus when referring to 'masculine' or 'feminine' traits, feminist economists are not stating that these are essentially 'more appropriate for' or 'more likely found in' persons of one sex or the other, but that they are traits that have been culturally, metaphorically gendered. The hierarchical nature of the dualism – the systematic devaluation of females and whatever is metaphorically understood as 'feminine' – is what Nelson identifies as sexism.

Turning to the definition of economics, there is certainly a diversity of endeavours, yet one central concept in mainstream economics is that of 'the market'. For Gary Becker (see, for example, 1981), the idealized market is a place where rational, autonomous, anonymous agents with stable preferences interact for the purpose of exchange. The prototypical market is one in which tangible goods or services are exchanged, with money facilitating the transactions, and in which the agents are individual persons. For an economics work to be accepted as 'being economics', it must bear a resemblance to this prototype, although it is wide enough to include research on dual labour markets, satisficing and aspects of finance, with other works deemed as 'on the fringe'. Discussions of comparable worth, for example, violate the centrality of the idea of allocation by market forces, so the subject is usually demoted to the realm of politics.

Economics, as a social endeavour, reflects some points of view, favoured by the group that makes the rules for the discipline, and neglects others. While diversity does exist around the fringes in economics, the central programme of economics is metaphorically linked with the hierarchical, dualistic conception of gender and a 'privileging' of a particular conception of masculinity (Nelson, 1992).

Consequently, accounting, with its many cues from economics, has emerged as a language, arch-commentator and social constructor of consciousness, society and environment that is 'hard, dry, impersonal, objective, explicit, outerfocused, action-oriented, analytical, dualistic, quantitative, linear, rationalist, reductionist and materialist' (Hines, 1992: 313). Through the gaze constructed by accounting, reality is seen to be divisible and quantifiable, named, identified, separated and delineated – assets, liabilities, expenses, revenues, capital – 'and these realities are combined, recombined, added and subtracted. In combination they create and delimit the boundaries of organizations, and determine the equity rights or "share" of reality to which people are entitled' (ibid.). The outcome is that 'accounting calculations and measures provide a basis for rational decision-making, enabling a rational, "efficient", profit-maximizing, allocation of resources. As well as being rationalist, accounting is profoundly materialist and reductionist' (ibid.: 314).

An accounting conceptualized in this manner sets the stage for the types of questions raised, the interpretation of data, and the limits of the discipline. Two instances are provided in the following section to exemplify the effect.

Women's work / if women counted

The Washington Feminist Faxnet reports on 17 February 1995, 'Women's work isn't counted – at least by the US government'. In contrast to the decision a decade ago when *Forward Looking Strategies for the Advancement of Women* (emerging out of the UN Decade for Women) recommended that 'Women's unwaged work should be counted when economic statistics on gross product are put together', the Clinton administration is hesitant. Laments US Secretary of Labor, Robert Reich, since economists can't agree on methodology, unwaged work should not be counted. Remarks the Washington Feminist Faxnet, 'When did we start waiting for economists to agree? Over 150 organizations worldwide have supported counting unwaged work, including many from the US concerned with pay equity.'

As in economics, in accounting practice in the US and elsewhere, discontinuities in measurement instruments and the lack of hard data are often cited as rationales for not including environmental, occupational safety and an array of quality-of-life measures in financial statements. Yet accounting standards are required for numerous difficult-to-measure transactions, such as pension contingencies and the cost to Employee Benefits Other than Pensions, which require actuarial estimates, future projections and a range of assumptions about cost behaviour. In sympathy here with Cooper, C. (1992), suggesting that to measure quality of life and environmental issues would be a travesty, and it would suit 'us' (activists, feminists, marginalized, outsiders) better to be out on the margin, not co-opted by an arcane measurement system, it would also seem important to question the very system that initiated the behaviours indicated. Demanding some form of accountability would be one form of activism.

Marilyn Waring's book, *If Women Counted: A New Feminist Economics* (1988) is a painstakingly precise illustration of the worldwide exclusion of women's contribution and production in society. In world census gathering, in construction of national accounts, in valuing time, 'work' and parenting, the contributions of women are either excluded or diminished. And as is frequently the case, the exclusion of female life practices from monetary amounts *does* matter. It has real material effects on the lives of women, and it matters when it speaks a message to women and men regarding the worth of women, and what women contribute to society.

Accounting's culpability in the process of excluding information which would serve the varied interests of women as a group receives limited articulation. This exclusion may be seen as the result of the factors observed above: the demand for hard data, the subjectivity of what is identified with masculinity-valued preferences, and the promotion of only certain groups' interests in the adoption of such a methodology. Recognizing the array of differences between women, I note however, that the exclusion of 'women's data' traverses ideological space, economic paradigms and culture. Hines concurs: 'The present world order, and the lived experience of most people in it, is substantially influenced by the concepts and consequences of accounting: management accounting, financial accounting, national and government accounting, and international accounting' (1992: 328).

Eastern paradoxes: business as usual

In the global context, accounting continues 'to matter'. The accounting gaze is inescapable for the countries of Eastern and Central Europe and the former Soviet Union; in transforming a centrally planned economy to a market one, a new language of accountability, ownership rights and claims to wealth is required – as part of the broader social, political and legal shifts. Familiar as we are with the term 'shock therapy' applied to the Russian economy, culture shock, culture clash, and culture backlash in the form of deep nationalism are also outcomes of the sudden introduction of market imperatives in a previously command economy. New social relations emerge from the new economic realities – a reconstitution of the worker–management relationship; an end to the long-time guarantee of employment, housing, education and child care; a focus on the individual and private world in contrast to communal life; and numerous additional shifts in religious, family, mass media and political practices.

Within this, 'Traditional Western accounting with its focus on calculation of profit and ownership plays an important part in creating a new economic reality' (de la Rosa and Merino, 1995: 2), in particular because 'Valuation and transferability of ownership are central to the discussion of privatization' (ibid.: 5). Yet, as the UN Commission on Transnational Corporations recognizes, the significance of accounting and the problematic nature of privatization arise 'because new accounting systems are imposed on old ones and/or the quality of the data is insufficient to produce useful information' (ibid.: 5–6).

Not only does the process of privatization impose incongruities but it is another significant economic activity marginalizing women. In debates over privatization and the setting of accounting standards, the impacts on women (as heads of household, for example) are largely ignored, and women are typically excluded from the circle of men making these crucial decisions, an exclusion pervasive in the new labour markets as well.

Behind closed doors: Russian style

Employment figures for women in the transforming economy are dismal. Official statistics in Russia report that two out of three of the unemployed are women, and in many regions over 85 per cent of the unemployed are women.[6] In Moscow, women represent 80 per cent of the newly un-employed; of this percentage, 54 per cent are women with higher education, 87 per cent have children under sixteen years of age, and 46 per cent are women aged thirty to forty-five. Women from all professions – engineers, doctors, educators, scientific researchers, journalists, bookkeepers and shop clerks – are included.

Widespread employment discrimination not only reflects policies of private enterprise, but is practised and tolerated across government agencies. Government employers openly express their preference for hiring men, and women are fired in disproportionate numbers as a strategy for streamlining their workforces. Government employment offices frequently advertise jobs for men only and refuse to refer women to jobs where the employer has indicated a preference for men. Public sector job interviewers often question women about children, and reject applicants on the basis of their sex, parental status or potential maternity.

The official sanctioning of such discrimination comes from high govern-ment posts: Gennady Melikyan, the Russian Labour Minister suggested (in 1993) that a solution to unemployment in Russia is for women to abandon their role in the workforce. 'Why should we try to find jobs for women when men are idle and on unemployment benefits?' he remarked. 'Let men work and women take care of the homes and their children.'

Significant cutbacks in social support such as enterprise child-care facilities assist in reversing the achievement of women's integration in the workforce, which had been 51 per cent in the former Soviet Union. This is not to deny discrimination in employment in Russia, where on average the wage rate for women was 70 per cent to a man's dollar (the average ratio being the same in much of the Western world). During the transition to a market economy this female to male wage ratio has dropped substantially, to a level of 40 per cent (Moscow Centre for Gender Studies, 1996, unpublished reports).

Mirror, mirror

What it means to be a virtuous, ideal, contemporary Russian woman is . . . challenging. Remarks Larissa Lissyutkina:

> Without skipping a beat, the image of the woman worker [as the ideal Soviet woman] was overthrown by the ideal of the woman as prostitute or beauty queen (Miss Russia). . . . Before our eyes, the granddaughters of the commissars, who in the 1980s were Pioneers straining in the kitchen and the home, willingly posed in bikinis before television cameras. (Lissyutkina, 1993: 275)

Such a transformation is clear to young women. Asked to write an essay on 'what they want to do in their future', a vast majority of high school women in a Moscow class answered, 'Marry a rich foreigner' (conversation with G. Negruesteva, 1994), while a poll of Moscow high-school seniors revealed that prostitution was regarded as the most prestigious profession. 'The prostitute, the lone entrepreneur breaking taboos, is the pioneer of the market economy, from which is supposed to come universal salvation' (Lissyutkina, 1993: 284). The transition to a free market in post-communist Russia may be graphically symbolized by the 'grotesque marriage of the hard currency "intourist girl" to the foreign businessman' (ibid.).

In literature, 'male writers reproach contemporary Soviet women for having allegedly betrayed their own ideal self, for having thrown themselves off the pedestal. . . . In present-day Russia, women no longer embody the spiritual and moral ideal. They have been demoted from "Mother Russia" to "Miss Russia"' (ibid.: 285).

Romanticizing the past of traditional Russian women contrasts the reality of Russian life where 'Violence within the family isn't considered a crime' (Pisklakova, in Meek, 1995: 23). 'This is a very Russian tradition which is very difficult to stop,' muses the head of a local police station in Moscow. 'To drink or beat your wife? . . . Both' (ibid.).[7]

Why work? Business and accounting incentives

Keeping women out of the economy has become a preoccupation for a variety of factions in contemporary Russia. The crises of spirituality, and unprecedented violence and crime among Russian youth, is used to victimize working women. Claiming that the absence of a 'proper' home for children has deprived society of women's essential domestic duties, a return to the role of homemaker is demanded. Where nationalists meet marketeers and radical reformists is in their essentialist view of women – women's place is in the home. Adopting a non-essentialist view of human nature goes against the grain of the Soviet consensus, and suggests a different role of women than the homemaker (Waters, 1993: 288–9).[8]

When Russian women do enter commerce, they are likely to be among male counterparts who '"see women in business in one role – as an elegant secretary who brings me coffee," says a leading Russian businessman echoing the prevailing male wisdom' (*The Economist*, 12 August 1995: 46).

Newspapers are full of advertisements for secretaries who are 'Young, blonde, long-legged and without inhibitions' (ibid.). Women with children are given every encouragement *not* to work; frequently employment advertisements exclude women over thirty-five, insist women wear miniskirts and bring a picture of themselves in a bathing suit to interviews, and that they should be prepared to 'entertain clients'.

'[I]t is already economics, trade and finance in terms of men, it is still rhetoric and pathos in terms of women . . . women are encouraged to remain helpful, pleasing, warm and kind. It is so natural, they say' (Kupryashkina, 1994: 2). When Tatyana Paramonova was made acting head of the Central Bank, several Russian newspapers seemed more interested in her views on cooking than on monetary policy (*The Economist* 12 August 1995: 46). Concludes *The Economist*: 'Russia is still a man's world'.

'What problems will need to be resolved in servicing Russian clientele?' was a question posed to a manager in a large Western accounting firm five years ago. 'The choices firms are making in hiring practices' were considered problematic (Anonymous, conversation with author, 1991). For the most part, predominantly male economists were being trained in Western accounting practices, despite the historical trend that women dominated the field of what loosely translates from the Russian into English as 'bookkeeper'. The Big 6 manager suggested one interpretation: Western firms were choosing male economists because accounting was becoming a profession in the former Soviet Union, and thus would be more respectable as a male domain.

'In the past, accountants were not considered part of senior managements. They performed routine clerical tasks. . . . In addition, accounting was perceived as a woman's occupation because of the clerical aspects' (Sherry and Vinning, 1995: 44–5). The status of women and accounting are linked: for women 'social elevation has not occurred in Russia . . . this perception is an impediment to raising the status of accounting as an important profession that can make significant contributions toward the successful transition to a market economy' (ibid.).[9] As in the US, the 'contribution' of accounting will be illusory and limited because the discipline privileges objectivity, analytics and profit maximization. Exporting this Western myopia is significant, as it provides the profession with an expanding influence. This influence is the basis of my concluding remarks.

Implications

The tendency to exclude significant domains of economic and social life in the practice of accounting transcends national boundaries. This exclusion is striking in the case of 'women's work' as Waring (1988) revealed: billions of dollars of productive women's labour throughout the globe is made invisible in the UN System of National Accounts. Another example is the case of environmental disclosure, where estimates exist that over $500 billion of environmental clean-up costs are not recorded on the financial statements of US publicly traded companies (Freedman and Stagliano, 1995) while a plethora of other environmental issues are relegated to the ambiguous status of 'externalities'. This exclusion becomes particularly disturbing as Western accounting practices become 'exported' to other nation states, with the implication that from West to East environmental aspects of business and governmental agencies will continue to defy scrutiny. This exclusion is considered an extension of the privileging of masculinities in accounting practice, manifest not only in overt discriminatory acts toward women, but in its silence on broad issues in social, corporate and global spheres.

Given Russia's sharp decline in industrial production since market reform, its high inflation rate, government deficit and decreasing real wage, one could argue there are many positive effects of maintaining a high proportion of women in the labour force (increased tax revenues, increase in consumption demands and thus production, and decrease in social payments of support). Yet statistics of national decline are used to rationalize closings of child-care centres, abandonment of affirmative action for women, preferential hiring for men, and an array of socially repressive policies for women. . . . Accounting matters.

Establishing the value of Soviet enterprises, for the purposes of privatization, and sale to investors (including Western investors) using Western accounting standards, imposes upon the Soviet accounting system the logocentric, materialistic, masculine assumptions of the Western system. It also requires some 'sympathy for the devil', an atmosphere that is conducive to the introduction of logocentric measures. There will certainly be resistance by an array of constituencies as well. The emergence of numerous independent feminist organizations within the former Soviet Union taking critical account of social and business practices marks one of these movements of hope.

Notes

Gratitude to, and inspiration from: David Collinson, Jeff Hearn, Nick Korol, Shana Penn, Anastasia Posadskaya, Vera Soboleva, the many supportive women of the Moscow Center for Gender Studies, the Network of East-West Women, and numerous other women's centres in the former Soviet Union. This chapter is dedicated to Esther Taubman, my grandmother, who, having reached her ninety-fifth birthday, has graced our world, both East and West.

1. Externalities, in this context, are used to define, for corporations, a cost or benefit not included or calculated as the corporations's 'responsibility'. Thus a corporation would not be held accountable for the cost of polluting the environment in the sense that the financial statements would not report all costs of prevention or clean-up. The external world would incur these costs (in environmental degradation, government clean-up, health impediments borne by citizens).

2. When we refer to 'women's position' (or that of men) we do not imply that all women (or men) are 'the same', but recognize the great heterogeneity of interests, rights and

perspectives of such groups. A diversity of groups have rightly held the US Women's Movement up to the mirror as being a privileged 'white' women's movement. This has allowed for reflection and change, and for the emergence of the movement to embrace many feminisms and many issues regarding race and class. Although race and class are not the 'focus' of this chapter, they are integral to the dilemmas posed herein.

3. Maupin and Lehman (1994) use the controversial Bem Sex-Role Inventory (BSRI), an instrument used to measure masculinity, femininity and androgyny (defined as a high propensity towards both feminine and masculine characteristics). Included as a masculine item would be 'acts as a leader'; the characteristic 'loves children' would be classified as feminine. 'Sex switching' refers to a male subject receiving a feminine score, or a female subject receiving a masculine score. The BSRI categories are clearly problematic, given the social construction of masculinity and femininity. Yet the usage of the BSRI categories helps, in fact, to measure the stereotypical sex roles permeating our organizations and our lives.

4. We do not suggest that women have 'succeeded' when they break the glass ceiling and become promoted to partnership position; yet without women in decision-making positions 'at the top' or in mentoring positions for young women and men, possibilities for transformations of hierarchies and socially positive changes are limited.

5. In the social construction of the self, the 'nature versus nurture' debate has occupied an important sphere of feminist debate. Although biology might not be destiny, one cannot deny biological differences in the sexes. 'If you are in any doubt about the effect of hormones on emotion, libido, and aggression, have a chat with a transsexual who must take hormones medically. He or she will set you straight' (Paglia quoted in Goodwin, 1995: 4). It is what a society chooses to *do* with these differences that really matters.

6. The 'Women Question' in Russia (and the former Soviet Union) has been researched, debated in the Kremlin, considered 'solved', and is complex and fascinating. Neither a Sovietologist nor a scholar in Russian feminist history, I provide here an account based on over a dozen visits to the FSU in the past five years, with an array of business, gender, governmental and educational organizations, my personal observations, as well as my enquiries into research and literature on the subject (see, for example, Buckley, 1989; Funk and Mueller, 1993; Goldman, 1989; de Grazia, 1992; Kruks et al., 1989; Lehman, 1992b; Molyneux, 1991; Rosenberg, 1991; Snitow, 1993; Szalai, 1991; *Women and Earth*, 1992).

7. During 1993, 14,500 Russian women were killed by their husbands, and a further 56,400 were disabled or badly injured in domestic attacks 'yet there is not a single refuge for battered women in the country' (Meek, 1995: 23). The Ministry of the Interior reports that there were more than 13,000 cases of rape in Russia last year. 'As in other countries, many victims – perhaps most – do not report the crime to the police, many of whom routinely accuse victims of "asking for it"' (*The Economist*, 12 August 1995: 44).

8. Numerous women and gender organizations have emerged in the past five years in the former Soviet Union, and many of these are particularly concerned with women's economic independence, women's right to be free of discrimination, the importance of women's participation in all aspects of civil society, and women's integration into the emerging market economy.

9. Greater hiring practices were being directed towards women on my more recent visits. Nevertheless, the potentially discriminatory practices observed from the earlier years remain problematic.

9

Multinational Masculinities and European Bureaucracies

Alison E. Woodward

A stylish stiletto heel dominates the poster. The text asks, 'Shouldn't your next boss be wearing these?' in one of the many languages of the European Union. This ad, designed to disarm masculine resistance to affirmative action policies in the administration of the European Union, raised a sea of protest, not from men, but from women from the northern countries. This sexually and nationally differentiated response to the symbolism of the feminine in an international organization illustrates how gender in international management is subject to construction. In fact, the southern European advertising agency that designed the campaign envisaged a certain kind of male viewer who needs to have his women distinctly 'feminized' and 'eroticized' by dress. Based on observation of the application of affirmative action policies within the European Union,[1] this chapter discusses the pressures in international settings towards a construction of masculinities in management which are 'stereotypically' masculine, and how these masculinities in return resist the introduction of the female 'other' into management.

These pressures in a multinational setting towards stereotypic and macho-masculine management are framed by the patriarchal logic of the strictly, and virtually ideal-typical bureaucratic structure of the European administrative institutions. The administration of the European Union was designed using 'rational' principles of bureaucratic practice to be above party and national loyalties. Despite the 'rational' ambitions of the designers of the structures for European administration, the practice is far from the neutral, in terms of nation, party and gender. In fact, the setting lends itself to a crystallization of a masculine corporate culture, expressed in the dominance of certain professional subcultures, language, and corporate material symbolism.

This chapter speculates that multinational settings which offer few promotion opportunities and in which promotion may be based on ascribed factors extraneous to job performance can crystallize misogynist forms of masculinity. Formal bureaucratic structures (calculated on a 'male' value roster) encourage masculine practices of resistance to female participation in leadership functions.

Theoretically, the issues in the case of the European Commission of the European Union raise a number of concerns also applicable to other organizations where nationalities meet. For example, where do we put gender culture in multinational settings? Which national versions of the masculine and feminine predominate and under what conditions? What can we expect in an organization where a number of cultural scripts are available? Which set of rules will guide the players, and which are more or less open to discussion?

This chapter first explores the interface between the concepts of organizational culture and gender in public administration. In particular, there is a need for a conceptual scheme to understand the realities of women working in international organizations with men whose masculinity is constructed in a multicultural setting. Such a model, as pointed out in other chapters of this book, is missing in the mainstream management and organizational literature.

These issues will then be related to the relative lack of progress in affirmative action schemes at the Commission of the European Union in Brussels. The Commission is an exceptionally suitable bureaucracy to examine here. It is an institution which distils characteristics of several national bureaucratic structures, and which has rapidly grown. Further, it is a place where bureaucrats from many different national cultures meet. Finally, for the purposes of this chapter, it is particularly interesting, for the Commission is masculinely dominated, both in terms of personnel hierarchies and in terms of organizational culture.

The European Commission, which serves administrative as well as legislative functions within the European Union, is characterized by strong vertical and horizontal gender segregation. About three-quarters of the tasks carried out by the administration are in areas that can be characterized as male dominated, in the fields of agriculture, economics and competition, scientific and foreign policy. The Directorate Generales, or departments that carry out these prestigious tasks are also dominated by men in the university-trained A-grade leadership functions. Even the political leadership, the appointed Commissioners who change every five years, has been almost exclusively male.[2] Women with university qualifications are relegated to the supporting departments of the Commission, the velvet ghettos (Ghiloni, 1988) of translators, the social departments and information offices. While the C-grade staff, which includes clerical functions is 81 per cent female, the A-grade posts are only 14 per cent female, despite more than five years of active affirmative action policy. Asked in an internal survey whether being a woman was an advantage for their career, 100 per cent of the A-level respondents answered 'No' (COPEC, 1994). The work on equality has met both overt and covert opposition within the Commission. Many of the features of daily practice in the Commission distil a certain kind of Euro-masculinity which subverts attempts to move away from the patriarchal logic that has grown in the organization.

For example, questions of performance evaluation and promotion, especially in the higher realm, are subject to many criteria besides 'rationally evaluated merit', and the informal practice many times obviates the formal rules. While merit is measured, issues such as party politics, nationality and personal loyalties enter into promotion decisions, possibly to an even greater degree than in similar private organizations. Affirmative action policies, which are tailored according to the same rational logic as bureaucratic organization and thus in themselves might be seen as a paradoxically masculinist response to increasing female presence,[3] add one more element to the cocktail, and may act as a catalyst to concretize masculine resistance and masculine power patterns in ways unthinkable in uninational settings.

Our growing understanding of the relation between theoretical work on gender and masculinities, organizational culture and public bureaucracies can help us better comprehend such male resistance to affirmative action in an international bureaucracy. The chapter concludes with a discussion of the implications of the slow pace of change in European institutions for understanding the gender gap in attitudes to the European Union.

The gender of organization/bureaucratic culture

Academic literature on international organizations has remained remarkably impervious to the tumultuous and often times fashion-plagued literature on gender, culture and management. To some extent this may reflect the state of research in public administration itself. It frequently provides mainly a reflexive response to developments in the mainstream management literature. Here, we will briefly consider the various trends in feminist, organization and cultural theory with an eye towards developing a perspective relevant to international bureaucracies and masculinities. The notion of heterogeneity in masculinities and femininities underlined in the work of the editors of this volume is even more at issue in multinational settings.

Feminist research and the insights of cultural and postmodern analysis have turned our understandings of organizations around. In general (although with some exceptions), they have attacked the dominant framework of organizational analysis from separate vantage points.[4]

The concept of organizational culture popularized by such authors as Deal and Kennedy (1982) or Peters and Waterman (1982) was curiously gender- and indeed nation-free. But feminists saw, perhaps sooner than public administration analysts, the necessity of the culture concept for the classification and understanding of complex organizations. The classic concepts of strategy, structure, environment and technology miss important dimensions of organizational life. Today culture has been elevated to its own status in the pantheon of organizational characteristics. The problem, of course, more so than with the other classic elements, is one of definition and identification. What is culture in an organization and how does one deal with its chimerical nature? Czarniawska-Joerges (1992) rejects the idea that culture is simply a metaphor, as Smircich (1983) and Morgan (1986) among others call it. Yet her own improvement doesn't help the researcher interested in gender even though she does introduce the important notion of power (1992: 31). She struggles with the issue of the layers of meaning and the problem of context, in her effort to demonstrate the value of anthropologically inspired approaches to understanding organizations. Ultimately she sides with a more cognitive approach in her definition, finding useful in a general sense an idea that 'culture is a bubble [of meaning] covering the world, a bubble that we both create and live within . . . the medium of social life' (1992: 287). In this she treads metaphorical territory, as does the popular author Hofstede, who sees culture as socially constructed, soft, difficult to change but finally and metaphorically 'the collective programming of the mind which distinguishes the members of one organization from another' (1991: 180). Hofstede's research on IBM is solely concerned with national cultures, but, in his dimensions, as we will see below, he attempts to characterize them in terms of their 'masculinities' or 'femininities' as well.

The culture concept lends itself to the discussion of gender (Mills, 1992). Putting concern for national cultural variety together with a concern for gender, class and power easily leads to seeing the need for a concept of culture that also deals with multiple layers and various degrees of tenacity. Both male and female authors have increasingly seen the need to include the issue of gender in any discussion of organizational culture, even if the way understandings of gender interact with other cultural understandings in the construction of behaviour may remain unclear.

Public bureaucracies, culture and masculine/feminine dimensions

Organizational culture was widely used to analyse problems in private management but seldom tackled the issue of public bureaucratic cultures. This parallels the rather long time it took for gender approaches to be applied to public bureaucracies. This is not to say that the issue of culture within state bureaucracies was unknown (Edelman, 1977; Wildavsky, 1987), but rather that the literature in political science seemed to develop in a separate Petri dish with little cross-fertilization of concepts. Czarniawska-Joerges identifies a split between what is called public administration and organization studies which occurred some time in the 1960s (1992: 75–6). Studying bureaucracies became increasingly the province of political scientists and legal specialists.

These studies were informed by questions such as whether bureaucracy in its pure Weberian type was capable of delivering rationality or was doomed to inefficiency, or the tension between the politician and the bureaucrat in terms of power (Lane, 1987). While those doing field studies of the relations between bureau officials, politicians and the public could not fail to be struck by the importance of culture as made visible in language and behaviour and problems in communication (Woodward et al., 1994), the tools for analysis frequently were limited to quantitative survey methods. Authors such as Aberbach et al. (1981) admitted to finding qualitative approaches frustrating. This is not to ignore the important tradition of studies in the genre of Crozier (1964), but to say that the culture concept did not blossom in studies of bureaucracy in the late 1970s.[5] Curiously, even in international bureaucracies, such as the UN or World Bank, where one might expect a focus on cultural conflict, the concept is seldom discussed, although Michelmann (1978) does try to change the classic concept of technology in organizations to 'cultural practice' to apply to the World Bank.

Just as the culture concept has taken time to penetrate work on public organizations, so too has gender. We first note work on gender and public bureaucracy from the United States and Australia including the two Eisensteins' (1984, 1991a) seminal work as well as empirical work on public bureaucracies (Ferguson, 1984; Grant and Tancred, 1992; Watson, 1992). Collections, such as Savage and Witz's important *Gender and Bureaucracy* (1992), are very recent in Europe. Undoubtedly, the political push for equal opportunity policies in these countries was in part instrumental in encouraging this work. Camilla Stivers (1993) attempts to integrate the ethnographic and sociological studies of women's experience working for the state with a theoretical connection to public administration literature on legitimacy. Studies such as Cockburn (1991) provide case evidence of the problems of affirmative action in the bureaucracy. Such work poses a feminist challenge to the state: its legitimacy rests in feminists' eyes in part on its own ability to live up to the democratic ethos. The state and its agents should be better at demonstrating equality in employment and practice than the private sector, but instead the state is implicated in the reproduction of oppressive gender relations.

It was only in the 1990s that the scholarship on corporate culture, feminism and life in public bureaucracies began to meet in a search for a framework that would address the concerns of organization theorists and feminist scholars alike. Insights from researchers working on masculinity have further spurred the search. Combining the new gender-conscious management theory with a cultural perspective provides a different framework for understanding bureaucracy and gender.

One fruitful hybrid approach is the Gender-Organization-System framework suggested by Ellen Fagenson (1993) which hints that conditions within and without the organization systematically structure the interplay of gender and organization. The insights provided by the 'gender-centred approach' looking at issues such as socialization and sex roles, and the insights contributed by authors such as Kanter (1977) who consider the structural issues in organizations, are combined with two new assumptions. First, an individual must be understood in the society (culture) in which he or she acts, works and lives, and (in multinational organizations) in terms of their original national identity. Second, change in one part of the system will generate other changes (Fagenson, 1993: 6). The Gender-Organization-

System (GOS) approach allows for contextual factors, and emphasizes the argument that organizational culture is best studied as process.

The elements of culture and power could be strengthened in the GOS framework. Geert Hofstede presciently identifies what he calls a 'masculine–feminine' dimension in *national* cultures, but there is little reason why this train of thought could not be followed into the organization itself. Hofstede classifies national cultures as masculine or feminine on the basis of a cluster of items including the importance of financial rewards, recognition and challenge (the more important, the more masculine the culture). The feminine pole underlines the importance of relationships with superiors, co-operation, security of employment and the value of living in a desirable area (1991: 82). In part, it seems that Hofstede decided to classify these traits as male or female because there was a gender gap on this particular cluster of items. He describes, using primarily anecdotal material, a stereotypic European conception of the masculine and feminine:

> masculinity pertains to societies in which social gender roles are clearly distinct (i.e. men are supposed to be assertive, tough and focused on material success whereas women are supposed to be more modest, tender and concerned with the quality of life; femininity pertains to societies in which social roles overlap (i.e. both men and women are supposed to be modest, tender and concerned with the quality of life). (1991: 82–3).

The masculinity here defined is of a stereotypically macho kind, and leaves undiscussed the undeniable fact that other kinds of masculinity may be expressed in different national cultures. Antal and Izraeli (1993: 64) ironically note that even the most 'feminine' national cultures of Sweden and the Netherlands have few women managers. Solidarities between male managers as men, even in 'feminine' cultures, keep women out.

Each national situation provides its own reference points for the construction and expression of masculinities and femininities. Those with highly patriarchal religious values, based for example on Roman Catholicism, may have strong masculine ratings according to Hofstede's measurement method (1991: 102), but one could equally assume that the individualism encouraged in Protestant countries might be translated into the aggressive hero conception of masculinity present in northern European organizations. Within every national culture there are values about the correct place and behaviour for men and women. These beliefs may go deeper than other cultural values, and be reinforced by relations of power between men, thereby colouring the patterns of expectation and rules of play inside an organization.

International organizations as gendered bureaucracies: nation versus sex?

International organizations present an obvious test case for some of the theoretical problems inherent in the notion of culture in organizational studies. If we (for the sake of convenience) look at culture as a 'variable' both external and internal, we see in the international organization a number of layers of cultural identity or values: those of the *national culture* that an individual may be carrying when he or she enters the organization, those of a professional, managerial or *occupational culture*, given that international civil servants are many times recruited as experts, and finally aspects of *gender, race* and *class culture* from a national setting, infiltrating each of the above-named layers. The international organization itself presents specific ways of doing things, what might have been called a 'corporate culture', but which we would prefer to think of as 'a daily way of life' or better, cultural practice (Michelmann, 1978).

The argument that I would like to make in the particular situation of the institutions of the European Union needs the notion of layering suggested by the Gender-Organization-System approach: understandings about the relations between men and women compose a resistant and basic foundation. National culture, although important in an international organization, is used by higher-level managers as a useful, but often expendable, aspect of identity. Most of the younger upper-level civil servants have considerable experience in other countries and are no longer stuck in a personal national groove. Interviewees related that they mobilize their national and regional identities primarily in micro-level situations. Professional subculture comes later in life and is less deep-seated, and organizational culture is the most dismissable. Clifford Geertz introduced the idea of deep culture years ago (1973). I would like to do a little violence to his concept by suggesting that practices about gender go deeper than many other cultural practices: each layer of culture is infiltrated by practices resulting from the recognition that one is a man or a woman, what Northcraft and Gutek (1993: 228) call the 'salience' of gender. In a multicultural situation with unclear rules, participants grasp for the stereotypical gender solutions and have strongly stereotypic expectations about gender. Further, with Martin (1993 and this volume, Chapter 10), we can argue that the domination of men at the top of a hierarchical structure facilitates the construction of male bonds – as the clear hierarchy is linked to gender, and offers a source of power.

How do these layers articulate themselves in a multinational organization? We can expect that they will take certain forms affected by the interplay of these cultural notions in a specific situation. For example, national culture frequently interlocks with professional practice as articulated in various national settings. Research on the civil service in different European settings makes this clear.

National culture in public bureaucracies

The literature on European bureaucracies is so general that one almost suspects that the only difference between bureaucracies is in matters of standard operating procedure (Page, 1987: 231). Certainly for the theme of this chapter, one common feature is the historical association of the civil service, whatever the nation, with male management (Stivers, 1993) – a connection which also socially constructs masculinities (Hearn, 1992b). But an assumption of cross-European consensus (beyond gender relations) in public service is clearly counter-intuitive. Unfortunately, there has been little sustained effort to compare across national boundaries (Page, 1987: 231), let alone to compare different international bureaucracies with each other. However, in collections which treat the public service country by country (Dogan, 1975; Kingdom, 1990; Page, 1985), as well as in the national culture literature, such as that of Barzini (1983), significant differences appear in the way countries do their public administration and in the people they trust to do it. As Kingdom writes:

> a civil service, perhaps more than any other institution, reflects the values and norms of the society it serves. . . . The role and nature of the civil service is in large measure shaped by the texture of the political culture, which defines the expectations and demands made of it . . . A political culture is essentially the sum of the attitudes and psychological orientations which citizens hold toward the political practices and institutions of the state. (1990: 5)

Bureaucracies vary so dramatically in the relationship they are expected to have with the polity and politicians, and in their recruitment, training and career patterns, that one can speak of different models. The differences go far beyond matters of style. Top British civil servants are still recruited from generalist backgrounds. Scandinavian, Dutch and German officials often have backgrounds in their own national law, while the French produce administrative specialists in policy analysis from specialized schools – the Grandes Ecoles and the Ecole Nationale d'Administration (ENA). In some countries the competitive examination and a strict career ladder are the only forms of personnel management present in the civil service, while in other countries ministries and administrations may pick and choose to find the most appropriate candidate for a job. Some countries encourage careers within the same technical area (Denmark) while others attempt to send their high-flyers through several policy areas in the early years of their career to produce all-rounders (UK). Some civil services have special corps that produce 'highly integrated subsets of individuals within the bureaucracy which have a pronounced organizational identity of their own' (Peters, 1987: 275). This is the all-purpose elite found in France, Italy or Spain. 'The personal contacts, prestige and knowledge that members of these corps obtain enables them to manage their own village very well, and the entire society not too badly' (ibid.).

National political culture also affects the distance that public servants are supposed to keep from the public. French culture puts its public officials on a pedestal. The training and recruitment process produces an elite or Mandarins (Dogan, 1975). Scandinavian culture demands that officials be accessible and understandable to the general public and democratically and representatively recruited, even across the gender gap.

It seems that such differences are incontrovertible, and that the practice of making public policy would also be affected by them. This is why the European experiment is so interesting, as from the beginning the European organs were created and staffed by officials with varying national backgrounds in part 'to have personnel in key organizational posts who are familiar with conditions in their own countries' (Michelmann, 1978: 478) and in part to ensure fairness. The European institutions are a new set of organizations reflecting beliefs about the way to manage political reality. Here we have a meeting of specific national traditions in relation to how bureaucracies should operate (hierarchical or egalitarian). The entering civil servants are people who have already received substantial professional training, thereby participating in an occupational subculture as well. There is also the necessity in the European integration process to develop a supranational cadre, which ideally is loyal to the organization rather than state of origin. Yet the results have been that 'the Commission *is* a remote, vaguely threatening and unintelligible institution to many European citizens . . . this [is] a fundamental defect in the Commission's legitimacy' (Ludlow, 1991: 25).

A discussion of the underlying assumptions of the organization has only recently become the order of the day,[6] thanks to the questions posed by increasing citizen recalcitrance to a European unity managed by the organs of the European Community. The people who start working for the European Community are often carriers of specific visions about 'the way we do things around here' from their own national settings. The Community worked consciously to try to create a cadre free from such loyalties, but the new institutions of intellectuals, bureau officials and technical experts are very far even from the most well-informed public. Evidence that this distance creates a legitimacy problem is to be found not only in the referendum behaviour and popular press, but also in the mushrooming of lobbyists and information bureaux in Brussels itself, where there are now more lobbying agencies than in any other city besides Washington, DC (Nonon and Clamen, 1991).

The institutions of the European Union

The hybrid of the bureaucratic traditions of the first five members of the European Community, hatched at the end of the 1950s, may be very far from some of the newer members' ideals of responsive public administration. Some officials have become aware recently that the way of organization itself expresses political culture: 'As the EC organizes, so shall it behave. If it organizes on a hierarchical basis, then one can expect quite a different outcome from an organization based on individualistic principles' (Shackleton, 1991: 583). Anthropologists have begun to question (Shore and Black, 1992; Abélès, 1992; Zetterholm, 1994) what this European culture might really be all about, and what values are being retained in the distillation, whether they are derived from national, professional or social structural (race, class, gender) sources. The institutions of the European Union grew in many ways like Topsy – responding at short notice to the insertion of new members and new tasks. While among upper-level civil servants some semblance of a 'European' identity has arisen, the gender dimension of that identity assumes a subordinate position for women and supports attitudes about women of the most stereotypical type, a kind of lowest common gender denominator. A possible hypothesis is that since national chauvinism is taboo, gender chauvinism among men becomes more pronounced.

One does not have to look hard for evidence of the male bias of the organizational culture – a visitor to the European Commission is handed a visitor's pass, in at least two languages, but the space for the name is preceded by for example, Herr, and M.(onsieur). Numerous elements in the way business is done can be characterized as favouring certain kinds of masculinity. Below we will treat the concrete issue of promotion, which fuels masculine competitive displays. First some general examples of cultural practices that are characteristic of the democratic deficit of the European institutions, but which can also be seen to be coloured by the masculinist management.

The departments of the European Commission are topped predominantly by men from professional cultures which are themselves highly masculine. Experts and officials deal primarily with science, economics and the legal regulation of trade, and the disciplines represented are engineering, natural science, law and economics (Rothacker and Colling, 1987). The Commission culture has been described by Ludlow (1991) as being very much 'of the book'. With increasing size this aspect will undoubtedly increase. The dominant national civil service cultures of France and Germany are used for this model, and it offers the path of least resistance. Commission employees remark that nationality presents few problems, because they all speak the same professional language. This language, created in engineering and law schools, is highly masculine, as pointed out by researchers such as Robinson and McIlwee (1991), McIlwee and Robinson (1992) and Epstein (1981).

Language is also an issue of gender games. The non-transparent Euro-speak, which resembles the official French/English primarily in its grammar, is composed heavily of acronyms, abbreviations and shorthand references. It is an organizational jargon every bit as opaque as that of stevedores or taxi-drivers. While such language may facilitate quick communication about the labyrinthine legal decision process, it also acts as an exclusionary mechanism, frequently favouring those in the position to stay up to date through informal contacts. Not incidentally, much informal communication occurs in settings where women are less likely to be present, such as beer cafés after work. That the images of language created in all-male settings are often strong constructors of a masculinized world view has been demonstrated by such work as that of Carol Cohn on the language of the defence industry and international politics (Cohn, 1987).

Feminist management literature warns about the dangers of informal channels of communication and setting, as well as the use of gender-biased common topics which exclude women. In the Commission, two frequently discussed casual topics are food and wine (reflecting the importance of the French bureaucratic tradition) and football (soccer). Football talk is considered an acceptable place to express legitimate national chauvinism, but also provides an opportunity to exhibit a particular form of masculinity.

An obvious material representation of the construction of femininities by masculinities in the Commission is in dress. A Scandinavian correspondent to the European institutions first noted how much she had changed in dress styles when sent to cover a farm story back home in Finland. Her high heels, the symbol of Eurocratic womanhood, proved a great handicap in covering the world outside the carpeted corridors of power (von Sydow, 1995). Women and men adopt a Euro-look, strongly influenced by the fashion from the southern member states. For women, the clothes are expensive, and confiningly feminine as the above-mentioned poster makes explicit, but men also generally adopt a sartorial code of designer suits and glasses.

For northern women the perception of the European institutions as being 'anti-woman' undoubtedly plays a large part in the undeniable gender gap in approval of increasing European integration. The Eurostat office interprets the gender gap from the perspective of southern women as in part a result of limited knowledge and low political interest (Melich, 1994). For northern women, the opposite is the case. The women are well informed, in particular about the gendered character of European institutions,[7] and this information provides one of the elements in the clear gap in approval between Scandinavian women and men in the recent European referenda (1992–4). What is especially embarrassing for the more progressively minded Europeans in Brussels is the fact that in general Europe has become less 'anti-feminist' since 1975 (Morgan and Wilcox, 1992) but the European institutions, with the exception of the somewhat toothless European Parliament, have had difficulty in following suit.

Recruiting and promoting Eurocrats: what are the results of asking the 'F' question of the European Commission?

The Eurocrat,[8] as a result of the recent European elections, and certainly influenced by the role of the popular English language press, is a well-known and not very popular figure. Eurocrats are full-time public officials, employed in the four institutions of the European Union. The organizational structure and traditions of these institutions have been heavily influenced by the hierarchical forms of the French public bureaucracy and the legalistic procedures of the German. On paper at least, one has a virtual ideal-typical Weberian bureaucracy, of full-time civil servants promoted on formal merits and making decisions on the basis of written rules, arranged in a hierarchy of authority with clear chains of command (Weber, 1968). The rules for recruitment, selection and promotion are highly 'bureaucratized', and reveal at present little of the new thinking that is currently revamping the public service in many of the member states (Page and Wouters, 1994).[9] Further, these rules can be expected to call forth certain kinds of masculinity in clearer and more dangerous forms than those already supported by the dominant organizational culture. Just as French and German public service traditions represented in the construction of the institutions have been late in considering the position of women, the European Union itself has had significant problems in achieving its own aims for affirmative action.

Gender analysis involves asking the 'feminist' F question of an organization (Calás and Smircich, 1992a), which may also lead to a better understanding of the two 'Ms' – masculinities and management. Although the Commission points to a proud tradition of stimulating equal opportunities policies in Europe at the supranational level (Commission of the European Communities, 1991b; Mazey, 1988; Cunningham, 1992), in its own house it provides a virtual laboratory of how bureaucracy can be gendered. At every step in its previous personnel policy it has shown indirect and sometimes direct discrimination against women. Its efforts to remedy the situation commenced in 1978 with the creation of a working party on equal opportunities, and escalated to the adoption of a second three-year positive action programme for female staff, and an autonomous unit for equal opportunities in the Personnel Directorate (Viqueira, 1993). The efforts remain frustrated by a lack of will at the top and encounter resistance from men at middle management level who feel threatened by action which they feel disadvantages them, such as announcements that 50 per cent of new unit heads will have to be women by the end of the year. A reading of this organization in terms of the aspects of masculinities expressed in a Gender-Organization-System proposed above can be illuminating.

Structuring femininities and masculinities in the European Commission

Working women in Europe are less well paid than males, seldom top managers, frequently part-time, and often on temporary contract (Maruani, 1992), in short, all the characteristics of the secondary labour circuit, and characteristics that should be poison to a well-run Weberian bureaucracy. On the surface, the situation of the European Commission's some 13,500 employees would seem to contrast with that of the European woman, but when one looks more closely it repeats, or even exaggerates, these features among its employees.

The Commission itself reports varying figures about total Commission functionaries.[10] About 45 per cent are female. Predictably, they are not evenly distributed throughout. Whereas 17 per cent of the male employees hold positions of responsibility, only 2 per cent of the female employees do (Viqueira, 1993: 9). Anecdotal reports from informants claim that a further 3–6,000 people are working in the scattered buildings of the Commission on temporary contracts or as national experts, or as cabinet personnel and, finally, in the fluctuating categories of trainees.[11] Here indeed is the first flight from Weberian bureaucratic ideal-typicality. Many Commission workers have employment contracts of short duration, with no sick leave and no holiday pay. Some of them with exceptional technical skills have managed to remain in temporary status for more than ten years. Among the less lucky (again, anecdotally, as there are no figures by sex) a rather high percentage is female. Many of these women are working in the clerical category C, secretarial staff, and are dependent on their direct bosses for renewal of their contract. It is little wonder that this category of staff has seemed to have the most victims of sexual harassment, as indicated in an internal survey. Colleagues working in other multinationals corroborate this observation, noting that male managers far from home see the secretarial pool as a legitimate 'poaching ground' to a much higher degree than in uninational settings.

A further aspect constructing a feminine subordinate mirror for domi-nant masculinities is the Brussels army of 'trailing' spouses, many with high educational qualifications, who lurch from one temporary position to another in the European institutions and are neither fish nor fowl for union, employer or politician. These vulnerable positions provide fodder for a stereotypical notion of the female as having a low commitment to the labour force, but are in fact a creation of the structural conditions of the Commission employment system. As the system itself cannot quickly respond to new tasks, informal solutions spring up, built on temporary personnel.

The 'regular' employees of the European Union are divided into four categories on the basis of required minimum education, ranging from the D grade which includes those doing janitorial work and delivery and security tasks, to the A grade which has a university degree as a basic prerequisite. The labour market segmentation common in the rest of Europe is also reflected in the Commission, with upper level women relegated to support-ing roles.

The mechanisms of employment policy – recruitment, socialization, reward (Harrison and Carroll, 1991) – play an important role in creating and transmitting organizational culture and constructing masculinities. These mechanisms are intended to attract and promote 'the right sort' and, as we will see below, the unstated norm of the 'right sort' is male with a certain sort of cultural baggage. The focus in what follows is on the top-level management, who can be considered to be the 'culture' bearers, although the gendered situation of the EU as a whole includes the stereo-typical relations of subordinance and dominance mirroring female and male jobs.

Recruitment

In practice, recruitment at top levels was initially carried out by hand-picking officials who agreed with the European vision. Gradually a meritocratic examination system was developed structured to obtain a certain sort of candidate. The system held traces not only of the British system of comparative weighing of merits, but also of the Belgian idea of creating a reserve list of candidates, and the Italian concept that the administration could in its final choice change the order of the candidates chosen by the comparative examinations (Ziller, 1988). One could argue that the successful candidate is already a culture bearer. The present selection procedure has been more and more vociferously criticized on counts not only of sexism but also class bias. In December 1993, Walker (1994) reports, some 56,000 sat for the first stage of the selection procedure, a multiple-choice exam of 120 items. Already at this stage women seem to have been at a disadvantage. The following stages, a demanding written exam, strict language tests and the final oral questioning, lead, through supposedly 'neutral' procedures, to a pool of primarily male candidates for the reserve lists. From these lists, about 70 per cent are eventually offered a job. One veteran of the Commission notes that as the recruitment process has become more and more competitive, the successful enter the service 'like young gods, assured that they are a golden elite'. Our interviews demonstrate that many have had some years of education in another country, or are the products of culturally mixed marriages. A 1987 study (Rothacker and Colling, 1987) indicated that 25 per cent of top Commission officials were educated outside their home country. This percentage will probably grow. Candidates also share a certain kind of educational background. Open exams, for generalists, are organized half as often as those for lawyers, economists and technicians. Further specialized institutions of training are springing up, both in universities providing programmes on Europe and in a special European University in Florence and an institute in Maastricht. The faculty of these institutions is skewed toward men, although the percentage of female students has been steadily increasing.

Given the special recruitment process, a slightly different type of civil servant emerges. He is more frequently a 'he' given the tasks of the Commission, older and often with a European profile before coming to Brussels. A-grade employees perceive no problems that can be chalked up to national cultural differences in their life at work. This result strengthens a conviction that recruitment focuses on people who will identify as Europeans. However, the same interviews indicate that if national differences are perceived on any dimension, it is that of gender. As noted above, internal survey results showed that women almost universally felt disadvantaged in the culture of the Commission, and the male interviewees in this study all indicated they would not be in their present positions if they had been born female. Both male and female interviewees definitely recognized national differences in attitudes to women and men and provided stories about sexual harassment, missed promotion chances and the charged atmosphere of the Commission which indicated that a pan-European gender identity is far from clear. The culture encourages masculinities that firmly identify women as a capital 'F' *Femme*, and therefore 'Other'.

In sum, since the first affirmative action efforts on the part of the Commission there has been concern about the clearly discriminatory effects of the present examination process, especially for A-level candidates. Somewhat fewer women enrol for the exam, but do poorly, even with revised exam schemes, on the elimination round of multiple-choice questions, which have been criticized as class biased (questions about opera, Latin) but also gender biased (never a question about cooking or child care). As the stages of selection proceed to the reserve list, the classic roadblocks for women in international careers also begin to appear. For A-level candidates with spouses, the trailing spouse problem discourages many from going further. Another consideration for international careers is the situation for children. Women informants frequently note the difficulties posed in raising children without one's normal social network of relatives (van Elsacker, 1991).

Socialization and training

Up until 1993, new entrants to the Commission received virtually no socialization at all. They were placed directly in a work situation and allowed to follow an introductory course about the structure of the European Community during their first few months. The Commission has decided to start doing intake twice a year to develop a greater *esprit de corps*. Reform attempts by the director of personnel Hays at the end of the 1980s aimed to bring some private sector ideas, including middle-level management training, into play.

> In the public service as a whole, training is not seen as having the importance which the private sector recognizes for it. In the Commission – which is a microcosm of the public service – rather than looking for profits people looked for efficiency and devotion to work which was of a largely political kind. At the senior level it was linked to European construction. In these cases motivation was seen largely in that aim, and people did not consider there was a technique which could be imported by training that could be useful. (Hays quoted in Tutt, 1989: 44)

Again access to training for higher-level functions has been primarily for men. Through the actions of the equal opportunity organs, some of the traditional courses about women in management and assertiveness have been added, in the face of what the union representative referred to as the 'ironic smiles of the men'. Only recently (Commission of the European Communities, 1991a, 1991b, 1992) have opportunities for training been opened to heavily female categories.

When no attempt is made to create an organizational culture holding certain basic values, socialization into the existing culture allows participants to grasp at the cultural survival straws they bring with them. The Commission makes an effort with its top civil servants to find people who will survive among the nations, but there is no effort to see that they will be equally tolerant of the sexes. The path of least resistance may be in polar and stereotypical gender presuppositions.

Careers: promotion and masculine norms

The ceiling in career paths is often low. In statistics provided by the Equal Opportunities Unit, only the lower A-levels of A7–A4 are included. That is because the glass ceiling for both men and women in the permanent positions begins there. The political and subtle national pressures at the top make it especially hard for women to break through, and the processes are as non-transparent as in the private sector. This may promote a negative attitude to the organization. While the EU is modelled on a justice system of career movement, in fact top positions are affected by geography and politics, much to the frustration of civil servants from the northern countries and the older member states. The Commission follows promotion practices at the top which defeat the meritocratic image of the bottom. Appointments above a certain level require – structurally and in practice – extensive lobbying. Because of this, cowboy-like masculinities are favoured and men elbow for high-visibility, interdepartmental tasks. While this leads to high competitiveness among men, the dynamic curiously also encourages male bonding to close out illegitimate competition such as that from women.

A second area of concern is what exactly the emerging culture and practice of the European Commission says about Europe. There is a fear, expressed most clearly in the Scandinavian debate about European institutions, that the common civil service denominator being chosen is very far from a democratic or feminist ideal.[12] Many countries have a political culture which finds a bureaucratic 'elite' very compatible with good government. Thus while forces for the last ten years have pushed affirmative action plans, the representation of women in the top functions of the Commission has remained the same and at some levels actually gone backwards. The low priority this and other issues of representation receive is taken to be indicative of the kind of administrative culture that has emerged. There is an increasing tendency toward what Shackleton calls the hierarchical model as the EU institutionally tries to solve the issue of who will do what (Shackleton, 1991: 594) Recruiting from the Grand Corps, and increasing political appointments work against a more egalitarian bureaucratic culture and practice and reinforce a male managerial hegemony.

The full-time salaried functionary – a male norm?

By asking about women in each stage of the personnel policy at the Commission it is easy to conclude that they have been disadvantaged.

Female Commission staff are well aware of this. As one informant said, 'You could probably ask any randomly chosen woman around here what has really changed since the work of the affirmative action groups began, and the answer would be "pitifully little".'

Even simple things such as the ability to work · part-time or to take a partial leave of absence for child care are made very difficult. Only eleven of the 3,800 or so A-level employees work part-time, and one respondent related a horror story related to getting a part-time job approved. The day of the European Commission is a Mediterranean one, while the Belgian setting is a northern one. The two-hour lunch breaks mean that higher Commission officials, even if not workaholics frequently have meetings commencing at 5.30, while children return from school at 4 p.m. Naturally, secretaries are also required at such meetings. Meetings could be much better planned, according to one informant, if the reality of families was taken into account. Without going into depth here, it is evident from the data in this project that women must make substantial adjustments to combine even a non-traditional family life with a job at virtually any level within the Commission. A recent study revealed that at the A level, 50 per cent of women are either unmarried or divorced; one level lower, at B, only 18 per cent were unmarried or divorced, while at C level once again the sacrifices of the long hours can be seen: just 52 per cent are married. Given that the age level of women at the top is higher, these are rather striking figures, as is the fact that 50 per cent of these A-grade women are childless. While it is true that women in management often must make hard choices, these figures are dramatic in an institution which should be an example for Europe (COPEC, 1994).

Conclusions

Using the lens of gender to examine the bureaucracy of the European Commission is an extremely useful exercise in revealing norms that have been in place since the nineteenth century (Ramsay and Parker, 1992). The assumptions made about the ideal 'bureaucrat', above both the interests of party and nation, are assumptions coloured by a world of gendered contexts where the male role is the rule. The above examination of some of the key areas of attention for affirmative action in the personnel policy of the Commission reveals that the Eurocrat idealized in the written rules would have a slightly harder time being a woman with a normal life cycle. The selection and promotion procedures, not to speak of the daily practice of the Commission, serve to reinforce the nineteenth-century masculine ideal of the European civil servant, and thus also to constrain the development of less polarized forms of masculinity.

At every step along the way, from selection to promotion, gender is written into the structure of the Commission, and has been part of the reason for the extremely skewed representation of women at the top. Yet many national bureaucracies twenty years ago were equally skewed, and in a number of countries commitment to equal opportunities has made gains. Why the recalcitrance in the Commission? It is both a 'new' and an expanding and changing organization, faced by increasingly loud external demands that it begin to look more 'representative' and should be able to respond to such demands.

Part of the explanation for the stagnation of equal opportunity efforts may perhaps be found in the Gender-Organization-Culture system where beliefs about and practices of gendering, lying at a deeper level, may be the last element of national heritage brought into the Commission to change. In a place where people of many different national backgrounds meet, there may be a tendency to grasp at the few things that unite, including assumed beliefs about gender. This may be compounded by the equal opportunities initiatives of the Commission. The dramatic targets translate into diminished promotional opportunities for men, and seem to threaten even the merit basis of the promotions up to the A4 grade. At higher levels the only way to achieve targets would be a 'woman-only' policy. Some men may experience a public–private warp, as they live in a traditional domestic set-up where a well-educated spouse has given up career aspirations to follow the husband. These same middle-management men now find their own career opportunities blocked by women. The resentment provides grounds for men to emphasize their shared interests in anti-woman displays of their masculinity.

As most research on affirmative action programmes has demonstrated, without a significant and dynamic will from the top, little will change (Hammond, 1993). In the Commission, the top is 98 per cent male, and women in middle management are actually decreasing, while the numbers of managers increase. In this situation, an international, and therefore blunter, masculine cultural norm of the mildly amused smile when any aspect of equal opportunity is discussed becomes a common denominator. Through male bonding, which occurs over and above the identities of nation, new forms of resistance develop that work against a European Administration of men and women on a more equal footing, let alone an administration that could have a 'feminist' face. The growing confluence of gender theory and organization theory can bring understanding and provide a hope for a women-friendly Europe rather than one that resuscitates stereotypes and anachronisms.

Notes

1. Interview material for this chapter is taken from the pilot project 'The Making of a Eurocrat', funded by the Belgian National Science Foundation. A total of 30 qualitative interviews with A-level functionaries of the European Commission have provided information.

2. Until 1995, with the entry of Sweden, Finland and Austria, who demanded a better policy on equality. Five of today's twenty Commissioners are female.

3. An insight from David Morgan Chapter 3 this volume.

4. Joan Acker, who also whistle-blew on the issue of social class and gender in the early 1970s, wrote a seminal article (Acker and van Houten, 1992) noting the blindness of several classic authors. Kanter's pathbreaking *Men and Women of the Corporation* opened a few more eyes in 1977, but the issue of organizational theory and gender did not really get on to the main agenda of organizational theorists until the 1980s with the work of theorists like Mills (1989, 1992), Morgan (1986), Hearn and Parkin (1992) or Burrell and Hearn (1989). For an extended discussion of the history of the intertwine, see Mills and Tancred (1992: Introduction), or Witz and Savage (1992).

5. Except perhaps in the Netherlands (Ringeling, 1985; Frissen, 1988; Frissen and van Westerlaak, 1990) and in Sweden (Ahrne, 1985; Daun, 1988). Here, given the political culture, an extreme distance between decision makers and the public is seen as problematic and as evidence of a culture that needed to be changed. In both of these countries the public sector has undertaken significant efforts to change the bureaucratic culture.

6. Academics such as Ness and Brechin (1988) call for a bridging of the gap in the disciplinary valley between law students studying the community and political scientists, while Hix (1994), in his review of political scientific approaches, argues for rescuing it from an entirely international relations approach. It is notable that there is virtually no literature looking at the institutions of the European Community from a gender perspective.

7. This refers not only to the relatively low percentual representation of women in the European Parliament (25% after elections in 1994 as opposed to 39% in Finland or Norway, 42% in Sweden in 1994) but also to the extremely low number of women in top positions.

8. The term was most likely coined by Spinelli (1966).

9. This is not to say that reforms have not been under discussion. It is clear to everyone involved that the eventual expansion of the Union with four new member states will make the present institutional arrangement impossible. Further the Treaty of Maastricht stipulates a thoroughgoing review of all the institutions of the Union in 1996 and the European Parliament has already begun filing away at the personnel situation, with a Conservative proposition that some services be privatized.

10. Hays reports 16,300 with 3,500 at A grade (Hays, 1989: 31), while Viqueira, (1993: 10) suggests 13,386. Journalist Walker gives us 18,000 (1994), while one week later colleague Watson gives 15,000 (1994). Figures presented to the COPEC committee on 14 June 1994 gave 12,976 effective officials and a recruitment list of 904.

11. A parliamentary enquiry surfaced some 3,165 employees in these sorts of statuses in 1993 (European Parliament, 1994: 11).

12. How that feminist public sector might work is illustrated by one of the submissions produced in the Swedish KOM project, 'Men and Women Working Together' (Swedish Working Environment Fund, 1994). Public bureaucrats speculated on how their work might be organized differently if women ran the show. The results were showcased for European administrators in the preparation for Swedish membership, and indicated that the Swedes hope significantly to change working arrangements in Brussels.

10

Gendering and Evaluating Dynamics: Men, Masculinities, and Managements

Patricia Yancey Martin

For five years, I served on the Athletic Policy Board of a large public university. Chaired by a faculty member and containing about a third faculty members, the board met monthly with the director of university athletics, a man, to make policy recommendations about varsity athletics to the university president. (Varsity athletics include intercollegiate sport competitions that are regulated by the National Commission on Athletics Accreditation.) As a woman, I was discomfited at these meetings on more than one occasion. One incident involved a conversation I overheard between two men – white, middle-aged professors with extensive publication records, considerable stature among their peers, and a history of involvement in varsity athletics. In the incident, one complained to the other about a dean who is widely respected and well liked – and a woman. He talked in an ostensible whisper that was, it seemed to me, intended for my ears about how terribly the dean was doing and how something had to be done. His comments were graphic, rude and hostile. Although I do not recall them exactly, I remember my reaction to them. The incident struck me as 'jockish' and woman-bashing; feeling that the comments were made for my benefit, I was repulsed. I could practically smell the 'locker-room sweat'.

In reflecting on my experiences several years hence, I still wonder what I saw. Did I witness a routine criticism of a dean's performance? Did the speaker direct his comments (in part) to me? Even if not, I believe he did not mind if I heard. He could have spoken softly or turned his eyes away. If his comments were intended to make me feel badly, they succeeded; if intended to turn me against the dean, they failed. If the speaker wanted me to 'care less' about varsity athletics, again he succeeded. Both men were 'insiders' and my thoughts were, 'If that's how they think and behave, they can have it! Not my cup of tea.' If the speaker was reminding me of men's power in the university, letting me know that 'guys get girls who get power', I got the message. My thoughts were: 'What am I doing here? Why should I participate in a context that exposes me to such abuse?'

Would two women criticize a male dean in such a quasi-public and vitriolic way? Would a man who overheard the comments see them as criticism of a man '*qua man*' or of a 'gender-free' dean? Why did I hear the comments as criticisms *of a woman*? I may have done so because my presence in a hyper-masculine athletic facility made me keenly aware of being a *wo-man, a non-man*. The speaker had been a candidate for the deanship himself. I had served on the Search Committee (of twenty members) and spoken on behalf of the woman who was chosen; but I had only one vote and the final decision was made by the university vice-president, who was a man. Did the man 'pay me back' for supporting someone besides himself, and a woman at that, for the deanship?

As with many work-related evaluational dynamics, competition was involved. Competition activates identity comparisons and often swells anxieties about the self in contrast with others, particularly for men on the job (Kimmel, 1992, 1993). Robert Weiss (1990) reports that middle-class men are obsessively concerned with how they compare to other men at work. His study of eighty professionally qualified men showed them as having 'pervasive anxiety' about their 'place in the community of work'.

> At work everyone is always on trial. It is hard to relax . . . because every performance yields an assessment to those who witness it. . . . A comment is listened to not only for its manifest meaning but also for its indication of personal stake . . . Often without being aware that this is what they are doing, men take notes on who has power and who is knowledgeable, who has inside information and who has sound intuition. They appraise alliances and enmities and the nuances of people's feelings about each other. . . . They are exquisitely alert to indications of others' appraisals of themselves, and so they speculate, sometimes obsessively, about what it means that an assignment was or wasn't made to them, or that a supervisor did or didn't ask them for a report, or that a colleague was or wasn't deferential in a meeting (Weiss, 1990: 19)

Men's concerns about their standing at work may reflect a fear of losing out – for example security of employment, security of manhood – more than a drive to win (cf. Stoltenberg, 1993). Perhaps my colleague was embarrassed at having lost the deanship competition; exacerbating the pain of his loss, the victor was a woman! His identity as a man and security in the [male] community of work may have been threatened. Worry that his associates would view him in a lesser light may have prompted his attack. Whatever else may be true, I believe I witnessed a 'gendering episode', an enactment of *competitive masculinity* (see Kerfoot and Knights, 1993; Collinson and Hearn, 1994) by a powerful man that framed a powerful woman as flawed and of dubious value to the organization.

Interpretive framework: deconstructing managerial evaluations by deconstructing masculinity(ies)

This episode allows me to pose questions about gender and hierarchy, specifically the ways in which masculinism (see below, p. 188ff.), men and hegemonic masculinities continue to dominate in the structure, culture and practices of work organizations (Connell, 1987; Burton, 1987; Reskin,

1988; Brittan, 1989; Acker, 1990; Martin, 1991; Hearn and Morgan, 1990; Kerfoot and Knights, 1993; Collinson and Hearn, 1994; Steinberg, 1995). It also introduces the topic of my chapter – that is, *evaluations*, both informal and formal, and the *interactional styles of men* who make evaluations in managerial contexts. Why, how and with what consequences do hegemonic masculinities (Connell, 1987) operate through *formal and informal evaluation decisions*? Evaluation and interaction are inextricably linked, as my data show, and the significance of evaluational processes in the reproduction of gender divisions and of organizational culture, structure and power relations more broadly is neglected in the literature. I explore the power of men as managers and of managers as men in an attempt simultaneously to problematize *hierarchy* and *gender* as forms of organizational power and control. Hierarchy and gender are embedded in the organizational practices of evaluation and interaction. My goal is to address ways that they are entangled, or conflated, in the *masculinist* discourse, perceptions and practices of organizational participants and in the *patriarchal relations* that this discourse justifies. According to Kerfoot and Knights (1993: 661, extending Brittan, 1989: 3–5), masculinism 'denotes the ideology that naturalizes and justifies men's domination over women; and patriarchy is the structure of unequal power relations sustained by this ideology'.[1]

Gender divisions, segregation and occupational sex-typing characterize labour markets around the globe (Adler and Izraeli, 1988a, 1993; Reskin and Roos, 1990; Jacobs, 1992; Lorber, 1994). Furthermore, men dominate the positions of power and often reproduce their power/authority, cultural values and sense of identity – as men and as managers – in segregated work contexts (Burton, 1987, 1991; Cockburn, 1991; McIlwee and Robinson, 1992; Acker, 1990; Reskin, 1988; Milkman and Townsley, 1994). As noted by Burton (1991), 'masculine values' permeate the cultures of most organizations (also see Kanter's 'masculine ethic' of management, 1977). Given this state of affairs, evaluational dynamics associated with men's managerial relations and practices are consequential. Managers select, reward and promote others through the conduct of routine 'evaluations' that are ostensibly gender free. Selection and promotion are central features of managerial discretion and power yet they are difficult to study because managers are loath to expose what they do to outsiders (including to sociologists; see Jackall, 1988; Leidner, 1993a; Kunda, 1992, regarding the difficulties of gaining research access in organizations). A theme of my analysis is that these dynamics – that is, managerial evaluations – are dominated by men, embody masculinism, and reproduce varying masculinities. Women's representation in work organizations, and in management, has increased dramatically over four decades – from 9 per cent in 1950 to 40 per cent in 1990 in the US – but their success at gaining senior posts in hierarchical organizations has improved minimally (Lorber, 1994; Jacobs, 1992; Reskin and Ross, 1995; also see Boyd et al., 1991, on Canada). My analysis suggests that men's enactments of masculinity(ies) in and through their enactments of management-related evaluations reproduce men's dominance, assert men's rights to the best jobs, positions, opportunities and honours, and frame women as less valued and less worthy of powerful statuses and options.

In hierarchical contexts, promotion entails competition for scarce positions, and competition intensifies the identity concerns of the evaluated and the power/authority of the evaluators (Weiss, 1990). Evaluation is inextricably united with interaction, as my case vignettes demonstrate. Informal evaluations comingle with formal processes and relations, thus muddling the alleged gender-neutrality of various 'objective' evaluational practices (Martin, 1982). My cases (below) show how informal processes that enact gender affect formalized evaluation and promotion procedures (see West and Fenstermaker, 1995). For example, a decision-maker selects a personal friend, who is also a man, over an arguably 'more qualified' candidate, who is a woman, to head a unit of a professional school; four men on a presidential selection committee skip the formal presentation of the only woman but skip none made by ten men candidates; a male chemist attacks his woman supervisor, causing her to fear for her life, because he cannot find a job. The cases show how interaction and gendered interactional styles play out in managerial hierarchies. Selection, judgement and related social processes are characterized by the simultaneous and compounded gendered and hierarchical power of men who are managers/managers who are men.

By *evaluation*, I refer to assessments of others' potential, talents, legitimacy, worthiness, skill and performance. I am concerned with evaluations *associated with managerial relations* (Collinson, 1992: 17–20 offers a broad and critical definition of management and managing). Managers evaluate subordinates; subordinates evaluate managers; peers evaluate each other; policy boards and committees evaluate candidates, officers and nominees, for example for honours and awards. Because managerial work routinely occurs in person-to-person encounters, the growth of managerial jobs multiplies the opportunities to enact gender at/through work. A substantial amount of the work of university professors and research scientists is done in committees, research groups, task forces and work teams. As my data suggest, these contexts provide many opportunities for men to *do* masculinity(ies) in the course of *do*ing work (Martin, 1995).

In seeking to problematize the evaluational and masculinities enactments of men, I make three assumptions: (a) gender is culturally and structurally *embedded* in organizational arrangements (Hearn, 1992b: Chapter 7; Acker, 1990, 1992; Roper, 1994a, and Chapter 11 in this volume); (b) power is a constitutive aspect of gender relations and dynamics in organizations (Coleman, 1990; Kondo, 1990; Cockburn, 1994); and (c) members are proactively *gendered* through the discursive, relational and material dynamics and arrangements of organizations (Coleman, 1990; Kerfoot and Knights, 1993; Roper, 1994a; Martin, 1991, 1995). By *gendering* activity, I mean the 'doing of gender' (West and Zimmerman, 1987; West and Fenstermaker,

1993, 1995; Fenstermaker et al. 1991) – that is, men's and women's *strategic assertions* (Kondo, 1990: Chapter 1) about their gender statuses, identities, characteristics, rights or privileges. I am especially interested in men's 'doings' of masculinity, or what Wil Coleman calls 'the doings of men' that entail masculinity(ies) enactments (Coleman, 1990: 195; Burton, 1991; Cockburn, 1991, 1994).

In a separate paper (Martin, 1995), I propose that (many) men *enact masculinity(ies)* in the course of enacting work activities and relations and, in so doing, conflate the two dynamics that are allegedly independent of each other. This *conflation of masculinity(ies) and working activities* affects women (and many men) who work with, for or around men in largely negative ways.[2] One consequence is women's relegation to the status of *other* or outsider, beyond the bounds of men's worlds, relations and dynamics (Hollway, Chapter 2 in this volume) and men's denial (and lack of awareness) that such relegation is occurring or is related to gender. Since (some) men hold nearly all of the powerful and high-status positions in work organizations, their behaviour is highly consequential for women.

Evaluational opportunities provide, in Coleman's terms, 'occasions' for men's 'doings of masculinity' (1990). Why is that? I seek to identify the conditions under which men mobilize masculinity(ies) in the course of evaluating others, particularly women, at work. With Kondo (1990: Chapter 1), I assume that gender, work and organization comprise shifting fields of power, meaning and identity that are conditioned by cultural influences and material relations associated with class, race, nation state and historical period and conditions. Each of my vignettes illustrates how men's enactments of masculinity(ies) in the course of doing evaluations devalue women. They also show the embeddedness of organizational relations and dynamics in a *gendered substructure* of relations and arrangements (see Acker, 1990; Goffman, 1977; West and Fenstermaker, 1995). Despite having arguably superior qualifications, Paula in the first vignette was passed over by Fred's supervisor and then by Fred when she applied for a job. In the second vignette, Jane was distressed when the woman candidate was not 'taken seriously' by powerful men on the presidential search committee. Vivien in the third vignette 'changed the subject' when a male colleague disparaged a woman prize-winner's qualifications and was frightened by her subordinate's anger when he failed to find a permanent job.

Complexity theory in physics claims that very small changes at an early point in a process, such as the trajectory of a falling feather, can produce very large differences in outcome (for a view of complexity theory's relevance to social science see Gregersen and Sailer, 1993). For example, two identical feathers can end up in very different places if, when dropped from a tall building, one encounters a wind current while the other does not. One may land in a river twenty miles away and the other on a canopy of the building from which both were dropped. Similar dynamics occur, I believe, in universities and research labs that are, we know from research, pervasively structured by gender divisions and sex-typing of jobs (Morgan,

1981; DiNitto et al., 1984; Traweek, 1988; also Jacobs, 1992; Tomaskovic-Devey, 1993). Paula's, Jane's and Vivien's experiences of men's masculinity enactments in 'work-related' meetings, similar to my experiences on the Athletic Board, may seem trivial. But their impact can be substantial. Clare Burton (1991) describes women's 'cumulative burden of trivial experiences' with male bias at work. As a result of such experiences, Paula may become cynical and leave the organization (which she in fact did); Jane may refuse to participate on future selection committees; Vivien may shun contact with co-workers who denigrate women, restricting her access to informal con-tacts and information. Acker (1990) notes, with others (Hearn, 1992b), that organizations are premised on a gendered substructure that situates women and men differently both inside and beyond the workplace. Many internal dynamics that frame and treat women and men 'the same' are actually male-preferential because they are premised on men's lives, men's bodies, men's time, men's expectations, and men's ability to valorize work over home, family and personal life (Acker, 1990; Milkman and Townsley, 1994). Over time, such dynamics direct men and women to different places, 'one in the river twenty miles away, one on the canopy of the building'. I discuss gender-based framing near the chapter's end.

Men can devalue women through behaving in a masculinist manner. For example, being autocratic or highly directive are 'leadership' styles norma-tively associated with men but not women (see Eagly and Johnson, 1990 for a meta-analysis of gender and leadership styles). Women engineers say the 'male style of interacting' they are expected to display, *not the work of engineering*, is the most difficult and disliked part of their job (McIlwee and Robinson, 1992).

> Where engineers as a group are powerful, the culture takes on a form strongly identified with the male gender role, emphasizing aggressive displays of technical self-confidence as the criteria for success. As such, it devalues the gender role attributes of women, *defining professional competence in strictly masculine terms*. (McIlwee and Robinson, 1992: 138; emphasis mine)

When a woman adopts a 'male interactional style', I have heard men describe her by saying: 'She kicks ass with the best of them' or 'She's as hard as nails.' But such compliments cut two ways. While acknowledging a woman's ability to 'act like a man', for example in mobilizing competitive masculinity, they acknowledge her violation of norms associated with 'emphasized femininity' and her status as woman (Connell, 1987). Yet men may view women's enactments of masculinities as illegitimate and/or unattractive (Martin, 1991; Pleck et al., 1994). The 'community of work' to which men orient their behaviour and concerns is a world of, by and for men; women may 'fit' uneasily in this community except in subordinate, supportive positions and roles (see Cockburn, 1991; Weiss, 1990).

In the opening example, a faculty member criticized a dean. From the standpoint of two privileged statuses – professor and *man* – the speaker may have believed he was commenting on a *gender-free* dean. But a professor in his audience, myself, experienced his comments as 'gendered', an attack *by* a man *on* a woman. Situating the incident within a masculinist athletic facility, and a university that has historically devalued women, the woman's – my – response is perhaps explained. Both the speaker and I enjoy privileged academic rank but we work in a university where men and masculinities are hegemonic (see Connell, 1987, 1995; Coleman, 1990; Kerfoot and Knights, 1993; Messerschmidt, 1993), where few women hold senior faculty or administrative positions. As a woman in this environment, I experienced a powerful man's criticism of a powerful woman as a show of patriarchal masculinity that defined both the dean and me as other and, as such, as devalued (cf. Roper, 1994a; Hollway, Chapter 2 in this volume; Messner et al., 1993).[3]

The cases below provide *evocative* examples (see Kondo, 1990) of masculinism and men's mobilizations of masculinity(ies) in evaluating men and women at work. Masculinism, or the valorization of men and masculinities over women and femininities, is played out in the cases through men's enactments of patriarchal practices that promote men and reject, exclude and/or blame women (see Kerfoot and Knights, 1993: 661–5). (The cases' failure to address men's competition with each other should not be interpreted as evidence that it is absent from the contexts I describe.)

Data and methods

The case study materials were gathered through open-ended interviews with women and men in two universities and a research and development laboratory of a multinational corporation. Collected in the early 1990s, the data are part of an ongoing project on gender and organizations (see Martin, 1995) that has included in-depth interviews (N = 22 – 12 women, 10 men, with one interview totalling 14 hours over four sessions), group interviews (N = 6, with groups ranging from two to six), observation of training and other meetings (N = 6, with number of participants ranging from 15 to 90), and the use of archival materials ranging from videotapes produced for promotional purposes (internal as well as external) to annual reports, policy statements, and internal letters and memoranda. (I have also interviewed the staff of three consulting firms that specialize in 'diversity' issues and sell their services, often in the form of training materials and sessions, to corporations.) Data in the first vignette came from interviews with all persons named in the story (and others not quoted). Data for the second and third vignettes are from one informant only, the woman in each case. My analysis strategy (similar to that of Kondo, 1990) is to *critically thematize and problematize* the data relative to my research questions – that is, masculinities and men, evaluations and managements. Other than Vivien who is a British Commonwealth native, my informants are native-born US citizens. All are white, hold advanced disciplinary or professional degrees and have secure jobs or favourable prospects. They differ most on gender, age and work-related experiences. Informants and employers are given pseudonyms to protect their identities.

The vignettes

Story 1: promoting men

Fred, Paula and George hold comparable educational and professional qualifications. They are the only three staff in a special unit of a professional school situated in a large, public university. (Professional schools in US universities include engineering, business, education, social work, law, public administration, medicine, music and theatre, pharmacy, dentistry, and so on.) Fred and Paula are in their early forties; George is several years younger. Fred and Paula are more experienced professionally than George is and Paula is much more experienced in the unit's specialty area; in fact, Paula has received national acclaim for her work in that area. Fred's area of expertise differs from the unit's; George aspires to specialize in the unit's area but at the time was minimally experienced. A crisis developed when Fred selected George over Paula for a teaching assignment – the opportunity to teach a formal course – that both George and Paula wanted and that involved the unit's specialty area. (Like Paula and George, Fred had never taught a formal university course but Fred did not want the assignment.) Fred's selection of George over Paula threatened to destroy the unit; that is, Paula threatened to bring a legal suit with a charge of sex discrimination. At the time I interviewed, the climate of the unit was chilly. Fred and George were not speaking to Paula; higher administration was angry with Fred and George; and Paula was upset with everyone.

Paula believed Fred based his selection of George over her on subjective, emotional grounds. Whereas Fred admitted he *liked* George more than Paula, he denied that his decision was based on his emotions. Fred said George's career merited the 'developmental opportunity' more than Paula's did. Fred ironically gave identical reasons for George's selection and Paula's rejection: *inexperience*. According to Fred, 'George would have benefited [from the new experience] and we [the unit] would not have lost much if he failed.' Fred rejected Paula's petition, saying 'she lacked experience in teaching' and did not *need* the opportunity for her career. Fred did not acknowledge the contradictions in his reasoning about the candidates' relative levels of inexperience and career aspirations.

Paula believed her experience and expertise made her the obvious choice for the job, 'on rational grounds'. She experienced Fred's selection of George as a putdown and an affront to her seniority and greater expertise, experience and professional standing. She believed she lost out to 'old boy cronyism', not to 'rational logic' or 'objective' considerations. Before he made the decision, Fred talked about it informally on many occasions with George but not with Paula. Fred did not interview either Paula or George about the assignment nor did he ask them about their vision or plans for teaching the course. His dislike of Paula influenced him to avoid talking with her; indeed, he tried to avoid seeing her at work. Paula learned about Fred's decision in a memorandum that Fred addressed to his supervisor. George knew what was coming; Paula had no idea. Fred had not asked Paula what she thought about his assigning the job to George in order to develop his career. Fred's announcement hit Paula like a bolt from the blue, a *fait accompli* that offended her sense of fair play. Paula complained to the dean that 'the boys ganged up on me', and the dean, after investigating, agreed with her and withdrew the opportunity from the unit.

Would Fred have informed a senior man by memo that he was *not* choosing him, without discussing it or finding out how the man would react if the outcome were not to his liking? Why did Fred assume he could do this with impunity where Paula was concerned? Fred took weeks to make the decision and was visited and lobbied daily by George about the matter. George, saying he pressured Fred to give him the assignment, stressed his need for the job, telling Fred: 'I *need* this chance [to teach] . . . it's critical for my career.' Paula and Fred agreed that Paula told Fred *once* that she wanted the assignment, at which time she offered to share it with one or both of them, if Fred thought that best. Paula did not remind Fred repeatedly, as George did, of her interest. Fred said he thought Paula would be disappointed but he did not expect her to 'have a fit.' Paula expected Fred to compare her and George's relative experience and expertise and find in her favour. Fred compared them but the outcome was not what Paula expected. Fred chose George in order to help *develop* him and rejected Paula because she did not *need to be developed*.

If George had been the older and higher-status suppliant, would Fred have selected younger Paula in order to develop her career? Or would Fred have chosen George in deference to George's greater age, status and reputation? Although we cannot know, I think Fred would have selected George, from a reluctance to offend George and a hedge against the future. George might be in a position to help Fred some day; as a woman, Paula's odds of attaining such a position are lower. If Fred had prioritized the students' interests in having the most qualified instructor, he might have selected Paula over George. In justifying his selection of George, Fred appears to have enacted *paternalistic masculinity* that prioritized George's need to develop his career over Paula's qualifications and the students' interest in being taught by the more knowledgeable and experienced person. As a man, Fred may have understood the central importance to George of his 'standing' in the (men's) 'community of work' (Weiss, 1990; Kimmel, 1993).

Fred and Paula both acknowledged Paula's superior qualifications, relative to Fred, for *Fred's job*. Paula was experienced in the unit's specialty area, indeed was nationally recognized in it. When both interviewed for the director's job, the faculty liked them both and the dean favoured Paula; but the decision maker, a male assistant dean, selected Fred. Fred said the assistant dean chose him because he is a man and because they were old friends (Fred failed to mention that they also shared a specialty area in their profession); Paula believed the assistant dean chose Fred over her for these same reasons. Fred had said he would not join the unit unless he was made director; Paula said she would join even if she were not made director.

Did Paula's 'resistance' to Fred cause him to frame her as less deserving of the teaching assignment? Did Fred select George because he identified with him as a fellow *man* whose career was primary in importance (cf. Weiss, 1990)? Was Paula right to accuse Fred of 'cronyism', of ignoring her 'objective' qualifications and selecting George on 'personal-liking' grounds? Why did Fred ignore Paula's offer to co-teach the course with George, which would probably have pacified her and been acceptable to George? Did Fred use the decision as an 'occasion for doing masculinity' (see Coleman, 1990), for asserting his gender and hierarchical superiority to Paula, to show who was boss?

Micro-gendering acts such as Fred's reflect and reinforce macro-structural patterns that sort women and men into different jobs, units, hierarchical positions, honours and opportunities. The gender-organized workplace that favours men over women for valued opportunities set a stage for the assistant dean to valorize Fred over Paula and for Fred to valorize George over Paula (cf. Acker, 1990). Gendered conditions and dynamics, past and current, affect evaluators' perceptions and actions and help reproduce gender inequality even when 'intentional gender bias' is absent on the evaluator's part (Collinson et al., 1990; Milkman and Townsley, 1994; Martin, 1995).

Story 2: rejecting women

Dr Jane Coats, a professor of humanities at a large, research university in the US, served on an advisory committee to search for a new president. The committee consisted of half internal faculty and staff and half external alumni and friends. All but two of eighteen external members were men who were financial supporters of the university's intercollegiate men's athletic programme. (Several of them had endowed athletic scholarships or influenced their firms to donate large sums of money to the programme). Jane said four men skipped the presentation of the only woman candidate on the short list.

In the first round of interviews, one candidate was a white woman, one a black man, nine were white men. The initial interview involved a 90-minute meeting during which the candidate made an opening statement (10 to 30 minutes) and Search Committee members asked questions. The woman, Anne Sims, was a sitting president of a small university in a distant state. Her campus did not have Division I athletic programme status and her curriculum vitae did not list many publications or administrative jobs. Still, some members felt Sims's success as a sitting president showed she merited consideration. Most committee members, including Jane, felt that Sims and the African American man were 'affirmative action' candidates, chosen to make the search process look 'politically correct'. Jane never thought Sims had a real chance at the job although, she said, Sims's first interview was 'outstanding'.

Four men on the committee who were major athletic supporters failed to attend Sims's initial 90-minute interview. Jane was stunned by their behaviour. The men missed no other presentations, including the one by the African American man. Jane describes their explanation for their absence.

> When I asked them where they had been, they said they were meeting with our [sitting] president because this was the only time he could see them that week. They said they'd explained to President Sims [beforehand] and promised to view her videotape at home [each candidate was videotaped during their initial visit]. While this explanation mollified me slightly, I still felt their willingness to miss the interview showed they didn't take Sims's candidacy seriously. If they thought she had a chance of being president, they would not have skipped the interview, I feel sure. . . . Their action infuriated me.

When she 'saw Sims through these men's eyes', Jane says her heart sank. They were a visible, vocal group who sat up front and dominated the question and answer sessions of the interviews. Their absence was noticed by everyone on the committee. Jane said the experience showed her that 'leaders can lead only if followers follow' and she saw that these men had no intention of 'following' Sims.

> The followers of a [university] president – the faculty, students, staff, alumni, boosters and friends – make him or her a failure or success. I saw [that] this woman could not succeed as president of my university because some of the followers whose hard work is required for success would not follow and work hard to *make* her a success. I realized I was a party to institutional sexism. I saw that President Sims's selection for my university would be a liability because the people she needed to 'make it work' would not 'make it work *for her*'. I concluded she *should* not be [the] president.

Jane said Sims did an excellent job in her first interview, among the best of any candidate. She invoked the values and philosophy of a liberal arts education (the institution is strongly committed to the liberal arts); showed she had read about the university; and knew more about the campus than any other candidate except one. Sims knew that one of the men who skipped her presentation had endowed a faculty chair in his family's name. Jane wanted to support Sims's candidacy but realized that Sims would be likely to fail at her university. Jane said her state-wide university system had had a woman chancellor who was not liked or supported by powerful politicians and that this had caused turmoil in the system for several years.

> While I would love to have a woman president, I saw that this woman could not do the job at my university. From self-interest, I wanted my university to have an effective leader. I became a partner with the athletic boosters in saying, 'This candidate is not right for this university at this time.' I joined them in opposing President Sims's candidacy, rather *in failing to favour* her. Perhaps they would not support *any woman*; I failed to support this one. I realized if powerful followers opposed any woman even the best woman would have a hard time being a success. What a depressing thought!

Jane said an affluent external member, in his mid-seventies, commented during the interview process, 'We have to look at the wives as much as the candidates.' Every time he said this, the chair politely asked him to say spouses or partners, not wives. The speaker never acknowledged the request and would, in time, repeat the comment. A male faculty member said he explained to the man that Sims was a 'real' candidate but the man said, 'No, no woman can do the job.' Jane thought the reference to wives was the older man's way of challenging Sims's and indeed all women's legitimacy for the job. Jane said everyone knew this man would not support a woman president. In contrast, several men on the committee said they *would* support the *right* woman. The men who skipped Sims's presentation showed their scepticism about her candidacy, Jane says, framing Sims as an 'affirmative action' candidate and no more.

This vignette suggests that women may have difficulty progressing in organizations because powerful men who select them view them as 'inappropriate' for the job. Men prefer men for these positions, for reasons of identity, culture and power. As Kanter (1977) and others have noted, men 'homosocially' reproduce themselves in many selection dynamics. In mobilizing masculinity that views only men as legitimate leaders in a university, (some) men reject women as a class. Powerful men do not have to actively oppose women's candidacy for such jobs; rather, they can allow women (and men of colour and other men who violate the prototype) to fail by withholding the support, attendance, guidance or help that are needed for success (Cockburn, 1991). In discriminating among candidates and deciding to support only those who possess certain hegemonic qualifications – white, male, tall, articulate, supportive of big-time varsity athletics – powerful men mobilized hegemonic masculinity and shut Sims out.

The white, middle-aged, tall, physically attractive man who was selected as president differed from Sims in two ways besides on gender. He was a sitting president of a state university, as she was, but the presidency was his second. At both institutions, furthermore, he had aggressively built intercollegiate athletic programmes. His record of support for intercollegiate athletics, combined with the experience of 'putting his pants on every morning as a [university] president' – as one male committee member described him – worked in his favour. Several men on the selection committee suspected Sims of not strongly supporting intercollegiate athletics, men's football and basketball in particular (cf. Messner, 1992 on masculinity(ies) and sports for US men). Ironically, the men who skipped Sims's interview did so to meet with the sitting president over their concerns about men's football at the university.

Story 3: blaming women

Dr Vivien Jackson, a research chemist in a large, multinational corporation, supervises other scientists and technicians in her laboratory. She distributes resources such as space, equipment and supplies, and she has authority to tell people what to do. Besides running the lab, she does research and has several patents to her credit (which in corporate research labs is both a guarantee and sign of high status). Vivien, respected by her peers and superiors, has been with Azura Corporation for twelve years. Sean Glaskens, a post-doctoral fellow from a small teaching college, spent a year in Jackson's lab. As the year ended, Sean had trouble finding a permanent job and began blaming women for his failure. Jackson described his hostile behaviour towards her when he was upset.

> I was his supervisor during this year . . . at Azura [the corporation]. He called me at home one night and blasted me. . . . He said women were the cause of all his troubles. . . . I felt threatened. I was actually afraid of him, he was so wound-up. He interpreted his problems [about finding a job] as related to women and vented his anger and frustration on me. I was totally taken aback by this. I talked to my boss and told him I was concerned because this guy was so wound-up.

Sean demanded that Vivien call a meeting with herself, her boss, and her boss's boss – both men – to discuss his concerns.

> I asked him, 'And what would the purpose of this meeting be? We don't have meetings just to talk; you have to have a goal you hope to achieve.' He said he just wanted to talk. . . . So I went to his office and he just blasted me. He spouted venom and anger until he sort of ran down. Later, I realized he kept saying that 'My wife is threatening to get a job.' He used the word threatening over and over. I didn't see it at the time but this guy was really feeling threatened and blaming it on women.

Sean obtained a job in academia, eventually. Vivien said he came to her office with the news and said, 'Well you know, [university chemistry department] doesn't have a single woman on faculty. I'm going to do something about that when I get there.' Vivien said, 'That hypocrite! I was fearful of violence from him! He was so worked up, I feared he might do something awful.' [Like shoot you?] 'Yes, like shoot me.'

Vivien believes Sean and the other men with whom she works evaluate men and women differently, viewing women in a dim light, failing to see their work as valuable.

> One guy . . . I work with a lot and he and I like each other. Well, just the other day, he was ranting and raving about this woman [scientist at a prestigious west coast university] who has just gotten all these awards and recognition 'that she doesn't deserve'. It just pisses him off something fierce and the other guys I work with too. The guys can't stand it because they say she's gotten it only because she's a woman and that lots of brighter men are . . . deprived [of] it because she got it. . . . This woman is about 5'4" tall, very shapely, very attractive, very capable. Maybe she's not brilliant but she's been around a long time and she's a solid chemist. And if the guys can't tell the difference between a woman who's attractive and been around a long time and one that is truly brilliant, well, I say, that's *their* problem. Is she supposed to say, 'Don't give me this prize or honour?' Does some guy say, 'No, please don't give me this $40,000 a year for three years, I don't deserve it'? Many guys get awards all the time they don't deserve but you don't see them turning them down and you don't see the other guys getting all that upset. . . . There's this one guy here who is basically incompetent as a

chemist. He's published some stuff that we now know is absolutely wrong but he won't retract it. And it's still being cited and the other guys know it. But they like him so much. George [a colleague] said one day, 'This guy is just so . . . charismatic.' Well, maybe he didn't use that word but that's what he meant. Just so charming, so fun and interesting. They tolerate this guy who is worthless as a chemist because he is charismatic. But they have a fit that some woman gets recognized with honours and awards. They don't see all the guys who don't deserve recognition [but get it anyway].

Vivien clarified her claim that men use different standards to evaluate women and men:

Men assume it's their innate destiny to do offbeat, unusual, creative things. It's against women's destiny for them to be here, working in chemistry. They [women] should not be here. . . . Men give each other the benefit of the doubt but they don't give it to women. . . . They [men] say, 'Let's give him a chance. It may not come to anything but who knows.' If it's men's destiny to do such things, something really good may come of it. But they do not see this kind of potential in women. Women are acting *against their destiny* on these things [emphasis mine].[4]

Actions such as the foregoing used to upset Vivien but she ignores them now, she said: 'They don't bother me any more. I just let them [the comments] roll off my back. I can't be bothered.' Her body language and animated manner belied her claim that she is not bothered, however, When I asked how she manages her relations with colleagues who disparage women, she said,

I change the subject. I know from experience there's no need trying to change them [their views or beliefs]. So, I wait for a convenient moment and switch topics. [Does that work?] Almost inevitably [*sic*]; they don't seem to realize what I've done.

The men express negative views of women, to a woman, without apology. To protect the relationship, Vivien changes the subject to avoid becoming upset. What kinds of masculinity(ies) do men mobilize when they criticize women's potential to another woman? At a minimum, they assert men's superiority to women and depict women as outsiders, as inferior *others*.

Vivien's story shows that some men, for example post-doctoral fellow Sean, hold women responsible for their problems at work. We cannot know if Sean was scapegoating because his wife's threat to 'go to work' threatened his identity as family 'provider', a true man (cf. Weiss, 1990). But Sean's actions raise questions about how men construct their identities and experiences at and through their work. Did Sean see Azura as a 'man's world' and Vivien as taking his job? Subordinate women who help men at work – secretaries, lab assistants – may pose no threat to men's *identities as men* but women who are bosses (or peers) may threaten them, particularly when the men's job security is at risk (see Coleman, 1990; Weiss, 1990; Kerfoot and Knights, 1993).[5]

Vivien's account of men's views on women who receive honours in chemistry suggests that men see 'accomplished' women as deviant. A scientist who merits honour and recognition is a man; an honoured woman takes the honour from a more deserving man. Vivien says the woman in her story is not brilliant. But *men* gave her the award and the woman deserves it as much as many men who have won prizes, Vivien believes. I call the form of masculinity mobilized here *male superiority* masculinity, with a dynamic that demarcates men from women and asserts their superiority to women, as a sex-class. This kind of masculinity is implicated in Hollway's (Chapter 2 in this volume) analysis of men's framing of women as 'other', as an exercise in devaluation. *Other* than men means less eminent, less deserving, less accomplished (cf. Hartsock, 1990; Messner et al., 1993).

The Vivien–Sean story reveals contradictory uses of the notion of 'threat'. Vivien feared for her safety from Sean; she felt he might shoot her. Sean complained about his wife's 'threat' – to take a job! Sean appears to have expected Vivien, his boss, to find him a job. When he demanded a meeting with her bosses, both men, was he demanding that *a man* come to his aid? Was he upset because the *paternalistic support* he sought from Vivien as his boss was unforthcoming? Why did Sean feel free to spew, fume and rail against Vivien? While she did not understand his behaviour, Vivien felt Sean saw her as having failed him and she believed his anger was prompted in part by her being a woman.

Evaluational frames: masculinism and patriarchal masculinities

In a discussion of power, Jeffrey Pfeffer (1992: Chapter 10) tells a story about Donald Regan, then CEO of the Merrill Lynch Corporation, that illustrates the power of *framing* in organizational contexts. (An *organizational frame* directs members' attention and offers a set of rules and routine practices that members use as guides for appropriate action. See Goffman, 1974; March and Olsen, 1989; Martin and Powell, 1994). Regan told the vice-presidents serving under his authority to tell him what they thought about a decision he was contemplating. They enumerated many problems with the decision, advising him against it. When they finished, he told them he had already decided and the option he chose was the one they saw problems with. Now, he said, tell me what you would do to overcome the problems you so eloquently articulated. Without missing a beat, the vice-presidents began offering solutions to the problems they had deplored and, indeed, solved many of them on the spot. Pfeffer uses the example to illustrate the power of *framing* by managers in hierarchical organizations.

The gender-based evaluational *frames* that are suggested in my data are, I believe, equally powerful in shaping men's perceptions of and behaviour towards women at work. In deconstructing masculinism and the varied masculinities that are conflated with managerial evaluations, my data show three evaluational frames that concern women's vs. men's (1) potential,

(2) legitimacy, and (3) performance. These gender-based frames 'pre-form' the interactional context, framing women's capacities, legitimacy for valued jobs, and performance relative to men's as less outstanding, effective or valuable. Unless men (and women) consciously act to counteract the *a priori* biases that are embedded in these frames, they will evaluate women less favourably while *believing* they are evaluating them 'objectively' (see Martin, 1995, for development of this thesis). Each vignette contains examples of all three frames. Each frame devalues women's talents, rights and contributions relative to men's, so their cumulative impact on women at work can be debilitating (cf. Burton, 1991).[6]

Frame 1. Differing potential: men's versus women's innate traits and capacities

One gender-based frame used by men in the vignettes to evaluate men and women concerns potential or, as described by Vivien Jackson, men's and women's 'innate destinies'. Members of organizations could claim that women and men are alike but, based on my research, they seldom do. Typically, they see women and men as different, with distinctive traits, potential and temperaments (see Leidner, 1991, 1993b; Hall, 1993). Given that frames are 'pre-evaluational', they are generally used without reflection or 'awareness' on the evaluator's part. Difference claims about gender pervade everyday life (see Tavris, 1992; Lorber, 1994 for reviews). Thus, at work, men may frame men as more 'naturally' skilled at chemical research; men may say a man *can* be a university president but a woman *cannot*. When men invoke such frames, they depict men's talents and capacities as more *consonant with more valued* jobs and opportunities. They can also frame women as 'naturally' more suited, relative to men, for undesirable jobs. Cockburn (1988) documents men's claims that women have greater tolerance for detailed, repetitive, place-bound work than do men. Managers in her study used such claims to justify assigning women to less valued and variable jobs (see Ong, 1987; Milkman, 1987).

Frame 2. Normative legitimacy and hierarchical rank: men's versus women's rights to hierarchical power

A second evaluational frame involves legitimacy and hierarchical authority: do men and women have equal 'rights' to hierarchical authority? The discourse and actions of some men in my vignettes suggest that they framed women as lacking legitimacy to hold powerful positions. The male professor who criticized the dean may have objected to her elevation in status; as a man, he has more 'right' to the job than she as a woman does. Fred insisted on being unit director and was chosen for the job over Paula; he complained that Paula 'resisted his supervision', implying that she should have embraced her subordinate status relative to him. The men on the search committee who skipped Sims's presentation and the elderly man who mentioned the candidates' wives actively *undermined* Sims's candidacy by framing her as lacking *legitimacy* for the job. A gender-based legitimacy frame asserts that men *should* have authority over other men and women; women *should not* have authority over men or in men's stead. When men enact such a frame, they mobilize a form of masculinity that overrides considerations based on the 'merit or objective qualifications' that allegedly inform managerial hiring and promotion decisions (cf. Acker, 1990). A legitimacy frame does not question women's *potential* for holding a position or job, but women's normative *right* to hold it.

Frame 3. Performance and gender: valuing men's and women's contributions and failures

The third frame concerns the fit between performance and gender: Due to men's superior gender status, their successes and contributions may be amplified and their limitations and mistakes minimized; due to women's inferiority on gender, their successes and contributions may be minimized and their limitations and mistakes amplified (and women may do this to themselves; for a review, see Major, 1989). As a result of this frame, men observe women's performance through a 'gender lens' (Rothschild and Davies, 1994) that, frequently, devalues it relative to men's. Women's excellent performance may be viewed as competent, their competent performance as average, their incompetent performance as unacceptable (Pugh and Wahrman, 1983). (Research on this issue is complex and mixed; see Wagner et al., 1986; Wood and Karten, 1986; Eagly, 1987; Ridgeway, 1991, 1993.) Gupta, Jenkins and Beehr (1983: 183) report that men *evaluate* women positively (and similarly to men) but still favour men in their actions, for example by promoting them rather than women. The Azura chemists did not see a woman chemist's work as prizeworthy yet they celebrated a male colleague whose work they knew to be wrong. The male professor who criticized the woman dean ignored her record of excellent work, focusing instead on her (alleged) mistakes. When the men skipped Sims's presentation, they questioned her record as a president of another university as evidence that she could do or should have their presidency job.

Gendered interactional styles: masculinities and interpersonal dynamics

The behavioural styles men employ in evaluational contexts can harm women if they entail masculinism and masculinities enactment. I identify four such interactional styles displayed by men in my vignettes.

Style 1: promotion of men, individual and collective

Men respond to evaluational contexts by promoting themselves, their needs, talents, worthiness and accomplishments – as individuals and as a group. (This behaviour parallels Collinson and Hearn's (1994) description of 'careerist masculinity', although my data suggest that men promote other men as well as themselves, extending the dynamic beyond self-promotion.) George, for example, did not wait for Fred to select him on 'objective' grounds; he put his case forward to Fred, repeatedly. Paula asked Fred for the job once and assumed he would offer it based on her 'objectively' superior qualifications. Sean demanded help from Vivien and her bosses in finding a job. Vivien's colleagues claimed a woman did not deserve a chemistry prize, asserting the superior accomplishments of men – indirectly including themselves – relative to women. The professor who was passed over for the deanship elevated himself by criticizing the woman who was selected 'over him'. The self-promotional styles that some men use in evaluational contexts elevate all men, relative to women, in formal organizations.

Style 2: requests for paternalist aid

Men in the vignettes, particularly the younger men, asked for help from powerful superiors based on their 'need for it', for the sake of their careers. George said to Fred: let me teach; I need the experience. Sean said to Vivien: you are failing me by not finding me a job; find me a job. Fred said to the assistant dead: make me director or I won't come to your university. The men on the search committee asked the sitting university president for help with a problem they had. Paula, Jane and Vivien appear, in contrast, to have expected that 'objective' performance and qualifications would form the basis for the evaluational decisions in which they were involved. Within the male 'community of work', younger men appear to assume that older men (and hierarchical superiors?) should help them because they *need* help whereas women do not appear to expect assistance from superiors based on their needs.

Style 3: open criticism of women, not of men

In each vignette in my data, men publicly criticized women; no woman criticized men in similarly open ways. The following comment from Christy Evans, a member of the all-women America3 America's Cup sailing team, shows that men openly criticize women in 'task' contexts in ways they refrain from doing to men.

> There is this difference: A man'll criticize a woman in front of the rest of the crew, whereas he won't criticize another guy. Once I made a mistake and was pulled off the bow; if I'd been a guy, that never would have happened. (Karbo, 1995: 38–9)

Men's superior gender status, combined with superior hierarchical status and the gender-based frames reviewed earlier, orient men to interactionally disparage women and womanly or feminine traits and actions (see

Traweek, 1988; Curry, 1991). As Vivien reported, one of her male friends disparaged a prize-winning woman to her, a woman. Men's interactional practice of disparaging women at work demeans all women and places them in a defensive posture relative to the men who engage in such behaviour and to other women who, through this practice, are collectively devalued.

Style 4: 'ganging up on a woman'

My data show multiple instances of men acting *in concert* to criticize or depreciate women. Four men skipped Sims's interview; the man professor included his male colleague in an harangue against the woman dean; Sean demanded that Vivien involve her male superiors in his gripe against her; Fred and George 'ganged up on' Paula, or so she felt. Cognitive frames that valorize men over women set a stage for men to act in concert, to 'gang up on women' in ways that harm women by questioning their legitimacy, talents and contributions to the organization. My data suggest that when men collectively frame women as different from themselves, they sometimes invoke gender-based frames that valorize men over women. Masculinist interactional styles and gender-based cognitive frames that depreciate women call forth and reinforce each other in evaluational contexts.

Discussion and conclusions

To understand their perceptions and actions, we must situate the men and women in my vignettes within a wider context of the bureaucratic work organization of the late twentieth century, a capitalist economy where competition and rationality are ideologically hegemonic, and a global gender system that materially and ideologically valorizes men and men's lives and bodies over women and women's lives and bodies (Milkman and Townsley, 1994; Acker, 1990; Ferree and Hall, 1996). So situated, Sean's attack on Vivien is more than an isolated complaint by a difficult worker to a supervisor. Sean, like George in another vignette, is a young *man* in a tenuous situation, concerned about his career.

Sean and George know that *some men* control the power levers in their organizations. Sean's attack on Vivien and George's beseeching of Fred to give him the teaching assignment are premised on a gender-stratified system that questions Vivien's and Paula's abilities, legitimacy and performance at work. Men's greater prevalence and legitimacy in positions of power suggest to Sean that a *proper* organization of work relative to gender benefits men. These conditions may have given Sean the confidence to challenge Vivien aggressively, even to threaten her. Because he cannot find a job, Sean may see Vivien as failing him (see Williams and Heiker, 1993 on men nurses' framing of women supervisors). Sean's rage may have been directed in part at Vivien's superiors who too were failing to find him a job. Irrespective of his motivations, I interpret Sean's behaviour as a sign, and result, of men's power as managers and managers' power as men. The masculinism of the organization joins with Sean's enactment of aggressive, careerist masculinities to *create* as well as *reflect* male privilege (see Collinson and Hearn, 1994). Sean and George who were not managers with official power were nevertheless able to mobilize power associated with their gender status to challenge the authority of women whose hierarchical and professional statuses were higher than their own.

I offer a parallel interpretation of the actions of the men on the presidential search committee. In skipping Sims's talk, four powerful men undermined her candidacy *and* the future candidacy of *any* woman. If they had attended her talk, the gender-based frame that questioned Sims's legitimacy *as a woman* would probably have oriented them – and others – to see her as 'less qualified' than her male competitors (cf. Ridgeway, 1991; Major, 1989). But although they would have questioned Sims's legitimacy, I doubt that the gender-based frames on which the questioning was based would have been openly acknowledged. When the men skipped Sims's interview, however, they *publicly enacted* masculinism, declaring for all to see their assumption that men are better (more important) than women. Their action brought the submerged gender-based frames to the surface of awareness and interaction. Their actions said to Jane Coats that any woman, not only Sims, would have problems winning the time, attention and support of powerful men. The men's actions made manifest the university's masculinism, usually 'masked' by rhetoric about merit, qualifications, performance and eminence (Martin, 1982; DiNitto et al., 1984). I suggest that the men's actions enriched masculinism, assuring its perpetuation. By *enacting* a form of masculinity that asserts men's superiority to women, the men enhanced their own power *and* the potency of masculinism in the university.

In pursuing a goal of *deconstructing* – exposing, making visible – the masculinism and masculinities that characterize managerial evaluations, I do not contend that *all* men do at work is enact masculinity nor that *all of* men's actions at work entail masculinism or masculinities enactments (cf. Coleman, 1990). I do suggest that some actions by men activate masculinism and masculinities, however, and that these actions are consequential for women – and men – when done by evaluators with hierarchical power, gender-based power, or, as is frequently the case, both kinds of power. While my vignettes provide only a slice of organizational reality, and a tiny fraction of events in the informants' lives, they can shed light on women's and men's experiences of evaluations in formal organizations. My analysis will, I hope, make more visible the masculinism and masculinities dynamics that are embedded in some of them.

None of the gender-based frames or interactional styles that I identify is particularly newsworthy. Most have been identified before (for example Cockburn, 1991). But my study makes a contribution, I believe, by linking explicit forms of masculinity and masculinism to interpersonal relations and dynamics associated with evaluations at work. My analysis breathes dynamics into otherwise static lists of 'barriers' and 'biases' that hinder women on the job (including some that I have produced: see Martin et al., 1983; DiNitto et al., 1984; Martin, 1991; and Burton, 1991). In exploring *interactional dynamics*, we gain insights into *how* men 'erect' barriers, *how* they 'enact' biases in evaluational contexts. Is a barrier or bias intentional on the initiator's part or does a context where men, men's lives, masculinism and hegemonic masculinities hold sway allow men to enact barriers and biases as a matter of routine, without giving women all that much thought (Martin, 1995; Milkman and Townsley, 1994)? Under what conditions are such enactments more or less probable?

My analysis (limited to a few evocative vignettes) suggests that men mobilize masculinism and hegemonic masculinity(ies) in evaluational contexts under two conditions: (1) when scarce and/or valued positions (jobs), resources and opportunities are at stake, for example the university presidency, chemistry prizes, or the chance to develop a new skill; and (2) when men's job security or identities as men are threatened, e.g. Sean's inability to obtain a job, the professor's failure to be chosen as dean. The linking of these conditions to the dynamics that 'produce' them helps us see how masculinism and masculinities are activated in concrete relations and exchanges. If women's talents, and the talents of most men, are to be fully utilized in work organizations, new standards, new ways of interacting, and new ways of evaluating may be required.

In other papers, I have discussed the characteristics and practices of feminist organizations and of feminist management in non-feminist organizations (Martin, P.Y., 1990, 1993; also Ferree and Martin, 1995).[7] While this analysis takes us far afield of the focus of this study, I would like to acknowledge feminism's potential for transforming management and work organizations. In my 1993 paper, I argue that feminist management promotes co-operation, democratic processes, sharing, responsibility and development over competition, control, exploitation and one-upmanship (Martin, 1993; also Strobel, 1995; Staggenborg, 1995; Remington, 1991). When feminism is framed as a project that seeks to value women equally with men, not to elevate women (or women's presumed 'traits') over men, feminism challenges inequality, oppression and masculinism on multiple fronts (see Taylor, 1989; Fraser, 1989). For example, it calls for *transformation through the promotion of democracy and co-operation* – of the self, the workplace, the society (see Wallace, 1991). It offers a vision of organizations and management that emphasizes empowerment and the obligation of managers to those in their charge rather than managers' right to control and exploit subordinates and organizational resources for their personal gain (Martin, 1993; Hartmann, 1993). In feminist organizations, and organizations guided by feminist practice, gender could be eliminated as a basis for assessing members' potential, legitimacy and performance. Interactional styles that elevate men over women could be replaced by styles that downplay competition and other masculinities and that frame women as legitimate equals rather than as inferior others. While a totally gender-free workplace may be impossible, I can envisage one that avoids valorizing men and masculinist practices that devalue women (see J. Martin, 1990; Calás and Smircich, 1992a, 1992b; Thorne, 1993; Hearn, 1994a).[8]

When a male lineworker for a telephone company refuses for days to ask his supervisor for help with a problem he cannot solve and makes fun of a woman lineworker who asks her supervisor after 'only half a day of failure', we must recognize that the job entails more than the straightforward repair and maintenance of telephone lines (see Martin, 1995). The male lineworker's equation of *asking* with a loss of autonomy and respect relative to another man, his boss, and the woman lineworker's equation of asking with a pragmatic strategy for solving a problem show distinctively gendered approaches to an 'objectively' common situation. The separation of tasks and jobs from the doers of jobs and the social contexts within which doers do their jobs has limited utility for organizational analysis and it produces distorted accounts of practice and effect. Acker (1995) argues that organizations do not – indeed, cannot – exist except through the agency of people who enact them; some*one* must perform tasks in an organization's name, on its behalf. I call for more attention to practice. By focusing on practice, the 'doings of managements', and becoming aware of the diverse ways people 'do' manage, including 'managing' themselves and their superiors, we can learn about the many layers of meaning and substance that most work tasks and relations entail.

A focus on doing and the relational contexts in which *doers do* will improve understanding of managerial relations and activities that involve evaluations. An appreciation of managers as men and of men as managers will help to sort out the intertwining of the two. Freed of its substructural grounding in masculinity(ies) and masculinism (Acker, 1990; Calás and Smircich, 1992a), managerial evaluations can be imagined anew as practices that facilitate growth and development while helping people, individually and collectively, pursue organizational goals in ways that are unfettered by gender privilege or disadvantage.

Notes

I thank David Collinson and Jeff Hearn for their generous help and encouragement. I also thank Judith Lorber, Barbara Reskin, Linda Smircich, Catherine Fobes, Robin Leidner, Elaine Hall, Myra Marx Ferree, Caroline Persell and Roberta Spalter-Roth for their suggestions and help with earlier versions of this chapter.

1. While space limitations prohibit a detailed discussion of masculinities as theorized over the past decade, I wish to acknowledge the substantial influence on my thinking of Candace West and Don Zimmerman (1987) and Robert Connell (especially 1987; but also 1990, 1993, 1995).

2. Men also are constrained at work by hegemonic masculinities that require them to act and speak in narrowly drawn ways (Connell, 1987; Hearn and Morgan, 1990), a fact that most men fail to recognize (see Weiss, 1990; and Jackall, 1988). Men take their masculinity enactments of/with each other 'for granted' and fail to see them as 'gendered' unless someone draws their attention to the point (Coleman, 1990; Stoltenberg, 1993). Men assume that the kinds of masculinities that are hegemonic at work are expressions of organizational power, inevitable or 'natural' aspects of the workplace, or of men and authority-relations generally (for example Collinson, 1992).

3. In commenting on Foucault's theory of power relative to gender and herself, Hartsock (1990) says Foucault's failure to recognize the power/dominance relations associated with gender makes her see the world as a 'profoundly alien' place.

4. We should not conclude from Vivien's account that all men support each other at Azura Corporation. She was referring to informal friendship alliances among *some men* in her lab. She acknowledged that most Azura men compete with each other routinely.

5. Sean's behaviour towards Vivien resembles that of male secretaries towards women bosses. Pringle (1988) found that men secretaries were less respectful, subordinate and compliant towards women than men bosses and than women secretaries were towards bosses of either gender. They criticized their bosses openly on their management styles, personalities and behaviour. The *illegitimacy* for a man of having a woman boss may influence him to mobilize masculinity to assert his gender superiority, to resist the double insult of hierarchical *and* gender subordination (cf. Ridgeway, 1991, 1993). A man secretary is unlikely to have learned 'emphasized femininity' and may find subordination, particularly to a woman, distasteful (Connell, 1987). If men routinely construct their identities and seek security through their paid work – as Weiss (1990), among others, says they do – having a woman boss may be demeaning.

6. Many women say male colleagues question their motives at work, making them feel 'different'. A US religion professor said a colleague asked her *why* she would want to study women in the Holocaust. A Swedish sociologist said a colleague commented that her interest in feminism was making him and other men in her department 'question her seriousness' (cf. Hochschild, 1989). A research physicist said she tries to talk physics with her colleagues but they repeatedly introduce their wives and children into their conversations. Through practices such as these, men call women's judgement into doubt and imply that their work is second-rate, outside the mainstream – or malestream – which, from men's standpoint *qua men*, it often is (see Coleman, 1990).

7. Bureaucracies exist in many forms and sizes. When they operate fairly and inclusively, they can facilitate democratic participation (Cafferata, 1982; Wallace, 1991). Some feminist organizations operate more democratically than those run by men or by non-feminist women (Knoke, 1990; see Barnett, 1995 on African American women and men in the US civil rights movement). Research on feminist organizations, some of which are bureaucratic (for example Staggenborg, 1988, 1989; Leidner, 1993a; Siriani, 1993; Bordt, 1995; Strobel, 1995; Christiansen-Ruffman, 1995), and on feminist mobilization within mainstream institutions (see Eisenstein, 1991b, 1995; Reinelt, 1995; Katzenstein, 1995) documents the successes of (some) feminists and feminist organizations in downplaying competition, exploitation, abuses of power, and in achieving a range of intended goals (see Acker, 1995; Gelb, 1995; Staggenborg, 1995).

8. In *Moral Mazes: The World of Corporate Managers* (1988), Robert Jackall reported that the managers he studied were, for the most part, dishonest, competitive, exploitative of the organization and self-serving. Few cared about ethical standards, honesty, saving the environment, helping subordinates, or achieving organizational goals. When I read the book, I wondered where the managers were who wanted to do right, achieve organizational goals, and help people. Jackall talked to a few of these but said they were outfoxed by the more self-serving and ambitious within their ranks. Jackall viewed ruthless managers as guided by the dictates of bureaucracy, the 'iron cage', that has invaded all aspects of modern life. I suggest a different explanation. The managers in Jackall's book – nearly all of whom were men (and Jackall treated the handful of women as if they were men too) – were driven, in my view, by

authoritarian and careerist masculinities, not by bureaucracy alone (see Collinson and Hearn, 1994). The corporate context is bureaucratic, unquestionably, but organizational politics are ongoing as well; many men engage in 'masculinity politics' at work, in contests over their identities, power, rank and privileges (for example, Weiss, 1990; Martin, 1995). In my view, Jackall's managers mobilized masculinities in the course of doing management and conflated masculinities with managing in ways that had negative consequences for themselves, those with whom they worked, and their organizations.

11

'Seduction and Succession': Circuits of Homosocial Desire in Management

Michael Roper

The place of organizations in men's lives is often, even characteristically, contradictory. They may offer status and meaning and threat and competition to men, as well as acting as *circuits* or *pyramids* of men's (suppressed) desire for men. (Hearn, 1992b: 205)

'The recovery of the irrational' has become something of a catch-cry in organization studies, as part of a growing backlash against classical theories (Albrow, 1992: 314; Flam, 1990a, 1990b; Reed, 1991). 'Rationalist' models have been criticized for characterizing the managerial process in terms of calculability, consistency and efficiency, as if these exhausted the vocabulary of human motivations (Flam, 1990a: 40–3). Thus the swath of literature since the late 1980s on gender, sexuality and emotions in organizations often commences with a critique of the post-war management classics and their 'instrumental way of thinking' (Burrell and Hearn, 1989: 11–14; Fineman, 1993: 1; Witz and Savage, 1992: 5). A general preoccupation of this literature is the attempt to move beyond what Helena Flam calls the 'soft edges' of rationalist models. Emotions, we are told, do not sit on top of an emotion-free bureaucratic machine, but are part of their 'inner wiring' (Hochschild, 1993: x).

Organization theorists have thus not only spotted gaps between the bars of Weber's iron cage, but have begun plotting conceptual escape routes. Even so, the legacy of neoclassical models remains substantial. A prime illustration of this is the lack of research on intimacy between men in management. Male bonding, John Stoltenberg has commented, 'is how men get . . . power, and male bonding is how it is kept' (quoted in Jackson, 1990: 168). Moreover – as Eve Kosofsky Sedgwick has argued in *Between Men* – this bonding often has an erotic aspect. Is there, she asks, a continuity between men promoting the interests of other men and men loving other men (Sedgwick, 1985: 3)?

This question is especially pertinent to management, which has remained a male-dominated occupation despite over two decades of equal opportunities legislation. Yet even the so-called 'new wave' writers on management have generally ignored the role of intimacy in perpetuating exclusionary networks. The masculine myth of the non-emotional 'organization man' retains a hold.

Why is this? On the one side, feminist researchers have mainly concentrated on women as 'emotion workers'. Arlie Hochschild's influential argument in *The Managed Heart* (1983) was that sexual and emotional divisions of labour uphold each other. Women frequently perform emotional labour in service occupations such as flight attendant, nurse, secretary or sales assistant. The emotion work which women do is an important aspect of their subordination.

However, this approach leaves many unanswered questions in relation to men, management and emotions. The 'managed heart' of Hochschild's title is a woman's heart. Although Hochschild alludes to men's role as the managers of emotional labour, it is not clear whether they also perform emotional work themselves. If so, is the same portion of the human heart – empathy and sexual charm – appropriated for commercial purposes? If a male manager performs emotion work, does it reinforce his subordination?

On the other side, some 'new wave' management theorists are in danger of forsaking one set of universalist assumptions for another. 'Emotional man' replaces 'rational man'. For example, Flam stresses the role of organizations as manipulators of feeling. They promote unwritten social guidelines called 'feeling rules' which specify expectations about the nature and quantity of emotional display (Flam, 1990a: 45). A corporate strategy is not only an expression of instrumental aims, but may prescribe particular kinds of emotions: 'corporate goals as "profit realisation" or "help to the needy" or "solidarity" can be seen as intentions to construct and sustain specific emotions' (Flam, 1990b: 226). Flam opens the way for research on the differences between organizations in their 'texture of affectivity' (Albrow, 1992: 326). But such approaches pay no attention to the gender order in which these feeling rules are created and enforced.[1] The Weberian split between rationality and emotion is rejoined, but with no recognition that it is often men who – as managers – create corporate rules about human feeling.

In any case, the criticisms of 'new wave' management theorists are not entirely justified. Some of the post-war classics did depict management as an emotional activity (for example Dalton, 1959; Gouldner, 1955a). The tension between rivalry and intimacy is an important theme in Gouldner's ethnographic study of management succession (Gouldner, 1955a, see esp. Chapter 3). Yet such studies – because they took male experience as the norm – were unable to account for the gendered character of the relationships they observed. Only in 1977, with Rosabeth Moss Kanter's landmark study of the US firm Indsco, did the germ of a different history emerge. Kanter attributed the exclusion of women from management to a 'masculine ethic' which represented the manager in non-emotional terms:

A 'masculine ethic' can be identified as part of the early image of managers. This 'masculine ethic' elevates the traits assumed to belong to some men to necessities for effective management: a tough-minded approach to problems; analytic abilities to abstract and plan; a capacity to set aside personal, emotional considerations in the interests of task accomplishment; and a cognitive superiority

in problem-solving and decision-making . . . when women tried to enter manage-
ment jobs, the 'masculine ethic' was invoked as an exclusionary principle.
(Kanter, 1977: 22)

More recent work has pointed to the role of organization studies itself in
fostering this ethic (Pringle, 1988; Bologh, 1990; Acker, 1990). The attack
on the classical model proceeds through a reading of its founding texts
which lays bare the alignment of masculinity with the rational and im-
personal. Rosemary Pringle, for example, comments that 'Weber's account
of "rationality" can be read in gender terms as a commentary on the
construction of a particular kind of masculinity based on the exclusion
of the personal, the sexual and the feminine from any definition of
"rationality"' (Pringle, 1989: 161).

Yet there is a risk that this stress on the role of managerial texts in
constructing an asexual, non-emotional vision of managerial masculinity
continues to obscure the intimacies between men. What is needed is an
approach that both acknowledges the discursive positioning of male
managers as 'rational' and reflects on their emotional relations. For as Jeff
Hearn has observed, the heterosexual, rationalist myth of the 'organiza-
tional monoculture' conceals relations of desire between men (Hearn,
1992b: 199–207). Decentring that myth requires that we focus on the
intimate practices of men in management, not just on dominant discourses
about organizational masculinities.

How can this best be accomplished? A major stumbling block is the
absence of terms which adequately capture all-male intimacy. Sometimes
men's networks are described as 'homosocial', and at others as 'homo-
sexual', with no clear conceptual reason given for the distinction. For
example, Kanter used the term 'homosexual reproduction' to describe men's
networks in management, even though she herself did not consider erotic
feeling as central to how they functioned (Kanter, 1977: 97). Kanter's term
was shorthand for a system in which managers counteracted the un-
certainties of business by selecting successors from backgrounds similar to
their own. Homosexual reproduction connoted the process by which men
'reproduce themselves in their own image' (Kanter, 1977: 48). Anne Witz
and Mike Savage (1992) have underlined Kanter's insight that 'shared
maleness' is a key mechanism in perpetuating male dominance in
management. However they argue that the phrase 'homosexual reproduc-
tion' was 'clumsily' applied by Kanter, since she was not really talking
about sexuality, but about a structural mechanism through which manage-
ment becomes a 'closed and gendered circle' (Witz and Savage, 1992: 15).
They opt for the term 'male homosociability', which they see as representing
both the way in which women are 'dispossessed of corporate power', and
the way access to organizational power is decided between men (ibid.: 16).

I believe that the term 'male homosociability' is as misconceived as
'homosexual reproduction'. In revising Kanter's definition, Witz and Savage
suppress the aspects of desire that give male bonding in management its
peculiar intensity (Roper, 1994a: esp. Chapter 3). This leaves no space for

the erotic subtext of all-male intimacies (Wood, 1987). A senior manager I interviewed evoked this subtext when he described his relationship with an older male manager as one in which 'high levels of energy' had flowed from 'the chemistry being right' (Roper, 1994a: 79). In male-dominated organizations, homoerotically charged feelings may influence decisions about who succeeds whom, contributing to the reproduction of gender segregation. Managers themselves are fascinated by this 'chemistry' and often allude to it, and yet it has been largely ignored in research on management. What is needed, then, is a term which captures rather than erases the ambiguities between the 'social' and the 'sexual' in men's networks. Sedgwick's concept of 'homosocial desire' does just this; identifying a distinctive category of intimacy in formally heterosexual settings which presents as non-sexual but which nevertheless involves potentially erotic desires.

The following account portrays homosocial desires in a management college. The setting is significant because of the pivotal role which business education has played in promoting a hegemonic 'masculine ethic' of management as a professional (and therefore non-intimate) activity. My aims are twofold. First, to show that homosocial desires flourish in precisely those settings where the masculine ethic of management as a calculative and instrumental activity is strong. The chapter illustrates Hearn's assertion that homosocial 'circuits of desire' commonly coexist with competition between men (Hearn, 1992b: 205). A second aim is to illustrate the fluidity of boundaries between friendship and desire in men's networks, thus – as Sedgwick puts it – drawing 'the homosocial back into the orbit of desire, of the potentially erotic' (Sedgwick, 1985: 1). Seduction has an unacknowledged place in the story of how power passes from one generation of male managers to the next.

Seduction and succession at Southey college

The research for this chapter is based on a visit to Southey management college in Australia during the early 1990s. My two main informants, John and Howard, had worked in the Industrial Policy Unit of the college as junior researchers. Their testimonies were supplemented by participant observation over a two-month period, during which I attended department seminars and social events.

Jobs in the college were vertically segregated along gender lines. Sixteen per cent of the academic staff were women and all the professors were men.[2] Women and men were also horizontally segregated in different teaching and research areas. Women staff were clustered in social science or applied departments such as marketing, while men predominated in finance and economics. The proportion of women staff in social science (25 per cent) was more than four times greater than that in the combined economics and finance areas.

The Industrial Policy Unit reflected this male domination of economics.

Fourteen of its seventeen academic staff were men.[3] Women and men were clustered at opposite ends of the seniority scale. All the teaching and senior research staff were men, whilst the three women were junior researchers on short-term contracts. The job of junior researcher was itself gendered, in that it offered greater mobility to men than women. Two of the women, married and in their late thirties, were amongst the longest-serving junior staff members in the unit. By contrast all but one of the male junior researchers were in their twenties, and had joined the college straight from university undergraduate or Master's degrees. Some have gone on to jobs in industry as consultants or financial analysts; others went into journalism or took up teaching posts. As Howard explained, for men the job of junior researcher was a 'staging post'.

This promise of male mobility was built into the department's routines. Parties paved the passage from semi-student to fully fledged professional man. A departing junior researcher began his farewell speech with a self-deprecating joke that illustrates the feminine connotation of lack of mobility. He was in danger of being 'left on the shelf', he explained, because he had seen twenty-nine people pass through the department in his four and a half years there. Departures were presaged by rumours about the starting salary, which served as a rough measure of the man concerned. Parties, gifts and the signing of cards prepared them for what one well-wisher described – in a message rich in phallic connotation – as 'life at the sharp end'.

This pattern of differential mobility cannot be fully understood by establishing the existence of structural mechanisms which advantaged men, for these mechanisms were embedded in a much wider exclusionary male culture. A shared background in economics, and expertise in articulating its discourse, was the element which unified men in the unit.[4] Economics was the basis of their professional status, but it also played a role in their self-presentations as men, representing an 'ideal type' of masculinity (see also Lehman, Chapter 8 in this volume). Staff in the unit regarded economics as superior to other disciplines. They defended this belief in gendered terms. Howard explained that econometrics and economic forecasting depended on methods which were 'hard' and therefore authoritative. As Howard put it, 'if you didn't subscribe to those assumptions, then things couldn't be proved, completely tested, in a rigorous and safe fashion. And in which case, then, it was suspect and open to derision.' The masculine nature of economics was implied through a contrast with the social sciences. Women were more common in social science, Howard explained, because it espoused broadly feminine values: 'sociology is more woolly and open and softer. It's got softer subjects.' As the 'social science person' amongst economists, I was jibbed about the 'wishy-washy' character of sociology at the seminars I attended.[5]

Status within the unit depended partly on the ability of staff to speak the calculative language of economics. Junior researchers would vie with each other for the head's approval in seminars by picking away at flaws in each other's arguments. John noted that 'it was a game in which what mattered wasn't what you were saying, how original it was, or the strength of the empirical evidence, but how logically you argued it'. The department's status within the college as a whole was also seen to derive from the predictive abilities or 'truth-effect' of their discipline (Knights and Morgan, 1991: 200). Images of masculinity were integral to this authority claim. This is illustrated by the junior researcher's comments about the 'old guard' of social scientists whom they had replaced. Professor Jones, a psychologist by training, was still formally attached to the unit, but was largely ignored by the staff. He would come in to get coffee in the mornings, but people rarely talked to him. Jones's academic marginalization went hand in hand with his marginalization as a man. A seminar paper he gave on organizational culture was described as 'wet' and 'touchy-feely'. He was also criticized for being a poor breadwinner for the unit. He 'never got anything out', explained one researcher, whilst another described him as 'dead wood'. Criticizing Jones's supposed lack of productivity and his inability to speak the 'hard' language of economics perhaps enabled the young men to underline their own potency as producers, bolstering their masculinity. Department members thus positioned themselves both individually and collectively in relation to a hegemonic masculine image of deductive logic and 'hard' quantitative methods.

The scene I have described above conforms closely to the version of managerial masculinity that Kanter called the 'masculine ethic', and Hearn calls the 'organizational monoculture' (Kanter, 1977: 22; Hearn, 1992b: 199). It confirms a vision of male-dominated organizations as unemotional places and of men as rational actors. Yet to concentrate on these dominant representations alone would be to miss their 'shadow structure': men in organizations are also emotive subjects (Connell, 1987: 114; Hearn, 1993: 142–3). I will illustrate this by focusing on Paul, the head of department's line manager and 'right-hand man'. His style of leadership suggests that, rather than erasing the erotic aspect of Kanter's term 'homosexual reproduction', we might explore more fully the role of seduction in men's networks.

Although only in his late twenties, Paul was the third most senior staff member in the unit. He had a long association with the head of department, having been taught by him as an undergraduate, and having worked as a junior researcher for him. Paul's role in the department was multi-faceted. On the one hand – as the unit's memos indicate – he sought to systematize its working procedures. He wrote a 'publications strategy' aimed at 'rationalizing the outputs to a more coherent structure'. Detailed guidelines were issued for answering telephone calls in a more 'efficient and professional' manner, which included a recommended optimum number of bell-rings before the receiver should be picked up, and a suggested greeting. Paul was the department's progress chaser, setting research schedules, monitoring work-in-progress and streamlining its intellectual products. His aim as Howard saw it was to 'extract efficiency, trying to make the department produce more'. Paul represented himself to the junior researchers as a skilled exponent of calculative rationality, a living example of the masculine ethic.

On the other hand his appearance and demeanour departed from the bureaucratic norm. For the post-war generation of 'organization men', the neutral image of the suit was one of its principal advantages. As Kanter argued, its 'tailored, conservative appearance' symbolized social conformity (Kanter, 1977: 37, 47). Instantly recognizable as the uniform of the manager, its predictable shape and cut had the effect of deflecting attention from the body. Such men could be recognized simply by their 'white collar'. The head of department's attire was typical:

> *M.R.*: What kinds of clothes did the head of department wear, a suit . . .?
> *John*: A suit. His suits always seemed rather too big for him; the pants were crinkled up at the bottoms, the jackets hung a bit low. . . . His shoes were often quite worn and scuffed, like he didn't bother to polish them often. And he used to wear really nondescript, not tatty, but totally bland ties. His suit was just a uniform.

By comparison, Paul's clothes were luxurious. He used the repertoire of the 'yuppy culture' (Mort, 1988) to full effect:

> *John*: In seminars he was a joy to watch. He used to command attention by showing his body off. He'd move continually whilst talking. He would walk up to the window, sit on the ledge, back straight, chalk in hand, making these expansive gestures. . . . Then he would pace up and down at the front of the room, stop, put his hands on his hips like this [*Gestures*]. . . . Seeming to say all the time 'Look at me, look at me.'
>
> He would wear the usual white shirt, tie and suit trousers, yet there was always some kind of personal twist. His shirts were more billowy than most, very luxurious looking. He would often wear a belt that had a polished silver buckle and tip on it. . . . Kind of like a cowboy belt, only it looked incredibly elegant. Paul's personal trademark was his ties. They were usually very colourful, floral, and quite dramatic. About halfway through my time in the college, he suddenly appeared with a new kind of knot on his tie. It would be gathered in tight at the neck, and then flare out wide, with the back piece just visible to one side, almost like a cravat.
>
> The funny thing was, after Paul began wearing this new knot, then in the following weeks the others started imitating Paul, tying their ties with this same sharp fold! . . . Sometimes he would walk into meetings with the top piece slung over his shoulder, like he'd just dashed inside on a windy day.

John's reaction to this performance is revealing. On the one hand he disliked Paul, as the slightly ironic tone of this passage indicates. On the other hand he admired his style and ability to win over an audience. Paul seems to have had a similarly ambivalent effect on the other young men. 'People didn't like John that much because he was Paul's mouthpiece,' Howard commented. Yet, as John notes, they were certainly impressed enough by his appearance to copy his tie knot *en masse*. What then was the basis of this attraction? The above description hints at the element of sexual play in Paul's performance: his generally decorative style, his attention to detail, and the vitality of his movements. Perhaps too, John's careful observation of Paul's gestures and body postures reveals something of his own homosocial desires.

Paul's powers of seduction extended right to the head of department, Stuart. The two men frequently worked together in Stuart's office into the evening. Paul would help rehearse the head of department's public appearances, acting as a sounding board for his ideas, and trying them out in seminars. John commented that 'you'd often see Stuart behind his desk, hands behind head, leaning back in his seat thinking or talking, while Paul paced about the room, throwing in suggestions, talking in this loud voice, laughing and so on'.

This kind of working relationship does not conform to the separation of person from office which is, in Weberian terms, the hallmark of professional organizations such as the business college. The neoclassical framework assumed that organizations consisted of rules and routines which were largely independent of human relationships. Yet the emotional climate of the department hinted at a different story, one in which systematic procedures played only a partial role in the negotiation of power. It was this tension which enabled Paul to use his sexuality to effect. His actions were not explicable or capable of regulation within the terms of bureaucratic rationality. At the same time it was the shared appreciation of Paul's covert sexual displays by men in the department – their homosocial desires – that sustained his leadership.

This cameo of succession suggests that the flow of power between men in organizations is not always one-way, from the senior to the junior manager. As Foucault puts it, 'Pleasure and power do not cancel or turn back against one another. . . . They are linked together by complex mechanisms and devices of excitation and incitement' (1980a: 48). Paul was the dominant partner in the expression of homosocial desire. He wooed the head of department. His physical appearance was the more prepossessing, a factor which counted for much in the media-orientated culture of the business college. In watching Paul, the head of department perhaps even found a model for his own public performances. Paul's sexually nuanced displays certainly do seem to have influenced senior staff. This is suggested by a story which both my informants told me about a meeting they had attended. Paul himself was absent, but halfway through it the head of department rose from his chair and began pacing up and down the room, moving and gesticulating in precisely the manner that Paul usually did. Soon his senior colleague – responding to this vigorous display – also got up from his chair, and began imitating the head of department. In imitating Paul the senior staff unconsciously confessed to their seduction. These men were highly attuned to each other's physical appearance and movement.

The displays of homosocial desire in this department were perhaps more open than in other male-dominated settings. This is partly due to the ambiguities surrounding Paul's sexuality. Publicly he alluded to previous relationships with women, but others, citing conversations with Paul, wondered if he was gay. The uncertainty of my informants is revealing. It would have been difficult for Paul to come out in an environment such as the management college, which – partly because of its dealings with senior managers – placed a strong emphasis on social conformity. Yet this ambivalence typifies the department as a whole, not just Paul. Paul's presence had a powerful effect on most of the senior managers and other staff. It is this shared culture of homosocial desire, rather than Paul's sexuality alone, that is significant.

The Southey case study – even if considered as an exception – is instructive about the depiction of masculinity in studies of management. These often emphasize the congruence between male-dominated sectors and stereotypically 'masculine' qualities.[6] Discussions of corporate symbolism, too, usually comment on the more obviously phallic metaphors (Knights and Morgan, 1991). In studies of management, as Alvesson and Due Billing (1992) comment, masculinity is too often depicted as a unitary and unchanging category. As I shall argue below, this exclusive concentration on the dominant representations of masculinity risks entrenching essentialist notions of gender. It takes little account of the highly localized self-presentations that may count as 'masculine' in a given organizational setting. More subtle – perhaps more usual – ways in which masculinity and men's managerial power enmesh are thus overlooked (Alvesson and Due Billing, 1992).

Masculinity and emotion management

The existing research on men and emotions in organizations can be divided into two areas. Organizations are sometimes seen as sites from which men's emotions in particular are suppressed or excluded. For example writers from a broadly 'men's studies' perspective have pointed to the role of organizations in reinforcing taboos on men's emotional expression (Ochberg, 1987; Seidler, 1992; Tolson, 1977). Alternatively, there is now a large literature on the processes through which – as Hochschild puts it – women workers 'make a resource out of feeling' (Hochschild, 1983: 163). The following section explores problems raised by these approaches: the first which excludes emotion from its account of masculinity in organizations, the second which excludes masculinity from the account of emotion work and its management.

Men's lack of emotional expressivity was a constant preoccupation in writings about masculinity during the 1970s and 1980s. A contemporary crisis in masculinity was felt to have resulted from the influence of feminism, which had exposed a 'silence at the heart of men's social relations' (Metcalf, 1985: 4). This literature owed much to Nancy Chodorow's account of the acquisition of gender identity, which was itself founded on the supposition that adult men are less likely than women to have access to their emotions. In *The Reproduction of Mothering* (1978), Chodorow attributed the asymmetry of emotional expression between men and women to the need for the infant male to give up its primary identification with the mother in order to establish a separate masculine identity. As a result of this suppression of feeling towards the mother, she argued, adult males subconsciously tend to suppress feelings in general.

Whilst Chodorow's most recent work stresses the need for appreciation of psychic variety *within* each sex, sociological reworkings of the 'early' Chodorow are common in accounts of gender segregation in organizations (Chodorow, 1994; Hochschild, 1983, 164–5; Williams, 1989). For example Victor Seidler laments the fact that men lack the 'words' and language with which to communicate intimacy. Work contributes to this emotional illiteracy, its competitive, jealous atmosphere prohibiting all but 'thin' relationships between men (Seidler, 1992: 17). Men *do* things together but 'feel uncomfortable when emotional issues emerge in our relationships with men and we will often stay silent about them' (ibid.: 18). Work and the personal investment in it functions as an escape, enabling men to 'hang out' together whilst avoiding emotional commitment (ibid.: 22).

This type of account confuses the 'myth of organizational monoculture', which represents men in unitary terms as non-emotional, with their actual experiences (Hearn, 1992b: 199–205). It conflates the *discursive* positioning of men in organizations as non-emotional, with how they are. Of course, as Hearn notes, there is 'some truth' in the view of men in organizations as unemotional (Hearn, 1993: 143). Yet Seidler, like many others, takes the 'masculine ethic' of men as non-emotional at face value. Two problems arise from this. First, the representation of work as a refuge from intimacy leaves no space for developing a view of men in organizations as emotional subjects. Secondly, one might argue in the case of management that the organizational monoculture, the presentation of men's networks as bureaucratic and non-subjective, has concealed exclusive and exclusionary affections between men.

In this sense the contrast with Arlie Hochschild's *The Managed Heart* could hardly be greater. Where many 'men's movement' writers depict organizations as largely non-intimate realms, Hochschild sets out to understand why women in organizations are overdetermined as emotional beings. For Hochschild, then, emotions are 'a permanent aspect of the workplace' (1993: x). Yet she is equivocal about the extent to which emotion work is gendered, and the role of managers in the 'Managed Heart'.

Hochschild depicts men and emotions in three quite different ways. First, she states categorically in one passage that 'the evidence seems clear that women do more emotion managing than men' (Hochschild, 1983: 164). Just as women's dependence upon men in the domestic sphere is repaid by 'affirming, enhancing and celebrating the well-being and status of others', so the airline stewardess does 'deep acting' for the (often male) customer, summoning up good feeling in return for a wage (Hochschild, 1983: 19, 165).[7] This transmutation of women's private 'emotion work' into paid 'emotional labour' locks women into servicing roles *vis-à-vis* men (Hochschild, 1990: 118). Not only are women more likely to perform emotional labour than men, but emotional labour is itself partly defined by the fact that women perform it.

Yet Hochschild also suggests that *both* women and men perform emotional labour, albeit of different kinds. As she comments, 'for each gender a different portion of the heart is enlisted for commercial use' (Hochschild, 1983: 163–4). Women are more likely to be required to exploit qualities of 'sexual beauty, charm and relational skills', whilst for men 'it is more often the capacity to wield anger and make threats that is delivered over to the company' (ibid.: 147, 164). Hochschild uses the example of the male debt collector, who deep-acts 'escalating aggression' in order to extract money from the debtor (ibid.: 139). In this conception both women and men do emotional labour, but of fundamentally dissimilar kinds.

Especially in her more recent writings, Hochschild positions men in a third way: as the managers who write and oversee feeling rules. This suggests an alternative view of emotional labour in which masculinity is crucial. Hochschild argues that whilst management is usually viewed in terms of cognitive processes, actually a large part of the manager's job is concerned with the management of emotions. Managerial divisions of labour are also emotional divisions of labour. Thus the emotional labour of the personnel manager, she suggests, involves getting to know and manipulate the company's 'emotional map': how to interpret jokes and insults, and how to handle staff quarrels or interdepartmental rivalry (Hochschild, 1993: x). The advertising executive carries out emotional labour in relation to external customers, reading the desires of the general public in order to sell products. As Hochschild asserts: 'As part of emotional labour, the manager also assesses feeling' (ibid.: ix).

Moreover, in contrast to the lower-level employee, managers may become so immersed in emotion work that they can no longer distinguish between the private and the public uses of feeling. The more senior the post, the 'deeper' the acting. Whilst supermarket checkout workers may be encouraged to smile and greet customers, this 'surface acting' can be done with the maintenance of some emotional distance. In contrast the salesperson may become so enthusiastic about their company or product that they 'transform their show of personality into a symbol of the company' (Hochschild, 1983: 154). This aptly describes Paul, whose lively visual performances became a symbol of departmental virility. At very senior levels, Hochschild argues, there may be an almost complete merging of self and organization. For corporate decision makers,

> the ties between self and work are many and diffuse. Here years of training and experience, mixed with a daily carrot-and-stick discipline, conspire to push corporate feeling rules further and further away from self-awareness. Eventually

these rules about how to see things and how to feel about them come to seem 'natural', a part of one's personality. The longer the employment and the more rewarding the work in terms of interest, power and pay, the truer this becomes. (Hochschild, 1983: 155)

This insight tips the Weberian story – at least its crude incarnation in organization studies – on its head. Emotions were supposed to have been regulated out of existence in the modern bureaucracy, yet Hochschild is suggesting here that for many managers their work identity *is* their self-identity. Instead of the bureaucracy resting on impersonal foundations, its rules about human feeling reach to the very core of subjectivity. In this respect it seems that, rather than men doing less emotional labour than women, managers in general – and men as the majority of managers – do the deepest acting of all.

Given the male domination of management, especially at the senior levels Hochschild is talking about, this insight raises a range of questions about how male managers shape their identities as men through work, and the nature of their emotional bonds with each other. The example of Paul suggests that emotional labour can be gendered in ways that do not confirm subordination. His success depended partly on labours which Hochschild would surely see as feminine in kind. He used his physical appearance to create a sense of well-being in others. In listening to the head of department and commenting on his work, he provided the kind of invisible support for which male professionals are said to depend on their wives (Finch, 1983). As progress chaser he absorbed the aggression of the junior researchers, shielding the head of department from internal tensions. In all these ways Paul might be said to have performed emotional labour. Yet it was through these skills that Paul consolidated his position within the unit. Illustrations such as this indicate that perhaps we need to consider the gendering of emotional labour in a rather less categorical way, rather than representing masculinity solely in terms of aggression, instrumental thinking or the denial of vulnerability. As Andrea Cornwall and Nancy Lindisfarne remind us, 'being masculine' – and assuming authority as a man – 'can involve self-presentations which include behaviour convention-ally associated with *both* masculinity and femininity' (Cornwall and Lindisfarne, 1994: 15).

Existing depictions of emotional labour raise as many questions as they answer in relation to management and masculinity.[8] On the one hand they present a model of gender hierarchies in which women are the principal subjects of the commercialization of feeling. On the other hand they present a model of managerial hierarchies in which emotional work becomes more deep-rooted and insidious the higher up one goes. These tensions exemplify the gaps that still remain in researching men, management and emotions in organizations. As I will argue below, making male managers visible as emotional subjects means bringing to light the full range of their intimate practices, rather than accepting the organizational monoculture and its non-emotional 'masculine ethic' at face value.

Management as 'homosexual reproduction'?

Just as researchers have been slow to recognize the role of emotion in men's networks, so they have understated the sexual aspects of male bonding. There are many reasons for this. In broadly liberal-feminist studies of women in management there has been a tendency to perceive sexuality as problematic mainly where women and men are. Attention has usually been fixed on heterosexual relations, specifically on identifying forms of sexual harassment of women by men (Pringle, 1988: 95). At the same time, networks between men in management have been regarded as strategic mechanisms rather than as institutionalized forms of intimacy.[9] Homosocial desire thus remained invisible on two counts: because it did not directly oppress women, and because networking was regarded as a normal – and therefore non-sexual – part of organizational routines.

Recent work has moved away from this conception of sexuality in terms of directly oppressive or harassing acts, to seeing it as an 'ordinary and frequent process of public life' (Burrell and Hearn, 1989: 13).[10] Even so there remains a silence around same-sex relations (ibid.). For example, in a summary of research on sexuality and organizational practices, Barbara Gutek describes the shift from seeing sexual behaviour mainly in terms of harassing acts (Gutek, 1989: 57).[11] Gutek highlights the fact that men's sexual behaviour has often gone unnoticed. She argues that, contrary to popular stereotypes, men more often than women use their sexuality to 'foster organizational goals'. Precisely because their behaviour is less likely to be interpreted as sexual, they possess the freedom to seduce women or offer them organizational rewards in return for sex (Gutek, 1989: 62–4). At the same time as Gutek strives to rectify the asymmetrical picture of men's and women's sexual behaviour, she perpetuates it through her focus on heterosexuality:

> Is it possible to create a social setting that actually conveys the message that 'sex is inappropriate here'? Probably not. This may be the reason why organizations like the military traditionally prefer only heterosexual men. Having only same-sex heterosexuals at least in theory precludes any sexual behaviour. (Gutek, 1989: 66)

Gutek here reflects a widespread presumption that sexual desire is ubiquitous between women and men, but not between formally heterosexual men. Moreover, despite her broadening of the definition of sex to include both consent and coercion, Gutek still views sexuality mainly in terms of practices and behaviour. Such an approach does not give any clues as to the intensity of affections and the aspects of desire that give men's networks their particular dynamism.

It is within broadly post-structuralist writing that the notion of management as a process of 'homosexual reproduction' is most fully developed. Perhaps the boldest attempt in this direction is Calás and Smircich's rereading of 'classic' texts on leadership (Calás and Smircich, 1991). They argue that seduction is a dominant form in organizational writings on leadership, but that this is suppressed by the textual construction of an opposition between 'leadership' as rational and 'seduction' as devalued and non-organizational. Seduction is embedded in the discourse of leadership (Calás and Smircich, 1991: 570). For example they deconstruct the text of Henry Mintzberg's *The Nature of Managerial Work* (1973), revealing the manager as one who 'will be preoccupied with the body and its carnal needs': who 'will bestow his favours and gifts to those placed in his possession'; and who 'will constantly stimulate, excite, arouse and penetrate' (Calás and Smircich, 1991: 586). Calás and Smircich's point is less that leadership *is* seduction than that writing about leadership itself has seductive effects on the reader. Moreover, it is homosexual seduction, since leadership discourse is a masculine discourse aimed at maintaining a 'homosocial system of organization'. Writings on leadership articulate 'a form of seduction which thrives on *sameness*' (Calás and Smircich, 1991: 571).

A deconstructive reading such as this neatly elicits the sexualized nature of male-dominated fields of knowledge and action. At the same time however, connections with actual sexual practices are lost. In deconstructive analyses, sexual discourses can be found just about everywhere: as master narratives which structure boss/secretary relations; even in the staid literature of management studies. Indeed it is the fact that leadership texts are devoid of sexual language which leads Calás and Smircich to interpret such texts as having seductive effects in the first place! If some writers on gender and management have tended to overlook the ubiquity of sexuality, mistakenly grouping men's networks under the banner of 'homosociality', the literary turn threatens to conflate all manner of intimacies into the category of the sexual. Organizational sexuality has gone from being nowhere to being present even when it is absent.

The example of Southey suggests that relations in male-dominated organizations often fall between the categories of the social and the sexual. Empowerment within such settings depends not only on the possession of technical skills or qualifications, but equally upon the ability to engage in the erotic aspects of male bonding. Finding the right words for these activities is thus important. Yet male bonding has often been described in terms of clumsy dichotomies such as social versus sexual or homosexual versus heterosexual. To describe it as 'homosocial' emphasizes its function in maintaining male monopolies but disregards the erotic energy that motivates it. Nor is 'homosexual reproduction' accurate: male bonding gains its particular ambience precisely because it does not involve explicit acts of sexual intimacy. Homosexual repression, as Lynne Segal observes, 'is central to male bonding' (Segal, 1990: 159).

Sedgwick's concept of 'homosocial desire' is helpful because it addresses these radical discontinuities between male heterosexuality and homosexuality. Such desires need to be revealed, she argues, because they are 'the affective or social force, the glue, even when its manifestation is hostility or hatred' that shapes relationships of empowerment (Sedgwick, 1985: 2, 27). At the same time, whilst one might talk of a circuit of desire or a 'lesbian continuum'[12] which extends from friendship to sexual relations between women, its visibility among men is radically disrupted by homophobia and the compulsory heterosexuality of institutions such as management (Sedgwick, 1985: 1–2).

Institutionalized homophobia has many effects. One is that men cannot easily engage in emotionally supportive and intimate relationships without raising questions about homosexuality (Nardi, 1992; Wood, 1987: 275). Another is that homosocial desires cannot be openly named. Sometimes they are alluded to via the language of heterosexual attraction. For example Howard described the effect of Paul's public performances on the men in the department as like that produced by a 'female flamenco dancer'. Alternatively, they may be evoked in terms – such as 'horseplay' or 'messing around' – which defuse their erotic resonance by limiting the sexual connotations of the act.[13]

Homoerotically charged behaviour in male-dominated workplaces is more commonplace than is usually recognized. In the nineteenth century the testicles of apprentice engineers were sometimes daubed with grease as part of their initiation to the trade. Nowadays – as Marc E. Burke shows in a recent book – straight policemen get their thrills by chasing gay men who are cottaging (Burke, 1993: 48). There is a narrow divide between homosocial and homosexual desire. Yet while homosocial desire may be especially significant in traditionally 'masculine' settings such as management, it remains concealed by homophobia and the cultural divide between heterosexuality and homosexuality.

Homosocial desire has remained largely unexplored even in studies of gender segregation in management, a function perhaps of the exclusive focus on women's position in early liberal-feminist studies. Intimacies between male managers are crucially important, however, because it is through them that 'exclusionary circles' are formed and maintained. Rosemary Pringle has commented that male sexuality in the workplace has to be 'made visible and accountable' (Pringle, 1994: 122). I would argue that this process should encompass both relations of heterosexuality and homosocial desire within management, so that exclusionary and inclusionary practices can be seen side by side.

Researchers have sometimes conspired in the view that intimacy between men is a private matter, one which pertains mainly to non-work domains, and especially not to management. Anthony Giddens introduces his survey of love and sexuality in the twentieth century, *The Transformation of Intimacy*, with the comment that 'Modern societies have a covert emotional history, yet to be fully drawn into the open. It is a history of the sexual pursuits of men, kept separate from their public selves' (Giddens, 1992: 2). At one level Giddens is absolutely right: men's intimacies have historically been excluded from their representation as public actors. And yet Giddens encapsulates an unresolved problem here, for he takes at face value the organizational monoculture of men in public as non-sexual. Rather than upholding the myth of men's 'public' and 'private' selves as separate, we could learn much by considering their public activities *as* forms of sublimated 'sexual pursuit'.

Notes

I would like to thank the following people for their helpful comments on this chapter: David Collinson, Jeff Hearn, John Land, David H. Morgan, Lyndal Roper, and especially Howard White. Audiences at Essex, City Business School, UMIST, Royal Holloway College and the University of North London also heard and constructively commented on various wild drafts of it. Please note that the names of individuals and institutions have been disguised so as to ensure anonymity.

1. A notable exception to this lack of attention to gender is Nicole Woolsey Biggart's study of direct selling organizations (DSOs) in America. Biggart argues that the success of DSOs hinges on the way that their managements exploit familial networks and ideologies. However, by emphasizing the distinctive logic of this organizational form, Biggart leaves unaltered the definition of 'conventional' workplaces – bureaucracies – as characterized by 'relatively impersonal relations' (Biggart, 1990: 6).

2. This is a slightly lower proportion than the national figure for British universities of over 20 per cent women academic staff and 4.9 per cent professors (Association of University Teachers, 1993: 1).

3. The department's recruitment practices assisted this. Six staff had been recruited from the university in which the head of department had previously taught, five of them men.

4. The importance placed on the 'instrumental-purposive' discourse of economics resulted partly from an earlier struggle over the unit's leadership (Knights and Morgan, 1991: 200). In the middle 1980s it had been staffed largely by social psychologists. With the appointment of a new head in the later 1980s who was a neoclassical economist, almost all the 'old guard' (as Howard called them) left. The new head had appointed economists in their place, and had shifted the direction of research away from topics such as corporate culture to competitive performance.

5. The tone of these jibes was similar to the tone of jokes which male shopfloor workers sometimes deploy against their middle-class managers (Collinson, 1992: Chapter 4).

6. See for example Collinson and Knights's study of insurance salesmen, or Collinson, Knights and Collinson on the ideology of the 'company breadwinner' amongst industrial managers (Collinson and Knights, 1986: 149; Collinson et al., 1990: 86).

7. Hochschild argues that '[a]s a matter of tradition, emotion management has been . . . more often used by women as one of the offerings they trade for economic support' (Hochschild, 1983: 20).

8. In more recent work Hochschild has posed many of the questions addressed in this chapter, arguing that '[i]f . . . we should bring men back into sociology, then we had better bring emotions back in with them' (Hochschild, 1990: 117). She flags many possible research agendas, including the extent to which the emotional labour of a secretary differs from that of an executive, or the extent to which all-male environments have different emotional cultures than all-female (Hochschild, 1990: 138).

9. The literature on women and 'mentoring' programmes in management provides a good example. Marilyn Davidson and Cary Cooper, in *Shattering the Glass Ceiling*, are cautious about cross-gender sponsorship programmes – especially where the senior partner is male – partly because they are liable to provoke 'gossip' about sexual liaisons (Davidson and Cooper, 1992: 100–4). In an earlier UK study, Clutterbuck and Devine also warned of the dangers of 'sexual innuendo' in cross-gender sponsorship, and the difficulty of warding off assumptions that the couple are 'motivated by sexual interest' (Clutterbuck and Devine, 1987). The

assumption here is that management networks become sexualized only when women are part of them. Such approaches perpetuate the asymmetrical visibility of men's and women's sexuality by concentrating solely on the stereotype of the woman manager who 'sleeps her way to the top'. Framed within a discourse of fairness, liberal-feminist approaches to women in management uphold the image of men's behaviour in organizations as the non-sexual norm.

10. This reflects the influence of post-structuralism on organization theory, particularly Foucault's notion of a 'wider politics of the body' in which institutions routinely promote discourses that incite and regulate sexuality (Witz and Savage, 1992: 55; Burrell and Hearn, 1989: 7–8).

11. Gutek's survey of Los Angeles workers found that the vast majority of women and men had experienced 'sexual overtures' or other forms of sexual behaviour in their present job which they did not consider to be harassment (Gutek, 1989: 57, 66).

12. Adrienne Rich's phrase describes a continuum among women which extends from friendship to sexual relations. Rich argues that women's common experience of and resistance to male oppression unites them in this continuum (Rich, 1984).

13. The first UK case involving sexual harassment of one man by another was taken in mid-1993. A security guard, Matthew Gates, claimed that on repeated occasions his boss had come 'up behind me, put one hand around my waist, the other around my neck and attempted to simulate sexual intercourse'. The judge ruled that the behaviour of the accused man went 'well beyond what a reasonable person would regard as horseplay' (*Guardian*, 15 July 1993). His comments suggest that a range of implicitly sexual behaviour between men has traditionally been accepted as within the realms of 'horseplay'.

12

Managing Universities: Is It Men's Work?

Craig Prichard

'Management' in conventional discourse is understood as various ways of attempting to exercise some directionality on, over or through the work of others (Daft, 1991; Hales, 1993; Watson, T., 1994). What is so often left out of conventional accounts of these relations is their gendered character. Managing invariably involves attempts to enable or disable particular gendered ways of being (identities, relations) and gendered ways of doing (activities of the body, ways of speaking). One consequence of this enabling and disabling is that certain occupations and sets of positions in organizations are dominated by men or women. For instance the senior posts of tertiary education internationally are held by men to a degree where they seem to be retained *for* men. In the UK at the time of writing there are just two women vice-chancellors in post at the apex of the seventy-two universities in England (both in post-1992 'new' universities).[1] However, as an indicator of some change and perhaps challenge to this practice, three women were expected to take up vice-chancellor posts in September 1995 (see Williams, 1995).[2] Nevertheless Miller notes in his review of his work on university management in three countries (Australia, Canada and the United Kingdom) that the 'most obvious, but often unreported, feature of the management of universities in all three countries is the sheer dominance of men and masculine styles' (1994: 30).

For Cockburn (1991) the dominance of men in organizations amounts to a fratriarchal sexual contract between men over women in work organizations. This is accomplished, she points out, through two strategies. First, women's work is partitioned off from, and awarded lower value than men's work, and second, where women achieve senior positions they supervise other women, or their executive management role is identified with the 'feminine' aspects of the organization's work, such as personnel management. It is through the daily enactment and reinforcing of these gendered processes, which interweave certain masculinities with the work of managing and can include intimidation and violence,[3] that men come to be dominant in organizations.

Yet this is not inevitably the case. Whilst this fratriarchal contract is deeply entrenched it is not inevitably reproduced. This chapter offers a discussion of the linkages between management and masculinities in tertiary education and a brief account of a challenge to these prevailing relationships in a post-1992 university. The account notes the way discourse practices surrounding the running of university committee meetings are supportive of dominant masculinities, and how these are being challenged by a group of women academic and administrative 'managers', drawing on 'new' management discourse. The chapter concludes by asking what possible future there may be for relations between men and women in the management and organization of tertiary education in the UK.

The empirical materials for this chapter are drawn from interviews with senior post-holders in two post-1992 universities (former local authority controlled polytechnics which as a result of successive legislation became universities in 1992) and two 'civic' universities which were well established by 1992. A similar sample of post-holders were interviewed in each institution. Of the nine interviewees from each organization, three were from what might be described as the vice-chancellor's group. This includes the vice-chancellor, a pro-vice-chancellor and either the director of finance, registrar or bursar. Three senior academic 'managers' were interviewed, usually a dean or equivalent and two heads of department. Three senior administrative managers were also interviewed including the directors of finance, personnel and estates. As a further indicator of the general absence of women senior post-holders in UK universities, of the thirty-five respondents interviewed, just six were women. One of the pre-1992 universities had no women members in its senior management team (directors of services, pro-vice chancellors, etc.), while the other pre-1992 university had two women members of this tier. Two of the six women interviewed for this study were directors of personnel in two institutions and three of the six, all from one of the two post-1992 universities, were respectively a head of department, a dean and a senior administrative head.[4]

Managing UK tertiary education: setting the scene

It is impossible to develop a feel for the conditions currently operative in university management, without briefly outlining something of the background to the changes under way in the UK's tertiary education sector. Prior to the 1980s the established universities enjoyed a quasi-autonomous status in which the unit of resource for a student was basically fixed, though subject to some erosion, and research resources were spread fairly evenly across institutions. Following the election of the Thatcher administration, the Department of Education pursued a strongly interventionist line (in which vice-chancellors have been complicit). Initially, there were major, selective cuts in the funding of universities based largely upon the quality of their intake (i.e. the grades achieved by school leavers). Subsequently, student numbers have been continuously expanded without an equivalent increase in resources, and research resources have been distributed according to 'objective' measures of performance (for example size of research grants, number of top journal publications, number of research students) rather than according to the numbers of academic staff employed (see Miller, 1995; Humphrey et al. 1995).

In 1992, competitive pressures were intensified by the wholesale conversion of polytechnics into universities, a move that made the former eligible to compete for research funding and provided an alternative model of administration and teaching provision to that traditionally pursued within the established universities. Without going into the detail of these changes (see Willmott, 1995; Parker and Jary, 1995), their effect has been to increase the pressures on senior academics and administrators – from vice-chancellors to heads of department – to demonstrate a capacity to organize and 'manage' their staff in ways that deliver the results that will ensure a flow of resources sufficient to sustain their existence and, ideally, to boost their prestige. While it could be argued that these post-1992 universities have a history of more explicit managerialism (compared to the established universities), their shift to become self-managing entities (April 1989) and then universities (1992) financed directly by the university funding councils brought with it the introduction of new management disciplines and an intensification of concern on the part of senior postholders for control over organizational activities. During 1992–3 the UK's further education sector (colleges offering predominantly vocational and university entry courses) went through a similar process to that of the former polytechnics. Colleges became self-managing organizations and senior post-holders were encouraged to see themselves as business people and their institutions as businesses engaged in an education market funded (in the main) by government agencies. This process of incorporation has introduced management disciplines into colleges and intensified the pressure on colleges to recruit and 'teach' more students for less cost (Reeves, 1995). One effect of this has been an intensive and drawn-out campaign by college employers to introduce a new and potentially more exploitative employment contract for lecturers. Thousands of college lecturers have to date refused to sign this. Non-signers were recently described by the head of the colleges' negotiating body as lecturers who 'may not be appropriate professionals to stay in the education sector' (Charter, 1995).

The key point is that tertiary education in the UK has seen rapid increases in student numbers which have not been matched by an equivalent level of resources. Alongside this, a set of programmes has been instituted which seek to measure and audit institutional performance. In this situation the work of senior post-holders is being repositioned. From being administrators of largely predictable and protected income flows, senior post-holders are now under pressure to take responsibility for the processes that are deemed to influence these flows. It is in the midst of this mêlée that some challenges are under way to the embedded linkages between masculinities and the management of tertiary education. For instance Brian Booth, rector and chief executive (the dual title is instructive of the changes taking place) of the post-1992 University of Central Lancashire (formerly Lancashire Polytechnic), noted:

The style of management in the former polytechnics has changed radically over the past three years through specification, via the articles of government, of the responsibilities placed on the head of the institution. The delegation of these responsibilities through clear line management structures and, in some institutions, the use of permanent rather than rotating posts at middle and senior management levels, has enabled significant career development for both women and men, in particular for women, who do not seem to get elected or nominated to rotating posts. (Booth, 1992)

Of course while Booth notes development in the careers of some women in the sector, most of the 'managers' of tertiary education continue to be men (Williams, 1995). Managing to these men tends to rely heavily for its efficacy and plausibility on particular established masculinities (Kerfoot and Whitehead, 1995; Whitehead, 1995; Wild, 1994; Heward, 1994; Thomas, 1994; Morley, 1994; Collinson and Hearn, 1994; Cockburn, 1991), such as a deeply embedded paternalism (Court, 1994), or emerging masculinities which seem increasingly aggressive, 'macho' and autocratic (Utley, 1995).

Nevertheless, as Yeatman (1995) argues, women's relative outsider positioning, their status as 'other' in the established masculine world at the apex of education institutions, means that in some cases, or at certain moments in an institution's history, they are used by senior men in attempts to change these organizations; to call attention to 'all the fustian, patriarchal inefficiencies of the old institutional culture' (ibid.: 200). Yeatman suggests that in the contemporary managerialist, competitive, results-based environment, opportunities have opened up for women to take up these change-agent positions in education management.

This chapter supports Yeatman's contention and attempts to add 'flesh' to it by providing an example of these relations at work. The argument here is that on the fringes of the tertiary education sector in the UK – on terrain where change is occurring rapidly, where gaps in the fustian fabric have opened up and where women have found jobs and some like-minded colleagues (both men and women) – some challenge is under way. In certain cases, women have been successfully incorporated into what might be seen as a reinvigorated masculine ethos, and become 'honorary' men. In others, small groups of women, now in quite senior positions, are attempting to create different patterns in the way these organizations are articulated and practised. The argument is that in the UK's 'new' post-1992 institutions (those former local authority organizations which adopted equal opportunities policies early: Heward and Taylor, 1992) it is possible to find groups of women challenging masculine taken-for-granted ways of doing and ways of being. Of course it is also possible to find men who are challenging these taken-for-granted dispositions. But it is *around* these groups of women that the incisions, the challenges and the new patterns are being worked out. To some extent it is 'new' managerialism (Clarke et al., 1994), the ascended or ascending discourse of authority in education settings (which is seen as a constraint and in some settings an attack on established academic and administrative identities and relations) that provides this opportunity for change (Newman, 1994).

Managerial practices, managerial masculinities

Using material from the interviews with the senior post-holders, this section seeks to describe some of the ways in which masculinities and the management of universities are linked. A number of authors have suggested that the plausibility of management discourse in education cannot be understood without reference to the ways in which it is supported by gender – particularly by certain contemporary masculinities (Blackmore, 1993; Court, 1994; Heward, 1994; Morley, 1994; Thomas, 1994). Kerfoot and Whitehead (1995) for instance stress, with regard to the further education (FE) sector, that the 'discourse of new managerialism in FE is consonant with, and constitutive of, a form of masculinity that achieves validation through control and power over others' (1995: 12).

Masculinities are various narratives, identities and ways of being in space and over time which construct relations between men and men, and men and women. For example, one faculty dean with whom I spoke talked about how the close long-term relations between himself and his colleagues made it largely impossible for him to be an autocratic 'jack-boot Führer' of a manager. This suggests that embedded in particular locales are relations between men that revolve significantly around homosociability or the male camaraderie of being 'mates'. The masculinity here is woven with a strong egalitarian ethic between men which flattens overt institutional differences, such as being a dean or a manager, and enforces an ethic where members don't 'get above themselves'. What this suggests is that fratriarchal loyalties are part of the 'cocktail' of resistances to the wholesale managerialization (Clarke et al., 1994) of the UK tertiary education sector.

A quite different example of these masculinities at work was described by one head of department interviewed during the research. He noted that further 'up' the organization, relations between men tended to be more aggressive and compliant:

> I think there is less mediation of instructions the further up you go. The deans get told in a fairly bloody-minded way to do this [or] do that by Tuesday. They mellow a bit as they tell us, or ask us, and so on down. The sort of brutalist approach gets more obvious at the top. What is very obvious is [that this is] a very *man-managed* institution.
>
>   C.P.: What do you mean by *man-managed*?
>
> Well I mean whatever the pretence and actually whether we talk about men or women it is very much a traditional image of tough males running the place. (emphasis mine)

'Man-management' seems to mean here that management in this organization relies heavily on a mix of what Collinson and Hearn (1994) describe as authoritarian and entrepreneurial masculinities. The head of department's comment suggests that masculinities at work among senior post-holders, especially in relations between deans and the senior team, are based on aggressive and dictatorial relations overlaid with perhaps a concern for organization targets, performance levels and efficiency. This was confirmed by comments from other heads in the institution. For instance a long-serving head of department offered a quick sketch of the senior post-holders:

> [the vice-chancellor] is very rigid in his approach and extremely inflexible. [The deputy vice-chancellor] is a very difficult character to deal with. He will not allow conversation and unfortunately I don't even think he is aware of it. He makes very pejorative remarks and statements like 'You are all academic heads so I'll explain this to you twice.' You know, is that supposed to be funny? It [the vice-chancellor's group] is very male dominated. They seem to be very task-orientated people. Perhaps they are overworked, perhaps it [the vice-chancellor's group] is insufficient [in number] but I think there is a definite need to have a more human-relations-orientated type of person in at that level and we also need to have a team of deans who are stronger than the current team we have now.

Men managers exercise their power and authority through discursive practices. These include displays of inflexibility, unwillingness to listen, unwillingness to allow others to talk, patronizing humour and derogatory remarks. All these serve to organize and reproduce managerial power relations in this organization. The above example shows how managerial relations of dominance and subordination are enacted and expressed through particularly masculine authoritarian, aggressive, and competitive practices.

Yet while the more managerialist educational site might rely on these aggressive and authoritarian masculine styles, a more paternalistic masculinity is also engaged in reproducing managerial relations in education institutions. As Morley (1994: 200) notes: 'The heterosexist model of the nuclear family with its gender-specific roles and responsibilities appears to reproduce itself in the academic workplace.' This 'model' appears in material collected from the four universities studied and, as might be expected, tends to revolve around relations between administrative and academic post-holders. The following comment suggests there is a dominant narrative (certainly not specific to universities) at work which positions men as the breadwinners (academics in this case), women as housekeepers (administrators) and students as the 'children'. One of the pro-vice-chancellors interviewed for this study said in relation to senior administrators:

> We are trying to treat them [the service heads] as equals, but they are unequal. The service people provide services and are therefore subservient in that way. They are not initiators or developers of the institution. They may develop new systems of finance or academic registry, but they don't see themselves as leading the institution. The deans meanwhile, leading the schools, certainly do and should do because everyone else is dependent on them bringing in the students.

One vital piece of information left out of the foregoing statement is that all the deans at this institution are men and the service heads have among them a high-profile group of women. One of these women had this to say about relations between these groups:

> Two or three years ago certainly the heads of service felt that they were on the periphery and were not being taken seriously. It is such a contrast that we are now just mainstream management. We are all affected by this and it has been quite a 'sea change'. [C.P.: 'Right, in whose eyes?'] I think both, you know, the heads of service now have much more confidence in themselves. If you feel inferior you tend to act in that way and I think the deans recognize the importance now of the infrastructure.

Clearly there is some contradiction between this and the above comment from the male pro-vice-chancellor at the same university. The two comments reveal a struggle over positioning in competing narratives. The first statement places academics, who are largely men, over service heads and service department workers, who in this case are women. This view reflects and reinforces assumptions about a traditional nuclear family narrative which is not far from its surface. The second, competing, narrative from the service head draws on management discourse to challenge the traditional arrangement. The generalizing and equalizing aspects of management discourse (highlighted here by the service head in the comment: 'We are now just mainstream management') is drawn upon to help reposition this group of women senior post-holders in relation to the dominant group of male academic heads. This also attempts to rewrite the paternalistic nuclear family narrative of the organization. The pro-vice-chancellor's comment meanwhile suggests that he is both struggling with and ultimately resistant to this rewriting. He begins his comments first by 'flagging up' this equalizing aspect of management discourse; for example: 'We are trying to treat them as equal.' But then he quickly repositions service heads as unequal by returning to the notion of the academics as the 'natural' leaders of the institution and· ascribing to administration a subservient position.

Another head of service added extra 'flesh' to the story of the masculinities engaged at senior levels across this university:

> The deans are all men at the moment. The interesting thing is probably that [the differences between them] depend on their academic background. The dean of arts and the dean of the business school, which has the professional women's development unit in it, are the softies if you like. And then you've got sciences, you know, real hard tough and yet he [dean of science] is in fact very good with his staff. Er, and then you have got the mixture in between. But yes I think one of the problems is that because they are all men there is a tendency for them to sort of [be] the boys together, the gang, and you know, we should all drink Newcastle Brown and pints.

The social spaces in which these masculinities are reproduced (of 'being the boys together') include senior post-holder committee meetings. Another service head describes how she saw these meetings:

> It has to be said that deans dominate these meetings because they're the ones who are used to spouting off and they don't think twice about whether their point is valid. And once one has said something the other deans have got to say something. . . . And heads of services tend to see that it is a game and think oh . . . I have got more important things to do back at base, you know.

These are not stand-alone comments. Such comments reflect an at times overt conflict between senior post-holders over the way power relations are exercised. To some extent the arrival of a woman pro-vice-chancellor at the university in the late 1980s helped to clarify the gendered character of this conflict. A service head offered some background to this:

> We have a woman pro-vice-chancellor who has an academic background. I work very very closely with her and we just have different ways of doing things. I think until she came [here] I hadn't realized just how uncomfortable I felt about some of the ways the committees worked and hadn't really had an opportunity to look at other ways of working because there was nobody else to work with in that way. . . . She has a very open way of chairing meetings and a very different kind of way. The first meeting she had, she ordered sticky buns and things like that, you know, ha ha, like people were just taken aback, didn't know what to do with it. It is sort of a very disarming kind of role a kind of um um leadership style which she has which is very interesting. It's very interesting seeing it work, much more relaxed and informal and yet still getting the work done.

Here the service head is referring to how the normalized hierarchical formality of organizational practices was challenged to some extent by the pro-vice-chancellor's more open, informal ways of operating. These allowed the service head to be more 'herself' in these settings and to experience a sense in which the previous practices had operated to position her as subordinate to others and had clearly helped to define and reinforce a paternalistic, nuclear family narrative of the university. These practices had allowed comments, such as those by the male pro-vice-chancellor recorded above ('[the service people] don't see themselves as leading the institution'), to be made 'common sense' in the university. In turn both the meeting practices, and this 'common sense' concerned with relations between academic and service heads, further reproduced men's dominance and women's sense of exclusion from the organization.

Coleman (1991) in her study of women's experiences of organizations highlights similar points. A major theme to emerge from her informants was a 'sense of being at odds with the prevailing "style" and value system of the organization, an awareness of difference' (1991: 41). Coleman goes on to say that 'overwhelmingly, the women I interviewed were expressing the ways in which they experience themselves as women being "different" in their organization from the prevailing male norm' (1991: 47). The service head and some of her colleagues above had similar experiences prior to the pro-vice-chancellor's arrival. The university's traditional meeting practices positioned the service head as different from the norm, and in being positioned as different, the norm-alized speaking and being practices which men used were not extended to her. The open, informal and deconstructing practices of the new pro-vice-chancellor served to open up this space for some reflection and later challenge. With this background in mind I will now briefly sketch out a particular point in this conflict over the dominant masculine way of organizing at this university.

Women's challenge to management masculinities

In 1993 a group of senior post-holders in this institution attempted to challenge the way the senior team organized its work. This group of women, who number just five among the senior tier of twenty-seven deans, heads of services and executives, proposed that committees in the university be replaced with task groups and special project teams. It was argued that these would be both more effective and more flexible ways of working at senior levels. They suggested that on a trial basis all regular committee meetings should be cancelled in the autumn term in favour of working groups and special project teams. The suggestion had the support of some men but more importantly drew on the current emphasis in management discourse on teams, teamworking and 'team ideology' (Sinclair, 1992).

The proposal was however rejected by other members of the senior staff tier. One of the proposers related that: 'It was just thrown out, "couldn't possibly entertain that suggestion".' The woman service head (S.H.) said:

Interestingly those who chaired the senior committees were totally against it. There was actually no way that they were going to allow that. You know 'what would we do? We would have half a week not in committees, oh dear me'.

C.P.: There is a temptation to suggest that men have got their identities very much tied into the committee structures. The 'chairman' and that kind of thing, whereas the women in the institution are happier working in a looser more informal way. Is that a fair, or is that too . . .?

S.H.: My experience is that men use committees more to make statements about their own power and their own power base and to make statements about themselves whereas I think women actually want to make [*pause*], you know perhaps we are just naive, I don't know. We [the women] tend to go there thinking this is the agenda, this is what we are going to talk about. I think often the senior management here have other agendas and they are trying to prove other things to other people and that is one of the problems with meetings. They don't actually talk about [*pause*] some of the agenda items just get sidetracked because somebody has got a personal agenda for that day and they are determined that whatever the meeting is about they are going to make their point about something and so lots of it is used very much as a power base.

Despite the proposal's failure at this time, the above example shows that in this university challenges to the links between certain masculinities and management practice (suggested here by the comment 'they [senior management] are trying to prove other things to other people') are being undertaken in overt and pragmatic ways. In this case the women, who to some extent drew on a feminist reading of organization, together with a set of alternative meeting practices, were able to present their proposals using management discourse. By putting the imperializing discourse of management to work for them, they sought to challenge one of the organization's control mechanisms (committee meetings) which reproduce particular gendered relations. If established in place of committee meetings, the suggested informal task groups and special project teams would have challenged to some extent the overlap between masculinities and management. The dominance of male chairs would probably have been questioned. The informal committee meeting practices that allow academic men to speak more and on off-agenda subjects (which work to maintain the link between masculine identities and control) is likely to have been problematized, and a whole regime of relations between bodies in enclosed rooms would have been challenged, with senior post-holders meeting in the more informal settings of offices rather than in formal meeting rooms.

Challenging management masculinities: some possible futures

The above discussion suggests that 'new' management discourse provides certain plausible opportunities through which alternative ways of organizing and managing, that challenge linkages between managing and masculinities, can be articulated (Coleman, 1991; Court, 1994; Newman, 1994). It shows that women in this university have to some extent positioned themselves as change agents and are engaged in an albeit slow process of reconstructing the character of managing in these environments. Could this mean that what is occurring is the slow 'feminization' of tertiary education management in the UK, and with this the unsettling of the embeddedness of masculinities in management? Or are examples such as that discussed above 'sideshows' to the major 'drama', which is the continuation and adaptation of the fratriarchal contract in a changing tertiary education sector? Part of any answer to these questions requires discussion of other examples of challenges from other institutions. It also requires a more in-depth analysis of the changing character of the sector as a whole.

It may be that current attempts to increase the level of control over the tertiary education sector, especially its curriculum and its 'learning facilitators' (its teachers and lecturers: see for example Bocock and Watson, 1994; Parker and Jary, 1995), will undermine and to some extent replace the established identities of the male academic manager. This could bring women to senior posts as *managers*. Yet this may, as Yeatman suggests, be part of a shift whereby research, particularly that which earns 'big dollars' (1995: 202), becomes the new patriarchal heartland of the university. In the midst of this process, management becomes 'feminized' just as administration has tended to be (Game, 1994). Another possibility is that both management *and* research in universities will continue to be mutually reinforcing patriarchal heartlands while isolated challenges to this fabric and its deeply interwoven threads of masculinities and management will remain just that – isolated. While such organizations as the Women in Higher Education Network (King, 1993; Utley, 1994b) might be working to challenge this 'hegemonic masculinity' (Connell, 1987), conditions across the tertiary sector, and the public sector generally, need to be considered as part of exploring these possibilities.

One feature of this is apparent. Changes to the patriarchal fabric are interdependent (in a variety of ways) with the changing character of the sector. Two aspects of this change are increasing levels of the commodification of work and increasing attention to control over the sector and its workers (Willmott, 1995; Parker and Jary, 1995; Winter, 1995; Miller, 1995; Prichard and Willmott, 1995). This suggests a complex situation where at certain points and moments across the sector's vast social terrain, these processes actually help to challenge embedded gender relations. Alternatively, as Whitehead's research (1995) suggests, these processes may reinvigorate the links between masculinities and management. Another aspect to be considered when addressing possible futures is the effect that changes across the tertiary sector generally might have, given the concentration of women in the lowest grades of teaching, research and administration (Heward and Taylor, 1992; Morley, 1994; Wild, 1994). It seems likely that in the context of this positioning women may be more intensely subjected to processes which seek to tighten control over academic and administrative labour. If this is the central outcome of the current changes, then the possibility seems rather remote that challenges such as that described above might upset the embedded masculine ethos of many of these organizations. Nevertheless, as I have sought to argue, it is not inevitable that changes occuring across the tertiary education sector in the UK will reinforce ties between existing or emerging masculinities and the practices of managers and managing. There are spaces and points at which challenges to these ties are both possible, and being made.

Notes

1. This figure of two women vice-chancellors does not include the woman head of the University of London's Birkbeck College.

2. There are 63 women principals of the 457 further education colleges (including sixth-form colleges) in the UK (Utley, 1994a, 1994b; Ward, 1995).

3. The intimidation may not necessarily occur between managers and staff, but between male and female staff with the unspoken acquiescence of managers. For instance conflict between, and the intimidation of, mainly women administrative staff by lecturing staff in many universities has a largely unspoken gender dimension. In one university where the author worked, male lecturing staff appeared to patrol the administrative offices in highly masculine ways, for instance by regularly standing over or behind the seated female administrative staff. They also regularly used apparently humorous comments, such as 'Where are the serving wenches, you can't get the staff these days', to reinforce their dominance. When the author attempted to challenge this by writing about it in a column in the university's newsletter it provoked an interesting response. While the faculty's senior administrative manager

congratulated the author on the column, the male lecturing staff sent a representative who bullyingly accused the author of 'selling out' and of 'joining the other side'. He also asserted that the department's female administrative workers 'did not know how lucky they were' as they would probably be worse off in the 'real world'.

4. The interviews lasted between 40 and 90 minutes and covered the following issues: the interviewees' current experience of work; past experience of work; changes in their experience of work; the consequences of these changes and anticipated future changes.

References

Abélès, M. (1992) *La vie quotidienne au Parlement Européen*. Paris: Hachette.

Aberbach, J.D., Putnam, R. and Rodman, B. (1981) *Bureaucrats and Politicians in Western Democracies*. Cambridge, MA: Harvard University Press.

Accountant (1915) 'The admission of women into the professions', 23 January: 127–9.

Acker, J. (1988) 'Class, gender, and the relations of distribution', *Signs: Journal of Women in Culture and Society*, 13(3): 473–97.

Acker, J. (1989) 'The problem with patriarchy', *Sociology*, 23(2): 235–40.

Acker, J. (1990) 'Hierarchies, jobs, bodies: a theory of gendered organizations', *Gender and Society*, 4(2): 139–58.

Acker, J. (1991) 'Hierarchies, jobs, bodies: a theory of gendered organization', in J. Lorber and S.A. Farrell (eds), *The Social Construction of Gender*. London: Sage. pp. 162–79.

Acker, J. (1992) 'Gendering organizational analysis', in A.J. Mills and P. Tancred (eds), *Gendering Organizational Analysis*. Newbury Park, CA and London: Sage. pp. 248–60.

Acker, J. (1994) 'The gender regime in Swedish banks', *Scandinavian Journal of Management*, 10(2): 117–30.

Acker, J. (1995) 'Feminist goals and organizing processes', in M.M. Ferree and P.Y. Martin (eds), *Feminist Organizations: Harvest of the New Women's Movement*. Philadelphia: Temple University Press. pp. 137–44.

Acker, J. and van Houten, D.R. (1992) 'Differential recruitment and control: the sex structuring of organizations', in A.J. Mills and P. Tancred (eds), *Gendering Organizational Analysis*. Newbury Park, CA: Sage. pp. 15–31. First published 1974.

Adler, N. and Izraeli, D.N. (eds) (1988) *Women in Management Worldwide*. Armonk, NY: M.E. Sharpe.

Adler, N. and Izraeli, D.N. (eds) (1993) *Competitive Frontiers: Women Managers in the Global Economy*. Cambridge, MA: Basil Blackwell.

Agger, B. (1975) 'On science as domination', in A. Kontos (ed.), *Domination*. Toronto: University of Toronto Press.

Ahrne, G. (1985) 'Den irriterade medborgaren. En undersökning om erfarenheter och upplevelser av byråkrati'. Arbetsrapport 2, Stockholm: Sociologiska institutionen, Stockholms Universitet.

Albrow, M. (1992) 'Sine ira studio – or do organizations have feelings?', *Organization Studies*, 13(3): 313–29.

Allen, S. and Truman, C. (1993) *Women in Business*. London: Routledge.

Allison, A. (1994) *Nightwork: Sexuality, Pleasure and Corporate Masculinity in a Tokyo Hostess Club*. Chicago: University of Chicago.

Alvesson, M. and Due Billing, Y. (1992) 'Gender and organization: towards a differentiated understanding', *Organization Studies*, 13(2): 73–102.

Anderson, G. (ed.) (1988) *The White Blouse Revolution: Female Office Workers since 1870*. Manchester: Manchester University Press.

Antal, A.B. and Izraeli, D.N. (1993) 'A global comparison of women in management: women managers in their homelands and as expatriates', in E.A. Fagenson (ed.), *Women in Management: Trends, Issues and Challenges in Managerial Diversity*, Vol. 4 Women and Work. Newbury Park, CA: Sage. pp. 52–96.

Anthony, P.D. (1986) *The Foundations of Management*. London: Tavistock.

Anthony, P.D. (1994) *Managing Culture*. Milton Keynes: Open University Press.

Armstrong, P. (1984) 'Competition between the organisational professions and the evolution of management control strategies', in K. Thompson (ed.), *Work, Employment and Unemployment*. Milton Keynes: Open University Press. pp. 97–120.

Armstrong, P. (1986) 'Management control strategies and inter-professional competition: the cases of accountancy and personnel management', in D. Knights and H. Willmott (eds), *Gender and the Labour Process*. Aldershot: Gower. pp. 19–43.

Armstrong, P. (1989) 'Limits and possibilities for HRM in an age of management accountancy', in J. Storey (ed.), *New Perspectives on Human Resource Management*. London: Routledge. pp 154–66.

Aron, C.S. (1987) *Ladies and Gentlemen of the Civil Service: Middle-Class Workers in Victorian America*. New York: Oxford University Press.

Arrington, C.E. and Francis, J.R. (1989) 'Letting the chat out of the bag: deconstruction, privilege and accounting research', *Accounting, Organizations and Society*, 14(1/2): 1–28.

Association of University Teachers (1993) *AUT Update*, 8 (June).

Austrin, T. (1980) 'The "lump" in the UK construction industry', in T. Nichols (ed.), *Capital and Labour*. Glasgow: Fontana. pp. 302–15.

Bacchi, C.L. (1990) *Same Difference: Feminism and Sexual Difference*. Sydney: Allen & Unwin.

Baritz, L. (1965) *Servants of Power*. Middletown, CT: Wesleyan University Press.

Barnard, C. (1938) *The Functions of the Executive*. Cambridge, MA: Harvard University Press.

Barnett, B.M. (1995) 'Black women's collectivist movement organizations: their struggles during the "doldrums"', in M.M. Ferree and P.Y. Martin (eds), *Feminist Organizations: Harvest of the New Women's Movement*. Philadelphia: Temple University Press. pp. 199–219.

Baron, A. (1992) 'Technology and the crisis of masculinity: the gendering of work and skill in the US printing industry, 1850–1920', in A. Sturdy, D. Knights and H. Willmott (eds), *Skill and Consent: Contemporary Studies in the Labour Process*. London: Routledge. pp. 67–95.

Barrett, M. (1980) *Women's Oppression Today*. London: Verso.

Barzini, L. (1983) *The Europeans*. Harmondsworth: Penguin.

Becker, G.S. (1981) *A Treatise on the Family*. Cambridge: Harvard University Press.

Beeton, I. (1861) *The Book of Household Management*. Facsimile 1968, London: Jonathan Cape.

Bell, E.L. and Nkomo, S.M. (1992) 'Re-visioning women managers' lives', in A. Mills and P. Tancred (eds), *Gendering Organizational Theory*. Newbury Park, CA: Sage. pp. 235–47.

Bendix, R. (1956) *Work and Authority in Industry*. Berkeley, CA: University of California Press.

Benhabib, S. (1992) *Situating the Subject*. London: Sage.

Beninger, J.R. (1986) *The Control Revolution*. Cambridge, MA: Harvard University Press.

Bennis, W. (1989) *On Becoming a Leader*. Wilmington, MA: Warren Bennis.

Benson, S.P. (1992) '"The clerking sisterhood": rationalization and the work culture of saleswomen in American department stores, 1890–1960', in A.J. Mills and P. Tancred (eds), *Gendering Organizational Analysis*. Newbury Park, CA: Sage. pp. 167–84.

Berle, A.A. and Means, G.C. (1932) *The Modern Corporation and Private Property*. New York: Macmillan.

Beynon, H. (1980) *Working for Ford*. Harmondsworth: Penguin.

Biggart, N.W. (1990) *Charismatic Capitalism. Direct Selling Organizations in America*. Chicago: University of Chicago Press.

Bilimoria, D. and Piderit, S.K. (1994) 'Board committee membership: effects of sex-based bias', *Academy of Management Journal*. 37(6): 1453–77.

Bittman, M. (1991) *Juggling Time: How Australian Families Use Time*. Canberra: Office of the Status of Women.

Bittner, E. (1973) 'The concept of organisation', in G. Salaman and K. Thompson (eds) *People and Organisations*. London: Longman. pp. 264–76. First published 1965.

Blackmore, J. (1993) '"In the shadow of men": the historical construction of administration as a "masculinist" enterprise,' in J. Blackmore and J. Kenway (eds), *Gender Matters in Education Administration and Policy*. London: Falmer Press. pp. 27–48.

Blainey, G. (1979) 'Introduction', in *125 Years of 'The Age'*. Melbourne: Nelson.

Blau, P.M. (1963) *The Dynamics of Bureaucracy*, revised edn. Chicago: University of Chicago Press.

Blau, P.M. and Schoenherr, R.A. (1973) 'New forms of power', in G. Salaman and K. Thompson (eds), *People and Organisations*. London: Longman. pp. 13–24. First published 1971.

Bocock, J. and Watson, D. (eds) (1994) *Managing the University Curriculum*. Buckingham: Open University and Society for Research into Higher Education.

Bologh, R.W. (1990) *Love or Greatness?: Max Weber and Masculine Thinking – A Feminist Inquiry*. London: Unwin Hyman.

Booth, B. (1992) 'More power to the ex-polys elbow', *Times Higher Education Supplement*, 2 October: 24.

Bordt, R. (1995) 'Form and content: an organizational analysis of women's nonprofits'. Ph.D. dissertation. Department of Sociology, Yale University, New Haven, CT.

Bornstein, K. (1994) *Gender Outlaw: On Men, Women and the Rest of Us*. New York: Routledge.

Boulgarides, J.D. (1984) 'A comparison of male and female business managers', *Leadership and Organisational Development Journal*. 5(5): 27–31.

Bourdieu, P. (1984) *Distinction*. Cambridge, MA: Harvard University Press.

Boyd, M., Mulvihill, M.A. and Myles, J. (1991) 'Gender, power, and postindustrialism: women and men in Canada's postindustrial transition', *Canadian Review of Sociology and Anthropology*, 28(4): 407–36.

Bradley, H. (1986) *Men's Work, Women's Work: A Sociological History of the Sexual Division of Labour in Employment*. Cambridge: Polity Press.

Braverman, H. (1974) *Labor and Monopoly Capital: The Degradation of Work in the Twentieth Century*. New York: Monthly Review Press.

Braybon, G. and Summerfield, P. (1987) *Out of the Cage: Women's Experiences in Two World Wars*. London: Pandora.

Brenner, J. and Ramas, M. (1984) 'Rethinking women's oppression', *New Left Review*. 144: 33–71.

Brittan, A. (1989) *Masculinity and Power*. Oxford: Basil Blackwell.

Brod, H. (ed.) (1987) *The Making of Masculinities. The New Men's Studies*. London and Boston: Allen & Unwin.

Brod, H. and Kaufman, M. (eds) (1994) *Theorizing Masculinities*. Thousand Oaks, CA: Sage.

Buckley, M. (1989) 'The "woman question" in the contemporary Soviet Union', in S. Kruks, R. Rapp and M.B. Young (eds), *Promissory Notes: Women in the Transition to Socialism*. New York: Monthly Review Press. pp. 251–81.

Burawoy, M. (1979) *Manufacturing Consent*. Chicago: University of Chicago Press.

Burawoy, M. (1985) *The Politics of Production*. London: Verso.

Burke, M.E. (1993) *Coming Out of the Blue. British Police Officers Talk about their Lives in 'The Job' as Lesbians, Gays and Bisexuals*. London: Cassell.

Burnham, J. (1945) *The Managerial Revolution*. Harmondsworth: Penguin.

Burns, T. (1994) 'Viewpoint', *Social Sciences: News from ESRC*, 24: 2.

Burns, T. and Stalker, G.M. (1961) *The Management of Innovation*. London: Tavistock.

Burrell, G. (1984) 'Sex and organizational analysis', *Organization Studies*, 5(2): 97–118.

Burrell, G. (1992) 'The organization of pleasure', in M. Alvesson and H. Willmott (eds), *Critical Management Studies*. London: Sage. pp. 66–89.

Burrell, G. and Hearn, J. (1989) 'The sexuality of organization', in J. Hearn, D.L. Sheppard, P. Tancred-Sheriff and G. Burrell (eds), *The Sexuality of Organization*. London: Sage. pp. 1–28.

Burris, B. (1983) *No Room at the Top: Underemployment and Alienation in the Corporation*. New York: Praeger.

Burris, B. (1986) 'Technocratic management: social and political implications', in D. Knights and H. Willmott (eds), *Managing the Labour Process*. London: Gower. pp. 166–85.

Burris, B. (1989a) 'Technocratic organization and control', *Organization Studies*, 10(1): 1–22.

Burris, B. (1989b) 'Technocracy and gender in the workplace', *Social Problems*, 36(2): 165–80.

Burris, B. (1989c) 'Technocratic organization and gender', *Women's Studies International Forum*, 12(4): 447–62.

Burris, B. (1992) 'Sexuality, sexual harassment, and non-sexual harassment in the workplace'. Paper presented at the 1992 SASE (Society for the Advancement of Socioeconomics) meeting, New York City, 19 March.

Burris, B. (1993) *Technocracy at Work*. Albany, NY: SUNY Press.

Burton, C. (1987) 'Merit and gender: organizations and the mobilization of masculine bias', *Australian Journal of Social Issues*, 22: 424–35.

Burton, C. (1991) *The Promise and the Price: The Struggle for Equal Opportunity in Women's Employment*. Sydney: Allen & Unwin.

Business Week (1992) 'The 250 richest women in Britain', October: 74–130.

Butler, J. (1990) *Gender Trouble: Feminism and the Subversion of Identity*. New York: Routledge.

Cadbury, E. (1914) 'Some principles of industrial organisation: the case for and against scientific management', *Sociological Review*, 7(2): 99–117.

Cafferata, G.L. (1982) 'The building of democratic organizations: an embryological metaphor', *Administrative Science Quarterly*, 27(2): 280–303.

Calás, M.B. and Smircich, L. (1991) 'Voicing seduction to silence leadership', *Organization Studies*, 12(4): 567–602.

Calás, M. and Smircich, L. (1992a) 'Using the "F" word: feminist theories and the social consequences of organizational research', in A.J. Mills, and P. Tancred (eds), *Gendering Organizational Analysis*. Newbury Park, CA: Sage. pp. 222–34.

Calás, M. and Smircich, L. (1992b) 'Re-writing gender into organization theorizing: directions from feminist perspectives', in M. Reed and M.D. Hughes (eds), *Rethinking Organizations: New Directions in Organizational Research and Analysis*. London: Sage. pp. 227–53.

Calás, M.B. and Smircich, L. (1993) 'Dangerous liaisons: the "feminine-in-management" meets "globalization"', *Business Horizons*, March/April: 71–81.

Campbell, D.F. and Bouma, G.D. (1978) 'Social conflict and the Pictou notables', *Ethnicity*, 5: 76–88.

Carrigan, T., Connell, R.W. and Lee, J. (1985) 'Toward a new sociology of masculinity', *Theory and Society*, 14(5): 551–604.

Chandler, A.D. (1977) *The Visible Hand: The Managerial Revolution in American Business*. Cambridge, MA: Harvard University Press.

Chapman, R. and Rutherford, J. (eds) (1988) *Male Order. Unwrapping Masculinity*. London: Lawrence & Wishart.

Charter, D. (1995) 'Silver book staff frozen out', *Times Higher Education Supplement*, 28 July: 2.

Chell, E., Haworth, J. and Brearley, S. (1991) *The Entrepreneurial Personality: Concepts, Cases and Categories*. London: Routledge.

Child, J. (1969) *British Management Thought*. London: Allen & Unwin.

Child, J. (1984) *Organization: A Guide to Problems and Practice*. London: Harper and Row.

Chodorow, N. (1978) *The Reproduction of Mothering. Psychoanalysis and the Sociology of Gender*. Berkeley: University of California Press.

Chodorow, N. (1994) *Femininities, Masculinities, Sexualities. Freud and Beyond*. London: Free Association Books.

Christiansen-Ruffman, L. (1995) 'Women's conceptions of the political: three Canadian women's organizations', in M.M. Ferree and P.Y. Martin (eds), *Feminist Organizations: Harvest of the New Women's Movement*. Philadelphia: Temple University Press. pp. 372–93.

Clarke, J., Cochrane, A. and McLaughlin, E. (eds) (1994) *Managing Social Policy*. London: Sage.

Clawson, D. (1980) *Bureaucracy and the Labor Process*. New York: Monthly Review Press.

Clegg, S.R. (1990) *Modern Organizations.* London and Newbury Park, CA: Sage.

Clements, R.V. (1958) *Managers: A Study of Their Careers in Industry.* London: Allen & Unwin.

Clough, P.T. (1992) *The End(s) of Ethnography: From Realism to Social Criticism.* Newbury Park, CA: Sage.

Clutterbuck, D. and Devine, M. (eds) (1987) *Businesswoman: Present and Future.* London: Macmillan.

Cockburn, C. (1983) *Brothers: Male Dominance and Technological Change.* London: Pluto Press.

Cockburn, C. (1985) *The Machinery of Dominance: Women, Men and Technical Know-how.* London: Pluto Press.

Cockburn, C. (1987) 'Restructuring technology, restructuring gender'. Paper presented at the American Sociological Association Meeting, Chicago.

Cockburn, C. (1988) *Machinery of Dominance: Women, Men, and Technical Know-How.* Boston, MA: Northeastern University Press.

Cockburn, C. (1991) *In the Way of Women: Men's Resistance to Sex Equality in Organizations.* London: Macmillan/Ithaca, NY: ILR Press.

Cockburn, C. (1994) 'Play of power: women, men, and equality initiatives in a trade union', in S. Wright (ed.), *Anthropology of Organizations.* London: Routledge. pp. 95–114.

Cohn, C. (1987) 'Sex and death in the rational world of defense intellectuals', *Signs*, 12(4): 687–712.

Cole, G.A. (1982) *Management: Theory and Practice.* Eastleigh, Hants: D.P. Publications.

Coleman, G. (1991) *Investigating Organisations: A Feminist Approach.* Bristol: School for Advanced Urban Studies University of Bristol, Occasional Paper 37.

Coleman, W. (1990) 'Doing masculinity/doing theory', in J. Hearn and D. Morgan (eds), *Men, Masculinities and Social Theory.* London: Unwin Hyman. pp. 186–99.

Collins, R. (1991) 'Women and men in the class structure', in R.L. Blumberg (ed.), *Gender, Family and Economy: The Triple Overlap.* Newbury Park, CA: Sage. pp. 52–73.

Collinson, D.L. (1987) 'Who controls selection?', *Personnel Management*, May: 32–5.

Collinson, D.L. (1992) *Managing the Shopfloor. Subjectivity, Masculinity and Workplace Culture.* Berlin: Walter de Gruyter.

Collinson, D.L. (1994) 'Strategies of resistance: power, knowledge and subjectivity in the workplace', in J. Jermier, D. Knights and W. Nord (eds), *Resistance and Power in Organizations.* London: Routledge. pp. 25–68.

Collinson, D.L. and Collinson, M. (1989) 'Sexuality in the workplace: the domination of men's sexuality', in J. Hearn, D. Sheppard, P. Tancred-Sheriff and G. Burrell (eds), *The Sexuality of Organization.* London and Newbury Park, CA: Sage. pp. 91–109.

Collinson, D.L. and Collinson, M. (1992) 'Mismanaging sexual harassment: blaming the victim and protecting the perpetrator', *Women in Management Review*, 7(7): 11–17.

Collinson, D.L. and Collinson, M. (1995) 'Corporate liposuction and the re-masculinization of management'. Keynote address at Gender and Life in Organizations Conference, University of Portsmouth, September.

Collinson, M. and Collinson, D.L. (1996) 'It's only Dick: the sexual harassment of women managers in insurance', *Work, Employment and Society*, 10(1): 29–56.

Collinson, D.L. and Hearn. J. (1994) 'Naming men as men: implications for work, organization and management', *Gender, Work and Organization* 1(1): 2–22.

Collinson, D.L. and Hearn, J. (1995) 'Men managing leadership', *International Review of Women and Leadership*, 1(2): 1–24.

Collinson, D.L. and Hearn, J. (1996) '"Men" at "work": multiple masculinities in multiple workplaces', in M. Mac An Ghaill (ed.), *Understanding Masculinities: Social Relations and Cultural Areas.* Buckingham: Open University Press. pp. 61–76.

Collinson, D.L. and Knights, D. (1986) '"Men only": theories and practices of job segregation in insurance', in D. Knights and H. Willmott (eds), *Gender and the Labour Process.* Aldershot: Gower. pp. 140–78.

Collinson, D.L., Knights, D. and Collinson, M. (1990) *Managing to Discriminate*. London: Routledge.

Commission of the European Communities (1991a) *A Career in the Commission of the European Communities*. Luxembourg: Office for Official Publications of the European Communities.

Commission of the European Communities (1991b) 'Equal opportunities for women and men', *Social Europe*, 3/91.

Commission of the European Communities (1992) 'Equal opportunities: second positive action programme for female staff of the Commission (1992–1996)'. Brussels: Commission of the European Communities, Equal Opportunities Unit, DG–IX–Personnel and Administration.

Connell, R.W. (1985) 'Theorizing gender', *Sociology*, 19(2): 260–272.

Connell, R.W. (1987) *Gender and Power: Society, the Person, and Sexual Politics*. Stanford, CA: Stanford University Press; Cambridge: Polity Press.

Connell, R.W. (1990) 'A whole new world: remaking masculinity in the context of the environmental movement', *Gender and Society*, 4: 452–78.

Connell, R.W. (1993) 'The big picture: masculinities in recent world history', *Theory & Society*, 22(5): 597–623.

Connell, R.W. (1995) *Masculinities*. Cambridge: Polity Press.

Cooper, C. (1992) 'The non and nom of accounting for (M)other Nature', *Accounting, Auditing & Accountability Journal*, 5(3): 16–39.

Cooper, C. and Davidson, M. (1992) *Shattering the Glass Ceiling: The Woman Manager*. London: Paul Chapman.

Cooper, R. (1992) 'Formal organization and representation: remote control, displacement, abbreviation', in M. Reed and M. Hughes (eds), *Rethinking Organization: New Directions in Organization Theory and Analysis*. London: Sage. pp. 254–72.

COPEC (Comité paritaire de l'égalité des chances) (1994) 'Rapport d'activités du COPEC pour 1993'. Brussels: Commission of the European Communities, COPEC (94)/D/023 revision 1.

Cornfield, D., Phipps, P., Bates, D., Carter, D., Coker, T., Kitzmiller, K. and Wood, P. (1987) 'Office automation, clerical workers, and labor relations in the insurance industry', in D. Cornfield (ed.), *Workers, Managers, and Technological Change*. New York: Plenum Press. pp. 111–34.

Cornwall, A. and Lindisfarne, N. (1994) 'Dislocating masculinity: gender, power and anthropology', in *Dislocating Masculinity. Comparative Ethnographies*. London: Routledge. pp. 11–48.

Coser, L.A. and Rosenberg, B. (eds) (1976) *Sociological Theory: A Book of Readings*, 4th edn. New York: Macmillan.

Court, M. (1994) 'Removing macho management', *Gender, Work and Organization*, 1(1): 33–49.

Craig, S. (ed.) (1992) *Men, Masculinity and the Media*. Newbury Park, CA: Sage.

Crozier, M. (1964) *The Bureaucratic Phenomenon*. Chicago: University of Chicago Press; London: Tavistock.

Cunningham, S. (1992) 'The development of equal opportunities theory and practice in the European Community', *Policy and Politics*, 20(3): 177–89.

Curry, T.J. (1991) 'Fraternal bonding in the locker room: a profeminist analysis of talk about competition and women', *Sociology of Sport Journal*, 8: 119–35.

Czarniawska-Joerges, B. (1992) *Exploring Complex Organizations: A Cultural Perspective*. London: Sage.

Daft, R.L. (1991) *Management*. London: Dryden Press.

Dalton, M. (1959) *Men Who Manage*. New York: John Wiley & Sons.

Daun, Å. (1988) 'Svenskhet som hinder i kulturmötet', in Å. Daun and B. Ehn (eds), *Bland Sverige, kulturskillnader och kulturmöten*. Stockholm: Carlssons Förlag.

Davidoff, L. and Hall, C. (1987) *Family Fortunes: Men and Women of the English Middle Class, 1780–1850*. London: Routledge.

Davidson, M. and Cooper, C. (1983) *Stress and the Woman Manager*. Oxford: Martin Robertson.

Davidson, M.J. and Cooper, C.L. (1992) *Shattering the Glass Ceiling. The Woman Manager.* London: Paul Chapman.

Davies, K. (1990) *Women and Time: Weaving the Strands of Everyday Life.* Aldershot: Avebury.

Davies, M. (1974) 'Women's place is at the typewriter: the feminization of the clerical labor force', *Radical America,* 8: 1–37.

Davies, N. (1992) *The Unknown Maxwell.* London: Pan Macmillan.

De Beauvoir, S. (1953) *The Second Sex.* London: Jonathan Cape. First published 1949.

De Grazia, V. (1992) *How Fascism Ruled Women, Italy, 1922–1945.* Berkeley: University of California Press.

De la Rosa, D.M. and Merino, B. (1995) 'Accounting as a facilitator in the transition from socialism to capitalism'. Paper presented at the Academy of Accounting Historians Annual Research Conference, Urbana, Illinois.

Deal, T.E. and Kennedy, A.A. (1982) *Corporate Culture: The Rites and Rituals of Corporate Life.* Reading, MA: Addison-Wesley.

Delphy, C. and Leonard, D. (1992) *Familiar Exploitation.* Cambridge: Polity Press.

Denham, D. (1991) 'Research note: the "macho" management debate and the dismissal of employees during industrial disputes', *Sociological Review,* 39(2): 349–64.

Dickson, T. and McLachlan, H.V. (1989) 'In search of "The Spirit of Capitalism": Weber's misinterpretation of Franklin', *Sociology,* 23(1): 81–9.

DiNitto, D., Martin, P.Y. and Harrison, D. (1984) 'Sexual inequality among social work faculty', *International Social Work,* 27: 27–36.

DiTomaso, N. (1988) *Ensuring Minority Success in Corporate Management.* New York: Plenum.

Dogan, M. (ed.) (1975) *The Mandarins of Western Europe. The Political Role of Top Civil Servants* New York: Wiley.

Donnell, S.M. and Hall, J. (1980) 'Men and women as managers: a significant case of no significant difference', *Organizational Dynamics,* 8: 60–77.

Drosnin, M. (1987) *Citizen Hughes.* New York: Henry Holt.

Drucker, P. (1979) *The Practice of Management.* London: Heinemann.

Drucker, P. (1985) *Innovation and Entrepreneurship.* London: Heinemann.

Due Billing, Y. (1994) 'Gender and bureaucracies – a critique of Ferguson's *The Feminist Case against Bureaucracy*', *Gender, Work and Organization,* 1(4): 179–93.

Eagly, A.H. (1987) *Sex Differences in Social Behavior: A Social Role Interpretation.* Hillsdale, NJ: Lawrence Earlbaum.

Eagly, A.H. and Johnson, B.T. (1990) 'Gender and leadership style: a meta-analysis', *Psychological Bulletin,* 108: 233–56.

Easlea, B. (1981) *Science and Sexual Oppression: Patriarchy's Confrontation with Woman and Nature.* London: Weidenfeld & Nicolson.

Economist (1995) 'The Feministki are coming', 12 August: 44–6.

Edelman, M. (1977) *Political Language: Words that Succeed and Policies that Fail.* New York: Academic Press.

Edwards, P.K. (1987) *Managing the Factory.* Oxford: Basil Blackwell.

Edwards, R.C. (1979) *Contested Terrain: The Transformation of the Workplace in the Twentieth Century.* London: Heinemann; New York: Basic Books.

Ehrenreich, B. and English, D. (1979) *For Her Own Good: 150 Years of the Experts' Advice to Women.* New York: Doubleday.

Eisenstadt, S.N. (1959) 'Bureaucracy, bureaucratization and debureaucratization', *Administrative Science Quarterly,* 4: 302–20.

Eisenstein, H. (1991a) *Gender Shock: Practising Feminism on Two Continents.* Sydney: Allen & Unwin.

Eisenstein, H. (1991b) 'Speaking for women: voices from the Australian femocratic experiment', *Australian Feminist Studies,* 14: 29–42.

Eisenstein, H. (1995) 'The Australian femocratic experiment: a feminist case for bureaucracy', in M.M. Ferree and P.Y. Martin (eds), *Feminist Organizations: Harvest of the New Women's Movement*. Philadelphia: Temple University Press.

Eisenstein, Z.R. (1984) *Feminism and Sexual Equality*. New York: Monthly Review Press.

Elder, D. (1967) *Ebenezer Syme and the 'Westminster Review'*, Melbourne: The Age.

Elliot, D. (1994) 'No market for grannies', *Newsweek*, 28 March: 37.

Elliott, O. (1959) *Men at the Top*. London: Weidenfeld & Nicolson.

Epstein, C. (1981) *Women in Law*. New York: Basic Books.

Equal Opportunities Commission (1992) *Women and Men in Britain*. London: HMSO.

Erickson, A.L. (1993) *Women and Property in Early Modern England*. London: Routledge.

Etzioni, A. (1965) 'Organizational control structure', in J.G. March (ed.), *Handbook of Organizations*. New York: Rand McNally. pp. 650–77.

Etzioni, A. (1975) *A Comparative Analysis of Complex Organizations*, revised edn. New York: Free Press.

European Parliament (1994) 'Session Document: report on the staff policy of the Community institutions: Committee on Budgets'. James Elles, UK, rapporteur, 15 April.

Ezzamel, M., Hoskin, K. and Macve, R. (1990) 'Managing it all by numbers: a review of Johnson & Kaplan's *Relevance Lost*', *Accounting and Business News*, 30(78): 153–66.

Fagenson, E.A. (1993) 'Diversity in management: introduction and the importance of women in management', in E.A. Fagenson (ed.), *Women in Management: Trends, Issues and Challenges in Managerial Diversity*. Vol. 4, Women and Work. Newbury Park, CA: Sage. pp. 3–19.

Fayol, H. (1949) *General and Industrial Management*. London: Pitman.

Feldberg, R. (1980) 'Technology and work degradation: re-examining the impacts of office automation'. Unpublished paper, Boston University.

Feldberg, R. and Glenn, E. (1983) 'Technology and work degradation', in J. Rothschild (ed.), *Machina ex Dea*. New York: Pergamon Press. pp. 59–78.

Feldberg, R. and Glenn, E. (1987) 'Technology and the transformation of clerical work', in R. Kraut (ed.), *Technology and the Transformation of White-Collar Work*. Hillsdale, NJ: Lawrence Erlbaum. pp. 77–98.

Feldman, D. and Klich, N. (1991) 'Impression management and career strategies', in R. Giacalone and P. Rosenfeld (eds), *Applied Impression Management*. Newbury Park, CA: Sage. pp. 67–80.

Fenstermaker, S., West, C. and Zimmerman, D. (1991) 'Gender inequality: new conceptual terrain', in R.L. Blumberg (ed.), *Gender, Family, and Economy: The Triple Overlap*. Newbury Park, CA: Sage. pp. 289–307.

Ferguson, K.E. (1984) *The Feminist Case against Bureaucracy*. Philadelphia, PA: Temple University Press.

Ferree, M.M. and Hall, E. (1996) 'Rethinking stratification from a feminist perspective: race, class, and gender in introductory textbooks', *American Sociological Review*, 61.

Ferree, M.M. and Martin, P.Y. (1995) 'Doing the work of the movement: feminist organizations', in M.M. Ferree and P.Y. Martin (eds), *Feminist Organizations: Harvest of the New Women's Movement*. Philadelphia: Temple University Press. pp. 3–23.

Fiedler, F.E. (1967) *A Theory of Leadership Effectiveness*. New York: McGraw-Hill.

Finch, J. (1983) *Married to the Job: Wives' Incorporation in Men's Work*. London: Allen & Unwin.

Fineman, S. (ed.) (1993) *Emotion in Organizations*. London: Sage.

Fischoff, E. (1959) 'The history of a controversy', in R.W. Green (ed.), *Protestantism and Capitalism: The Weber Thesis and its Critics*. Lexington, MA: D.C. Heath. pp. 107–14.

Fitzgerald, L.F. (1992) 'Sexual harassment in higher education: concepts and issues', Unpublished manuscript, University of Illinois at Champaign.

Fitzgerald, R.T. (1967) *The Printers of Melbourne: the History of a Union*. Melbourne: Sir Isaac Pitman & Sons.

Flam, H. (1990a) 'Emotional "man": I. The emotional "man" and the problem of collective action', *International Sociology*, 5(1): 39–56.

Flam, H. (1990b) 'Emotional "man": II. Corporate actors as emotion-motivated emotion managers', *International Sociology*, 5(2): 225–34.

Ford, H. (1923) *My Life and Work*. London: William Heinemann.

Foucault, M. (1980a) *The History of Sexuality, Volume One. An Introduction*. Harmondsworth: Penguin.

Foucault, M. (1980b) *Power/Knowledge*, ed. Colin Gordon. Brighton: Harvester.

Foucault, M. (1988) 'On power' and 'social security' in L.D. Kritzman (ed.). *Foucault . . . Interviews and Other Writings 1977–1984*. London: Routledge.

Fraser (1989) *Unruly Practices: Power, Discourse, and Gender in Contemporary Social Theory*. Minneapolis: University of Minnesota Press.

Freedman, M. and Stagliano, A. (1995) 'Disclosure of environmental cleanup costs: the impact of the Superfund Act', *Advances in Public Interest Accounting*, 6: 163–76.

Freud, S. (1938) *Totem and Taboo*. Harmondsworth: Penguin.

Friedan, B. (1963) *The Feminine Mystique*. New York: Dell.

Friedman, A.L. (1977) *Industry and Labour*. London: Macmillan.

Friedrich, C.J. (1952) 'Some observations on Weber's analysis of bureaucracy', in R.K. Merton, A.P. Gray, B. Hockey and H.C. Selvin (eds), *Reader in Bureaucracy*. Glencoe, IL: Free Press. pp. 27–33.

Friedson, E. (1984) 'The changing nature of professional control', *Annual Review of Sociology*, 10: 1–20.

Frissen, P.H.A. (1988) 'Organisatiecultuur: Een overzicht van benaderingen', *Mens en Organisatie*, 40(6): 532–45.

Frissen, P.H.A. and van Westerlaak, J.M. (1990) *Organisatiecultuur van toverwoord tot bruikbaar begrip*. Schoonhoven: Academic Service, Bedrijfskundige signalementen 90/1.

Fromm, E. (1978) *To Have Or To Be*. London: Jonathan Cape.

Frosh, S. (1987) *The Politics of Psychoanalysis*. London: Macmillan.

Fuller, L. and Smith, V. (1991) 'Consumers' reports: management by customers in a changing economy', *Work, Employment and Society*, 5(1): 1–16.

Fulop, L. (1991) 'Middle managers: victims or vanguard of the entrepreneurial movement?', *Journal of Management Studies*, 28(1): 25–44.

Funk, N. and Mueller, M. (eds) (1993) *Gender Politics and Post Communism: Reflections from Eastern Europe and the Former Soviet Union*. New York: Routledge.

Gabriel, E.P. and Martin, L. (1993) 'Women in the work force: a business imperative', *Deloitte & Touche 1993 Annual Report*: 16–21.

Gallese, L.R. (1985) *Women Like Us*. New York: William Morrow.

Game, A. (1991) *Undoing the Social: Towards a Deconstructive Sociology*. Milton Keynes: Open University Press.

Game, A. (1994) 'Matter out of place: the management of academic work', *Organization*, 1(1): 47–50.

Gane, M. (1993) *Harmless Lovers? Gender, Theory and Personal Relationships*. London: Routledge.

Garson, B. (1981) 'The electronic sweatshop: scanning the office of the future', *Mother Jones*, July: 32–6.

Geertz, C. (1973) *The Interpretation of Cultures. Selected Essays*. New York: Basic Books.

Gelb, J. (1995) 'Feminist organization success and the politics of engagement', in M.M. Ferree and P.Y. Martin (eds), *Feminist Organizations: Harvest of the New Women's Movement*. Philadelphia: Temple University Press. pp. 128–34.

Gellerman, S.W. (1966) *The Management of Human Relations*. Illinois: Holt, Rinehart and Winston.

Geneen, H.S. (1985) *Managing*. London: Collins.

Gerth, H. (1940) 'The Nazi party: its leadership and composition', *American Journal of Sociology*, 45: 517–41.

Gerth, H.H. and Mills, C.W. (1948) *From Max Weber: Essays in Sociology*. London: Routledge & Kegan Paul.

Gherardi, S. (1995) *Gender, Symbolism and Organizational Culture*. London: Sage.

Ghiloni, B. (1988) 'The velvet ghetto: women, power and the corporation', in W. Domhoff and T.R. Dye (eds), *Power Elites and Organizations*. Newbury Park, CA: Sage. pp. 21–36.

Gibbings, S. (1990) *The Tie: Trends and Traditions*. London: Studio Editions.

Giddens, A. (1992) *The Transformation of Intimacy. Sexuality, Love and Eroticism in Modern Societies*. Cambridge: Polity Press.

Gildea, M.C. (1952) 'Women's place in accounting', *The Illinois Certified Public Accountant*, March: 48–52.

Gilligan, C. (1982) *In a Different Voice*. Cambridge, MA: Harvard University Press.

Glennon, L. (1979) *Women and Dualism*. New Brunswick, NJ: Transaction Books.

Goffee, R. and Scase, R. (1985) *Women in Charge: The Experiences of Female Entrepreneurs*. London: Allen & Unwin.

Goffee, R. and Scase, R. (1987) *Entrepreneurship in Europe*. London: Croom Helm.

Goffman, E. (1959) *The Presentation of Self in Everyday Life*. Harmondsworth: Penguin.

Goffman, E. (1961) *Asylums*. New York: Anchor.

Goffman, E. (1974) *An Essay on the Organization of Experience: Frame Analysis*. Boston, MA: Northeastern University Press.

Goffman, E. (1977) 'The arrangement between the sexes', *Theory & Society*, 4(3): 301–31.

Goldman, P. and van Houten, D.R. (1979) 'Bureaucracy and domination: managerial strategy in turn-of-the-century American industry', in D. Dunkerley and G. Salaman (eds), *International Yearbook of Organization Studies*. London: Routledge & Kegan Paul.

Goldman, W.Z. (1989) 'Women, the family, and the new revolutionary order in the Soviet Union', in S. Kruks, R. Rapp and M.B. Young (eds), *Promissory Notes: Women in the Transition to Socialism*. New York: Monthly Review Press. pp. 59–81.

Goldthorpe, J., Lockwood, D., Bechoffer, F. and Platt, J. (1969) *The Affluent Worker: Industrial Attitudes*. Cambridge: Cambridge University Press.

Goodwin, C.E. (1995) 'Transgender identity: art and subversion'. Paper presented at the International Congress on Gender, Cross Dressing and Sex Issues, Center for Sex Research, Institute for Social and Behavioral Sciences, California State University, Northridge.

Gordon, F. and Strober, M. (eds) (1975) *Bringing Women into Management*. New York: McGraw-Hill.

Gouldner, A.W. (1952) 'Red tape as a social problem', in R.K. Merton, A.P. Gray, B. Hockey and H.C. Selvin (eds), *Reader in Bureaucracy*. Glencoe, IL: Free Press. pp. 410–18.

Gouldner, A.W. (1955a) *Patterns of Industrial Bureaucracy*. London: Routledge & Kegan Paul/New York: Free Press.

Gouldner, A.W. (1955b) 'Metaphysical pathos and the theory of bureaucracy', *American Political Science Review*, 49: 496–507.

Grant, J. and Tancred, P. (1992) 'A feminist perspective on state bureaucracy', in A.J. Mills and P. Tancred (eds), *Gendering Organizational Analysis*. Newbury Park, CA: Sage. pp. 112–28.

Gray, R., Owen, D. and Maunders, K. (1987) *Corporate Social Reporting: Accounting, and Accountability*. Hemel Hempstead: Prentice Hall.

Gregersen, H. and Sailer, L. (1993) 'Chaos theory and its implications for social science research', *Human Relations*, 46: 777–802.

Grey, C. (1994) 'Career as a project of the self and labour process discipline', *Sociology*, 28(2): 479–98.

Grint, K. (1995) *Management: A Sociological Introduction*. Cambridge: Polity Press.

Gupta, N., Jenkins, G.D. Jnr., and Beehr, T.A. (1983) 'Employee gender, gender similarity and supervisor–subordinate cross-evaluations', *Psychology of Women Quarterly*, 8: 174–84.

Gutek, B. (1983) 'Women's work in the office of the future', in J. Zimmerman (ed.), *The Technological Woman*. New York: Praeger. pp. 159–68.

Gutek, B. (1989) 'Sexuality in the workplace. Key issues in social research and organizational practice', in J. Hearn, D.L. Sheppard, P. Tancred-Sheriff and G. Burrell (eds), *The Sexuality of Organization*. London: Sage, pp. 56–70.

Guzzardi, W. (1966) *The Young Executives: How and Why Successful Managers Get Ahead*. New York: Mentor Books.

Hacker, S. (1983) 'Mathematization of engineering: limits on women', in J. Rothschild (ed.), *Machina ex Dea*. New York: Pergamon. pp. 38–58.

Hacker, S. (1989) *Pleasure, Power, and Technology*. Boston: Unwin Hyman.

Hacker, S. (1990) *Doing It the Hard Way*, ed. D. Smith and S. Turner. Boston: Unwin Hyman.

Hagan, J. (1966) *Printers and Politics: A History of the Australian Printing Unions 1850–1950*. Canberra: Australian National University Press.

Hales, C.P. (1986) 'What do managers do? A critical review of the evidence', *Journal of Management Studies*. 23(1): 88–115.

Hales, C.P. (1993) *Managing through Organizations: The Management Process, Forms of Organizations and Work of Managers*. London: Routledge.

Hall, C. (1992) *White, Male and Middle Class: Explorations in Feminism and History*. Cambridge: Polity Press/New York: Routledge.

Hall, E. (1993) 'Waitering/waitressing: engendering the work of table service', *Gender and Society*, 7: 325–46.

Hammond, V. (1993) 'Opportunity 2000: Gelijke kansen door cultuurverandering', *HRM select*, 3: 59–71.

Hannaway, J. (1989) *Managers Managing*. New York: Oxford University Press.

Hansard Society (1990) *Women at the Top*. London: Hansard Society.

Harlow, E., Hearn, J. and Parkin, W. (1995) 'Gendered noise: organizations and the silence and din of domination', in C. Itzin and J. Newman (eds), *Gender, Culture and Organizational Culture*. London: Routledge. pp. 89–105.

Harrison, J.R. and Carroll, G.R. (1991) 'Keeping the faith: a model of cultural transmission in formal organizations', *Administrative Science Quarterly*, 36(4): 552–81.

Hartmann, H. (1979a) 'Capitalism, patriarchy, and job segregation by sex', in Z. Eisenstein (ed.), *Capitalist Patriarchy and the Case for Socialist Feminism*. New York: Monthly Review Press.

Hartmann, H. (1979b) 'The unhappy marriage of Marxism and feminism: towards a more progressive union', *Capital and Class*, 8(2): 1–33.

Hartmann, H. (1993) 'Commentary', in E. Fagenson (ed.), *Women in Management: Trends, Issues, and Challenges in Managerial Diversity*, Vol. 4. Newbury Park, CA: Sage. pp. 297–301.

Hartsock, N. (1990) 'Foucault on power: a theory for women?' in L.J. Nicholson (ed.), *Feminism/Postmodernism*. New York and London: Routledge.

Harvey Jones, J. (1991) *Getting it Together*. London: BBC Books.

Hays, R. (1989) *The European Commission and the Administration of the Community*. Brussels: Office for Official Publications of the European Communities, 3/1989.

Hearn, J. (1985) 'Men's sexuality at work', in A. Metcalf and M. Humphries (eds), *The Sexuality of Men*. London: Pluto Press. pp. 110–28.

Hearn, J. (1987) *The Gender of Oppression: Men, Masculinity and the Critique of Marxism*. Brighton: Wheatsheaf; New York: St Martin's.

Hearn, J. (ed.) (1989) 'Men, masculinities and leadership: changing patterns and new initiatives', Special Issue, *Equal Opportunities International*, 8(1).

Hearn, J. (1990) 'State Organisations and Men's Sexuality in the Public Domain 1870–1920', in L. Jamieson and H. Corr (eds) *State, Private Life and Political Change*. London: Macmillan. pp. 50–72.

Hearn, J. (1992a) 'Changing men and changing managements: a review of issues and actions', *Women in Management Review and Abstracts*, 7(1): 3–8.

Hearn, J. (1992b) *Men in the Public Eye. The Construction and Deconstruction of Public Men and Public Patriarchies*. London and New York: Routledge.

Hearn, J. (1993) 'Emotive subjects: organizational men, organizational masculinities and the (de)construction of "emotions"', in S. Fineman (ed.), *Emotion in Organizations*. London: Sage. pp. 142–66.

Hearn, J. (1994a) 'Changing men and changing managements: social change, social research and social action', in M.J. Davidson and R.J. Burke (eds), *Women in Management – Current Research Issues*. London: Paul Chapman. pp. 192–209.

Hearn, J. (1994b) 'Research in men and masculinities: some sociological issues and possibilities'. *Australian and New Zealand Journal of Sociology*, 30(1): 40–60.

Hearn, J. (1996) 'Is masculinity dead? A critique of the concept of masculinity/masculinities', in M. Mac an Ghaill (ed.), *Understanding Masculinities. Social Relations and Cultural Arenas*. Buckingham: Open University Press. pp. 202–17.

Hearn, J. and Collinson, D.L. (1994) 'Theorizing unities and differences between men and between masculinities', in H. Brod and M. Kaufman (eds), *Theorizing Masculinities*. Newbury Park, CA and London: Sage. pp. 148–62.

Hearn, J. and Morgan, D.H.J. (eds) (1990) *Men, Masculinities and Social Theory*. London and Boston: Unwin Hyman.

Hearn, J. and Parkin, W. (1987) *'Sex' at 'Work': The Power and Paradox of Organization Sexuality*. Brighton: Wheatsheaf; New York: St Martin's.

Hearn, J. and Parkin, W. (1988) 'Women, men and leadership: a critical review of assumptions, practices and change in the industrialized nations', in N.J. Adler and D. Izraeli (eds), *Women in Management Worldwide*. New York: M.E. Sharpe pp. 17–40.

Hearn, J. and Parkin, W. (1992) 'Gender and organizations: a selective review and a critique of a neglected area', in A.J. Mills and P. Tancred (eds), *Gendering Organizational Analysis*. London: Sage. pp. 46–66. First published 1983.

Hearn, J. and Parkin, W. (1995) *'Sex' at 'Work': The Power and Paradox of Organisation Sexuality*. London: Prentice-Hall/Harvester Wheatsheaf; New York: St. Martin's. Rev. edn.

Hearn, J., Sheppard, D., Tancred-Sheriff, P. and Burrell, G. (eds) (1989) *The Sexuality of Organization*. London: Sage.

Hebert, R.F. and Link, A.N. (1989) 'In search of the meaning of entrepreneurship', *Small Business Economics*, 1: 39–49.

Hekman, S.J. (1990) *Gender and Knowledge: Elements of a Postmodern Feminism*. Cambridge: Polity Press.

Helgesen, S. (1990) *The Female Advantage: Women's Ways of Leadership*. New York: Doubleday.

Hennessey, R. (1993) *Materialist Feminism and the Politics of Discourse*. New York and London: Routledge.

Henriques, J., Hollway, W., Urwin, C., Venn, C. and Walkerdine, V. (1984) *Changing the Subject*. London: Methuen.

Heward, C. (1994) 'Academic snakes and merit ladders: reconceptualising the "glass ceiling"', *Gender and Education*, 6(3): 249–62.

Heward, C. and Taylor, P. (1992) 'Women at the top in higher education: equal opportunities policies in action?', *Policy and Politics*, 29(2): 111–21.

Hickson, D. and Pugh, D. (1995) *Management Worldwide*. Harmondsworth: Penguin.

Hines, R.D. (1992) 'Accounting: filling the negative space', *Accounting, Organizations and Society*, 17(3/4): 313–42.

Hix, S. (1994) 'The study of the European Community: the challenge to comparative politics', *West European Politics*, 17(1): 1–30.

Hochschild, A.R. (1983) *The Managed Heart. Commercialization of Human Feeling*. Berkeley: University of California Press.

Hochschild, A.R. (1989) *The Second Shift*. New York: Avon Books.

Hochschild, A.R. (1990) 'Ideology and emotion management: a perspective and path for future research', in T.D. Kemper (ed.), *Research Agendas in the Sociology of Emotions*. New York: SUNY Press.

Hochschild, A.R. (1993) 'Preface', in S. Fineman (ed.), *Emotion in Organizations*. London: Sage. pp. ix–xiii.

Hodson, R. (1988) 'Good jobs and bad management: how new problems evoke old solutions in high-tech settings', in P. England and G. Farkas (eds), *Sociological and Economic Approaches to Labor Markets*. New York: Plenum Press. pp. 247–79.

Hofstede, G. (1991) *Cultures and Organizations: Software of the Mind*. London: McGraw-Hill.

Hofstede, G. (1993) 'Cultural constraints in management theories', *Academy of Management Executive*, 7(1): 81–93.

Hollander, E.P. and Offerman, L.R. (1990) 'Power and leadership in organizations', *American Psychologist*, 45(2): 179–89.

Hollway, W. (1984a) 'Gender difference and the production of subjectivity', in J. Henriques, W. Hollway, C. Urwin, C. Venn and V. Walkerdine, *Changing the Subject: Psychology, Social Regulation and Subjectivity*. London: Methuen. pp. 227–63.

Hollway, W. (1984b) 'Women's power in heterosexual sex', *Women's Studies International Forum*, 7(1): 63–8.

Hollway, W. (1989) *Subjectivity and Method in Psychology: Gender, Meaning and Science*. London: Sage.

Hollway, W. (1991) *Work Psychology and Organizational Behaviour: Managing the Individual at Work*. London: Sage.

Hollway, W. (1993) 'Efficiency and welfare: industrial psychology at Rowntree's Cocoa Works', *Theory and Psychology*, 3(3): 303–22.

Hoskin, K.W. (1990) 'Using history to understand theory: a re-consideration of the historical genesis of "strategy"'. Paper delivered at the EIASM Workshop on Strategy, Accounting and Control, Venice, October.

Hoskin, K.W. and Macve, R.H. (1986) 'Accounting and the examination: a genealogy of disciplinary power', *Accounting, Organizations and Society*, 11(2): 105–36.

Hoskin, K.W. and Macve, R.H. (1988) 'Cost accounting and the genesis of managerialism: the Springfield Armory episode'. Paper presented at the Second Interdisciplinary Perspectives in Accounting Conference, University of Manchester, 11–13 July.

Hoskin, K.W. and Macve, R.H. (1993) 'Accounting as discipline: the overlooked supplement', in E. Messer-Davidow, D. Shumway and D. Sylvan (eds), *Knowledges: Historical and Critical Perspectives on Disciplinarity*. Charlottesville: University of Virginia Press. pp. 25–53.

Hoxie, R.F. (1915) *Scientific Management and Labor*. New York: Appleton.

Humphrey, C., Moizer, P. and Owen, D. (1995) 'Questioning the value of the research selectivity process in British university accounting', *Accounting, Auditing and Accountability Journal*. 8(3): 139–62.

Hyman, R. (1987) 'Strategy or structure? Capital, labour and control', *Work, Employment and Society*, 1(1): 25–55.

Iacocca. L. (1984) *Iacocca: an Autobiography*. New York: Bantam.

Ibarra, H. (1995) 'Race, opportunity, and diversity of social circles in managerial networks', *Academy of Management Journal*, 38(3): 673–703.

Institute of Management (1995) *National Management Salary Survey*. Kingston upon Thames: Institute of Management.

Jackall, R. (1988) *Moral Mazes: The World of Corporate Managers*. New York: Oxford University Press.

Jackson, D. (1990) *Unmasking Masculinity. A Critical Autobiography*. London: Unwin Hyman.

Jacobs, J.A. (1992) 'Women's entry into management: trends in earnings, authority, and values among salaried managers', *Administrative Science Quarterly*, 37: 282–301.

Jaques, E. (1947–8) 'On the dynamics of social structure: a contribution to the psycho-analytic study of social phenomena', *Human Relations*, 1: 3–23.

Jaques, E. (1951) *The Changing Culture of a Factory*. London: Tavistock.

Jaques, E. (1955) 'Social systems as a defence against persecutory anxiety', in M. Klein, P. Hyman and R.E. Money-Kyrle (eds), *New Directions in Psycho-analysis*. London: Tavistock. pp. 478–98.

Jefferson, T. (1994) 'Theorizing masculine subjectivity', in T. Newburn and E.A. Stanko (eds), *'Just Boys Doing Business'. Men, Masculinities of Crime*. London and New York: Routledge. pp. 10–31.

Jelinek, M. and Adler, N.J. (1988) 'Women: world-class managers for global competition', *Academy of Management Executive*, 11(1): 11–19.

Jermier, J., Knights, D. and Nord, W. (eds) (1994) *Resistance and Power in Organizations*. London: Routledge.

Josefowitz, N. (1983) 'Paths to power in high technology organizations', in J. Zimmerman (ed.), *The Technological Woman*. New York: Praeger. pp. 191–200.

Kanter, R.M. (1977) *Men and Women of the Corporation*. New York: Basic Books.

Kanter, R.M. (1983) *The Change Masters: Innovation for Productivity in American Corporations*. New York: Simon & Schuster.

Kanter, R.M. (1993) *Men and Women of the Corporation*. New York: Basic Books. 2nd edn.

Karbo, K. (1995) 'Polite, feminine, can bench-press Dennis Conner', *Outside*, January: 34–40, 96–8.

Katzenstein, M.F. (1995) 'Discursive politics and feminist activism in the Catholic Church', in M.M. Ferree and P.Y. Martin (eds), *Feminist Organizations: Harvest of the New Women's Movement*. Philadelphia: Temple University Press. pp. 35–52.

Keller, E.F. (1983) *A Feeling for the Organism: The Life and Work of Barbara McClintock*. New York: Freeman.

Keller, E. Fox (1985) *Reflections on Gender and Science*. London and New Haven, CT: Yale University Press.

Kelly, J. (1985) 'Management's redesign of work: labour process, labour markets and produce markets', in D. Knights, H. Willmott and D. Collinson (eds), *Job Redesign*, Aldershot: Gower. pp. 197–226.

Kelly, P. (1992) *The End of Certainty*. Sydney: Allen & Unwin.

Kennedy, C. (1980) *The Entrepreneurs*. London: Scope.

Kerfoot, D. and Knights, D. (1993) 'Management, masculinity and manipulation: from paternalism to corporate strategy in financial services in Britain', *Journal of Management Studies*, 30(4): 659–79.

Kerfoot, D. and Knights, D. (1994) 'Into the realm of the fearful: power, identity and the gender problematic', in H.L. Radtke and H.J. Stam (eds), *Power/Gender: Social Relations in Theory and Practice*. London: Sage.

Kerfoot, D. and Knights, D. (1995) 'Empowering the quality worker?': the seduction and contradiction of the total quality phenomenon', in A. Wilkinson and H.C. Willmott (eds), *Making Quality Critical*. London: Routledge.

Kerfoot, D. and Whitehead, S. (1995) '"And so say all of us": the problematics of masculinity and managerial work'. Paper presented at the Gender and Life in Organizations conference, University of Portsmouth Business School.

Kimmel, M. (1992) 'Integrating content on men and masculinity in courses on gender'. Presentation at American Sociological Association annual meeting, Pittsburgh.

Kimmel, M. (1993) 'What do men want?', *Harvard Business Review*, November/December: 50–63.

Kimmel, M.S. and Messner, M.A. (eds) (1989) *Men's Lives*. New York: Macmillan.

King, C. (ed.) (1993) *Through the Glass Ceiling: Effective Senior Management Development for Women*. Kent: Tudor Business Publications.

Kingdom, J.E. (ed.) (1990) *The Civil Service in Liberal Democracies: An Introductory Survey*. London: Routledge.

Kirkham, L.M. (1992) 'Integrating herstory and history in accountancy', *Accounting, Organizations and Society*, 17(3/4): 287–98.

Kirkham, L.M. and Loft, A. (1993) 'Gender and the construction of the professional accountant', *Accounting, Organizations and Society*, 18(6): 507–58.

Knights, D. and Morgan, G. (1990) 'The concept of strategy in sociology: a note of dissent', *Sociology*, 24(3): 475–83.

Knights, D. and Morgan, G. (1991) 'Corporate strategy, organizations, and subjectivity: a critique', *Organization Studies*, 12(2): 251–73.

Knights, D. and Odih, P. (1995) '"It's about time!": the significance of gendered time for financial services consumption', *Time & Society*, 4(2): 205–31.

Knights, D. and Willmott, H. (eds) (1986) *Managing the Labour Process*. Aldershot: Gower.

Knights, D. and Willmott, H. (eds) (1990) *Labour Process Theory*. London: Macmillan.

Knoke, D. (1990) 'The mobilization of members in women's associations', in L.A. Tilly and P. Gurin (eds), *Women, Politics, and Change*. New York: Russell Sage. pp. 383–410.

Kohn, M. (1971) 'Bureaucratic man: a portrait and an interpretation', *American Sociological Review*, 36: 461–74.

Kondo, D. (1990) *Crafting Selves: Power, Gender, and Discourses of Identity in a Japanese Workplace*. Chicago: University of Chicago Press.

Kotter, J. (1982) *The General Manager*. New York: Free Press.

Kraft, P. (1977) *Programmers and Managers: the Routinization of Computer Programming in the United States*. New York: Springer-Verlag.

Krause, D.G. (1995) *The Art of War for Executives*. London: Nicholas Brealey.

Kreitner, R. (1989) *Management*. Boston, MA: Houghton Mifflin.

Kruks, S., Rapp, R. and Young, M.B. (eds) (1989) *Promissory Notes: Women in the Transition to Socialism*. New York: Monthly Review Press.

Kunda, G. (1992) *Engineering Culture: Control and Commitment in a High-Tech Corporation*. Philadelphia: Temple University Press.

Kupryashkina, S. (1994) 'From East to West: new values and where they stand'. Working paper, Ukranian Center for Gender Studies.

Lane, J.E. (ed.) (1987) *Bureaucracy and Public Choice*. London: Sage.

LaNuez, D. and Jermier, J. (1994) 'Sabotage by managers and technocrats: neglected patterns of resistance at work', in J. Jermier, D. Knights and W.R. Nord (eds), *Resistance and Power in Organizations*. London: Routledge. pp. 219–51.

Larson, M.S. (1977) *The Rise of Professionalism*. Berkeley: University of California Press.

Lawrence, P.R. and Lorsch, J.W. (1967) *Organization and Environment*. Cambridge, MA: Harvard Business School.

Lawson, T. (1981) 'Paternalism and labour market segmentation theory', in F. Wilkinson (ed.), *The Dynamics of Labour Market Segmentation*. London: Academic Press. pp. 47–66.

Leapman, M. (1983) *Barefaced Cheek: The Apotheosis of Rupert Murdoch*. London: Hodder & Stoughton.

Leapman, M. (1985) *Arrogant Aussie: The Rupert Murdoch Story*. Secaucus, NJ: Lyle Stewart.

Lee, J.A. (1982) 'The social science bias in management research', *Business Horizons*, November–December: 21–31.

Lee, J.A. (1985) 'After fads and advocative, ideological social science, Whither OD?', *International Journal of Manpower*, 6(4): 11–20.

Legge, K. (1987) 'Women in personnel management: uphill climb or downhill slide?', in A. Spencer and D. Podmore (eds), *In a Man's World*. London: Routledge. pp. 33–60.

Lehman, C.R. (1992a) 'Herstory in accounting: the first eighty years', *Accounting, Organizations and Society*, 17(3/4): 261–86.

Lehman, C.R. (1992b) 'Fe[men]inists' account', *Accounting, Auditing, and Accountability Journal*, 5(3): 4–15.

Leidner, R. (1991) 'Serving hamburgers and selling insurance: gender, work, and identity in interactive service jobs', *Gender and Society*, 5: 154–77.

Leidner, R. (1993a) 'Constituency, accountability, and deliberation: reshaping democracy in the National Women's Studies Association', *NWSA Journal*, 5: 4–27.

Leidner, R. (1993b) *Fast Food, Fast Talk*. Berkeley, CA: University of California Press.

Levinson, D. (1973) 'Role, personality and social structure in the organizational setting', in G. Salaman and K. Thompson (eds), *People and Organisations*. London: Longman. pp. 223–37. First published 1959.

Lewis, P.M. (1991) 'Mummy, matron and the maids: Feminine presence and absence in male institutions, 1934–63', in M. Roper and J. Tosh (eds), *Manful Assertions: Masculinities in Britain since 1800*. London: Routledge. pp. 168–89.

Likert, R. (1961) *New Patterns of Management*. New York: McGraw-Hill.

Lind, M. (1995) 'A managing elite is storming the developed world', in *The Sunday Times*, 27 August: 11.

Linstead, S. (1995) 'Averting the gaze: gender and power on the perfumed picket line', *Gender, Work and Organization*, 2(4): 192–206.

Linstead, S., Grafton Small, R. and Jeffcutt, P. (eds) (1996) *Understanding Management*. London: Sage.

Lissyutkina, L. (1993) 'Soviet women at the crossroads of perestroika', in N. Funk and M. Mueller (eds), *Gender Politics and Post Communism: Reflections from Eastern Europe and the Former Soviet Union*. New York: Routledge. pp. 274–86.

Littler, C.R. (1982) *The Development of the Labour Process in Capitalist Societies*. London: Heinemann.

Littler, C.R. and Salaman, G. (1984) *Class at Work: The Design, Allocation and Control of Jobs*. London: Batsford Academic and Educational.

Loden, M. (1985) *Feminine Leadership: Or How to Succeed in Business without Being One of the Boys*. New York: Random House.

Lorber, J. (1994) *Paradoxes of Gender*. New Haven, CT: Yale University Press.

Lowe, M. and Hubbard, R. (1983) *Woman's Nature: Rationalizations of Inequality*. New York: Pergamon Press.

Lown, J. (1983) 'Not so much a factory, more a form of patriarchy: gender and class during industrialisation', in E. Gamarnikow, D.H.J. Morgan, J. Purvis and D.E. Taylorson (eds), *Gender, Class and Work*. London: Heinemann. pp. 28–45.

Ludlow, P. (1991) 'The European Commission', in R.O. Keohane and S. Hoffman (eds), *The New European Community: Decision Making and Institutional Change*. Boulder, CO: Westview Press. pp. 85–132.

Mac an Ghaill, M. (1993) 'Irish masculinities and sexualities in England: social and psychic relations'. Working paper, University of Birmingham.

Mac an Ghaill, M. (1994) 'The making of black English masculinities', in H. Brod and M. Kaufman (eds), *Theorizing Masculinities*. Thousand Oaks, CA: Sage.

Maccoby, M. (1977) *The Gamesman: The New Corporate Leaders*. London: Secker & Warburg.

Macdonald, R. (1982) *David Syme*. Melbourne: Vantage House.

MacIntyre, A. (1981) *After Virtue: A Study in Moral Theory*. London: Duckworth.

Macintyre, S. (1991) *A Colonial Liberalism: The Lost World of Three Victorian Visionaries*. Melbourne: Oxford University Press.

Mackay, L. (1986) 'The macho manager: it's no myth', *Personnel Management*, January: 25–7.

MacKinnon, C.A. (1987) *Feminism Unmodified*. Cambridge, MA: Harvard University Press.

MacPherson, C.B. (1962) *The Political Theory of Possessive Individualism*. Oxford: Clarendon Press.

Major, B. (1989) 'Gender differences in comparisons of entitlement: implications for comparable worth', *Journal of Social Issues*, 45: 99–115.

Mangham, I.L. and critics (1995) 'Macintyre and the manager', *Organization*. 2(2): 181–242.

Mant, A. (1977) *The Rise and Fall of the British Manager*. London: Macmillan.

March, J.G. and Olsen, J. (1989) *Rediscovering Political Institutions: The Organizational Basis of Politics*. New York: Free Press.

Marglin, S.A. (1974) 'What do bosses do? The origin and functions of hierarchy in capitalist production', *The Radical Review of Political Economics*. 6: 33–60.

Marshall, G. (1982) *In Search of the Spirit of Capitalism: An Essay on Max Weber's Protestant Ethic Thesis*. London: Hutchinson.

Marshall, G. (1990) *In Praise of Sociology*. London: Unwin Hyman.

Marshall, J. (1995) *Women Managers Moving On*. London: Routledge.

Marshall, S. (ed.) (1989) *Women in Reformation and Counter-Reformation Europe*. Indianapolis: Indiana University Press.

Martin, J. (1990) 'Deconstructing organizational taboos: the suppression of gender conflict in organizations', *Organizational Science*, 1(4): 339–59.

Martin, P.Y. (1982) '"Fair Science": test or assertion? A response to Cole's "Women in Science"', *Sociological Review*, 30: 478–508.

Martin, P.Y. (1990) 'Rethinking feminist organizations', *Gender and Society*, 4: 182–206.

Martin, P.Y. (1991) 'Gender, inequality, and interaction in organizations', in C. Ridgeway (ed.), *Gender, Interaction, and Inequality*. New York: Springer-Verlag. pp. 208–31.

Martin, P.Y. (1993) 'Feminism and the practice of management', in E.A. Fagenson (ed.), *Women in Management: Trends, Issues, and Prospects*. Newbury Park, CA: Sage. pp. 274–96.

Martin, P.Y. (1995) 'Mobilized masculinities and glass ceilings'. Unpublished ms, Department of Sociology, Florida State University, Tallahassee.

Martin, P.Y., Dinitto, D., Byington, D. and Maxwell, M.S. (1992) 'Organizational and community transformation: a case study of a rape crisis center', *Administration in Social Work*, 16(2): 123–45.

Martin, P.Y., Harrison, D. and DiNitto, D. (1983) 'Advancement for women in hierarchical organizations: a multilevel analysis of problems and prospects', *Journal of Applied Behavioural Science*, 25: 451–70.

Martin, P.Y. and Powell, M. (1994) 'Accounting for the "second assault": legal organizations' framing of rape victims', *Law & Social Inquiry*, 19: 853–90.

Martin, R. and Fryer, R.H. (1973) *Redundancy and Paternalist Capitalism: A Study in the Sociology of Work*. London: Allen & Unwin.

Maruani, M. (ed.) (1992) 'La place des femmes sur le marché du travail – Tendence et évolutions dans les douze pays de la Communauté européenne 1983–1990', *Femmes d'Europe*, 36.

Maupin, R.J. and Lehman, C.R. (1994) 'Talking heads: stereotypes, status, sex-roles and satisfaction – an analysis of female and male auditors', *Accounting, Organizations and Society*, 19(4/5): 427–37.

Mayo, E. (1930) 'Changing methods in industry', *The Personnel Journal*, 8.

Mayo, E. (1949) *The Social Problems of an Industrial Civilization*. London: Routledge & Kegan Paul.

Mazey, S. (1988) 'European Community action on behalf of women: the limits of legislation', *Journal of Common Market Studies*, 27(1): 63–83.

McGregor, D. (1960) *The Human Side of Enterprise*. New York: McGraw-Hill.

McIlwee, J.S. and Robinson, J.G. (1992) *Women in Engineering: Gender, Power, and Workplace Culture*. Albany, NY: SUNY Press.

McMahon, A. (1993) 'Male readings of feminist theory: the psychologization of sexual politics in the masculinity literature', *Theory & Society*, 22(5): 675–95.

McMylor, P. (1994) *Alisdair MacIntyre: Critic of Modernity*. London: Routledge.

Meek, J. (1995) 'Moscow wakes up to the toll of violence in the home', *The Guardian*, 22 June: 23.

Melich, A. (1994) 'Women's attitudes towards European integration – the Member States – presentation of Eurobarometer data'. Paper presented at conference Women and European Integration, Centre for European Policy Studies, Brussels, 25 May.

Menzies, I. (1960) 'A case study in the functioning of social systems as a defense against anxiety', *Human Relations*, 13: 95–121. Reprinted in I. Menzies-Lyth (1988) *Containing Anxiety in Institutions: Selected Essays*. London: Free Association Books.

Merton, R.K. (1957) *Social Theory and Social Structure*. revised edn. Glencoe IL: Free Press.

Merton, R.K., Gray, A.P., Hockey, B. and Selvin, H.C. (eds) (1952) *Reader in Bureaucracy*. Glencoe, IL: Free Press.

Messerschmidt, J. (1993) *Masculinities and Crime: Critique and Reconceptualization of Theory*. Totowa, NJ: Rowman & Littlefield.

Messner, M.A. (1992) *Power at Play: Sports and the Problem of Masculinity*. Boston, MA: Beacon Press.

Messner, M.A. (1993) '"Changing men" and feminist politics in the United States', *Theory & Society*, 22(5): 723–37.

Messner, M.A., Duncan, M.C. and Jensen, K. (1993) 'Separating the men from the girls: the gendered language of televised sports', *Gender and Society*, 7(1): 121–37.

Metcalf, A. (1985) 'Introduction', in A. Metcalf and M. Humphries (eds), *The Sexuality of Men*. London: Pluto Press. pp. 1–14.

Michelmann, H.J. (1978) 'Multinational staffing and organizational functioning in the Commission of the European Communities', *International Organization*, 32(2): 477–96.

Middleton, P. (1992) *The Inward Gaze. Masculinity and Subjectivity in Modern Culture*. London and New York: Routledge.

Milkman, R. (1987) *Gender at Work: The Dynamics of Job Segregation by Sex during World War II*. Urbana: University of Illinois Press.

Milkman, R. and Townsley, E. (1994) 'Gender and the economy', in N.J. Smelser and R. Swedberg (eds), *Handbook of Economic Sociology*. Princeton, NJ: Princeton University Press. pp. 600–19.

Mill, J.S. (1848) *Principles of Political Economy, Vol II*. Boston: Charles C. Little and James Brown.

Miller, E. and Gwynne, G.V. (1972) *A Life Apart*. London: Tavistock.

Miller, H. (1994) 'Management and change in universities: Australia, Canada and the United Kingdom', *Association of Commonwealth Universities Bulletin of Current Documentation*, 115: 30–4.

Miller, H. (1995) *Management of Change in Universities: Universities, State and Economy in Australia, Canada and the United Kingdom*. Buckingham: Open University Press and the Society for Research into Higher Education.

Miller, P. and Rose, N. (1990) 'Governing economic life', *Economy and Society*, 19(1): 1–31.

Millett, K. (1977) *Sexual Politics*. London: Virago.

Mills, A.J. (1989) 'Gender, sexuality and organizational theory', in J. Hearn, D. Sheppard, P. Tancred-Sheriff and G. Burrell (eds), *The Sexuality of Organization*. Newbury Park, CA: Sage. pp. 29–44.

Mills, A.J. (1992) 'Organization, gender and culture', in A.J. Mills and P. Tancred (eds), *Gendering Organizational Analysis*. London: Sage. pp. 93–111. First published 1988.

Mills, A.J. and Tancred, P. (eds) (1992) *Gendering Organizational Analysis*. Newbury Park, CA: Sage.

Mills, C.W. (1956) *The Power Elite*. New York: Oxford University Press.

Mintzberg, H. (1973) *The Nature of Managerial Work*. New York: Harper & Row.

Mintzberg, H. (1975) 'The manager's job: folklore and fact', *Harvard Business Review*, July/August: 49–61.

Mintzberg, H. (1979) *The Structuring of Organizations*. Englewood Cliffs, NJ: Prentice-Hall.

Mintzberg, H. (1983) *Power in and Around Organizations*. Englewood Cliffs, NJ: Prentice-Hall.

Mintzberg, H. (1989) *Mintzberg on Management*. New York: Macmillan.

Molyneux, M. (1991) 'The "woman question" in the age of perestroika', in R. Blackburn (ed.), *After the Fall: The Failure of Communism and the Future of Socialism*. New York: Verso. pp. 47–77.

Morgan, A. and Wilcox, C. (1992) 'Anti-feminism in Western Europe 1975–1987', *West European Politics*, 15(4): 151–69.

Morgan, D.H.J. (1981) 'Men, masculinity, and the process of sociological enquiry', in H. Roberts (ed.), *Doing Feminist Research*. London: Routledge & Kegan Paul. pp. 83–113.

Morgan, D.H.J. (1992) *Discovering Men*. London: Routledge.

Morgan, G. (1986) *Images of Organization*. Beverly Hills, CA: Sage.

Morley, L. (1994) 'Glass ceiling or iron cage: women in UK academia', *Gender, Work and Organization*, 1(4): 194–204.

Mort, F. (1988) 'Boys own? Masculinity, style and popular culture', in R. Chapman and J. Rutherford (eds), *Male Order. Unwrapping Masculinity*. London: Lawrence & Wishart. pp. 193–224.

Mulholland, K. (1993) 'The marginalisation of women and the process of wealth creation', in A. Sinfield (ed.), *Poverty, Inequality and Justice*. Edinburgh: New Waverly Press, University of Edinburgh.

Mulholland, K. (1996) 'Gender power and property relations within entrepreneurial wealthy families', *Gender, Work and Organization*, 3(2): 78–102.

Munster, G. (1985) *A Paper Prince*. Melbourne: Penguin Viking.

Murphree, M.C. (1984) 'Brave new office: the changing world of the legal secretary', in K. Sacks and D. Remy (eds), *My Troubles are Going to Have Trouble with Me*. New Brunswick, NJ: Rutgers University Press. pp. 140–59.

Nardi, P. (1992) '"Seamless souls". An introduction to men's friendships', in P. Nardi (ed.), *Men's Friendships*. Newbury Park, CA: Sage. pp. 1–14.

National Research Council (1986) *Women's Work, Men's Work*. Washington, DC: National Academy Press.

Neale, A. (1995) 'The manager as hero'. Paper presented at Labour Process Conference, Blackpool, April.

Neimark, M. (1994) *The Hidden Dimensions of Annual Reports: Sixty Years of Social Conflict at General Motors*. Princeton: Markus Wiener.

Nelson, J.A. (1992) 'Gender, metaphor, and the definition of economics', *Economics and Philosophy*, 8: 103–25.

Ness, G.D. and Brechin, S.R. (1988) 'Bridging the gap: international organizations as organizations', *International Organization*, 42(2): 245–73.

Newman, J. (1994) 'The limits of management: gender and the politics of change', in Clarke, J., Cochrane, A. and McLaughlin, E. (eds), *Managing Social Policy*. London: Sage. pp. 182–209.

New York Times (1993) 'Women pay more for success', 4 July: 25.

Nichols, T. (1970) *Ownership, Control and Ideology*. London: Allen & Unwin.

Niven, M.M. (1967) *Personnel Management 1913–1963*. London: Institute of Personnel Management.

Nonon, J. and Clamen, M. (1991) *L'Europe et ses couloirs; lobbying et lobbyistes*. Paris: Dunod.

Nord, W. and Jermier, J. (1992) 'Critical social science for managers', in M. Alvesson and H. Willmott (eds), *Critical Theory of Management Science*. London: Sage. pp. 202–22.

Norris, G.M. (1978) 'Industrial paternalist capitalism and local labour markets, *Sociology*, 12: 469–89.

Northcraft, G. and Gutek, B. (1993) 'Point-counterpoint: discrimination against women in management – going, going, gone or going but never gone?', in E.A. Fagenson (ed.), *Women in Management: Trends, Issues and Challenges in Managerial Diversity*. Vol. 4, Women and Work. London: Sage. pp. 219–45.

Noyelle, T.J. (1987) *Beyond Industrial Dualism*. Boulder, CO: Westview Press.

O'Brien, M. (1981) *The Politics of Reproduction*. London: Routledge & Kegan Paul.

Oakes, L.S. and Hammond, T.A. (1993) 'Biting the epistemological hand: feminist perspectives on science and their implications for accounting research', *Critical Perspectives on Accounting*, 6(1): 49–75.

Ochberg, R. (1987) 'The male career code and the ideology of role', in H. Brod (ed.), *The Making of Masculinities*. London and Boston: Allen & Unwin. pp. 193–210.

Offe, C. (1976) *Industry and Inequality*. London: Edward Arnold.

Ohlott, P., Ruderman, M. and McCauley, C. (1994) 'Gender differences in managers' developmental job experiences', *Academy of Management Journal*, 37(1): 46–67.

Ong, A. (1987) *Spirits of Resistance and Capitalist Discipline: Factory Women in Malaysia*. Albany, NY: SUNY Press.

Ortner, S. (1974) 'Is female to male as nature is to culture?', in M.Z. Rosaldo and L. Lamphere (eds), *Woman, Culture and Society*. Stanford: Stanford University Press. pp. 67–87.

Page, E. (1985) *Political Authority and Bureaucratic Power: A Comparative Analysis*. Brighton: Harvester.

Page, E. (1987) 'Comparing bureaucracies', in J.-E. Lane (ed.), *Bureaucracy and Public Choice*. London: Sage. pp. 230–54.

Page, E. and Wouters, L. (1994) 'Paying the top people in Europe', in C. Hood and B.G. Peters (eds), *Rewards at the Top: A Comparative Study of High Public Office*. London: Sage. pp. 201–14.

Pahl, R. (1995) *After Success: 'Fin-de-Siècle' Anxiety and Identity*. Cambridge: Polity Press.

Palm, G. (1977) *The Flight from Work*. Cambridge: Cambridge University Press.

Parker, M. and Jary, D. (1995) 'The McUniversity: organisation, management and academic subjectivity', *Organization*, 2(2): 319–38.

Parkin, D. and Maddock, S. (1993) 'Gender cultures', *Women in Management Review*, 8(2): 3–9.

Parkin, F. (1982) *Max Weber*. Chichester: Ellis Horwood.

Pateman, C. (1988) *The Sexual Contract*. Cambridge: Polity Press.

Pedersen, J. (1992) 'Liberal ideals and feminist organization in Victorian England: one cause or many?'. Paper presented to Third Conference of the International Society for the Study of European Ideas, Aalborg University, Denmark.

Penrose, E. (1980) *The Theory of the Growth of the Firm*. Oxford: Basil Blackwell.

Peters, B.G. (1987) 'Politicians and bureaucrats in the politics of policy making', in J.-E. Lane (ed.), *Bureaucracy and Public Choice*. London: Sage. pp. 256–81.

Peters, T.J. and Waterman, R.H. (1982) *In Search of Excellence*. New York: Harper & Row.

Pfeffer, J. (1992) *Managing with Power: Politics and Influence in Organizations*. Boston, MA: Harvard Business School Press.

Phillips, A. and Taylor, B. (1980) 'Sex and skill: notes towards a feminist economics', *Feminist Review*, 6(7): 79–88.

Piore, M.J. and Sabel, C. (1984) *The Second Industrial Divide*. New York: Basic Books.

Pleck, J. (1989) 'Men's power with women, other men, and society', in M. Kimmel and M. Messner (eds), *Men's Lives*. New York: Macmillan.

Pleck, J.H., Sonenstein, F.L. and Ku, L.C. (1994) 'Attitudes toward male roles among adolescent males: a discriminant validity analysis', *Sex Roles*, 30: 481–501.

Poggi, G. (1983) *Calvinism and the Capitalist Spirit*. London: Macmillan.

Pollard, S. (1965) *The Genesis of Modern Management: A Study of the Industrial Revolution in Great Britain*. London: Edward Arnold.

Pollert, A. (1981) *Girls, Wives, Factory Lives*. London: Macmillan.

Pollitt, K. (1995) *Reasonable Creatures: Essays on Women and Feminism*. New York: Vintage Books.

Potter, M. (1986) 'Gender equality and gender hierarchy in Calvin's theology', *Signs: A Journal of Women in Culture and Society*, 11(41): 726–9.

Powell, G.N. (1988) *Women and Men in Management*. Newbury Park, CA: Sage.

Pratt, A. (1908) *David Syme: The Father of Protection in Australia*. Melbourne: Ward Lock.

Prichard, C. and Willmott, H. (1995) *Targets and Tactics: the Managerial Challenge to Professional Locales in UK Universities*, (ESRC Professions in Late Modernity Series 5). London: The Management School, Imperial College, London.

Pringle, R. (1988) *Secretaries Talk: Sexuality, Power and Work*. Sydney: Allen & Unwin. Published 1989, London: Verso.

Pringle, R. (1989) 'Bureaucracy, rationality and sexuality: the case of secretaries', in J. Hearn, D.L. Sheppard, P. Tancred-Sheriff and G. Burrell (eds), *The Sexuality of Organization*. London: Sage. pp. 158–77.

Pringle, R. (1994) 'Office affairs', in S. Wright (ed.), *Anthropology of Organizations*. London: Routledge. pp. 115–23.

Pugh, D.S. and Hickson, D.J. (1973) 'The comparative study of organisations', in G. Salaman and K. Thompson (eds), *People and Organisations*. London: Longman. pp. 50-66. First published 1968.

Pugh, M.D. and Wahrman, R. (1983) 'Neutralizing sexism in mixed-sex groups: do women have to be better?', *American Journal of Sociology*, 88: 746–62.

Purcell, J. (1982) 'The rediscovery of the management prerogative: the management of labour relations in the 1980s', *Oxford Review of Economic Policy*, 7(1): 33–43.

Ram, M. (1994) *Managing to Survive*. Oxford: Basil Blackwell.

Ramsay, K. and Parker, M. (1992) 'Gender, bureaucracy and organizational culture', in M. Savage and A. Witz (eds), *Gender and Bureaucracy*. Oxford: Blackwell. pp. 253–78.

Reckman, B. (1979) 'Carpentry: the craft and trade', in A. Zimbalist (ed.), *Case Studies on the Labor Process*. New York: Monthly Review Press.

Reed, M. (1989) *The Sociology of Management*. London: Harvester Wheatsheaf.

Reed, M. (1991) 'Scripting scenarios for a new organization theory and practice', *Work, Employment and Society*, 5(1): 119–32.

Reed, R. (1987) 'Making newspapers pay: employment of women's skills in newspaper production', *The Journal of Industrial Relations*, 29(1): 25–40.

Reed, R. (1988) 'From hot metal to cold type printing technology', in E. Willis (ed.), *Technology and the Labour Process: Australasian Case Studies*. Sydney: Allen & Unwin. pp. 33–50.

Reed, R. (1990) *Strategies of Regulation: Labour Market Segmentation in the Melbourne Newspaper Industry*. Industrial Relations Research Centre Monograph No. 27. Sydney: University of New South Wales IRRC.

Reed, R. (1991a) 'Intra-organisational strategies of professionalisation: *Age* journalists', *Media Information Australia*, 61, August: 42–9.

Reed, R. (1991b) 'Calvinism, the Weber thesis and entrepreneurial behaviour: the case of David Syme', *Journal of Religious History*, 16(3): 292–303.

Reed, R. (1993) *Women in Printing: Employers' Attitudes to Women in Trades*. Canberra: AGPS.

Reeves, F. (1995) *The Modernity of Further Education*. Wolverhampton: Bilston Community College Publications.

Regan, S. (1976) *Rupert Murdoch: A Business Biography*. London: Angus & Robertson.

Reinelt, C. (1995) 'Moving onto the terrain of the state: the battered women's movement and the politics of engagement', in M.M. Ferree and P.Y. Martin (eds), *Feminist Organizations: Harvest of the New Women's Movement*. Philadelphia: Temple University Press. pp. 84–104.

Reiter, S.A. (1995) 'Theory and politics: lessons from feminist economics', *Accounting, Auditing and Accountability Journal*, 8(3): 34–59.

Remington, J. (1991) *The Need to Thrive: Women's Organizations in the Twin Cities*. St Paul: Minnesota Women's Press.

Remy, J. (1990) 'Patriarchy and fratriarchy as forms of androcracy', in J. Hearn and D. Morgan (eds), *Men, Masculinities and Social Theory*. London: Unwin Hyman. pp. 43–54.

Reskin, B.F. (1988) 'Bringing the men back in', *Gender and Society*, 2: 58–81.

Reskin, B.F. and Roos, P.A. (1990) *Job Queues, Gender Queues: Explaining Women's Inroads into Men's Occupations*. Philadelphia: Temple University Press.

Reskin, B.F. and Ross, C.E. (1995) 'Job segregation, authority, and earnings: the continuing significance of sex', in J.A. Jacobs (ed.), *Gender Inequality at Work*. Newbury Park, CA: Sage. pp. 127–51.

Rich, A. (1984) 'Compulsory heterosexuality and lesbian experience', in A. Snitow, C. Stansell and S. Thompson (eds), *Desire, The Politics of Sexuality*. London: Virago. pp. 212–41.

Ridgeway, C. (1991) 'The social construction of status value: gender and other nominal characteristics', *Social Forces*, 70: 367–86.

Ridgeway, C. (1993) 'Gender, status, and the social psychology of expectations', in P. England (ed.), *Theory on Gender, Feminism on Theory*. New York: Aldine/de Gruyter. pp. 175–97.

Ringeling, A.B. (ed.) (1985) *Ambtelijke cultuur en verandering van het openbaar bestuur*. s'Gravenhage: VUGA Uitgeverij.

Roberts, J. and Coutts, J.A. (1992) 'Feminization and professionalization: a review of an emerging literature on the development of accounting in the United Kingdom', *Accounting, Organizations and Society*, 17(3/4): 379–96.

Robinson, J. and McIlwee, J. (1991) 'Men, women and the culture of engineering', *Sociological Quarterly*, 32(3): 403–21.

Roethlisberger, F.J. (1949) *Management and Morale*. Boston, MA: Harvard University Press. First Published 1941.

Roethlisberger, F.J. (1954) *Training for Human Relations*. Boston, MA: Harvard University Press.

Roethlisberger, F.J. and Dickson, W.J. (1970) *Management and the Worker*. Boston, MA: Harvard University Press. First published 1939.

Rogers, B. (1988) *Men Only: An Investigation into Men's Organizations*. London: Pandora.

Roper, M.R. (1991) 'Yesterday's model: product fetishism and the British company men 1945–85', in M.R. Roper and J. Tosh (eds,) *Manful Assertions. Masculinities in Britain since 1800*. London and New York: Routledge. pp. 190–211.

Roper, M.R. (1994a) *Masculinity and the British Organization Man since 1945*. Oxford: Oxford University Press.

Roper, M.R. (1994b) 'Gender and organizational change', in S. Wright (ed.), *Anthropology of Organizations*. London: Routledge. pp. 87–94

Roper, M.R. and Tosh, J. (eds) (1991) *Manful Assertions: Masculinities in Britain since 1800*. London: Routledge.

Rose, J. (1987) 'Femininity and its discontents', in Feminist Review (eds), *Sexuality: A Reader*. London: Virago. pp. 177–98.

Rosenberg, D.J. (1991) 'Shock therapy: GDR women in transition from a socialist welfare state to a social market economy' *Signs: Journal of Women in Culture and Society*, 17(1): 129–51.

Rosener, J. (1990) 'Ways women lead', *Harvard Business Review*, 68(6): 119–25.

Rothacker, A. and Colling, M. (1987) 'The Community's top management: a meritocracy in the making', in *Courrier du Personnel EC Commission*, October.

Rothschild, J. and Davies, C. (1994) 'Organizations through the lens of gender: introduction to the special issue', *Human Relations*, 47: 583–90.

Saco, D. (1992) 'Masculinity as signs: post-structuralist feminist approaches to the study of gender', in S. Craig (ed.), *Men, Masculinity and the Media*. London: Sage. pp. 23–40.

Salaman, G. and Thompson, K. (eds) (1973) *People and Organisations*. Milton Keynes: Open University Press.

Sampson, R. (1965) *Managing the Managers*. New York: McGraw-Hill.

Savage, M. and Witz, A. (eds) (1992) *Gender and Bureaucracy*. Oxford: Basil Blackwell.

Sawer, M. (1990) *Sisters in Suits*. Sydney: Allen & Unwin.

Sayers, C.E. (1965) *David Syme: A Life*. Melbourne: F.W. Cheshire.

Sayles, L. (1964) *Managerial Behavior*. New York: McGraw-Hill.

Scase, R. and Goffee, R. (1989) *Reluctant Managers*. London: Unwin Hyman.

Schein, V.E. (1976) 'Think manager – think male', *Atlanta Economic Review*, March–April: 21–4.

Scott, J. (1989) 'Ownership and employer control', in D. Gallie (ed.), *Employment in Britain*. Oxford: Basil Blackwell. pp. 437–64.

Seccombe, W. (1986) 'Patriarchy stabilised: the construction of the male breadwinner norm in nineteenth century Britain', *Social History*, 11(1): 53–76.

Sedgwick, E.K. (1985) *Between Men. English Literature and Male Homosocial Desire*. New York: Columbia University Press.

Segal, L. (1990) *Slow Motion: Changing Masculinities, Changing Men*. London: Virago/New Brunswick, NJ: Rutgers University Press.

Seidler, V.J. (1989) *Rediscovering Masculinity: Reason, Language and Sexuality*. London: Routledge.

Seidler, V.J. (1992) 'Rejection, vulnerability and friendship', in P. Nardi (ed.), *Men's Friendships*. Newbury Park, CA: Sage. pp. 15–34.

Seidler, V.J. (1994) *Unreasonable Men: Masculinity and Social Theory*. London: Routledge.

Sekaran, U. and Leong, F.T. (1992) *Womanpower*. London: Sage.

Selznick, P. (1966) *TVA And the Grass Roots: A Study in the Sociology of Formal Organization*. New York: Harper & Row. First published 1949.

Sennett, R. and Cobb, J. (1977) *The Hidden Injuries of Class*. Cambridge: Cambridge University Press.

Shackleton, M. (1991) 'The European Community between three ways of life: a cultural analysis', *Journal of Common Market Studies*, 29(6): 575–601.

Shaw, M. (1990) 'Strategy and social process: military context and sociological analysis', *Sociology*, 24(3): 465–73.

Sheppard, D.L. (1989) 'Organizations, power and sexuality: the image and self-image of women managers', in J. Hearn, D. Sheppard, P. Tancred-Sheriff and G. Burrell (eds) *The Sexuality of Organization*. London: Sage. pp. 139–57.

Sherrod, D. (1987) 'The bonds of men: problems and possibilities in close male relationships', in H. Brod (ed.), *The Making of Masculinities*. London and Boston: Allen & Unwin. pp. 213–40.

Sherry, G. and Vinning, R. (1995) 'Accounting for perestroika', *Management Accounting*, April: 42–6.

Sherwood, R. (1980) *The Psychodynamics of Race: Vicious and Benign Spirals*. Brighton: Harvester.

Shore, C. and Black, A. (1992) 'Citizen's Europe and the construction of European identity'. Paper presented at conference: Anthropology of Europe: 1992 and After, 25–6 June, Anthropology Department, Goldsmiths' College, University of London.

Silverman, K. (1992), *Male Subjectivity and the Margins*. London and New York: Routledge.

Simon, H. (1945) *Administrative Behaviour*. London: Macmillan.

Sinclair, A. (1992) 'The tyranny of team ideology', *Organization Studies*, 13(4): 611–26.

Sinclair, A. (1995) 'Sex and the MBA', *Organization*, 2(2): 295–319.

Siriani, C. (1993) 'Learning pluralism: democracy and diversity in feminist organizations', in J. Chapman and I. Shapiro (eds), *Democratic Community: NOMOS XXXV*. New York: New York University Press. pp. 283–312.

Smircich, L. (1983) 'Concepts of culture and organizational analysis', *Administrative Science Quarterly*, 28(3): 339–58.

Smith, V. (1990) *Managing in the Corporate Interest: Control and Resistance in an American Bank*. Berkeley and Los Angeles, CA: University of California Press.

Snitow, A. (1993) 'Feminist futures in the former East bloc', *Peace and Democracy*, 7(1): 40–4.

Sofer, C. (1970) *Men in Mid-Career: A Study of Managers and Technical Specialists*. Cambridge: Cambridge University Press.

Souter, G. (1981) *Company of Heralds*. Melbourne: Melbourne University Press.

Southall, I. (1967) *Softly Tread the Brave*. Sydney: Angus & Robertson.

Spinelli, A. (1966) *The Eurocrats*. Baltimore, MD: Johns Hopkins University Press.

Staggenborg, S. (1988) 'The consequences of professionalization and formalization in the pro-choice movement', *American Sociological Review*, 53: 585–606.

Staggenborg, S. (1989) 'Stability and innovation in the women's movement: a comparison of two movement organizations', *Social Problems*, 36: 75–92.

Staggenborg, S. (1995) 'Can feminist organizations be effective?', in M.M. Ferree and P.Y. Martin (eds), *Feminist Organizations*. Philadelphia: Temple University Press. pp. 339–55.

Stead, B.A. (1985) *Women in Management*. Englewood Cliffs, NJ: Prentice-Hall.

Steinberg, R. (1995) 'Gendered instructions: cultural lag and gender bias in the Hay system of job evaluation', in J.A. Jacobs (ed.), *Gender Inequality at Work*. Newbury Park, CA: Sage. pp. 57–92.

Stewart, R. (1976a) *Contrasts in Management*. London: McGraw-Hill.

Stewart, R. (1976b) *The Reality of Management*. Harmondsworth: Penguin.

Stewart, R. (1986) *The Reality of Management*. London: Heinemann. 2nd edn.

Still, L. (1990) *Enterprising Women*. Sydney: Allen & Unwin.

Stivers, C. (1993) *Gender Images in Public Administration: Legitimacy and the Administrative State*. London: Sage.

Stoltenberg, J. (1993) *The End of Manhood: A Book for Men of Conscience*. New York: Dutton.

Storey, J. (1983) *Managerial Prerogative and the Question of Control*. Boston, MA: Routledge & Kegan Paul.

Strauss, A. (1978) *Negotiations*. San Francisco, CA: Jossey-Bass.

Strobel, M. (1995) 'Organizational learning in the Chicago Women's Liberation Union', in M.M. Ferree and P.Y. Martin (eds), *Feminist Organizations*. Philadelphia: Temple University Press. pp. 145–64.

Strober, M. and Arnold, C. (1987) 'Integrated circuits/segregated labor: women in computer-related occupations and high-tech industries', in National Research Council (eds), *Computer Chips and Paper Clips*, Vol. II. Washington, DC: National Academy Press. pp. 136–84.

Sward, K. (1948) *The Legend of Henry Ford*. New York: Russell & Russell.

Swedish Working Environment Fund (1994) 'Men and Women Working Together: The Kom Programme'. Uppsala: Arbetsmiljöfonden.

Sydie, R.A. (1987) *Natural Women, Cultural Men: A Feminist Perspective on Sociological Theory*. Milton Keynes: Open University Press.

Sydney Morning Herald (1987) 'Ranald Macdonald's long haul back', *Sydney Morning Herald*, 21 February: 7.

Szalai, J. (1991) 'Some aspects of the changing situation of women in Hungary', *Signs: Journal of Women in Culture and Society*, 17(1): 152–70.

Tavris, C. (1992) *The Mismeasure of Women*. New York: Simon & Schuster.

Tawney, R.H. (1938) *Religion and the Rise of Capitalism: A Historical Study*. London: Penguin.

Taylor, F.W. (1911) *Principles of Scientific Management*. New York: Harper.

Taylor, F.W. (1947) *Scientific Management*. New York: Harper and Row.

Taylor, V. (1989) 'The future of feminism in the 1980s: a social movement analysis', in L. Richardson and V. Taylor (eds), *Feminist Frontiers II*. New York: Random House. pp. 434–51.

Thane, P. (1992) 'The history of the gender division of labour in Britain: reflections on *"Herstory" in Accounting: The First Eighty Years*', *Accounting, Organizations and Society*, 17(3/4): 299–312.

Tharenou, P., Latimer, S. and Conroy, D. (1994) 'How do you make it to the top? An examination of influences on women's and men's advancement', *Academy of Management Journal*, 37(4): 899–931.

Thomas, A.B. (1993) *Controversies in Management*. London: Routledge.

Thomas, R. (1994) 'Gendered cultures and performance appraisal: the experience of women academics'. Paper presented to the British Academy of Management conference, Lancaster University, September.

Thompson, P. and McHugh, D. (1995), *Work Organisations*. London: Macmillan.

Thorne, B. (1993) *Gender Play: Girls and Boys in School*. Rutgers, NJ: Rutgers University Press.

Tinker, T. (1985) *Paper Prophets: A Social Critique of Accounting*. London: Holt, Rinehart & Winston.

Tinker, T. and Neimark, M. (1987) 'The role of annual reports in gender and class contradiction at General Motors: 1917–1976', *Accounting, Organizations and Society*, 12: 71–88.

Tolson, A. (1977) *The Limits of Masculinity*. London: Tavistock.

Tomaskovic-Devey, D. (1993) *Gender and Racial Inequality at Work: The Sources and Consequences of Job Segregation*. Ithaca, NY: ILR Press.

Traweek, S. (1988) *Beamtimes and Lifetimes: The World of High Energy Physics*. Cambridge, MA: Harvard University Press.

Tsokhas, K. (1984) *A Class Apart?: Businessmen and Australian Politics 1960–1980*. Melbourne: Oxford University Press.

Turkle, S. (1984) *The Second Self: Computers and the Human Spirit*. New York: Simon & Schuster.

Tutt, N. (1989) *Europe on the Fiddle: The Common Market Scandal*. London: Christopher Helm.

Tyra, A.I. (1969) 'Letters to the journal', *Journal of Accountancy*, June: 28.

Ulrich, L. (1982) *Good Wives: Image and Reality in the Lives of Women in Northern New England, 1650–1750*. New York: Oxford University Press.

Utley, A. (1994a) 'Single minded feel the squeeze', *Times Higher Education Supplement*, 29 April: 6.

Utley, A. (1994b) 'Opportunity knocks for women managers', *Times Higher Education Supplement*, 4 October: 4.

Utley, A. (1995) 'Managers get more macho', *Times Higher Education Supplement*, 9 June: 6.

Van Elsacker, G. (1991) 'De positie van de vrouw in de Europese Commissie; evaluatie van het positieve actie beleid in een communautaire instelling', Unpublished Licentiaat thesis, Antwerp: Universitaire Instelling Antwerpen.

Veblen, T. (1925) *Theory of the Leisure Class*. London: Allen & Unwin.

Venn, C. (1984) 'The subject of psychology', in J. Henriques, W. Hollway, C. Urwin, C. Venn and V. Walkerdine, *Changing the Subject: Psychology, Social Regulation and Subjectivity*. London: Methuen.

Viqueira, L. (ed.) (1993) 'Positive action at the Commission', Equal Opportunities Unit, DG–IX, Personnel and Administration, Commission of the European Communities.

Vogel, L. (1993) *Mothers on the Job: Maternity Policy in the US Workplace*. New Brunswick, NJ: Rutgers University Press.

Von Sydow, E. (1995) 'If the shoe fits', *The Bulletin*, 22, 1 June: 33.

Vroom, V.H. and Yetton, P.W. (1973) *Leadership and Decision-Making*. Pittsburgh, PA: University of Pittsburgh Press.

Wagner, D.G., Ford, R.S. and Ford, T.W. (1986) 'Can gender inequalities be reduced?', *American Sociological Review*, 51: 47–61.

Wajcman, J. (1991) 'Patriarchy, technology, and conceptions of skill', *Work and Occupations*, 18(1): 29–45.

Walby, S. (1986a) 'Gender, class and stratification: towards a new approach', in R. Crompton and M. Mann (eds), *Gender and Stratification*. Cambridge: Polity Press. pp. 22–37.

Walby, S. (1986b) *Patriarchy at Work*. Cambridge: Polity Press/Minneapolis: University of Minnesota Press.

Walby, S. (ed.) (1988) *Gender Segregation at Work*. Milton Keynes: Open University Press.

Walby, S. (1990) *Theorizing Patriarchy*. Oxford: Basil Blackwell.

Walker, L. (1994) 'Name that vegetable and we've got a job for you', *European*, 1–7 April.

Walker, M. (1982) *Powers of the Press*. London: Quartet Books.

Wallace, R.A. (1991) *They Call Her Pastor*. Albany, NY: SUNY Press.

Ward, L. (1995) 'Women who surf the Gender Network', *Times Education Supplement*, 1 December: 25.

Waring, M. (1988) *If Women Counted: A New Feminist Economics*. San Francisco: Harper Collins.

Waters, E. (1993) 'Finding a voice: the emergence of a women's movement', in N. Funk and M. Mueller (eds), *Gender Politics and Post Communism: Reflections From Eastern Europe and the Former Soviet Union*. New York: Routledge. pp. 287–302.

Watson, R. (1994) 'Brussels advisers make the best of taking a fall', *European*, 8–14 April.

Watson, S. (1992) 'Femocratic feminisms', in M. Savage and A. Witz (eds), *Gender and Bureaucracy*. Oxford: Blackwell. pp. 186–204.

Watson, T. (1994) *In Search of Management: Culture, Chaos and Control in Managerial Work*. London: Routledge.

Weber, M. (1930) *The Protestant Ethic and the Spirit of Capitalism*. London: Allen & Unwin.

Weber, M. (1947) *The Theory of Social and Economic Organization*. Glencoe, IL: Free Press.

Weber, M. (1968) 'Bureaucracy', in H. Gerth and C. Wright Mills (eds), *From Max Weber*. London: Routledge & Kegan Paul.

Weber, M. (1978) *Economy and Society: An Outline of Interpretive Sociology*, (ed.) G. Roth and C. Wittich, Vols I & II. Berkeley, CA: University of California Press.

Weisel, M.S. (1991) 'Employer's burden of proof in "Mixed Motive" Title VII litigation and available remedies: *Hopkins v. Price Waterhouse* one year later', *Labor Law Journal*, 42(1): 45–51.

Weiss, R.S. (1990) *Staying the Course: The Emotional and Social Lives of Men Who Do Well at Work*. New York: Free Press.

Wensley, R. (1996) 'Isabella Beeton: management as "everything in its place"', *London Business School Business Strategy Review*, 7(1): 37–46.

West, C. and Fenstermaker, S. (1993) 'Power, inequality, and the accomplishment of gender: an ethnomethodological view', in P. England (ed.), *Theory on Gender/Gender on Theory*. New York: Aldine de Gruyter. pp. 151–74.

West, C. and Fenstermaker, S. (1995) 'Doing difference', *Gender and Society*, 9: 8–37.

West, C. and Zimmerman, D. (1987) 'Doing gender', *Gender and Society*, 1: 125–51.

Westwood, S. (1984) *All Day Every Day: Factory, Family, Women's Lives*. London: Pluto Press.

Whitehead, S. (1995) 'Men managers: the gendered/gendering subject'. Paper presented to the Understanding the Social World conference, University of Huddersfield.

Whitley, R. (1986) 'The transformation of business finance into financial economics: the roles of academic expansion and changes in US capital markets', *Accounting, Organizations and Society*, 11(2): 171–92.

Whyte, W.H. (1956) *The Organization Man*. New York: Doubleday Anchor.

Wild, R. (1994) 'Barriers to women's promotion in further education', *Journal of Further and Higher Education*, 18(3): 83–98.

Wildavsky, A. (1987) 'Cultural theory of responsibility', in J.-E. Lane (ed.), *Bureaucracy and Public Choice*. London: Sage. pp. 283–93.

Wilensky, H. (1964) 'The professionalization of everyone?', *American Journal of Sociology*, 70(2): 137–58.

Williams, C.L. (1989) *Gender Differences at Work. Women and Men in Nontraditional Occupations*. Berkeley: University of California Press.

Williams, C.L. and Heiker, E.J. (1993) 'The importance of researchers' gender in the in-depth interview: evidence from two case studies of male nurses', *Gender and Society*, 7: 280–91.

Williams, E. (1995) 'Lipstick and white collars', *Times Higher Education Supplement*, 28 July: 18–19.

Williams, P.F. (1989) 'The logic of positive accounting research', *Accounting, Organizations and Society*, 13(5/6): 455–68.

Williams, R. (1976) *Keywords*. Glasgow: Fontana.

Willis, P. (1977) *Learning to Labour*. Farnborough, UK: Saxon House.

Willis, P. (1979) 'Shopfloor culture, masculinity and the wage form', in J. Clarke, C. Critcher and R. Johnson (eds), *Working Class Culture*. London: Hutchinson. pp. 185–98.

Willmott, H. (1984) 'Images and ideals of management work', *Journal of Management Studies*, 21(3): 349–68.

Willmott, H. (1987) 'Studying managerial work: a critique and a proposal', *Journal of Management Studies*, 24(3): 249–70.

Willmott, H. (1993) 'Strength is ignorance, slavery is freedom: managing culture in modern organizations', *Journal of Management Studies*, 30(4): 515–52.

Willmott, H. (1995) 'Managing the academics: commodification and control in the development of university education in the UK', *Human Relations*, 48(9): 1–35.

Winter, R. (1995) 'The University of Life plc: the "industrialisation" of higher education?' in J. Smyth (ed.), *Academic Work*. Buckingham: Open University Press and the Society for Research into Higher Education. pp. 129–43.

Witz, A. (1986) 'Patriarchy and the labour market: occupational control strategies and the medical division of labour', in D. Knights and H. Willmott (eds), *Gender and the Labour Process*. Aldershot: Gower. pp. 14–35.

Witz, A. and Savage, M. (1992) 'The gender of organizations', in M. Savage and A. Witz (eds), *Gender and Bureaucracy*. Oxford: Basil Blackwell. pp. 3–62.

Wolf, N. (1991) *The Beauty Myth: How Images of Beauty Are Used against Women*. New York: Doubleday.

Women and Earth: A Feminist Magazine in English and Russian (1992) 1(1), 8 March.

Wood, S. (ed.) (1982) *The Degradation of Work*. London: Hutchinson.

Wood, S. (1987) '*Raging Bull*: the homosexual sub-text in film', in M. Kaufman (ed.), *Beyond Patriarchy. Essays by Men on Power, Pleasure and Change*. Toronto: Oxford University Press. pp. 266–76.

Wood, W. and Karten, S.J. (1986) 'Sex differences in interaction style as a product of perceived sex differences in competence', *Journal of Personality and Social Psychology*, 50: 341–7.

Woodward, A., Ellig, J. and Burns, T.R. (1994) *Municipal Entrepreneurship: A Five Nation*

Study of Energy Politics, Innovation and Social Change. Philadelphia, PA: Gordon & Breach.

Yeatman, A. (1995) 'The gendered management of equity-oriented change in higher education', in J. Smyth (ed.), *Academic Work*. Buckingham: Open University Press and the Society for Research into Higher Education. pp. 194–205.

Zetterholm, S. (ed.) (1994) *National Culture and European Integration*. Oxford: Berg.

Ziller, J. (1988) *Egalité et mérite*. Maastricht: European Institute of Public Administration.

Zimmerman, D. (1973) 'The practicalities of rule use', in G. Salaman and K. Thompson (eds), *People and Organisations*. London: Longman. pp. 250–63.

Zimmerman, J. (1983) *The Technological Woman*. New York: Praeger.

Zuboff, S. (1982) 'New worlds of computer-mediated work', *Harvard Business Review*, 60(2): 142–52.

Zuboff, S. (1988) *In the Age of the Smart Machine*. New York: Basic Books.

Index